THE SPIRIT
OF AMERICAN PHILOSOPHY

THE SPIRIT
OF AMERICAN PHILOSOPHY

THE SPIRIT
OF WESTERN CIVILIZATION
GENERAL EDITOR
Charles M. Sherover

The Spirit
of American Philosophy

An Anthology, selected,

edited and with introductions by

Gerald E. Myers

Capricorn Books
New York

To Barton Myers

CONTENTS

PREFACE

American philosophy is presented here not as an isolated professional activity but as a part of American culture. The spirit of American philosophy is identified with the culture's traditional respect for the individual and with its effort to define the contexts in which individuality can flourish. Jefferson, Lincoln, Thoreau, Holmes, and Veblen are therefore among those included with Dewey, James, Cohen, and Lewis as major American philosophers.

Each chapter has an introduction discussing the themes that organize the readings, and this prefatory note makes no attempt to recapitulate the six introductory essays. But a word here about the general organization of the book may be helpful.

Seventeenth-century America believed that individuality could flourish only in an appropriate religious context, and this continuing feature of the American philosophic outlook is the focus of the first chapter. Representative essays in the philosophy of government constitute the second chapter; with an eye to the contemporary scene, discussion of the traditional place of dissent in our culture is included here. The third chapter traces the attempt by the individual to define a suitable moral context for himself, emphasizing how this effort is complicated, for example, by the necessary extension of moral consideration to the proper role of government in the economic affairs of state and nation. Chapter Four presents the traditional American respect for education, illustrating how American history is in part the attempt to define a context for the individual in which the rule of reason is obligatory.

But we also note a different philosophic spirit in American life, something more metaphysical, sometimes occult and irrational. This phenomenon is the subject of Chapter Five, in which we point out that our philosophical heritage has encouraged the individual to define himself in a metaphysical rather than merely an everyday context. Professional philosophical concern with this and with the individual's attempt to define his situation philosophically, appealing to the concepts of Life, Experience, and Reality, is the focus of Chapter Six. What is culturally significant here is the pluralism of contemporary professional philosophy in America.

What promises to be the temper of tomorrow's American philosophy and its role in the culture? This book makes no prediction, but it was put together in the old idea that, in guessing where a culture is headed philosophically, you ought to know its philosophic performances heretofore. This book represents what we think ought to be remembered in any speculating about the future spirit of American philosophy and about the future philosophic spirit of American culture.

THE SPIRIT
OF AMERICAN PHILOSOPHY

I. *Religion*

INTRODUCTION

The spirit of culture is its traditions. One of the pervasive traditions of American culture is that Puritanism which was planted in colonial Massachusetts. It was a religion, a philosophy, and a way of life. Its Christian theology explained the purpose of human existence; its philosophic reflection explored ways in which to fulfill it.

The purpose of human life is to please God; in order to fulfill it a man had to agree to two covenants or contracts, one with God and another with his fellowmen. The covenant with God is remarkable since it demonstrates His willingness to tell man the terms of eternal salvation and to promise that He will never abrogate those conditions. The Bible, as the word of God, is the statement of the terms of the covenant to which God and man become voluntary parties. God in the covenant satisfies man that human and divine conceptions of values—of what is right, wrong, and just—are in basic agreement; a man can conduct his life with the assurance that he knows what the deity wants of him and that his own finite evaluations have divine recognition.

Simultaneously, a man must enter a second covenant with his fellows to create a society which pleases God. The famous Mayflower Compact is the earliest American document illustrating this second contract; ten years later, in 1630, a similar version of it was formulated by John Winthrop on board the *Arbella*. This compact stipulates that one has voluntarily joined in creating a community and abides by its policies in appreciation of the benefits obtained from belonging to it. The Puritans believed that communal existence was superior to proud isolation in a primitive "state of nature," and that men could not serve the demands of God unless they ministered to one another; the example of the life of Jesus was sufficient to resolve any doubt on this. But the Puritan covenant was not identical with the earlier versions of the social contract theory which defined social right and wrong by social agreement. That one thing is right and another thing is wrong, the Puritans insisted, is not the result of merely human agreement; basic

1

moral definitions are eternal fact mutually agreed to by God and man; which things are right and which are wrong are mainly revealed in the Scriptures.

The Puritans championed freedom and individuality, of course, to the extent that they insisted on church reforms in England and Europe, maintained their own convictions despite persecutions, and founded New England in the face of incredible hardship. They brought to America lessons already learned in England about ways of achieving enlightened self-government. They taught that an individual can meet God on his own, without priestly intermediaries, and that mystical experiences are rare but do occur. But their emphasis was less upon individuality and freedom as such (as shown by their treatment of Roger Williams and by the Salem witch trials) than upon the particular kind of individual they believed one ought to become and the particular cause in behalf of which they believed one ought to use one's freedom.

Most of God's demands referred to relationships. True individuality could flourish only in the context of a theocracy or Holy Commonwealth. God's business on earth required more than scattered, individual efforts. If God's will was to be satisfied, dedicated communities of people were needed, in which all accepted the same religious goal and pulled together as a team. The Puritan thinkers were entirely aware of the mission they had mounted. As John Winthrop announced, by rejoicing together, mourning together, laboring and suffering together, we insure that "the God of Israel is among us"; men will then say of "succeeding plantations" that they should emulate the Holy Commonwealth of New England, "for we must consider that we shall be as a city upon a hill, the eyes of all people are upon us." The Christian success of each individual clearly depended, in their own eyes, upon the successful establishment of a Christian commonwealth.

Covenant doctrine indicated an interesting attitude toward the role of the individual in society—a role analogous to the "businessman" whose life is a constant affair of negotiating and signing agreements. Considerable importance, of course, was attached to the fact that both God and man *volunteer* to enter the covenant; but since this is so obviously what one ought to do, the fact of its being done freely tended to slide from notice. What became emphasized instead was the serious business of life, the consequent demand for a businesslike *initiative* in approaching the negotiating and finalizing of a contract, and a firm sense of responsibility to all the terms agreed to. Dealing with God and dealing with fellowmen are both of the same pattern, initiating the agreement which the evidence shows to be both morally and practically the best, and abiding by the contract in a spirit of honesty and basic commitment to its clauses. If one wondered how conscience, guilt, remorse, and duty were to be understood, these could always be explained by alluding to the psychological complications which can occur in adhering to the terms of a contract which one may occasionally find taxing. From the outset the American ethic and the American conception of life held that life is a profoundly serious business to conduct, and one's frame of mind is essentially the same whether working out contracts with God or man. Initiative, responsibility, and successful conduct of life's business became more prominent as virtues in such an ethic than liberty and individuality.

The Puritan ethic, however, always insisted that initiative was in the service of God, and that, accordingly, it must be tempered by faith and humility and not permitted to balloon into arrogant ambition; this was stressed by John Cotton in his characterization of the "goat-type" of man who would "outshoot God in his own bow." Not ambition but one's true "calling" in life is the genuine quest. John Cotton's statement is reminiscent of a main thesis of Plato's *Republic;* namely, that a man lives justly if he finds what he is best equipped to do and restricts himself to that. Indeed, it has often been remarked that the Puritan concept of society was essentially Plato's, modified by Christian theology. Its basic assumption was that a harmonious society depended upon each man's using his own God-given gifts and talents, whether as joiner, wheelwright, or governor, for the good of the whole. Each person's mission was to contribute, quietly and diligently, in his own special way to his community and thereby acquire the measure of dignity and esteem due him.

A few, like John Wise, interpreted this to imply that democracy is the preferred form of government. But Wise was in a minority in the emphasis he placed upon freedom, individuality, and democracy. Most of the New England founders accepted Plato's thesis that the ideal republic is an aristocracy. Winthrop spoke for the majority: "God Almighty in his most holy and wise providence hath so disposed of the condition of mankind, as in all times some must be rich, some poor, some high and eminent in power and dignity; others mean and in subjection." Some individuals have a higher calling than others, and their word counts more heavily in fashioning social policy.

Apart from the impetus provided by their own struggles for independence of outlook, there were certain features of the Puritan philosophy which were calculated to assist the ideals of democracy and freedom. The doctrine of the convenant coincided with the doctrines of original sin and man's natural depravity; man's primitive or natural state is one of wickedness, and the covenant with God is a necessary if not sufficient condition for receiving grace. This, incidentally, is a decidely un-Platonic note in Puritanism since Plato's writings strongly indicate that the whole notion of sin was foreign to his thought. But the Puritans employed the doctrine of original sin, according to which no man is born quite innocent, to explain why political power corrupts, why, therefore, something like democratic checks must be placed upon those holding public office. As Samuel Eliot Morison pointed out,

> . . . a further check on autocracy was established by a body of laws and a bill of rights. Winthrop and his elected assistants who served also as judges, liked to pass judgments based on their intuition and the Bible. The people observed that this allowed too much discretion to the judges. Hence the Massachusetts "Body of Liberties" adopted in 1641, and the "General Fundamentals" of Plymouth Colony which may have been earlier, contained the classic safeguards of English liberty, such as jury trial, no taxation without representation, free elections, nobody to be deprived of life, liberty, or property save by due process of law, or compelled to incriminate himself. These are the same principles later incorporated in the Bill of Rights of the Federal Constitution. In certain aspects, the Body of Liberties was ahead of English practice. Torture and cruel and barbarous punishments were prohibited, feudal dues were abolished, foreigners were assured equal protection of the law (as they already had been in Virginia), and cruelty to animals was forbidden. Cruelty to wives, too; a husband was forbidden to beat his wife "unless it be in his own defense upon her assault!*

One of the most important features of Puritan philosophy was its respect for education, exemplified by the founding of Harvard College. What is significant was the role of the laity in religion; they contributed to the support and education of their clergy, and they joined with the clergy in erudite discussions of subtle theological problems. Religion was eminently a subject for general discussion and open to rational scrutiny. Religion in America began as part of man's search for greater and greater rationality in coping with existence. Although an occasional irrationalism inevitably appeared in various guises, religion was not

---

* Samuel Eliot Morison, *The Oxford History of the American People* (New York, Oxford University Press, 1965), pp. 66–7.

believed to be a collection of mysteries designed to bewilder human finitude; it was rather conceived as the inspirational focus of an essentially rational theory of the cosmos.

Various forces—commerce, immigration, politics, internal conflicts, movements of the frontier—gradually undermined the self-contained character of Puritan theocracy. As the original vitality faded, a religious restlessness appeared, culminating in a twenty-year phenomenon known as the Great Awakening, a wave of religious revival meetings across the colonies. The most famous representative of the Great Awakening and one who contributed to its beginnings in the early 1730's was Jonathan Edwards, generally conceded to be America's first distinguished philosopher. Given the complexity and flavor of Edwards' philosophy of religion, it is less remarkable that he was dismissed in 1750 by his congregation in Northampton, Massachusetts, than that they listened to him for twenty-four years. Edwards was the thin-lipped spokesman for that kind of gloomy sketch of man and his world which is capable of triggering a short, intense revival but can hardly survive it.

In "The Christian Pilgrim" Edwards spoke eloquently to the approving understanding of his audiences. We must see "this life only as a journey towards heaven," perhaps grateful for the joys which earthly existence affords, but we should not settle for them since the danger is one of investing too much in a life which is too little. Existence on earth is preparation for another type in heaven; the only justification for mortal duration is its being an anticipation of immortal life. Everyone could appreciate this view, as well as the suggestion that it is absurd to grieve immoderately for those dear friends who have completed their pilgrimage to heaven. Edwards' thrilling restatement of the Calvinist notion of man's depravity in accordance with the doctrine of original sin was also readily comprehended, and the looming vision of hell was agreed to: "Thus the bulk of mankind are hastening onward in the broad way to destruction; which is, as it were, filled up with the multitude that are going in it with one accord. And they are every day going to hell out of this broad way by thousands. Multitudes are constantly flowing down into the great lake of fire and brimstone, as some mighty river constantly disembogues its water into the ocean." The Northampton congregation, like hundreds of others, could respond passionately to sermons detailing the imminent horrors of hell, feeling that it was indeed a Great Awakening and a refinding of the religious vitality which founded America. It was a time when one could joyfully rediscover the rich potentialities contained in being a sinner.

The emphasis placed by Edwards upon religious *experience*, of conversion and rediscovery of faith, indeed the sort of experience which his sermons were intended to rouse, could also be appreciated by his audience even if deplored by more conservative clergymen in Boston. This valuing of individual experience partook of the general climate of the time; it was marked by a restlessness characteristic of the transition from an older and more consolidated order into an expanding and increasingly fragmented type of society. New churches and colleges were founded, and new denominations were set up which eventually became Baptists and Methodists. Religion seemed available, in a revitalized way, to the common man. He could again understand its essential message of heaven and hell. He could better appreciate the significance of his own work through coming to know himself as a sinner who was capable of the ineffable experience of conversion. It has been said of the Great Awakening, which Edwards helped arouse:

> It stimulated a fresh interest in religion, caused hundreds of new churches to be founded, strengthened the movement of religious liberty, gave the common man a new sense of his significance, and thus indirectly contributed to the American Revolution. Most important, the Great Awakening brought it about that Christianity expanded with the frontier, and that the new independent American, like the old dependent colonist, inherited a strong Christian tradition.*

But, on the whole, Edwards' philosophy of religion was too complex and too gloomy for his parishioners, too severe in its personal rebukes to them. Edwards' views of predestination, of the true nature of virtue, of infant damnation, were too harsh to live with and too intricate to reason through. Man could not even deserve God's love, he argued, and he gave no place for the doctrine of the covenant which had originally yielded respite from the doctrine of natural depravity. Thus Edwards' theological philosophy, intended as a defense of Calvinism, actually served to contribute to its decline. Whatever technical aspects of it attract attention today, his philosophy thus ceased to be a candidate for representing the spirit of American culture.

The mid-eighteenth century brought the Enlightenment to America. The development of science, technology, and renewed respect for the capacities of human reason produced a religious philosophy very different from that of Edwards although it drew heavily on the same

* *Ibid.*, p. 151.

Puritan source. Among those objecting to old-line Calvinism and pointing toward the emergence of Unitarianism and Transcendentalism was
William Ellery Channing. He urged that claims based upon revelation
or upon readings of the Scriptures be subjected to thorough rational
examination. The doctrines of natural depravity and predestination,
for instance, he argued could not be made logically consistent with
God's goodness and equity. The *unity* of God was proclaimed on the
grounds that the doctrine of the Trinity was both "unscriptural" and
"irrational." Nevertheless, despite the contradictions which Channing
entered against specific doctrines of the Puritan and Calvinist
philosophy, there are respects in which his reliance upon a "reasoned"
interpretation of the Bible is closer to the seventeenth-century Puritan
attitude than was the more "enthusiastic" attitude of Jonathan Edwards.
Although Channing did not revive the old convenant theology, he
preserved a significant development of convenant doctrine: Man is
spiritually made in the image of God, such that he can *know*, to some
extent, the nature of his maker. God is not an unknowable whose
terrible wrath we must fear in sheer ignorance of His will. This was
never a religious conception really congenial to American minds.
Channing's statement that "The idea of God, sublime and awful as it
is, is the idea of our own spiritual nature, purified and enlarged to
infinity . . ." outraged some wearers of the cloth; but it expressed for
his audiences what had seemed to the Puritans a highly reasonable
position—that God was a Person with whom man could do business,
with whom he could have some idea of where he stood. The influence of
the Scottish commonsense philosophy, to which he had been introduced
at Harvard, was manifested in Channing's philosophy of religion.

What "Likeness to God" (1828) insists upon is the resemblance of
a parent to a child, the likeness of a kindred nature. We comprehend
the Deity only through our own nature, our own souls, which afford
clues to His nature, the idea of God being "first developed in ourselves, and thence transferred to our creator." It is because of the essential homogeneity of ourselves with God that we are capable of receiving
His instructions and that He can appreciate our prayers. There is even
a touch of infinity in the human mind, a depth in human love which is
"unfathomable," and these echo similar features, on a grander scale,
in the Deity.

Channing's devotion to causes marking him a social reformer
required a humanitarian religion, stressing the gentle, parental nature
of God. His call to man is to enter a fellowship "in his philanthropy

. . . he has placed you in social relations for the very end of rendering you ministers and representatives of his benevolence . . . and to advance the sublimest purpose of his goodness, the redemption of the human race, by extending the knowledge and power of Christian truth." Channing's philosophy of religion sought a context in which the individual could hopefully respond to a world which had seen the American and French revolutions, the Industrial Revolution in England with its harbingers of what was to happen in nineteenth-century America, the development of secular politics, and the rapid growth of the sciences. In such a world one must remain in the world:

> To resemble our creator we need not fly from society, and entrance ourselves in lonely contemplation and prayer. Such processes might give a feverish strength to one class of emotions, but would result in disproportion, distortion, and sickliness of mind. Our proper work is to approach God by the free and natural unfolding of our highest powers—of understanding, conscience, love, and the moral will.

Channing perpetuated the earliest American tradition in finding God through oneself because of likeness to Him and through community of likeness of men to one another. American tradition has encouraged the legend of the Colorado cowboy as an enviable "loner," but it never sponsored the picture of the solitary man of religion riding off, happy with his melancholy, into the sunset. As the frontier expanded, as successive generations of immigrants arrived, as the "melting-pot" America took shape, it became increasingly important to identify the religious community with which one's ethnic name and heritage coincided.

Professional philosophy in America reflected this tradition of the individual seeking to define himself in terms of a religious community and simultaneously to define that community, in some part at least, by virtue of what he, as a unique person, requires of it. Josiah Royce, whose religion was also challenged by the post-Darwinian thinking of the late nineteenth century, employed various arguments to show the necessary interdependence of individual and community. But, besides, Royce offered an argument to demonstrate the necessary interdependence of man and God; and this argument, because of the philosophic and religious notice it received, was an important, if somewhat curious, continuation of the tradition of rational religion, of arguing for theological conclusions, not by appeal to revelation, sacred Scriptures, or mystical experience, but rather by rational considerations alone. His startling suggestion was that the existence of God can be proved by a purely logical argument, by an argument containing no theological premises; indeed, the only premises needed are very prosaic.

The argument begins by noting that one often forms an opinion, which is either true or false. But what does it mean to form an opinion at all? Royce answered that it means that one is trying to anticipate "what a wider view, a larger experience of your present situation, a fuller insight into your present ideas, and into what they mean, would show you, if you now had that wider view and larger experience." If you believe that war will occur next week, then, according to Royce, you are not merely predicting the occurrence of war next week; you are presuming what a wider and more comprehensive knowledge would already know as true. The point is that one who knows whether the opinion is true or false is obviously better informed than one merely holding the opinion; the informed person may be said to have a "wider" or "larger" experience; if the person merely holding the opinion could now have the perspective of the informed person, it would illuminate his whole *present* outlook as well as insure what specifically to expect. Further, even if we know of no such informed person who could now confirm that war will occur next week, we nevertheless are trying to comprehend what his perspective would be like if he did exist, and how it would illuminate our present outlook. It will not do to suggest that such a perspective is merely hypothetical. "Everything that you regard as possible has to be conceived as somehow based upon what you regard as actual. And so, in fact, your opinions are always appeals to some form of wider or larger or deeper or richer insight which, in the act of appealing to it, you regard as a present or as a past or as a future reality—in brief, as a live and perfectly concrete insight to whose verdict you appeal." So, in just holding an opinion, even an erroneous one, one is appealing to what a larger perspective than one's own would show for one's present situation; one is trying to view one's present from the point of view of *another though larger self*. Without appeal to this other self larger than oneself, one could not even err since one could not hold any belief at all. By an appropriate synthesis of ever larger perspectives, Royce concluded that "The world is the object of an all-inclusive and divine insight, which is thus the supreme reality." God, therefore, identified as the ultimate and all-inclusive perspective, is shown to be the logical consequence of the human ability to err! What man strives for, even when deficient, indicates his dependence upon a superhuman self or experience. Royce's argument thus is that the very ability to hold fallacious opinions proves God's existence. This unique argument immediately attracted wide attention and was the subject of philosophic debate.

Royce's philosophy was, in part, an effort to make religion rational and respectable in answer to skeptical challenges, apart from appeals to authority or mystic kinds of experience. Some of his reasoning was narrowly intellectual and certainly unrepresentative of the mainstream of American culture. But his general position was important and traditional insofar as it continued the Puritan thesis that reason was not inherently hostile to religion. For reason demonstrated that it could only find its own fulfillment and completion in the all-inclusive concept of God. Royce supported the common belief that science and faith are compatible by arguing that logic itself required religion. People might not always grasp the argument, but they welcomed the conclusion.

Another famous thinker, deserving to be included in the American roster, since his reputation as a philosopher was made at Harvard after retiring as professor of mathematics in England, was Alfred North Whitehead. His statement, "Religion is what the individual does with his own solitariness," is often quoted but without remembering what more Whitehead intended by it. Whitehead did not claim to prove the truth of any religion but rather to point up an important feature of what he called "rational religion" and under which he included Christianity as well as Buddhism. As he put it,

> The moment of religious consciousness starts from self-valuation, but it broadens into the concept of the world as a realm of adjusted values, mutually intensifying or mutually destructive. . . . In its solitariness the spirit asks what, in the way of value, is the attainment of life? And it can find no such value till it has merged its individual claim with that of the objective universe. Religion is world-loyalty.

Whitehead's point is that religion does originate in genuine solitariness, not in communion of any sort; religion originates in the loneliness of self-regard. But this value which an individual places upon himself immediately introduces associated concepts: the value of different individuals for one another and the value of the "objective world which is a community derivative from the interrelations of its component individuals, and also necessary for the existence of each of these individuals." Finding oneself valuable and important necessarily points beyond itself. Confucianism, Buddhism, Hinduism, and Christianity agree, according to Whitehead, that God is inferred rather than intuited. The great religions are wise in so agreeing, for they appreciate how many contradictory opinions are generated if religion is declared to originate in private and direct intuition of a Deity. The intuition which unites the concept of one's own value with the value of other persons and with the worth of the objective world, is rather an intuition into the ultimate character of the universe, an intuition that there is a "permanent rightness" in the nature of things. This intuition cannot be more fully conceived to anyone who has not shared it. But the point is that it is an intuiting of the *value* attaching, not to just oneself, but in fact to the world; it is an intuiting of a value which is universal rather than a direct vision of a person of any sort. Dwelling upon the idea of intuiting a person or God, *as a starting point*, tends to leave one with something personal rather than universal; but, if one begins with an intuition of *value* instead, one has something capable of being universalized. One then begins to value also the community as the required context in which the individual can thus grow from self-valuation into devoutness, which is always necessarily social in nature. Whitehead's main point is that when religions appeal to personal gods, they become isolated cults. All religions speak alike, however, when they describe *devoutness* thus: It is the process by which the individual finds that the sense of his own value implies the existence of profound values in other people and in the cosmos itself. Thus understood, religion is universal and the same everywhere.

However difficult and obscure the reasoning of Royce and Whitehead may seem, their philosophies of religion reformulated and carried forward more fervent episodes from America's religious thought. But to conclude that this is all would be to offend their own sentiments toward religion and its role in American culture. The philosophic tradition, which Royce and Whitehead helped to sustain, keeps foremost in mind the need, even for the most independent of truth-seeking persons, to respect the role played by religion in shaping a communal context in which individuality may flourish. They represent a tradition which appreciates how a philosophical exploration of American religious culture may itself succeed in detecting and marking for survival what ought to be preserved.

MAYFLOWER COMPACT, 1620

In the name of God, Amen, We, whose names are underwritten, the loyal subjects of our dread Sovereign Lord King James, by the Grace of God, of Great Britain, France, and Ireland, King, Defender of the Faith, &c. Having undertaken for the glory of God and advancement of the Christian faith, and the honor of our king and country, a voyage to plant the first colony in the northern parts of Virginia; do by these presents, solemnly and mutually, in the presence of God and one another, convenant and combine ourselves together into a civil body politic, for our better ordering and preservation, and furtherance of the ends aforesaid: And by virtue hereof do enact, constitute, and frame, such just and equal laws, ordinances, acts, constitutions, and officers, from time to time, as shall be thought most meet and convenient for the general good of the colony; unto which we promise all due submission and obedience. In witness whereof we have hereunto subscribed our names at Cape Cod the eleventh of November . . . Anno Domini, 1620.

JOHN COTTON

John Cotton (1584–1652), born and educated in England, was a distinguished minister. When John Winthrop's contingent sailed from England for America in 1630, Cotton gave the farewell sermon. Three years later he was compelled to resign from the Church of England because of his controversial theological views. After migrating to New England, he became perhaps the most important theologian in Boston, and his works provided the definitive formulations of Congregationalism. The following selections are excellent examples of seventeenth-century Puritan thought. The first two are from *The New Covenant*, or *A Treatise, unfolding the order and manner of the giving and receiving of the Covenant of Grace to the Elect*, London, 1654. The third and fourth are taken from *The Way of Life*, London, 1641.

Swine and Goats

All the men in the world are divided into two ranks, Godly or Ungodly, Righteous or Wicked; of wicked men two sorts, some are notoriously wicked, others are Hypocrites: Of Hypocrites two sorts (and you shall find them in the Church of God) some are washed Swine, others are Goats.

1.   The *Swine* are those of whom our Saviour Christ saith, *That they returne unto their wallowing in the mire;* like unto these are such men who at the hearing of some Sermon have been stomach sick of their sins, and have rejected their wicked courses, but yet the swines heart remaineth in them, as a Swine when he cometh where the puddle is, will readily lye down in it: so will these men wallow in the puddle of uncleannesse when their conscience is not pricked for the present: But these are a grosser kind of Hypocrites.

2.   There is another sort that goe far beyond these, and they are *Goats*, so called, *Matth.* 25. 32, 33. and these are clean Beasts such as chew the cudd, meditate upon Ordinances, and they divide the hoofe, they live both in a generall and particular calling, and will not be idle; they are also fit for sacrifice; what then is wanting? Truly they are not *sheep* all this while, they are but *Goats*, yet a Goat doth loath that which a Swine will readily break into; but where then doe they fall short of the nature of sheep? A difference there is, which standeth principally in these particulars.

1. The Goat is of a Capricious nature, and affecteth Eminency, his gate also is stately, *Prov.* 30. 30. *Agur* reckoneth the He-goat among the 4 things that are comely in going: And they are full of Ambition, they cannot abide swamps and holes, but will be climbing upon the tops of mountains; there is not that plain lowly sheepish frame that attendeth unto the voyce of the Shepheard, to be led up and downe in fresh pastures: they attend upon their ends, and will outshoot God in his own Bowe, and therefore when they have done many things for Christ, he will say unto them, *Depart from me, ye workers of iniquity*. More Eminency they did affect, then they were guided unto. Thus it was with *Jehu*, who in his zeal for God thought to promote himselfe, and herein he will not be perswaded of his sin, and therefore going into crooked wayes, he cometh at length to cleave unto the sins of *Jeroboam* the Son of *Nebat*, who made *Israel* to sin; yet notwithstanding, you may rec[e]ive a Goat into Church-fellowship for all his capricious nature, and he will be a clean creature, and of much good use. The five foolish *Mat.* 25. 2. were all of them *Virgins*, all of them abhorring Idolatry, and all go forth to meet the Bridegroome, and yet they are foolish and never shall you make them wise, to be all for Christ, only hearing and obeying his voyce.

2. They are of a Rankish nature all of them, specially the old Goats will have an unsavory relish, far from that pleasant sweetnesse that is in a sheep; and herein Hypocrites are greatly different from the sheep of Christ, as the Prophet speaketh, *Ezek.* 34. 21. and they marre the Pastures with their feet, and will be at length mudling the faire waters of the Sanctuary also; and in your best sanctification they fall far short of a sheep-like frame of spirit, diligently to heare the voyce of the Shepheard, this will not be found in the sanctification of the best Hypocrite under Heaven, they may goe far and yet fall away, and this is no Arminianism, but if you search the Scriptures diligently, you will find these things to be true.

Hypocrites and Saints

Truly it is hard to perceive when men differ, and therefore it is not an easie matter to make such use of Sanctification, as by it to beare witnesse unto Justification: and it will be a very hard case and much more difficult, when men cannot feele the presence of spirituall gifts, but want spirituall light: and when they doe finde faith in themselves, they doe find it in hypocrites also, even in hypocrites also, even faith to seeke the Lord, & faith to waite upon him, and faith to apply him, saying, *My God*, and faith to stay upon the *God of Israel;* and yet these men doe vanish away in hypocrisie; this hypocrites may doe; seeing therefore what easines of errour may befall Christians, whether this or that grace be of the right stampe or no, it will behove Christians to be wary, for even Eagle-eyed Christians will have much adoe so to discerne of sanctification in themselves, before they see their justification, as to cut off all hypocrites from having the like in them, for the sanctified frame of Gods children, and that which seemeth to be like it in hypocrites, both of them spring from the holy Ghost, and both from faith: but now the Spirit of God hath further worke in his own people, beyond what he worketh upon others, though he melteth both, yet hypocrites are melted as iron, which will returne againe to his former hardnes, but his owne people are melted into flesh, which will never returne to his hardnes more, neither can they rest in any measure of softnes unto which they have attained, but still are carryed toward Jesus Christ: so that the one is a temporary faith, and the other persevereth: though both worke in the name of Christ, yet this difference will be found between them, not only when hypocrites come to be blasted, but even in the middest of their profession: As for the faith of the Gospell of Jesus Christ, it is never president of its own power, but his strength lyeth out of himselfe in Christ; whereas hypocrites and legall Christians are confident of their faith, that they can make use of it unto such and such ends, they think they need no more but look up to Christ, and their worke is at an end; and such strength they finde in themselves, as that they doe not feare, but that they shall carry an end all their worke to Gods glory and their own: whereas the strongest faith even of the *Thessalonians* (whose faith was such, as none of all the Churches went before them) if it be not supplyed and strengthened, they know, & the Apostle *Paul* knoweth that it will warpe & shrinke. This may we see by comparing, 1 *Thes*. 1. 3. with *Chap*. 3, 2, 10. And the faithfull people of God, *Isa*. 26, 12. acknowledge Him to *worke all their works for them*. And therefore as there is a reall difference in the presence of the Spirit; so also in the worke of faith in hypocrites, and the children of God, for the one putteth confidence in himselfe in the gift received, and the other in *Jehovah*. This is the first difference of Sanctification.

2.   There is Difference also in the Rule whereby they are guided, though both seeke to the word of God & take delight in that, insomuch as you shall not be able to difference them there, yet a great difference

there is in the apprehension of the word: the one is so confident of the comfort that he hath in the word, and he will be ready to take it ill at Gods hand, if he finde not acceptance before him: Now the other see the need they have of the Lord to maintaine their comfort for them. This manner of affection we finde in *David*, when the Lord had brought him and his people into a sweet frame and temper of spirit to offer willingly towards the building of the Temple; what saith *David* now? Doth he thinke this to be enough? No, no, but he prayeth to the Lord, 1 *Chron.* 29. 18. *O Lord God of Abraham, Isaack, and Israel our fathers keepe this for ever in the imagination of the thoughts of the heart of thy people, and prepare their heart unto thee.* Thus is he sensible that these comforts would soone faile them, & they should againe waxe barren and uncomfortable. And here is the nature of true Consolation in Christ to looke up unto the Lord to preserve and maintaine it, and so he is still drawne neerer & neerer to Christ. But now though both attend unto the Word, as their Rule of Sanctification, if you take it in the way, in which the one and the other hold it forth, yet there is a great difference. *Psal.* 119. 6. *Then shall I not be ashamed,* &c. Here is a Rule; what, may not hypocrites walke according to this rule? Truly they professe no lesse, and they think it enough, if they have but a Rule in their eye, and therfore under a spirit of bondage they are confident and say, *What soever the Lord commandeth us, we will heare it and doe it,* Deut. 5. 27. And what saith *Balaam; Though* Balaack *would give me an house full of silver and gold, I cannot goe beyond the Commandement of the Lord,* Numb. 22. 18. and yet he loved the wages of iniquity; and indeed those that undertake so much in their owne strength, they come afterward to be weary of the Lord, and weary of his Commandements: as *Amos* 8. 5. and they say at last, *It is in vaine to serve God, and what profit is it that we have kept his ordinances?* Mal. 3. 14. These are but like washed swine, that will crop grasse for a while in a faire Pasture, but if you keepe them long there, they will not delight in such manner of feeding, but will rather choose to go into the mire; but as for goats they will delight in the Commandments of the Lord, *Isa.* 58. 2. It is not a very hard thing unto them, nor grievous for them to keep solemne fasting dayes together, they come willingly, they delight to come, therefore the difference will be hardly discovered, and unles you be a Christian of a very cleere discerning, you will not finde the difference.

Wading in Grace

For further encouragement hereunto, consider that place, *Ezech.* 47. 3, 4, 5. It shewes you the marvailous efficacy of the spirit of Grace in the dayes of the Gospel: First a Christian wades in the rivers of God his grace up to the ankles, with some good frame of spirit; yet but weakly, for a man hath strength in his ankle bones, *Acts* 3. and yet may have but feeble knees, *Heb.* 12. 12. So farre as you walk in the waters, so far are you healed; why then in the next place, he must wade till he come to the knees, goe a thousand Cubits, a mile further, and get more strength to pray, and to walk on in your callings with more power and strength.

Secondly, but yet a man that wades but to the knees, his loynes are not drenched, for nothing is healed but what is in the water. Now the affections of a man are placed in his loynes, God tries the reines; a man may have many unruly affections, though he be padling in the wayes of grace; he may walk on in some eavennesse, and yet have many dis-tempered passions, and may have just cause to complaine of the rottennesse of his heart in the sight of God: why then, thou hast waded but to the knees, and it is a mercy that thou art come so farre; but yet the loynes want healing, why, wade a mile further then; the grace of God yet comes too shallow in us, our passions are yet unmortified, so as we know not how to grieve in measure, our wrath is vehement and immoderate, you must therefore wade untill the *loynes bee girt with a golden girdle;* wade an-end, & think all is not well untill you be so deep, & by this you may take a scantling, what measure of grace is poured out upon you. And if thou hast gone so farre, that God hath in some measure healed thy affections, that thou canst be angry and sin not, &c. it is well, and this we must attain to. But suppose the loyns should be in a good measure healed, yet there is more goes to it then all this; and yet when a man is come thus farre, he may laugh at all temptations, and blesse God in all changes: But yet goe another thousand Cubits, and then you shall swimme; there is such a measure of grace in which a man may swimme as fish in the water, with all readinesse and dex-terity, gliding an-end, as if he had water enough to swimme in; such a Christian doth not creep or walk, but he runs the wayes of Gods Commandements; what ever he is to doe or to suffer he is ready for all, so every way drenched in grace, as let God turn him any way, he is never drawn dry. . . .

Christian Calling

... *Vse* 1. From hence you see a just reproofe of the infidelity found in them that live without a calling, they either want faith, or the exercise of faith; if thou beest a man that lives without a calling, though thou hast two thousands to spend, yet if thou hast no calling, tending to publique good, thou art an uncleane beast; if men walke without a cloven hoofe, they are uncleane: and hast thou a Calling, and art never so diligent in it, it is but *dead worke*, if thou want faith. It likewise reproves such Christians, as consider not what gifts they have for this and that calling; he pleads for himselfe, his wife and children, further then himselfe he respects no calling; and this is want of faith in a Christians calling: or if men rest in the strength of their owne gifts, for the performing of their callings, and will serve God in some things, and themselves and theirs in other some, or if we can tell how to be eye-servants, it is but a dead worke, for want of faith; or if thou lose thy selfe, and thy heart is carnall, and not heavenly minded, thou mayest have faith, but that is but a dead worke. And if thou cast not all thy care and burthen upon God, thou wilt be very dead when ill successes fall out; but had we faith, it would support us in our worst successes; and if better successes come, if faith be wanting, our vaine heart will be lifted up; and if Christians be confounded before God and men, when they are to resigne up their callings, it is a signe that either they have no faith, or it puts not forth life and courage into them; and if it so fall out, know that the root of it springs from an unbeleeving heart.

Vse 2. It is an Use of instruction to every Christian soule that desires to walke by faith in his calling. If thou wouldst live a lively life, and have thy soule and body to prosper in thy calling, labour then to get into a good calling, and therein live to the good of others; take up no calling, but that thou hast understanding in, and never take it unlesse thou mayest have it by lawfull and just meanes, and when thou hast it, serve God in thy calling, and doe it with cheerfulnesse, and faithful-nesse, and an heavenly minde; and in difficulties and dangers, cast thy cares and feares upon God, and see if he will not beare them for thee; and frame thy heart to this heavenly moderation in all successes to sanctifie Gods name; and if the houre and power of darknesse come, that thou beest to resigne up thy calling, let it bee enough that con-science may witnesse to thee, that thou hast not sought thy selfe, nor this world, but hast wrought the Lords workes; thou mayest then have comfort in it, both before God and men.

Vse 3. It is a word of consolation to every such soule, as hath beene acquainted with this life of faith in his calling, Bee thy calling never so meane and homely, and never so hardly accepted, yet, if thou hast lived by faith in thy calling, it was a lively worke in the sight of God, and so it will be rewarded when thy change shall come; Many a Christian is apt to be discouraged and dismaid if crosses befall him in his calling, but be not afraid, let this cheare up thy spirit, that what ever thy calling was, yet thou camest into it honestly, and hast lived in it faithfully, your course was lively and spirituall, and therefore you may with courage looke up for recompence from Christ.

JOHN WINTHROP

John Winthrop (1588—1649) was an important attorney descended from an affluent English family. Interested in religion as a youth, he became attached to Puritanism. Finally convinced that the cause could not flourish in England, he joined the Massachusetts Bay Colony, of which he was elected Governor. Sailing on the *Arbella*, Winthrop's group arrived at Salem in 1630, and in the following year he moved to Boston. Thenceforth, Winthrop was the most prominent citizen of the colony during his lifetime. He formulated the theocratic policy of the colony and, opposed to thorough democracy, sternly opposed Anne Hutchinson and her fellow Quakers. The following selection* illustrates the theory of theocracy.

A Modell of Christian Charity

Written
On Boarde the Arrabella,
On the Attlantick Ocean.
By the Honorable John Winthrop Esquire.

In His passage, (with the great Company of Religious people, of which Christian Tribes he was the Brave Leader and famous Governor); from the Island of Great Brittaine, to New-England in the North America.

Anno 1630.
CHRISTIAN CHARITIE.
A Modell Hereof.

God almightie in his most holy and wise providence hath soe disposed of the Condicion of mankinde, as in all times some must be rich some poore, some highe and eminent in power and dignitie; others meane and in subieccion.

The Reason Hereof.

1.　Reas: *First*, to hold conformity with the rest of his workes, being delighted to shewe forthe the glory of his wisdome in the variety and differance of the Creatures and the glory of his power, in ordering all these differences for the preservacion and good of the whole, and the glory of his greatnes that as it is the glory of princes to haue many

* From Winthrop Papers, Vol. II (Boston: Massachusetts Historical Society, 1931). Used by permission.

officers, soe this great King will haue many Stewards counting himselfe more honoured in dispenceing his guifts to man by man, then if hee did it by his owne immediate hand.

2. Reas: *Secondly*, That he might haue the more occasion to manifest the worke of his Spirit: first, vpon the wicked in moderateing and restraineing them: soe that the riche and mighty should not eate vpp the poore, nor the poore, and disposed rise vpp against their superiours, and shake off theire yoake; 2ly in the regenerate in exerciseing his graces in them, as in the greate ones, theire loue mercy, gentlenes, temperance etc., in the poore and inferiour sorte, theire faithe patience, obedience etc:

3. Reas: *Thirdly*, That every man might haue need of other, and from hence they might be all knitt more nearly together in the Bond of brotherly affeccion: from hence it appeares plainely that noe man is made more honourable then another or more wealthy etc., out of any perticuler and singuler respect to himselfe but for the glory of his Creator and the Common good of the Creature, Man; Therefore God still reserues the propperty of these guifts to himselfe as Ezek: 16. 17. he there calls wealthe his gold and his silver etc. Prov: 3. 9. he claimes theire seruice as his due honour the Lord with thy riches etc. All men being thus (by divine providence) rancked into two sortes, riche and poore; vnder the first, are comprehended all such as are able to liue comfortably by theire owne meanes duely improued; and all others are poore according to the former distribution. There are two rules whereby wee are to walke one towards another: JUSTICE and MERCY. These are allwayes distinguished in theire Act and in theire obiect, yet may they both concurre in the same Subiect in eache respect; as sometimes there may be an occasion of shewing mercy to a rich man, in some sudden danger of distresse, and allsoe doeing of meere Justice to a poor man in regard of some perticuler contract etc. There is likewise a double Lawe by which wee are regulated in our conversacion one towardes another: in both the former respects, the lawe of nature and the lawe of grace, or the morrall lawe or the lawe of the gospell, to omitt the rule of Justice as not propperly belonging to this purpose otherwise then it may fall into consideracion in some perticuler Cases: By the first of these lawes man as he was enabled soe withall [is] commaunded to loue his neighbour as himselfe vpon this ground stands all the precepts of the morrall lawe, which concernes our dealings with men. To apply this to the works of mercy this lawe requires two things first that every man afford his help to another in every want or distresse. Secondly,

That hee performe this out of the same affeccion, which makes him carefull of his owne good according to that of our Saviour Math: [7. 12.] Whatsoever ye would that men should doe to you. This was practised by Abraham and Lott in entertaineing the Angells and the old man of Gibea.

The Lawe of Grace or the Gospell hath some differance from the former as in these respects first the lawe of nature was giuen to man in the estate of innocency; this of the gospell in the estate of regeneracy: 2ly, the former propounds one man to another, as the same fleshe and Image of god, this as a brother in Christ allsoe, and in the Communion of the same spirit and soe teacheth vs to put a differencc betweene Christians and others. Doe good to all especially to the household of faith; vpon this ground the Israelites were to putt a difference betweene the brethren of such as were strangers though not of the Canaanites. 3ly. The Lawe of nature could giue noe rules for dealeing with enemies for all are to be considered as freinds in the estate of innocency, but the Gospell commaunds loue to an enemy. proofe[:] If thine Enemie hunger feede him; Loue your Enemies doe good to them that hate you Math: 5. 44.

This Lawe of the Gospell propoundes likewise a difference of seasons and occasions there is a time when a christian must sell all and giue to the poore as they did in the Apostles times. There is a tyme allsoe when a christian (though they giue not all yet) must giue beyond theire abillity, as they of Macedonia. Cor: 2. 6. likewise community of perills calls for extraordinary liberallity and soe doth Community in some speciall seruice for the Churche. Lastly, when there is noe other meanes whereby our Christian brother may be releiued in this distresse, wee must help him beyond our ability, rather then tempt God, in putting him upon help by miraculous or extraordinary meanes. . . .

1.   For the persons, wee are a Company professing our selues fellow members of Christ, In which respect onely though wee were absent from eache other many miles, and had our imploymentes as farre distant, yet wee ought to account our selues knitt together by this bond of loue, and liue in the exercise of it, if wee would haue comforte of our being in Christ, this was notorious in the practise of the Christians in former times, as is testified of the Waldenses from the mouth of one of the adversaries Aeneas Syluius, mutuo [solent amare] pene antequam norint, they vse to loue any of theire owne religion even before they were acquainted with them.

2ly. for the worke wee haue in hand, it is by a mutuall consent through a speciall overruleing providence, and a more then an ordinary approbation of the Churches of Christ to seeke out a place of Cohabitation and Consorteshipp vnder a due forme of Government both ciuill and ecclesiasticall. In such cases as this the care of the publique must oversway all private respects, by which not onely conscience, but meare Ciuill pollicy doth binde vs; for it is a true rule that perticuler estates cannott subsist in the ruine of the publique.

3ly. The end is to improue our liues to doe more seruice to the Lord the comforte and encrease of the body of Christe whereof wee are members that our selues and posterity may be the better preserued from the Common corrupcions of this euill world to serue the Lord and worke out our Salvacion vnder the power and purity of his holy Ordinances.

4ly for the meanes whereby this must bee effected, they are 2fold, a Conformity with the worke and end wee aime at, these wee see are extraordinary, therefore wee must not content our selues with vsuall ordinary meanes whatsoever wee did or ought to haue done when wee liued in England, the same must wee doe and more allsoe where wee goe: That which the most in theire Churches maineteine as a truthe in profession onely, wee must bring into familiar and constant practice, as in this duty of loue wee must loue brotherly without dissimulation, wee must loue one another with a pure hearte feruently wee must beare one anothers burthens, wee must not looke only on our owne things, but allsoe on the things of our brethren, neither must wee think that the lord will beare with such faileings at our hands as hee dothe from those among whome wee haue liued. . . .

Thus stands the cause betweene God and vs, wee are entered into Covenant with him for this worke, wee haue taken out a Commission, the Lord hath giuen vs leaue to drawe our owne Articles wee haue professed to enterprise these Accions vpon these and these ends, wee haue herevpon besought him of favour and blessing: Now if the Lord shall please to heare vs, and bring vs in peace to the place wee desire, then hath hee ratified this Covenant and sealed our Commission, [and] will expect a strickt performance of the Articles contained in it, but if wee shall neglect the observacion of these Articles which are the ends wee haue propounded, and dissembling with our God, shall fall to embrace this present world and prosecute our carnall intencions seekeing greate things for our selues and our posterity, the Lord will surely breake out in wrathe against vs be revenged of such a periured people and make vs knowe the price of the breache of such a Covenant.

Now the only way to avoyde this shipwracke and to provide for our posterity is to followe the Counsell of Micah, to doe Justly, to loue mercy, to walke humbly with our God, for this end, wee must be knitt together in this worke as one man, wee must entertaine each other in brotherly Affeccion, wee must be willing to abridge our selues of our superfluities, for the supply of others necessities, wee must vphold a familiar Commerce together in all meekenes, gentlenes, patience and liberallity, wee must delight in eache other, make others Condicions our owne reioyce together, mourne together, labour, and suffer together, allwayes haueing before our eyes our Commission and Community in the worke, our Community as members of the same body, soe shall wee keepe the vnitie of the spirit in the bond of peace, the Lord will be our God and delight to dwell among vs, as his owne people and will commaund a blessing vpon vs in all our wayes, soe that wee shall see much more of his wisdome power goodness and truthe then formerly wee haue beene acquainted with, wee shall finde that the God of Israell is among vs, when tenn of vs shall be able to resist a thousand of our enemies, when hee shall make vs a prayse and glory, that men shall say of succeeding plantacions: the lord make it like that of New England: for wee must Consider that wee shall be as a Citty vpon a Hill, the eies of all people are vppon vs; soe that if wee shall deale falsely with our god in this worke wee haue vndertaken and soe cause him to withdrawe his present help from vs, wee shall be made a story and a by-word through the world, wee shall open the mouthes of enemies to speake euill of the wayes of god and all professours for Gods sake; wee shall shame the faces of many of gods worthy seruants, and cause theire prayers to be turned into Cursses vpon vs till wee be consumed out of the good land whether wee are goeing: And to shutt vpp this discourse with that exhortacion of Moses that faithfull seruant of the Lord in his last farewell to Israell Deut. 30. Beloued there is now sett before vs life, and good, deathe and euill in that wee are Commaunded this day to loue the Lord our God, and to loue one another to walke in his wayes and to keepe his Commaundements and his Ordinance, and his lawes, and the Articles of our Covenant with him that wee may liue and be multiplyed, and that the Lord our God may blesse vs in the land whether wee goe to possesse it: But if our heartes shall turne away soe that wee will not obey, but shall be seduced and worshipp . . . other Gods our pleasures, and proffitts, and serue them; it is propounded vnto vs this day, wee shall surely perishe out of the good Land whether wee passe over this vast Sea to possesse it;

Therefore lett vs choose life,
that wee, and our Seede,
may liue; by obeyeing his
voyce, and cleaueing to him,
for hee is our life, and
our prosperity.

JOHN WISE

John Wise (1652–1725), born in Massachusetts, was an important American clergyman and an eloquent spokesman for
democratic Congregationalism. He was removed from his
ministerial office for a time by Governor Andros because he
persuaded his fellow townsmen not to pay taxes that violated their
charter rights. He was opposed to Increase Mather and Cotton
Mather in their plan to organize the different churches under the
supervision of a group of ministers. Wise played a role in stopping
the witch hunts and signed a petition to acquit those who had been
condemned. He was a constant representative of democratic
principles, and though few details of his career are known, his
writings were influential long after his death. The following
selection, which shows the democratic temper of Wise's thought,
is from the first edition of the *Vindication of the Government of
New-England Churches*, 1717.

The Light of Nature

Chap. II.

. . . I shall consider Man in a state of Natural Being, as a Free-Born
Subject under the Crown of Heaven, and owing Homage to none but
God himself. It is certain Civil Government in General, is a very
Admirable Result of Providence, and an Incomparable Benefit to Man-
kind, yet must needs be acknowledged to be the Effect of Humane
Free-Compacts and not of Divine Institution; it is the Produce of Mans
Reason, of Humane and Rational Combinations, and not from any
direct Orders of Infinite Wisdom, in any positive Law wherein is drawn
up this or that Scheme of Civil Government. Government . . . is neces-
sary—in that no Society of Men can subsist without it; and that Particular Form of Government is necessary which best suits the Temper and
Inclination of a People. Nothing can be Gods Ordinance, but what he
has particularly Declared to be such; there is no particular Form of
Civil Government described in Gods Word, neither does Nature
prompt it. The Government of the *Jews* was changed five Times.
Government is not formed by Nature, as other Births or Productions;
If it were, it would be the same in all Countries; because Nature keeps
the same Method, in the same thing, in all Climates. If a Common
Wealth be changed into a Monarchy, is it Nature that forms, and brings
forth the Monarch? Or if a Royal Family be wholly Extinct (as in

Noah's Case, being not Heir Apparent from Descent from *Adam*) is it Nature that must go to work (with the King Bees, who themselves alone preserve the Royal Race in that Empire) to Breed a Monarch before the People can have a King, or a Government sent over them? And thus we must leave Kings to Resolve which is their best Title to their Crowns, whether Natural Right, or the Constitution of Government settled by Humane Compacts, under the Direction and Conduct of Reason. But to proceed under the head of a State of Natural Being, I shall more distinctly Explain the State of Humane Nature in its Original Capacity, as Man is placed on Earth by his Maker, and Cloathed with many Investitures, and Immunities which properly belong to Man separately considered. As,

1.   The Prime Immunity in Mans State, is that he is most properly the Subject of the Law of Nature. He is the Favourite Animal on Earth; in that this Part of Gods Image, *viz.* Reason is Congenate with his Nature, wherein by a Law Immutable, Instampt upon his Frame, God has provided a Rule for Men in all their Actions, obliging each one to the performance of that which is Right, not only as to Justice, but likewise as to all other Moral Vertues, the which is nothing but the Dictate of Right Reason founded in the Soul of Man. . . . That which is to be drawn from Mans Reason, flowing from the true Current of that Faculty, when unperverted, may be said to be the Law of Nature; on which account, the Holy Scriptures declare it written on Mens hearts. For being indowed with a Soul, you may know from your self, how, and what you ought to act, Rom. 2. 14. *These having not a Law, are a Law to themselves.* So that the meaning is, when we acknowledge the Law of Nature to be the dictate of Right Reason, we must mean that the Understanding of Man is Endowed with such a power, as to be able, from the Comtemplation of humane Condition to discover a necessity of Living agreeably with this Law: And likewise to find out some Principle, by which the Precepts of it, may be clearly and solidly Demonstrated. The way to discover the Law of Nature in our own state, is by a narrow Watch, and accurate Contemplation of our Natural Condition, and propensions. Others say this is the way to find out the Law of Nature. *scil.* If a Man any ways doubts, whether what he is going to do to another Man be agreeable to the Law of Nature, then let him suppose himself to be in that other Mans Room; And by this Rule effectually Executed. A Man must be a very dull Scholar to Nature not to make Proficiency in the Knowledge of her Laws. But more Particularly in pursuing our Condition for the discovery of the Law of

Nature, this is very obvious to view, *viz.*

1. A Principle of Self-Love, & Self-Preservation, is very predominant in every Mans Being.

2. A Social Disposition.

3. An Affection or Love to Man-kind in General. And to give such Sentiments the force of a Law, we must suppose a God who takes care of all Mankind, and has thus obliged each one, as a Subject of higher Principles of Being, then meer Instincts. For that all Law properly considered, supposes a capable Subject, and a Superiour Power; And the Law of God which is Binding, is published by the Dictates of Right Reason as other ways: Therefore says *Plutarch, To follow God and obey Reason is the same thing.* But moreover that God has Established the Law of Nature, as the General Rule of Government, is further Illustrable from the many Sanctions in Providence, and from the Peace and Guilt of Conscience in them that either obey, or violate the Law of Nature. But moreover, the foundation of the Law of Nature with relation to Government, may be thus Discovered. *scil.* Man is a Creature extreamly desirous of his own Preservation; of himself he is plainly Exposed to many Wants, unable to secure his own safety, and Maintenance without the Assistance of his fellows; and he is also able of returning Kindness by the furtherance of mutual Good; But yet Man is often found to be Malicious, Insolent, and easily Provoked, and as powerful in Effecting mischief, as he is ready in designing it. Now that such a Creature may be Preserved, it is necessary that he be Sociable; that is, that he be capable and disposed to unite himself to those of his own species, and to Regulate himself towards them, that they may have no fair Reason to do him harm; but rather incline to promote his Interests, and secure his Rights and Concerns. This then is a Fundamental Law of Nature, that every Man as far as in him lies, do maintain a Sociableness with others, agreeable with the main end and disposition of humane Nature in general. For this is very apparent, that Reason and Society render Man the most potent of all Creatures. And Finally, from the Principles of Sociableness it follows as a fundamental Law of Nature, that Man is not so Wedded to his own Interest, but that he can make the Common good the mark of his Aim: And hence he becomes Capacitated to enter into a Civil State by the Law of Nature; for without this property in Nature, *viz.* Sociableness, which is for Cementing of parts, every Government would soon moulder and dissolve.

2. The Second Great Immunity of Man is an Original Liberty Instampt upon his Rational Nature. He that intrudes upon this Liberty, Violates the Law of Nature. In this Discourse I shall wave the Consideration of Mans Moral Turpitude, but shall view him Physically as a Creature which God has made and furnished essentially with many Enobling Immunities, which render him the most August Animal in the World, and still, whatever has happened since his Creation, he remains at the upper-end of Nature, and as such is a Creature of a very noble Character. For as to his Dominion, the whole frame of the Lower Part of the Universe is devoted to his use, and at his Command; and his Liberty under the Conduct of Right Reason, is equal with his trust. Which Liberty may be briefly Considered, Internally as to his mind, and Externally as to his person.

1. The Internal Native Liberty of Mans Nature in general implies, a faculty of Doing or Omitting things according to the Direction of his Judgment. But in a more special meaning, this Liberty does not consist in a loose and ungovernable Freedom, or in an unbounded Licence of Acting. Such Licence is disagreeing with the condition and dignity of Man, and would make Man of a lower and meaner Constitution then Bruit Creatures; who in all their Liberties are kept under a better and more Rational Government, by their Instincts. Therefore as *Plutarch* says, *Those Persons only who live in Obedience to Reason, are worthy to be accounted free: They alone live as they Will, who have Learnt what they ought to Will.* So that the true Natural Liberty of Man, such as really and truely agrees to him, must be understood, as he is Guided and Restrained by the Tyes of Reason, and Laws of Nature; all the rest is Brutal, if not worse.

2. Mans External Personal, Natural Liberty, Antecedent to all Humane parts, or Alliances must also be considered. And so every Man must be conceived to be perfectly in his own Power and disposal, and not to be controuled by the Authority of any other. And thus every Man, must be acknowledged equal to every Man, since all Subjection and all Command are equally banished on both sides; and considering all Men thus at Liberty, every Man has a Prerogative to Judge for himself, *viz.* What shall be most for his Behoof, Happiness and Wellbeing.

3. The Third Capital Immunity belonging to Mans Nature, is an equality amongst Men; Which is not to be denied by the Law of Nature till Man has Resigned himself with all his Rights for the sake of a Civil State; and then his Personal Liberty and Equality is to be cherished, and preserved to the highest degree, as will consist with all just distinctions

amongst Men of Honour, and shall be agreeable with the publick Good. For Man has a high valuation of himself, and the passion seems to lay its first foundation (not in Pride, but) really in the high and admirable Frame and Constitution of Humane Nature. The Word Man, says my Author, is thought to carry somewhat of Dignity in its sound; and we commonly make use of this as the most proper and prevailing Argument against a rude Insulter, *viz. I am not a Beast or a Dog, but am a Man as well as your self.* Since then Humane Nature agrees equally with all persons; and since no one can live a Sociable Life with another that does not own or Respect him as a Man; It follows as a Command of the Law of Nature, that every Man Esteem and treat another as one who is naturally his Equal, or who is a Man as well as he. There be many popular, or plausible Reasons that greatly Illustrate this Equality, *viz.* that we all Derive our Being from one stock, the same Common Father of humane Race. . . .

3. A Democracy. This is a form of Government, which the Light of Nature does highly value, & often directs to as most agreeable to the Just and Natural Prerogatives of Humane Beings. This was of great account, in the early times of the World. And not only so, but upon the Experience of several Thousand years, after the World had been tumbled, and tost from one Species of Government to another, at a great Expence of Blood and Treasure, many of the wise Nations of the World have sheltered themselves under it again; or at least have blendished, and balanced their Governments with it.

It is certainly a great Truth, *scil.* That Mans Original Liberty after it is Resigned, (yet under due Restrictions) ought to be Cherished in all wise Governments; or otherwise a man in making himself a Subject, he alters himself from a Freeman, into a Slave, which to do is Repugnant to the Law of Nature. Also the Natural Equality of Men amongst Men must be duly favoured; in that Government was never Established by God or Nature, to give one Man a Prerogative to insult over another; therefore in a Civil, as well as in a Natural State of Being, a just Equality is to be indulged so far as that every Man is bound to Honour every Man, which is agreeable both with Nature and Religion, 1 Pet. 2, 17. *Honour all Men.*—The End of all good Government is to Cultivate Humanity, and Promote the happiness of all, and the good of every Man in all his Rights, his Life, Liberty, Estate, Honour, &c. without injury or abuse done to any. Then certainly it cannot easily be thought, that a company of Men, that shall enter into a voluntary Compact, to hold all Power in their own hands, thereby to use and improve their united force, wisdom, riches and strength for the Common and Particular good of every Member, as is the Nature of a Democracy; I say it cannot be that this sort of Constitution, will so readily furnish those in Government with an appetite, or disposition to prey upon each other, or imbezle the common Stock; as some Particular Persons may be apt to do when set off, and Intrusted with the same Power. And moreover this appears very Natural, that when the aforesaid Government or Power, settled in all, when they have Elected certain capable Persons to Minister in their affairs, and the said Ministers remain accountable to the Assembly; these Officers must needs be under the influence of many wise cautions from their own thoughts (as well as under confinement by their Commission) in their whole Administration: And from thence it must needs follow that they will be more apt, and inclined to steer Right for the main Point, *viz*. The peculiar good, and benefit of the whole, and every particular Member fairly and sincerely. And why may not these stand for very Rational Pleas in Church Order?

For certainly if Christ has settled any form of Power in his Church he has done it for his Churches safety, and for the Benefit of every Member: Then he must needs be presumed to have made choice of that Government as should least Expose his People to Hazard, either from the fraud, or Arbitrary measures of particular Men. And it is as plain as day light, there is no Species of Government like a Democracy to attain this End. There is but about two steps from an Aristocracy, to a Monarchy, and from thence but one to a Tyranny; an able standing force, and an Ill-Nature, *Ipso facto*, turns an absolute Monarch into a Tyrant; this is obvious among the Roman *Caesars*, and through the World. And all these direful Transmutations are easier in Church affairs (from the different Qualities of things) then in Civil States. For what is it that cunning and learned Men can't make the World swallow as an Article of their Creed, if they are once invested with an Uncontroulable Power, and are to be the standing Oratours to Mankind in matters of Faith and Obedience?

JONATHAN EDWARDS

Jonathan Edwards (1703–58) became one of America's most distinguished theologians and ministers. After graduating from Yale, he studied theology, and in 1727 joined his grandfather, Solomon Stoddard, in the ministry at Northampton, Massachusetts. Here he developed his famous defences of Calvinism and preached the fiery sermons about the terror of hell, which helped to set off the Great Awakening, a religious revival that swept over the colonies from 1730 to 1750. In 1750 his congregation dismissed him, and he moved to Stockbridge, Massachusetts, where he preached to a small congregation and tutored Indian youngsters. In 1757 he was named president of Princeton, but he died shortly afterward. This selection, which shows how Edwards conceived mortal existence, is taken from Edwards, *Works* (ed. Dwight, 1829), Vol. VII.

The Christian Pilgrim

SECTION II
Why the Christian's life is a journey or pilgrimage?

1.   This world is not our abiding place. Our continuance here is but very short. Man's days on the earth, are as a shadow. It was never designed by God that this world should be our home. Neither did God give us these temporal accommodations for that end. If God has given us ample estates, and children, or other pleasant friends, it is with no such design, that we should be furnished here, as for a settled abode; but with a design that we should use them for the present, and then leave them in a very little time. When we are called to any secular business, or charged with the care of a family, if we improve our lives to any other purpose, than as a journey toward heaven, all our labour will be lost. If we spend our lives in the pursuit of a temporal happiness; as riches, or sensual pleasures; credit and esteem from men; delight in our children, and the prospect of seeing them well brought up, and well settled, &c.—All these things will be of little significancy to us. Death will blow up all our hopes, and will put an end to these enjoyments. "The places that have known us, will know us no more": and "the eye that has seen us, shall see us no more." We must be taken away for ever from all these things; and it is uncertain when: it may be soon after we are put into the possession of them. And then, where will be all our worldly employments and enjoyments, when we are laid in the

silent grave! "So man lieth down, and riseth not again, till the heavens be no more."*

2. The future world was designed to be our settled and everlasting abode. There it was intended that we should be fixed; and there alone is a lasting habitation, and a lasting inheritance. The present state is short and transitory; but our state in the other world, is everlasting. And as we are there at first, so we must be without change. Our state in the future world, therefore, being eternal, is of so much greater importance than our state here, that all our concerns in this world should be wholly subordinated to it.

3. Heaven is that place alone where our highest end, and highest good is to be obtained. God hath made us for himself. "Of him, and through him, and to him are all things." Therefore, then do we attain to our highest end, when we are brought to God: but that is by being brought to heaven; for that is God's throne, the place of his special presence. There is but a very imperfect union with God to be had in this world, a very imperfect knowledge of him in the midst of much darkness: a very imperfect conformity to God, mingled with abundance of estrangement. Here we can serve and glorify God, but in a very imperfect manner; our service being mingled with sin, which dishonours God.—But when we get to heaven, (if ever that be,) we shall be brought to a perfect union with God, and have more clear views of him. There we shall be fully conformed to God, without any remaining sin: for "we shall see him as he is." There we shall serve God perfectly; and glorify him in an exalted manner, even to the utmost of the powers and capacity of our nature. Then we shall perfectly give up ourselves to God: our hearts will be pure and holy offerings, presented in a flame of divine love.

God is the highest good of the reasonable creature; and the enjoyment of him is the only happiness with which our souls can be satisfied.—To go to heaven fully to enjoy God, is *infinitely* better than the most pleasant accommodations here. Fathers and mothers, husbands, wives, or children, or the company of earthly friends, are but shadows; but the enjoyment of God is the substance. These are but scattered beams; but God is the sun. These are but streams; but God is the fountain. These are but drops; but God is the ocean.—Therefore it becomes us to spend this life only as a journey towards heaven, as it becomes us to make the seeking of our highest end and proper good, the whole work of our lives; to which we should subordinate all other

* Job xiv. 12.

concerns of life. Why should we labour for, or set our hearts on any thing else, but that which is our proper end, and true happiness?

4. Our present state, and all that belongs to it, is designed by him that made all things, to be wholly in order to another world.—This world was made for a place of preparation for another. Man's mortal life was given him, that he might be prepared for his fixed state. And all that God has here given us, is given to this purpose. The sun shines, and the rain falls upon us; and the earth yields her increase to us for this end. Civil, ecclesiastical, and family affairs, and all our personal concerns, are designed and ordered in subordination to a future world, by the maker and disposer of all things. To this therefore they ought to be subordinated by us.

SECTION III

Instruction afforded by the consideration, that life is a journey or pilgrimage, towards heaven.

1. This doctrine may teach us moderation in our mourning for the loss of such dear friends, who, while they lived, improved their lives to right purposes. If they lived a holy life, then their lives were a journey towards heaven. And why should we be immoderate in mourning, when they are got to their journey's end? Death, though it appears to us with a frightful aspect, is to them a great blessing. Their end is happy, and better than their beginning. "*The day of their death, is better than the day of their birth.*"* While they lived, they desired heaven, and chose it above this world, or any of its enjoyments. For this they earnestly longed, and why should we grieve that they have obtained it?—Now they have got to their Father's house. They find more comfort a thousand times, now they are got home, than they did in their journey. In this world they underwent much labour and toil; it was a wilderness they passed through. There were many difficulties in the way; mountains and rough places. It was laborious and fatiguing to travel the road; and they had many wearisome days and nights: but now they have got to their everlasting rest. "And I heard a voice from heaven, saying unto me, Write, blessed are the dead which die in the Lord from henceforth: yea, saith the Spirit, that they may rest from their labours; and their works do follow them."† They look back upon the difficulties, and sorrows, and dangers of life, rejoicing that they have surmounted them all.

* Eccles. vii. 1.
† Rev. xiv. 13.

We are ready to look upon death as their calamity, and to mourn, that those who were so dear to us, should be in the dark grave; that they are there transformed to corruption and worms; taken away from their dear children and enjoyments, &c. as though they were in awful circumstances. But this is owing to our infirmity; they are in a happy condition, inconceivably blessed. They do not mourn, but rejoice with exceeding joy: their mouths are filled with joyful songs, and they drink at rivers of pleasure. They find no mixture of grief that they have changed their earthly enjoyments, and the company of mortals, for heaven. Their life here, though in the best circumstances, was attended with much that was adverse and afflictive: but now there is an end to all adversity. "They shall hunger no more, nor thirst any more; neither shall the sun light on them, nor any heat. For the Lamb which is in the midst of the throne, shall feed them and shall lead them unto living fountains of waters: and God shall wipe away all tears from their eyes."*

It is true, we shall see them no more in this world, yet we ought to consider that we are travelling towards the same place; and why should we break our hearts that they have got there before us? We are following after them, and hope, as soon as we get to our journey's end, to be with them again, in better circumstances. A degree of mourning for near relations when departed is not inconsistent with Christianity, but very agreeable to it; for as long as we are flesh and blood, we have animal propensities and affections. But we have just reason that our mourning should be mingled with joy. "But I would not have you to be ignorant, brethren, concerning them that are asleep, that ye sorrow not, even as others that have no hope:"† (*i.e.*) that they should not sorrow as the Heathen, who had no knowledge of a future happiness. This appears by the following verse; "*for if we believe that Jesus died and rose again, even so them also which sleep in Jesus, will God bring with him.*"

2. If our lives ought to be only a journey towards heaven; how ill do they improve their lives, that spend them in travelling towards hell?—Some men spend their whole lives, from their infancy to their dying day, in going down the broad way to destruction. They not only draw nearer to hell as to time, but they every day grow more ripe for destruction; they are more assimilated to the inhabitants of the infernal world. While others press forward in the straight and narrow way to

* Rev. vii. 16. 17.
† 1 Thess. iv. 13.

life, and laboriously travel up the hill toward Zion, against the inclinations and tendency of the flesh; these run with a swift career down to eternal death. This is the employment of every day, with all wicked men; and the whole day is spent in it. As soon as ever they awake in the morning, they set out anew in the way to hell, and spend every waking moment in it. They begin in early days. "The wicked are estranged from the womb, they go astray as soon as they are born, speaking lies."* They hold on it with perseverance. Many of them who live to be old, are never weary in it; though they live to be an hundred years old, they will not cease travelling in the way to hell, till they arrive there. And all the concerns of life are subordinated to this employment. A wicked man is a servant of sin; his powers and faculties are employed in the service of sin; and in fitness for hell. And all his possessions are so used by him as to be subservient to the same purpose. Men spend their time in treasuring up wrath against the day of wrath. Thus do all unclean persons, who live in lascivious practices in secret; all malicious persons; all profane persons, that neglect the duties of religion. Thus do all unjust persons; and those who are fraudulent and oppressive in their dealings. Thus do all backbiters and revilers; all covetous persons, that set their hearts chiefly on the riches of this world. Thus do tavern-haunters, and frequenters of evil company; and many other kinds that might be mentioned. Thus the bulk of mankind are hastening onward in the broad way to destruction; which is, as it were, filled up with the multitude that are going in it with one accord. And they are every day going to hell out of this broad way by thousands. Multitudes are continually flowing down into the great lake of fire and brimstone, as some mighty river constantly diembogues its water into the ocean.

3. Hence when persons are converted they do but begin their work, and set out in the way they have to go.—They never till then do any thing at that work in which their whole lives ought to be spent. Persons before conversion never take a step that way. Then does a man first set out on his journey, when he is brought home to Christ; and so far is he from having done his work, that his care and labour in his Christian work and business, is then but begun, in which he must spend the remaining part of his life.

Those persons do ill, who when they are converted, and have obtained a hope of their being in a good condition, do not strive as earnestly as

* Psalm xlviii. 4.

they did before, while they were under awakenings. They ought, henceforward, as long as they live, to be as earnest and laborious, as watchful and careful as ever; yea, they should increase more and more. It is no just excuse, that now they have obtained conversion. Should not we be as diligent that we may serve and glorify God, as that we ourselves may be happy? And if we have obtained grace, yet we ought to strive as much that we may obtain the other degrees that are before, as we did to obtain that small degree that is behind. The apostle tells us, that he forgot what was behind, and reached forth towards what was before.*

Yea, those who are converted, have now a further reason to strive for grace; for they have seen something of its excellency. A man who has once tasted the blessings of Canaan, has more reason to press towards it than he had before. And they who are converted, should strive to "make their calling and election sure." All those who are converted are not sure of it; and those who are sure, do not know that they shall be always so; and still seeking and serving God with the utmost diligence, is the way to have assurance, and to have it maintained.

* Phil. iii. 13.

WILLIAM ELLERY CHANNING

William Ellery Channing (1780–1842) was born in Newport, Rhode Island, and was graduated from Harvard, where he had studied theology. He was ordained minister at the Federal Street Church in Boston at the age of twenty-three, and he remained there for his lifetime. His influence was considerable, and those indebted to him include Ralph Waldo Emerson, Henry David Thoreau, and William Cullen Bryant. Besides influencing later Transcendentalism in New England, he was instrumental in founding the American Unitarian Association in 1825. His writings and sermons, which were widely read in Europe, show him to have been a humanitarian, a liberal in his views on slavery, war, labor, and education. His *Negro Slavery*, published in 1835, signaled the commencement of antislavery activities. The following selection, which epitomizes the controversial theology he espoused, is taken from a discourse at the Ordination of the Reverend F. A. Farley, Providence, Rhode Island, 1828.

Human Likeness to God

Ephesians V, 1: "Be ye therefore followers of God, as dear children."

To promote true religion is the purpose of the Christian ministry. For this it was ordained. On the present occasion, therefore, when a new teacher is to be given to the church, a discourse on the character of true religion will not be inappropriate. I do not mean that I shall attempt, in the limits to which I am now confined, to set before you all its properties, signs, and operations; for in so doing I should burden your memories with divisions and vague generalities as uninteresting as they would be unprofitable. My purpose is to select one view of the subject which seems to me of primary dignity and importance; and I select this because it is greatly neglected, and because I attribute to this neglect, much of the inefficacy and many of the corruptions of religion.

The text calls us to follow or imitate God, to seek accordance with or likeness to him; and to do this not fearfully and faintly, but with the spirit and hope of beloved children. The doctrine which I propose to illustrate is derived immediately from these words, and is incorporated with the whole New Testament. I affirm and would maintain, that true religion consists in proposing, as our great end, a growing likeness to the Supreme Being. Its noblest influence consists in making us more and more partakers of the Divinity. For this is it to be preached. Religious instruction should aim chiefly to turn men's aspirations and efforts to that perfection of the soul which constitutes it a bright image of God. Such is the topic now to be discussed; and I implore Him whose glory I seek to aid me in unfolding and enforcing it with simplicity and clearness, with a calm and pure zeal, and with unfeigned charity.

I begin with observing, what all indeed will understand, that the likeness to God, of which I propose to speak, belongs to man's higher or spiritual nature. It has its foundation in the original and essential capacities of the mind. In proportion as these are unfolded by right and vigorous exertion, it is extended and brightened. In proportion as these lie dormant, it is obscured. In proportion as they are perverted and overpowered by the appetites and passions, it is blotted out. In truth, moral evil, if unresisted and habitual, may so blight and lay waste these capacities, that the image of God in man may seem to be wholly destroyed.

The importance of this assimilation to our Creator is a topic which needs no labored discussion. All men, of whatever name, or sect, or opinion, will meet me on this ground. All, I presume, will allow that no good in the compass of the universe, or within the gift of omnipotence, can be compared to a resemblance of God, or to a participation of his attributes. I fear no contradiction here. Likeness to God is the supreme gift. He can communicate nothing so precious, glorious, blessed as himself. To hold intellectual and moral affinity with the Supreme Being, to partake his spirit, to be his children by derivations of kindred excellence, to bear a growing conformity to the perfection which we adore,—this is a felicity which obscures and annihilates all other good.

It is only in proportion to this likeness that we can enjoy either God or the universe. That God can be known and enjoyed only through sympathy or kindred attributes, is a doctrine which even Gentile philosophy discerned. That the pure in heart can alone see and commune with the pure Divinity, was the sublime instruction of ancient sages as well as of inspired prophets. It is indeed the lesson of daily experience. To understand a great and good being, we must have the seeds of the same excellence. How quickly, by what an instinct, do accordant minds recognize one another! No attraction is so powerful as that which subsists between the truly wise and good; whilst the brightest excellence is lost on those who have nothing congenial in their own breasts. God becomes a real being to us in proportion as his own nature is unfolded within us. To a man who is growing in the likeness of God, faith begins even here to change into vision. He carries within himself a proof of a Deity, which can only be understood by experience. He more than believes, he feels the Divine presence; and gradually rises to an intercourse with his Maker, to which it is not irreverent to apply the name of friendship and intimacy. The Apostle John intended to express this truth, when he tells us that he in whom a principle of divine charity or benevolence has become a habit and life "dwells in God and God in him."

It is plain, too, that likeness to God is the true and only preparation for the enjoyment of the universe. In proportion as we approach and resemble the mind of God, we are brought into harmony with the creation; for in that proportion we possess the principles from which the universe sprung: we carry within ourselves the perfections of which its beauty, magnificence, order, benevolent adaptations, and boundless purposes are the results and manifestations. God unfolds himself in his works to a kindred mind. It is possible that the brevity of these hints may expose to the charge of mysticism what seems to me the calmest and clearest truth. I think, however, that every reflecting man will feel that likeness to God must be a principle of sympathy or accordance with his creation; for the creation is a birth and shining forth of the Divine Mind, a work through which his spirit breathes. In proportion as we receive this spirit we possess within ourselves the explanation of what we see. We discern more and more of God in every thing, from the frail flower to the everlasting stars. Even in evil, that dark cloud which hangs over the creation, we discern rays of light and hope, and gradually come to see, in suffering and temptation, proofs and instruments of the sublimest purposes of wisdom and love.

I have offered these very imperfect views that I may show the great importance of the doctrine which I am solicitous to enforce. I would teach that likeness to God is a good so unutterably surpassing all other good, that whoever admits it as attainable must acknowledge it to be the chief aim of life. I would show that the highest and happiest office of religion is to bring the mind into growing accordance with God; and that by the tendency of religious systems to this end their truth and worth are to be chiefly tried.

*   *   *

That man has a kindred nature with God, and may bear most important and ennobling relations to him, seems to me to be established by a striking proof. This proof you will understand by considering, for a moment, how we obtain our ideas of God. Whence come the conceptions which we include under that august name? Whence do we derive our knowledge of the attributes and perfections which constitute the Supreme Being? I answer, we derive them from our own souls. The divine attributes are first developed in ourselves, and thence transferred to our Creator. The idea of God, sublime and awful as it is, is the idea of our own spiritual nature, purified and enlarged to infinity. In ourselves are the elements of the Divinity. God, then, does not sustain a figurative resemblance to man. It is the resemblance of a parent to a child, the likeness of a kindred nature.

We call God a Mind. He has revealed himself as a Spirit. But what do we know of mind but through the unfolding of this principle in our own breasts? That unbounded spiritual energy which we call God is conceived by us only through consciousness, through the knowledge of ourselves. We ascribe thought or intelligence to the Deity, as one of his most glorious attributes. And what means this language? These terms we have framed to express operations or faculties of our own souls. The Infinite Light would be for ever hidden from us did not kindred rays dawn and brighten within us. God is another name for human intelligence raised above all error and imperfection, and extended to all possible truth.

The same is true of God's goodness. How do we understand this but by the principle of love implanted in the human breast? Whence is it that this divine attribute is so faintly comprehended, but from the feeble development of it in the multitude of men? Who can understand the strength, purity, fulness, and extent of divine philanthropy, but he in whom selfishness has been swallowed up in love?

*   *   *

I regard this view of religion as infinitely important. It does more than all things to make our connection with our Creator ennobling and happy; and, in proportion as we want it, there is danger that the thought of God may itself become the instrument of our degradation. That religion has been so dispensed as to depress the human mind, I need not tell you; and it is a truth which ought to be known, that the greatness of the Deity, when separated in our thoughts from his parental character, especially tends to crush human energy and hope. To a frail, dependent creature, an omnipotent Creator easily becomes a terror, and his worship easily degenerates into servility, flattery, self-contempt, and selfish calculation. Religion only ennobles us, in as far as it reveals to us the tender and intimate connection of God with his creatures, and teaches us to see in the very greatness which might give alarm the source of great and glorious communications to the human soul. You cannot, my hearers, think too highly of the majesty of God. But let not this majesty sever him from you. Remember that his greatness is the infinity of attributes which yourselves possess. Adore his infinite wisdom; but remember that this wisdom rejoices to diffuse itself, and let an exhilarating hope spring up at the thought of the immeasurable intelligence which such a Father must communicate to his children. In like manner adore his power. Let the boundless creation fill you with awe and admiration of the energy which sustains it. But remember that God has a nobler work than the outward creation, even the spirit within yourselves; and that it is his purpose to replenish this with his own energy, and to crown it with growing power and triumphs over the material universe. Above all, adore his unutterable goodness. But remember that this attribute is particularly proposed to you as your model; that God calls you both by nature and revelation, to a fellow-ship in his philanthropy; that he has placed you in social relations for the very end of rendering you ministers and representatives of his benevolence; that he even summons you to espouse and to advance the sublimest purpose of his goodness, the redemption of the human race, by extending the knowledge and power of Christian truth. It is through such views that religion raises up the soul, and binds man by ennobling bonds to his Maker.

To complete my views of this topic, I beg to add an important caution. I have said that the great work of religion is to conform ourselves to God, or to unfold the divine likeness within us. Let none infer from this language that I place religion in unnatural effort, in straining after excitements which do not belong to the present state, or in any thing separate from the clear and simple duties of life. I exhort you to no extravagance. I reverence human nature too much to do it violence. I see too much divinity in its ordinary operations to urge on it a forced and vehement virtue. To grow in the likeness of God we need not cease to be men. This likeness does not consist in extraordinary or miraculous gifts, in supernatural additions to the soul, or in any thing foreign to our original constitution; but in our essential faculties, unfolded by vigorous and conscientious exertion in the ordinary circumstances assigned by God. To resemble our Creator we need not fly from society, and entrance ourselves in lonely contemplation and prayer. Such processes might give a feverish strength to one class of emotions, but would result in disproportion, distortion, and sickliness of mind. Our proper work is to approach God by the free and natural unfolding of our highest powers,—of understanding, conscience, love, and the moral will...

JOSIAH ROYCE

Josiah Royce (1855–1916) came from a humble background in California. Encouraged by his mother, he achieved an education, graduating from the University of California in 1873. Royce studied philosophy at Johns Hopkins and in Germany, and then taught at the University of California. William James was responsible for bringing Royce to Harvard in 1882, where he taught for the remainder of his life. He became one of America's most distinguished writers of philosophy, representing the tradition of post-Kantian Idealism. Reality, he argued, is the experience of an absolute mind or God, and man's essential relation is to the Absolute. His range of interests was remarkable, from mathematical logic to philosophy of religion. The following selection* presents Royce's famous argument to prove God's existence.

How Reason Proves God

An opinion of yours may be true or false. But when you form an opinion, what are you trying to do? You are trying to anticipate, in some fashion, what a wider view, a larger experience of your present situation, a fuller insight into your present ideas, and into what they mean, would show you, if you now had that wider view and larger experience. Such an effort to anticipate what the wider view would even now show, if you were possessed of that view, involves both what are usually called theoretical interests and what pragmatists, such as James himself, have often characterised as practical interests. One can express the matter by saying, that you are trying, through your opinions, to predict what a larger insight, if it were present to you, would show or would find, that is, would experience. You can also say that you are trying to define what a fuller apprehension and a fairer estimate of your present purposes, and intentions, and interests, and deeds, and of their outcome, and of their place in life, would bring before your vision. In brief (whether you lay more stress upon deeds and their outcome, or upon experiences and their contents), any expression of opinion, made at any time, is an appeal of the self of the moment to the verdict, to the estimate, to the experience of a larger and better informed insight, in the light of which the self of the moment proposes to be judged. The special criteria by which your momentary opinion is tested, at the time

* From *The Sources of Religious Insight*, pages 107–16; copyright 1912 the Trustees of Lake Forest University; renewal copyright 1940. Reprinted with the permission of Charles Scribner's Sons.

when you form that opinion, vary endlessly with your mood and your training and your feelings, and with the topics and tasks in which you happen to be interested. But the universal form in which any opinion comes to your consciousness, and gets its definition for your own mind, is this form of an appeal to an insight that is superior in grasp, in unity, in coherence, in reasonableness to your momentary insight.

Now you can indeed say: "When I form and express an opinion, I appeal from my present experiences to some wider insight that I view *as if it were* possible. My opinion asserts that *if I were* permitted to see what I just now do not directly experience, I should find the facts to be so and so." But no such account of the matter is quite complete. Everything that you regard as possible has to be conceived as somehow based upon what you regard as actual. And so, in fact, your opinions are always appeals to some form of wider or larger or deeper or richer insight that, in the act of appealing to it, you regard as a present or as a past or as a future reality—in brief, as a live and perfectly concrete insight to whose verdict you appeal. Philosophers often express this by saying that all opinions are nothing but efforts to formulate the real contents of experience. This view I accept.

So then, as I insist, whatever your opinions, your expression of them is an appeal to some wider insight that you regard as real, and that you view as a live insight which comprehends your ideas, and which sees how they are related to genuine experience. This, I affirm, is the universal form which all opinion takes. A true opinion is true, because in fact it expresses what the wider insight confirms. A false opinion is false, because it is refuted by the light of this same wider view. Apart from such a confirmation or refutation in the light of such a larger view, the very concepts of truth and error, as applied to opinions which are not wholly confirmed or set aside by the instantaneous evidence of the moment when the opinions are formed or uttered, have no meaning. True is the judgment that is confirmed by the larger view to which it appeals. False is the assertion that is not thus confirmed. *Upon such a conception the very ideas of truth and error depend. Without such a conception truth and error have no sense.* If such a conception is not itself a true view of our situation, that is, if there is no wider insight, our opinions have neither truth nor error, and are all of them alike merely meaningless. When you are ignorant, you are ignorant of what the wider view makes clear to its own insight. If you blunder or are deluded, your blunder is due to a defective apprehension which the wider view confirms. And thus, whether you are ignorant or blundering, wise or foolish, whether the truth or the falsity of your present opinion is supposed to be actual, one actuality is equally and rationally presupposed, as the actuality to which all your opinions refer, and in the light of which they possess sense. *This is the actuality of some wider insight with reference to which your own opinion gets its truth or its falsity.*

To this wider insight, to this always presupposed vision of experience as it is, of the facts as they are, you are always appealing. Your every act of assertion displays the genuineness of the appeal and exemplifies the absolute rational necessity of asserting that the appeal is made to an insight that is itself real.

Frequently you do, indeed, call this insight merely the common-sense of mankind. But, strange to say, this common-sense of mankind is always and inevitably conceived by you in terms that distinguish it from the fleeting momentary views of any or of all merely individual men. Men—if I may judge them by my own case, and by what I hear other men confess—men, when taken merely as individuals, always live from moment to moment in a flickering way, normally confident, indeed, but clearly seeing at any one instant very little at a time. They are narrow in the span of the more direct insight. They grasp data bit by bit, and comprehend, in their instantaneous flashes of insight, only little scraps and tiny bundles of ideas. I who now speak to you cannot hold clearly and momentarily before my mind at once even all of the meaning that I try to express in two or three of my successive sentences. I live looking before and after, and pining for what is not, and grasping after unity; and I find each moment crumbling as it flies; and each thought and each sentence of my discourse drops into momentary forgetfulness so soon as I have carefully built up its passing structure. In our life all thus flows. We fly from one flash of insight to another.

But nevertheless our opinions, so we say, reflect sometimes the common-sense of mankind. They conform to the verdict of humanity. But who amongst us ever goes beyond thus confidently holding that he reflects the common-sense of mankind? Who among us personally and individually experiences, at any moment, the confirmation said to be given by the verdict of humanity? The verdict of humanity? What man ever finds immediately presented to his own personal insight that totality of data upon which this verdict is said to depend? The common-sense of mankind? What mortal man is there who ever finds incorporated in his flickering, fleeting, crumbling, narrow moments of personal experience the calm and secure insight which this common-sense of mankind, or of enlightened mankind, is said to possess?

No, the common-sense of mankind is, for us all, a sort of super-individual insight, to which we appeal without ourselves fully possessing it. This "*common*"-sense of mankind is just the sense *which no man of us all ever individually possesses.* For us all it is, indeed, something superhuman. We spend part of our busy little lives in somewhat pretentiously undertaking to report its dicta. But it is simply one of the countless forms in which we conceive the wider insight to be incorporated. *The true rational warrant for this confidence of ours lies in the fact that whatever else is real, some form of such a wider insight, some essentially super-individual and superhuman insight is real.* For unless it is real our opinions, including any opinion that we may have that doubts or questions or denies its reality, are all equally meaningless. Thus even when we appeal to common-sense we really appeal to a genuine but super-human insight.

Let us not here spend time, however, upon analysing this or that special form in which we are accustomed, for one special purpose or another, to conceive the wider insight. What is clear is that we constantly, and in every opinion, in every confession of ignorance appeal to such an insight. That such an insight is real, must be presupposed even in order to assert that our present opinions are errors. What interests us most at this point is, however, this, that whatever else the whole real universe is, the real universe exists only in case it is the object, and the very being, of such an insight, of such an inclusive experience, of such a view of what is. For, when you hold any opinions whatever about the real world, or about any of its contents, characters, or values, your opinions are either true or false, and are true or false by virtue of their actual conformity to the live insight which experiences what makes them true or false, and which therefore *ipso facto* experiences what the real world is. If there is *no* such world-possessing insight, then, once more, your opinions about the world are neither true nor false. Or, otherwise stated, if there is no such inclusive insight there is no world. To the real world, then, this insight which comprehends the world, and which knows whatever is true to be true, and whatever is false about the world to be false—to the real world this insight, I say, belongs. And the whole world belongs to it and is its object and essence. Whatever is real is real for that insight, and is in its experience, and exists as its possession, and as its well-known and well-comprehended content, and as its image and expression and meaning.

All this I say, as you may note, not because I hold in high esteem any of our private human opinions, but only because, *except in the light of such an all-seeing comprehension of facts as they are, our individual opinions about the world cannot even be false.* For opinion, in all its fleeting blindness and in its human chaos of caprices, is ceaselessly an appeal to the judge, to the seer, to the standard experience, to the knower of facts as they are, to the wider view, to the decisive insight. And opinions about reality in its wholeness, about the world, about the all, are appeals to the all-judging insight, to the all-seeing view, to the knowledge and experience that grasps the totality of facts, to the widest outlook, to the deepest insight, to the absolute rational decision. If this be so, then an opinion to the effect that there exists no such widest and deepest insight, and no such final view, is itself just such an appeal to the final insight, simply because it is an opinion about reality. To assert then that there is no largest view, no final insight, no experience that is absolute, is to assert that the largest view observes that there is no largest view, that the final insight sees that there is no such insight, that the ultimate experience is aware that there is no ultimate experience. And such an assertion is indeed a self-contradiction.

This, I assert, is the only rational way of stating the nature of opinion, of truth or error, and consequently of reality. This is the synthesis which reason inevitably accomplishes whenever it rightly views the nature and the implications of even our most flickering and erroneous and uncertain opinions. We can err about what you will. But if we err, we simply come short of the insight to which we are aiming to conform, and in the light of which our ideas get absolutely all of their meaning. In every error, in every blunder, in all our darkness, in all our ignorance, we are still in touch with the eternal insight. We are always seeking to know even as we are known.

I have sought in this sketch to vindicate the general rights of rational insight as against mere momentary or fragmentary intuition. I have also tried to show you what synthesis of reason gives us a genuinely religious insight.

"My first penitent," said the priest of our story, "was a murderer." "And I," said the nobleman, "was this priest's first penitent."

"I am ignorant of the vast and mysterious real world"—thus says our sense of human fallibility and weakness when we are first awakened to our need of rational guidance. The saying is true. The mystery is appalling. "I am ignorant of the real world." Yes; but reason, reflecting upon the nature and the essential meaning of opinion, of truth, of error, and of ignorance, points out to us this thesis: "That of which I am ignorant is that about which I can err. But error is failure to conform my momentary opinion to the very insight which I mean and to which I am all the while appealing. Error is failure to conform to the inclusive insight which overarches my errors with the heaven of its rational clearness. Error is failure to grasp the very light which shines in my darkness, even while my darkness comprehends it not. That of which I am ignorant is then essentially the object of a super-human and divine insight."

"I am ignorant of the world. To be ignorant is to fail to grasp the object of the all-inclusive and divine insight." That is the expression of our situation. Reason easily makes the fitting synthesis when it considers the priest and the nobleman. I ask you to make the analogous synthesis regarding the world and the divine insight. This synthesis here takes form in concluding that the world is the object of an all-inclusive and divine insight, which is thus the supreme reality.

I have but sketched for you the contribution of reason to our quest. This contribution will seem to many of you too abstract and too contemplative to meet vital religious needs. In fact, what I have said will mean little to you unless you come to see how it can be translated into an adequate expression in our active life. To this task of such a further interpretation of the mission of the reason as a guide of life my next lecture shall be devoted.

ALFRED NORTH WHITEHEAD

Alfred North Whitehead (1861–1947), a graduate of Trinity College, Cambridge, established his reputation as a mathematician while teaching at Cambridge and at the University of London. He collaborated with Bertrand Russell in *Principia Mathematica* (1910), a work designed to show the reducibility of mathematics to logic. In 1924 Whitehead became professor of philosophy at Harvard. His writings comprise technical essays in metaphysics (utilizing material from logic), mathematics, and the philosophy of science. His work in the philosophy of religion has received considerable attention from theologians as well as from philosophers. He is known as one of the foremost of "process philosophers." This selection* illustrates Whitehead's conception of the relation between the individual and the universal in religion and the way in which rational religion originates.

The Origin of Religion

". . . Religion is what the individual does with his own solitariness."

This point of the origin of rational religion in solitariness is fundamental. Religion is founded on the concurrence of three allied concepts in one moment of self-consciousness, concepts whose separate relationships to fact and whose mutual relations to each other are only to be settled jointly by some direct intuition into the ultimate character of the universe.

These concepts are:

1.   That of the value of an individual for itself.

2.   That of the value of the diverse individuals of the world for each other.

3.   That of the value of the objective world which is a community derivative from the interrelations of its component individuals, and also necessary for the existence of each of these individuals.

The moment of religious consciousness starts from self-valuation, but it broadens into the concept of the world as a realm of adjusted values, mutually intensifying or mutually destructive. The intuition into the actual world gives a particular definite content to the bare notion of a principle determining the grading of values. It also exhibits emotions,

* From *Religion in the Making*, Chapter II—"Religion and Dogma" (New York: The Macmillan Company, 1926, copyright renewed 1954 by Evelyn Whitehead). Used by permission.

purposes, and physical conditions, as subservient factors in the emergence of value.

In its solitariness the spirit asks, What, in the way of value, is the attainment of life? And it can find no such value till it has merged its individual claim with that of the objective universe. Religion is world-loyalty.

The spirit at once surrenders itself to this universal claim and appropriates it for itself. So far as it is dominated by religious experience, life is conditioned by this formative principle, equally individual and general, equally actual and beyond completed act, equally compelling recognition and permissive of disregard.

This principle is not a dogmatic formulation, but the intuition of immediate occasions as failing or succeeding in reference to the ideal relevant to them. There is a rightness attained or missed, with more or less completeness of attainment or omission.

This is a revelation of character, apprehended as we apprehend the characters of our friends. But in this case it is an apprehension of character permanently inherent in the nature of things.

There is a large concurrence in the negative doctrine that this religious experience does not include any direct intuition of a definite person, or individual. It is a character of permanent rightness, whose inherence in the nature of things modifies both efficient and final cause, so that the one conforms to harmonious conditions, and the other contrasts itself with an harmonious ideal. The harmony in the actual world is conformity with the character.

It is not true that every individual item of the universe conforms to this character in every detail. There will be some measure of conformity and some measure of diversity. The whole intuition of conformity and diversity forms the contrast which that item yields for the religious experience. So far as the conformity is incomplete, there is evil in the world.

The evidence for the assertion of general, though not universal, concurrence in the doctrine of no direct vision of a personal God, can only be found by a consideration of the religious thought in the civilized world. Here the sources of the evidence can only be indicated.

Throughout India and China religious thought, so far as it has been interpreted in precise form, disclaims the intuition of any ultimate personality substantial to the universe. This is true for Confucian philosophy, Buddhist philosophy, and Hindoo philosophy. There may be personal embodiments, but the substratum is impersonal.

Christian theology has also, in the main, adopted the position that there is no direct intuition of such an ultimate personal substratum for the world. It maintains the doctrine of the existence of a personal God as a truth, but holds that our belief in it is based upon inference. Most theologians hold that this inference is sufficiently obvious to be made by all men upon the basis of their individual personal experience. But, be this as it may, it is an inference and not a direct intuition. This is the general doctrine of those traditionalist churches which more especially claim the title of Catholic; and contrary doctrines have, I believe, been officially condemned by the Roman Catholic Church: for example, the religious philosophy of Rosmini.

Greek thought, when it began to scrutinize the traditional cults, took the same line. In some form or other all attempts to formulate the doctrines of a rational religion in ancient Greece took their stand upon the Pythagorean notion of a direct intuition of a righteousness in the nature of things, functioning as a condition, a critic, and an ideal. Divine personality was in the nature of an inference from the directly apprehended law of nature, so far as it *was* inferred. Of course, there were many cults of divine persons within the nature of things. The question in discussion concerns a divine person, substrate to the nature of things.

This question of the ultimate nature of direct religious experience is very fundamental to the religious situation of the modern world. In the first place, if you make religious experience to be the direct intuition of a personal being substrate to the universe, there is no widespread basis of agreement to appeal to. The main streams of religious thought start with direct contradictions to each other. For those who proceed in this way, and it is a usual form of modern appeal, there is only one hope— to supersede reason by emotion. Then you can prove anything, except to reasonable people. But reason is the safeguard of the objectivity of religion: it secures for it the general coherence denied to hysteria.

Another objection against this appeal to such an intuition, merely experienced in exceptional moments, is that the intuition is thereby a function of those moments. Anything which explains the origin of such moments, in respect to their emotional accompaniments, can then fairly be taken to be an explanation of the intuition. Thus the intuition becomes a private psychological habit, and is without general evidential force. This is the psychological interpretation which is fatal to evidence unable to maintain itself at all emotional temperatures amid great variety of environment.

Here a distinction must be drawn. Intuitions may first emerge as distinguished in consciousness under exceptional circumstances. But when some distinct idea has been once experienced, or suggested, it should then have its own independence of irrelevancies. Thus we may not know some arithmetical truth, and require some exceptional help to detect it. But when known, arithmetic is a permanent possession. The psychological interpretation, assigning a merely personal significance, holds when objective validity is claimed for an intuition which is only experienced in a set of discrete circumstances of definite specific character. The intuition may be clearer under such circumstances, but it should not be confined to them.

The wisdom of the main stream of Christian theology in refusing to countenance the notion of a direct vision of a personal God is manifest. For there is no consensus. The subordinate gods of the unrationalized religions—the religions of the heathen, as they are called—are not to the point; and when the great rationalized religions are examined, the majority lies the other way. As soon, however, as it comes to a question of rational interpretation, numbers rapidly sink in importance. Reason mocks at majorities.

But there is a large consensus, on the part of those who have rationalized their outlook, in favour of the concept of a rightness in things, partially conformed to and partially disregarded. So far as there is conscious determination of actions, the attainment of this conformity is an ultimate premise by reference to which our choice of immediate ends is criticised and swayed. The rational satisfaction or dissatisfaction in respect to any particular happening depends upon an intuition which is capable of being universalized. This universalization of what is discerned in a particular instance is the appeal to a general character inherent in the nature of things.

This intuition is not the discernment of a form of words, but of a type of character. It is characteristic of the learned mind to exalt words. Yet mothers can ponder many things in their hearts which their lips cannot express. These many things, which are thus known, constitute the ultimate religious evidence, beyond which there is no appeal.

II. *Government*

INTRODUCTION

The American Revolution, in its making and in its culmination, produced an extraordinary literature in the philosophy of government. Most of it echoed English theory and experience as well as the influence of Montesquieu, and virtually every major political figure regarded the functioning English constitution as the model to be consulted. The Founding Fathers, if not especially original in their political philosophy, were nevertheless remarkable in their thoughtful absorption of English thinking for application in the colonies. They fully appreciated the uniqueness of the possibility before them and were prepared to utilize every clue from the past. John Adams, like Governor Winthrop earlier, proclaimed it, in 1776, a once-in-a-lifetime opportunity:

> You and I, my dear friend, have been sent into life at a time when the greatest lawgivers of antiquity would have wished to live. How few of the human race have ever enjoyed an opportunity of making an election of government, more than of air, soil, or climate, for themselves or their children! When before the present epocha, had three millions of people full power and a fair opportunity to form and establish the wisest and happiest government that human wisdom can contrive?

Jefferson considered John Adams to be a monarchist like Hamilton. Adams, despite his protests, never succeeded in shaking the charge, because some things he had said certainly sounded monarchistic. But what Adams wrote in *Thoughts on Government* tends to justify his claim that he was not. For he wrote there that political wisdom does not reside in any single social class, that political wisdom is rather what we might call "the wisdom of the whole." This point is easily overlooked in interpreting Adams' political philosophy if one notices only his main argument for the separation of powers in the constitution he proposed for the colonies. As contemporary scholarship rightly emphasizes, the Founding Fathers were highly practical men, aware of the complex mechanics with which an effective government must program itself and

53

of how those mechanics must reflect the inevitable conflict of economic interests within the society. The most important governmental principle, according to Adams, was the separation of executive, legislative, and judicial powers, since this separation tends to forestall those greatest dangers to a society—tyranny by one class or interest of the society, and civil war. However, according to one scholar, Adams was *less* concerned with the separation of governmental functions than with "the equilibrium of the democratic, aristocratic, and monarchic elements. He remembered well from Bolingbroke, 'It is by mixture of monarchical, aristocratical, and democratical power, blended together in one system, and by these three estates balancing one another, that our free constitution of government hath been preserved so long inviolate.' "[1] The doctrine of separation of governmental powers was really, on this interpretation, a consequence of Adams' belief that class and economic conflict must define any society, and that government must supervise the struggle within the confines of a controllable tension. A Senate, in fact, is required for the very protection of the people. "The rich, the well born, and the able acquire an influence among the people that will soon be too much for simple honesty and plain sense, in a house of representatives. The most illustrious of them must, therefore, be separated from the masses, and placed by themselves in a senate; this is, to all honest and useful intents, an ostracism."[2]

The evidence clearly indicates how much Adams feared the despotism resulting from the domination of any single economic interest or class. But it seems equally clear that the American tradition of political philosophy which Adams helped to establish has never seen the main function of government to be *merely* regulation of economic conflict. The tradition rather holds that each of the elements in the society approximating the monarchial, aristocratic, and democratic has its own spirit or "genius." The best society allows the voice of each to be heard so that the wisdom, which guides the state, does not belong to any single societal interest but is instead a function of the interaction of the different interests.

In *Thoughts on Government* Adams moved far from Plato's aristocratic republic and its conception of the philosopher-king, far from the idea that political wisdom resides in the heads of the talented few. What Adams urged was a method of representing all people and

[1]Zoltàn Haraszti, *John Adams and the Prophets of Progress* (New York: Grosset & Dunlap, Universal Library Edition, 1964), p.30. The present account is indebted to this work.

[2]Quoted by Haraszti, *Ibid.*, p.36.

interests in such a way that the representative assembly "should be in miniature an exact portrait of the people at large. It should think, feel, reason, and act like them. That it may be the interest of this assembly to do strict justice at all times, it should be an equal representation, or, in other words, equal interests among the people should have equal interests in it." The wisdom of a good society is not in one of its parts; it is more than their sum; it is the wisdom of the whole which emerges from the colliding dialogue between the different parts. That this was the main thrust of Adams' thought is not contradicted by the reminder that he excluded women and the very poor from the franchised; he was indeed biased in his notion of what constituted a responsible citizen. But the point remains that he realized that a society is always many-sided and must always govern itself with a many-sided perspective. The aim is not merely the negative one of mitigating economic and class struggle; it is rather to introduce "knowledge among the people," to inspire them with a "conscious dignity becoming freemen; a general emulation takes place, which causes good humor, sociability, good manners, and good morals to be general." In short, the individual is not merely protected but actively assisted by the sort of government which understands that *practical* wisdom is always the *many-sided* perspective of a *whole* society.

James Madison joined Adams in describing what government must in particular avoid—the usurpation of power by a single class or economic interest. In one of his most cited defenses of the proposed Federal Constitution, Article Number 10 in the *Federalist Papers*, Madison noted that the instability of popular governments results from warring factions within the society. His essay is often but misleadingly described as a protest against "factionalism." He accepted factionalism or political lobbying by special interests as unavoidable, and thus sought a way to prevent any faction from controlling the government for itself. Like Adams, Madison believed the cause of factionalism to be economic, due to unequal distribution of property. "A landed interest, a manufacturing interest, a mercantile interest, a moneyed interest, with many lesser interests, grow up of necessity in civilized nations, and divide them into different classes, actuated by different sentiments and views." This division of a society into different factions, especially into the propertied and propertyless, is the *natural* result of men being possessed of different capabilities; therefore, government should not vainly attempt to abolish factions but only to regulate their effects.

What Madison especially feared, again with Adams, was "majority despotism," the tyranny occurring when the *majority faction* seizes government; freedom for minorities is not only desirable but indispensable for the maintenance of checks and balances between conflicting interests. The existence of minority groups, whose voices are effectively heard in government, is a necessary condition for a popular government which is not to succumb to majority tyranny. Egalitarian proposals, like the equal distribution of property, are "wicked" because they seek to define a society in terms of one interest alone, to reduce the desirable heterogeneity of the society to a common denominator. Moreover, a representative republic is superior to a "pure democracy," which consists of people assembling and administrating their government in person, as in the traditional New England town meeting. A republic is representative government, delegating power to the few individuals elected by the rest. An immediate advantage of a republic is

> to refine and enlarge the public views, by passing them through the medium of a chosen body of citizens, whose wisdom may best discern the true interest of their country, and whose patriotism and love of justice will be least likely to sacrifice it to temporary or practical considerations . . . it may well happen that the public voice, pronounced by the representatives of the people, will be more consonant to the public good than if pronounced by the people themselves, convened for the purpose.

But this ought not to be confused with a Platonic concept of government by "enlightened statesmen"; such men will not always "be at the helm." Consequently a republic must be a government of laws, not of men, which will effectively sustain conflicting interests while also regulating their effects. Representative government should tend to create enlightened statesmen, but in bleak periods it must, by its own structure, be able to survive their temporary absence. Moreover, a republic, unlike a pure democracy, can function for greater numbers of people and over a vaster geography, and is thus more likely to absorb a greater variety of minority interests.

Madison's plea for a stronger centralized government to replace the loose confederation of states was argued on similar lines. Control of factions is better managed by a large rather than small republic. The elected representatives, to whom powers of government are delegated, will tend to transcend local prejudices; the public good, as opposed to the satisfaction of a single faction, is more likely to be promoted. Though factious leaders may at times exercise considerable influence in their local states, such influence tends to remain localized under a national government dedicated to the proposition that "wisdom is in the whole." The liberty and happiness of the individual are preserved most effectively by a government which respects the faction to which he belongs but only as one faction among others; the individual demanding more for his faction is undermining his own freedom. Realizing this, Madison argued, citizens should also recognize the need to ratify the proposed Federal Constitution since "In the extent and proper structure of the Union, therefore, we behold a republican remedy for the diseases incident to republican government."

Until the Constitution became active in 1789, the Congress, under the Articles of Confederation (submitted in 1778 by the Continental Congress to the states for ratification as a method of permanent alliance), was the guiding force of the Union. Alexander Hamilton, despite his monarchistic bias and consequent reservations about the proposed Constitution, vigorously urged its ratification in his *Federalist* articles, as in Number 15 where he emphasized the need for a national government with the power to legislate for and superintend the *individuals* of the different states; the great weakness, according to Hamilton, of the existing Confederation was its indirect relation to the individual citizen, being forced to negotiate through the channels of each state government. The role of a national government is not merely one of regulating the effects of competing factions to which individuals belong; besides, "we must extend the authority to the persons of the citizen—the only proper objects of government." This proposal to establish a direct relation between a national government and the individual citizen, with the former enjoying the power to coerce the latter directly, aroused considerable opposition. It is perhaps for this reason that only six signers of the Declaration of Independence were also signers of the Constitution.[3] The representatives to the Constitutional Convention of 1787 were largely "conservatives," representing the mercantile, landed, and financial interests of the states; revolutionaries like Sam Adams and Patrick Henry were absent.[4]

From that time on, American political tradition has accepted the concept of a national government—stronger than a mere league of

[3] *See* Richard Hofstadter, *The American Political Tradition* (New York: Vintage Books, 1954), p. 12.

[4] *See* Charles A. Beard, *The Enduring Federalist* (New York: Frederick Ungar Publishing Co., 1948), p. 28. This fact and its implications were developed by Beard in earlier works, causing substantial controversies in the wake of their publication.

states, by virtue of its power to legislate and enforce laws in a direct relationship to the individual citizen of any state—though there has also remained an important subtradition in America of dissent and reluctant acceptance of the emergence of a strong federal power.

Abraham Lincoln was correct in saying, in his First Inaugural Address,

> The Union is much older than the Constitution. It was formed, in fact, by the Articles of Association in 1774. It was matured and continued by the Declaration of Independence in 1776. It was further matured, and the faith of all the then thirteen states expressly plighted and engaged that it should be perpetual, by the Articles of Confederation in 1778. And finally, in 1787, one of the declared objects for ordaining and establishing the Constitution was "to form a more perfect Union."

Lincoln would have accurately stated the matter, according to Charles Beard, had he said that the Union was even older than the 1774 Articles of Association, for these reasons: The different commonwealths had never been like sovereign nations; they had always been subject to Great Britain; the colonies won their independence by joint rather than separate action designed to achieve sovereign status for each; in jointly expressing their grievances to Great Britain and in the series of moves toward revolution, the colonies behaved as a Union.[5]

Lincoln, like all successful politicians, was a practical man employing a many-sided perspective. He disliked slavery intensely, but he was not an abolitionist; in fact, he had reproved Ohio Republicans for urging a repeal of the fugitive-slave law, and he promised in his First Inaugural to respect a proposed Constitutional amendment prohibiting federal interference with slavery in the South. Lincoln was firmly opposed to the extension of slavery, but as Richard Hofstadter has emphasized, Lincoln's concern was less for the Negro's plight as such than it was, as he said in speaking to white workers, for the "immediate 'danger' that slavery would become a nation-wide American institution if its geographical spread were not severely restricted at once."[6] In any event, the main concern of the First Inaugural Address, one of the most carefully composed documents in political history, was not the issue of slavery but, given the secession of seven Southern states, the preservation of the Union. The speech was a poignant plea for negotiation and compromise. Despite its immediate concern with a desperate situation, it remains an eloquent contribution to the philosophy of government.

[5] *Ibid.*, pp. 26–7.
[6] Hofstadter, *op. cit.*, p. 115.

By the mid-nineteenth century, when America had witnessed men like Andrew Jackson and Abraham Lincoln succeeding to the Presidency, the cause of the common man was more respectable than it had been in the post-Revolutionary period. Lincoln, like his predecessors, naturally understood the danger of majority despotism, of the necessity for legislative reins on a majority faction; yet in pledging to fulfill his Constitutional function in preserving the Union, he appealed to the concept of majority rule. Secession was held insufferable because it violates that concept. "A majority held in restraint by constitutional checks and limitations, and always changing easily with deliberate changes of popular opinions and sentiments, is the only true sovereign of a free people. Whoever rejects it does of necessity fly to anarchy or to despotism." In 1861 the fear of Lincoln was not of majority but of minority despotism.

The First Inaugural was an appeal to the American people to recomprehend the fact that their government belonged to them, that the chief executive derived his authority from them exclusively, that they had never given him power to arrange for secession or separation of the states, and that, moreover, they enjoyed the right of revolution. "This country, with its institutions, belongs to the people who inhabit it. Whenever they shall grow weary of the existing government, they can exercise their constitutional right of amending it, or their revolutionary right to dismember or overthrow it." But the problem for a chief executive who promises the right of extreme dissent while pledging himself to uphold the traditional order is more than delicate; it becomes seemingly insoluble because it involves moral, legal, psychological, and logical inconsistencies. As Hofstadter has summed up the situation,

> . . . Lincoln suppressed secession and refused to acknowledge that the right of revolution he had so boldly accepted belonged to the South. The same Lincoln . . . refused almost to the last minute even to suppress rebellion by revolutionary means. The contradiction is not peculiar to Lincoln; Anglo-Saxon history is full of it.[7]

Lincoln's First Inaugural is a memorable tribute to the main tradition of "The Union, above all else" and to the subtradition of very reluctant acceptance, a subtradition of defending the right to dissent to a prime tradition which enthusiastically agrees in word, and sometimes, even if bewilderedly, in deed.

The American subtradition of dissent found a spokesman, Henry David Thoreau, notably in his "Civil Disobedience" of 1849. The immediate

[7] *Ibid.*, p. 103.

issues for Thoreau were the Mexican War, which he thought was but a perverse attempt to extend slavery, and the institution of slavery itself. Thoreau thought of himself as fundamentally an anarchist, but being practical, as he put it, he was content to ask, not for the cessation of central government but for the immediate improvement in the national administration. He spoke for that perennial cult of individualists who agree that "that government is best which governs least," and who feel that it is a pity to require the protection of the state. Thoreau spoke for those who believe that dissent must at times be translated into civil disobedience if social and legislative changes are to occur. "I know this well, that if one thousand, if one hundred, if ten men whom I could name—if ten *honest* men only—ay, if *one* honest man, in the State of Massachusetts, *ceasing to hold slaves*, were actually to withdraw from the co-partnership [*i.e.*, from the government by refusing to pay taxes—Ed.], and be locked up in the county jail therefor, it would be the abolition of slavery in America." At the outbreak of the Civil War there were almost 4,000,000 persons in slavery and at its end more than 180,000 Negroes in the Union Army; Thoreau detested the slavery system and, like others in the subtradition of dissent, believed that civil liberties could be achieved only through some form of civil disobedience. Thoreau is still read, not only for his Transcendentalist rhetoric about Nature but for his defense of the American tradition of the individual's right to dissent in deed as well as word.

The problem remains of how a government can be strong while specifying conditions for dissent to itself. It is insoluble by the executive branch and is often rashly resolved by the legislative. It thus becomes an interpretative issue for the judicial; and, just as naturally, the history of the judiciary toward dissenting activity has been one of uncertainty, split decisions, and minority reports. Justice Oliver Wendell Holmes, Jr., known as The Great Dissenter because of his famous minority opinions, was a remarkable contributor to the shaping of an American philosophy of law.[8] The First World War generated difficult legal questions because

[8] One distinguished writer has said that even if no "branch of American law can be said to have been molded by him . . . the essential soundness of Holmes' main views on the nature of law . . . give his work an enduring quality, so that it seems unquestionable that future students of the law will come back to his writings as to those of no other American jurist. At any rate, the latest school of American jurisprudence seems to start from one of his dicta: to wit, that the law is not a brooding omnipresence in the sky but our prediction of what courts will decide—a dictum which some have taken too literally."

Morris R. Cohen, *American Thought* (Glencoe, Illinois: The Free Press, 1954), pp. 168–9.

of actual or potential conflict between security measures, on the one hand, and traditional individual liberties, on the other. One of Holmes' most celebrated dissenting opinions was in 1919 in *Abrams v. United States*, in which his concept of "clear and present danger" as a limitation on free speech under the First Amendment (a concept which has since become a general rule by the Supreme Court) was invoked. The case resulted from the tossing of leaflets, by Jacob Abrams and other Russian emigrants, from a rooftop into the streets of Manhattan's garment district. Abrams was convicted under the Espionage Act of 1917, which was designed to counter German espionage, and received a twenty-year sentence. His conviction was upheld by the Supreme Court, with Justices Holmes and Brandeis dissenting.

Holmes argued, against the majority decision, that the import of Abrams' leaflets was only to urge American workers not to produce weapons for possible interference with the Russian Revolution, and no "intent" had been proved to hinder the United States in its war with Germany. Of considerable significance was Holmes' insistence that, to convict a person of an "intent" to produce a certain result, it is not sufficient to show merely that the person knew at the time of his action that the result, said to be intended, would occur. "It may be obvious, and obvious to the actor, that the consequence will follow, and he may be liable for it even if he forgets it, but he does not do the act with intent to produce it unless the aim to produce it is the proximate motive of the specific act, although there may be some deeper motive." This interpretation of "intent" as "proximate motive" is justified insofar as it sees intent as the conscious and deliberate purpose of the act entertained just before doing it; it makes conviction of intent less simple if only because the occurrence of a proximate motive is less easy to prove than merely the probable possession of knowledge about the probable consequences of certain acts. Since the Espionage Act, as amended, specified the matter of intent, the issue was all-important. Holmes never doubted that free speech can be abused; when it presents a clear and immediate danger to the public interest, it is therefore punishable; but *only* in such a case does the limitation apply. "Congress certainly cannot forbid all effort to change the mind of the country." But in the case of Abrams, argued Holmes, "nobody can suppose that the surreptitious publishing of a silly leaflet by an unknown man, without more, would present any immediate danger that its opinions would hinder the success of the Government arms or have any appreciable tendency to do so."

In closing his report, Holmes warned against efforts to suppress the expression of "opinions that we loathe and believe to be fraught with death," against excessive confidence in one's own opinion. The best ideas are those retaining our trust and confidence after having been thoroughly exposed to debate.

> . . . when men have realized that time has upset many fighting faiths, they may come to believe even more than they believe the very foundations of their own conduct that the ultimate good desired is better reached by free trade in ideas—that the best test of truth is the power of the thought to get itself accepted in the competition of the market, and that truth is the only ground upon which their wishes safely can be carried out. That, at any rate, is the theory of our Constitution.[9]

The American theme of individualism is not, of course, identical with the right to dissent; it includes, besides, the original Protestant Ethic of initiative, thrift, self-reliance, and duty to work for reasons ultimately religious; it includes a whole scheme of values respecting the farmer, the inventor, the small businessman, and the process of individual growth through one's own persistent efforts; it includes the feeling that one's world can be large yet private, that the usually alternating choices of togetherness and isolation are entirely voluntary. But the industrialization and urbanizing of the nation, characteristic of the transition into the twentieth century, seemed to many to signal the end of a whole outlook subsumed under the old-fashioned expression "rugged individualism." John Dewey expressed the reaction:

> the United States has steadily moved from an earlier pioneer individualism to a condition of dominant corporateness. The influence business corporations exercise in determining present industrial and economic activities is both a cause and a symbol of the tendency to combination in all phases of life. Associations tightly or loosely organized more and more define the opportunities, the choices and the actions of individuals.

It is true that Dewey, in his essay "The United States, Incorporated," spoke of the "sad" decline of the farmer, of the "plight of the uncombined and unintegrated," and of a society in which mass production,

---

[9] Ralph Barton Perry has noted how "pragmatic" Holmes' concept of truth was, remarking further that it was the Pragmatism in the thought of his friend, William James, which Holmes preferred to everything else. *The Thought and Character of William James*, Vol. II (Boston: Little, Brown and Company, 1935), pp. 458–9. Max Lerner has described this passage as "the greatest utterance on intellectual freedom by an American, ranking in the English tongue with Milton and Mill." *The Mind and Faith of Justice Homes* (New York: The Modern Library, 1943), p. 306.

resulting in a mass education, submerges individual capacity and skill. Dewey was also troubled by what he regarded as the decline of privacy, evidenced by the character of contemporary apartments and subways; more importantly, individualism surrenders to any form of mass suggestion, the publicity agent being perhaps the "most significant of our present social life."

Nevertheless, Dewey also insisted that his main concern was not to praise or blame the effects of an increasingly corporate society but only to portray the "decline of an individualistic philosophy of life, and the formation of a collectivistic scheme of interdependence, which finds its way into every cranny of life, personal, intellectual, emotional, affecting leisure as well as work, morals as well as economics." Increasing standardization and mass uniformity are justly criticized in the new corporate society, but they are not, said Dewey, the whole of that society. He was himself too much of a representative of the post-Darwinian era, believing in the inevitability of change and the prospects of social evolution, to utter a merely cranky response to such a large-scale social revolution as was occurring in America. What concerned Dewey was, in Toynbee's terms, the nature of the response to be made by Americans to the challenge of corporate industry and the new urbanization. He believed that it required an individuality of a new type, endowed with the appropriate intelligence and sentiment. What is needed, he claimed, is a society where the traditional balance of opposed forces is maintained, where the "balance of the individual and the social will be organic" instead of artificial and arbitrary as is necessarily the case during a period of acute transition. The cause of the individual must be carefully protected in the new America. There was reason to be concerned and reason to be hopeful, but at least, Dewey thought, the general problem could be identified and the criteria for its resolution agreed to.

JOHN ADAMS

John Adams (1735–1826), second President of the United States, was born in Massachusetts. He graduated from Harvard, became a lawyer, and entered politics. A vigorous opponent of the Stamp Act of 1765, Adams in 1774 was a delegate to the First Continental Congress. At the Second Continental Congress he nominated George Washington as Commander in Chief. In 1776 he wrote *Thoughts on Government*, describing a proposed constitution for the colonies in which the separation of governmental powers is a major feature. Adams defended before Congress the Declaration of Independence, prepared by Jefferson. He succeeded Washington as President, barely defeating Jefferson. His son, John Quincy Adams, was to be elected President in 1824. The following selection represents one of the most influential statements of a philosophy of government by an American statesman. It is taken from John Adams, *Works*, IV, C. F. Adams, ed., Boston, 1851, pp. 193–200.

The Proper End of Government

We ought to consider what is the end of government before we determine which is the best form. Upon this point all speculative politicians will agree, that the happiness of society is the end of government, as all divines and moral philosophers will agree that the happiness of the individual is the end of man. From this principle it will follow, that the form of government which communicates ease, comfort, security, or, in one word, happiness, to the greatest number of persons, and in the greatest degree, is the best.

All sober inquirers after truth, ancient and modern, pagan and Christian, have declared that the happiness of man, as well as his dignity, consists in virtue. Confucius, Zoroaster, Socrates, Mahomet, not to mention authorities really sacred, have agreed in this.

If there is a form of government, then, whose principle and foundation is virtue, will not every sober man acknowledge it better calculated to promote the general happiness than any other form?

Fear is the foundation of most governments; but it is so sordid and brutal a passion, and renders men in whose breasts it predominates so stupid and miserable, that Americans will not be likely to approve of any political institution which is founded on it.

Honor is truly sacred, but holds a lower rank in the scale of moral excellence than virtue. Indeed, the former is but a part of the latter, and consequently has not equal pretensions to support a frame of government productive of human happiness.

The foundation of every government is some principle or passion in the minds of the people. The noblest principles and most generous affections in our nature, then, have the fairest chance to support the noblest and most generous models of government.

A man must be indifferent to the sneers of modern Englishmen, to mention in their company the names of Sidney, Harrington, Locke, Milton, Nedham, Neville, Burnet, and Hoadly. No small fortitude is necessary to confess that one had read them. The wretched condition of this country, however, for ten or fifteen years past, has frequently reminded me of their principles and reasonings. They will convince any candid mind, that there is no good government but what is republican. That the only valuable part of the British constitution is so; because the very definition of a republic is "an empire of laws, and not of men." That, as a republic is the best of governments, so that particular arrangement of the powers of society, or, in other words, that form of government which is best contrived to secure an impartial and exact execution of the laws, is the best of republics.

Of republics there is an inexhaustible variety, because the possible combinations of the powers of society are capable of innumerable variations.

As good government is an empire of laws, how shall your laws be made? In a large society, inhabiting an extensive country, it is impossible that the whole should assemble to make laws. The first necessary step, then, is to depute power from the many to a few of the most wise and good. But by what rules shall you choose your representatives? Agree upon the number and qualifications of persons who shall have the benefit of choosing, or annex this privilege to the inhabitants of a certain extent of ground.

The principal difficulty lies, and the greatest care should be employed, in constituting this representative assembly. It should be in miniature an exact portrait of the people at large. It should think, feel, reason, and act like them. That it may be the interest of this assembly to do strict justice at all times, it should be an equal representation, or in other words, equal interests among the people should have equal interests in it. Great care should be taken to effect this, and to prevent unfair, partial, and corrupt elections. Such regulations, however, may be better made in times of greater tranquillity than the present; and they will spring up themselves naturally, when all the powers of government come to be in the hands of the people's friends. At present, it will be safest to proceed in all established modes, to which the people have been familiarized by habit.

A representation of the people in one assembly being obtained, a question arises, whether all the powers of government, legislative, executive, and judicial, shall be left in this body? I think a people cannot be long free, nor ever happy, whose government is in one assembly. My reasons for this opinion are as follows:—

1. A single assembly is liable to all the vices, follies, and frailties of an individual; subject to fits of humor, starts of passion, flights of enthusiasm, partialities, or prejudice, and consequently productive of hasty results and absurd judgments. And all these errors ought to be corrected and defects supplied by some controlling power.

2. A single assembly is apt to be avaricious, and in time will not scruple to exempt itself from burdens, which it will lay, without compunction, on its constituents.

3. A single assembly is apt to grow ambitious, and after a time will not hesitate to vote itself perpetual. This was one fault of the Long Parliament; but more remarkably of Holland, whose assembly first voted themselves from annual to septennial, then for life, and after a course of years, that all vacancies happening by death or otherwise, should be filled by themselves, without any application to constituents at all.

4. A representative assembly, although extremely well qualified, and absolutely necessary, as a branch of the legislative, is unfit to exercise the executive power, for want of two essential properties, secrecy and despatch.

5. A representative assembly is still less qualified for the judicial power, because it is too numerous, too slow, and too little skilled in the laws.

6. Because a single assembly, possessed of all the powers of government, would make arbitrary laws for their own interest, execute all laws arbitrarily for their own interest, and adjudge all controversies in their own favor.

But shall the whole power of legislation rest in one assembly? Most of the foregoing reasons apply equally to prove that the legislative power ought to be more complex: to which we may add, that if the legislative power is wholly in one assembly, and the executive in another or in a single person, these two powers will oppose and encroach upon each other, until the contest shall end in war, and the whole power, legislative and executive, be usurped by the strongest.

The judicial power, in such case, could not mediate, or hold the balance between the two contending powers, because the legislative would undermine it. And this shows the necessity, too, of giving the executive power a negative upon the legislative, otherwise this will be continually encroaching upon that.

To avoid these dangers, let a distinct assembly be constituted, as a mediator between the two extreme branches of the legislature, that which represents the people, and that which is vested with the executive power.

Let the representative assembly then elect by ballot, from among themselves or their constituents, or both, a distinct assembly, which, for the sake of perspicuity, we will call a council. It may consist of any number you please, say twenty or thirty, and should have a free and independent exercise of its judgment, and consequently a negative voice in the legislature.

These two bodies, thus constituted, and made integral parts of the legislature, let them unite, and by joint ballot choose a governor, who, after being stripped of most of those badges of domination, called prerogatives, should have a free and independent exercise of his judgment, and be made also an integral part of the legislature. This, I know, is liable to objections; and, if you please, you may make him only president of the council, as in Connecticut. But as the governor is to be invested with the executive power, with consent of council, I think he ought to have a negative upon the legislative. If he is annually elective, as he ought to be, he will always have so much reverence and affection for the people, their representatives and counsellors, that, although you give him an independent exercise of his judgment, he will seldom use it in opposition to the two houses, except in case the public utility of which would be conspicuous; and some such cases would happen.

In the present exigency of American affairs, when, by an act of Parliament, we are put out of the royal protection, and consequently discharged from our allegiance, and it has become necessary to assume government for our immediate security, the governor, lieutenant-governor, secretary, treasurer, commissary, attorney-general, should be chosen by joint ballot of both houses. And these and all other elections, especially of representatives and counsellors, should be annual, there not being in the whole circle of the sciences a maxim more infallible than this, "where annual elections end, there slavery begins."

These great men, in this respect, should be, once a year,

> Like bubbles on the sea of matter borne,
> They rise, they break, and to that sea return.

This will teach them the great political virtues of humility, patience, and moderation, without which every man in power becomes a ravenous beast of prey.

This mode of constituting the great offices of state will answer very well for the present; but if by experiment it should be found inconvenient, the legislature may, at its leisure, devise other methods of creating them, by elections of the people at large, as in Connecticut, or it may enlarge the term for which they shall be chosen to seven years, or three years, or for life, or make any other alterations which the society shall find productive of its ease, its safety, its freedom, or, in one word, its happiness.

A rotation of all offices, as well as of representatives and counsellors, has many advocates, and is contended for with many plausible arguments. It would be attended, no doubt, with many advantages; and if the society has a sufficient number of suitable characters to supply the great number of vacancies which would be made by such a rotation, I can see no objection to it. These persons may be allowed to serve for three years, and then be excluded three years, or for any longer or shorter term.

Any seven or nine of the legislative council may be made a quorum, for doing business as a privy council, to advise the governor in the exercise of the executive branch of power, and in all acts of state.

The governor should have the command of the militia and of all your armies. The power of pardons should be with the governor and council.

Judges, justices, and all other officers, civil and military, should be nominated and appointed by the governor, with the advice and consent of council, unless you choose to have a government more popular; if you do, all officers, civil and military, may be chosen by joint ballot of both houses; or, in order to preserve the independence and importance of each house, by ballot of one house, concurred in by the other. Sheriffs should be chosen by the freeholders of counties; so should registers of deeds and clerks of counties.

All officers should have commissions, under the hand of the governor and seal of the colony.

The dignity and stability of government in all its branches, the morals of the people, and every blessing of society depend so much upon an upright and skillful administration of justice, that the judicial power ought to be distinct from both the legislative and executive, and independent upon both, that so it may be a check upon both, as both should be checks upon that. The judges, therefore, should be always men of learning and experience in the laws, of exemplary morals, great patience, calmness, coolness, and attention. Their minds should not be distracted with jarring interests; they should not be dependent upon any man, or body of men. To these ends, they should hold estates for life in their offices; or, in other words, their commissions should be during good behavior, and their salaries ascertained and established by law. For misbehavior, the grand inquest of the colony, the house of representatives, should impeach them before the governor and council, where they should have time and opportunity to make their defence; but, if convicted, should be removed from their offices, and subjected to such other punishment as shall be thought proper.

A militia law, requiring all men, or with very few exceptions besides cases of conscience, to be provided with arms and ammunition, to be trained at certain seasons; and requiring counties, towns, or other small districts, to be provided with public stocks of ammunition and intrenching utensils, and with some settled plans for transporting provisions after the militia, when marched to defend their country against sudden invasions; and requiring certain districts to be provided with field-pieces, companies of matrosses, and perhaps some regiments of light-horse, is always a wise institution, and, in the present circumstances of our country, indispensable.

Laws for the liberal education of youth, especially of the lower class people, are so extremely wise and useful, that, to a humane and generous mind, no expense for this purpose would be thought extravagant.

The very mention of sumptuary laws will excite a smile. Whether our countrymen have wisdom and virtue enough to submit to them, I know not, but the happiness of the people might be greatly promoted by them, and a revenue saved sufficient to carry on this war forever. Frugality is a great revenue, besides curing us of vanities, levities, and fopperies, which are real antidotes to all great, manly, and war-like virtues.

But must not all commissions run in the name of a king? No. Why may they not as well run thus, "The colony of   to A. B. greeting," and be tested by the governor?

Why may not writs, instead of running the name of the king, run thus, "The colony of   to the sheriff," &c., and be tested by the chief justice?

Why may not indictments conclude, "against the peace of the colony of   and the dignity of the same"?

A constitution founded on these principles introduces knowledge among the people, and inspires them with a conscious dignity becoming freemen; a general emulation takes place, which causes good humor, sociability, good manners, and good morals to be general. That elevation of sentiment inspired by such a government, makes the common people brave and enterprising. That ambition which is inspired by it makes them sober, industrious, and frugal. You will find among them some elegance, perhaps, but more solidity; a little pleasure, but a great deal of business; some politeness, but more civility. If you compare such a country with the regions of domination, whether monarchical or aristocratical, you will fancy yourself in Arcadia or Elysium.

If the colonies should assume governments separately, they should be left entirely to their own choice of the forms; and if a continental constitution should be formed, it should be a congress, containing a fair and adequate representation of the colonies, and its authority should sacredly be confined to these cases, namely, war, trade, disputes between colony and colony, the post-office, and the unappropriated lands of the crown, as they used to be called.

These colonies, under such forms of government, and in such a union, would be unconquerable by all the monarchies of Europe.

You and I, my dear friend, have been sent into life at a time when the greatest lawgivers of antiquity would have wished to live. How few of the human race have ever enjoyed an opportunity of making an election of government, more than of air, soil, or climate, for themselves or their children! When, before the present epocha, had three millions of people full power and a fair opportunity to form and establish the wisest and happiest government that human wisdon can contrive? I hope you will avail yourself and your country of that extensive learning and indefatigable industry which you possess, to assist her in the formation of the happiest governments and the best character of a great people. For myself, I must beg you to keep my name out of sight; for this feeble attempt, if it should be known to be mine, would oblige me to apply to myself those lines of the immortal John Milton, in one of his sonnets:—

> "I did but prompt the age to quit their clogs
> By the known rules of ancient liberty,
> When straight a barbarous noise environs me
> Of owls and cuckoos, asses, apes, and dogs."

ALEXANDER HAMILTON

Alexander Hamilton (1757?–1804) asserted the date of his birth in the British West Indies to be 1757, but recent scholarship indicates that it was probably a year or two earlier. Though born illegitimate and left by his father in trying circumstances, he exhibited sufficient talent and energy as a youth to be sent by a friend to the colonial mainland for an education. He entered King's College (Columbia) in 1774, having also become immediately active in Revolutionary activities, during and following the Boston Tea Party. He was a member of Washington's staff, writing speeches for Washington during his Presidency, and was appointed Secretary of the Treasury in 1789. In 1804 he was killed by Aaron Burr in a duel. The following selection is Hamilton's *Federalist* article number 15, in which is stated the nature of a true national government and the need for it. An important document in American political philosophy, it was published originally in the *Independent Journal*, December 1, 1787, and, like the other *Federalist* articles, it can be found in *The Federalist: A Collection of Essays Written in Favor of The New Constitution*, New York, 1788.

Government and the Citizen

We may indeed with propriety be said to have reached almost the last stage of national humiliation. There is scarcely anything that can wound the pride or degrade the character of an independent nation which we do not experience. Are there engagements to the performance of which we are held by every tie respectable among men? These are the subjects of constant and unblushing violation. Do we owe debts to foreigners and to our own citizens contracted in a time of imminent peril for the preservation of our political existence? These remain without any proper or satisfactory provision for their discharge. Have we valuable territories and important posts in the possession of a foreign power which, by express stipulations, ought long since to have been surrendered? These are still retained, to the prejudice of our interests, not less than of our rights. Are we in a condition to resent or to repel the aggression? We have neither troops, nor treasury, nor government.[1] Are we even in a condition to remonstrate with dignity? The just im-

[1] "I mean for the Union."

putations on our own faith, in respect to the same treaty, ought first to be removed. Are we entitled by nature and compact to a free participation in the navigation of the Mississippi? Spain excludes us from it. Is public credit an indispensable resource in time of public danger? We seem to have abandoned its cause as desperate and irretrievable. Is commerce of importance to national wealth? Ours is at the lowest point of declension. Is respectability in the eyes of foreign powers a safeguard against foreign encroachments? The imbecility of our government even forbids them to treat with us. Our ambassadors abroad are the mere pageants of mimic sovereignty. Is a violent and unnatural decrease in the value of land a symptom of national distress? The price of improved land in most parts of the country is much lower than can be accounted for by the quantity of waste land at market, and can only be fully explained by that want of private and public confidence which are so alarmingly prevalent among all ranks, and which have a direct tendency to depreciate property of every kind. Is private credit the friend and patron of industry? That most useful kind which relates to borrowing and lending is reduced within the narrowest limits, and this still more from an opinion of insecurity than from the scarcity of money. To shorten an enumeration of particulars which can afford neither pleasure nor instruction, it may in general be demanded, what indication is there of national disorder, poverty, and insignificance that could befall a community so peculiarly blessed with natural advantages as we are, which does not form a part of the dark catalogue of our public misfortunes?

This is the melancholy situation to which we have been brought by those very maxims and councils which would now deter us from adopting the proposed Constitution; and which, not content with having conducted us to the brink of a precipice, seem resolved to plunge us into the abyss that awaits us below. Here, my countrymen, impelled by every motive that ought to influence an enlightened people, let us make a firm stand for our safety, our tranquillity, our dignity, our reputation. Let us at last break the fatal charm which has too long seduced us from the paths of felicity and prosperity.

It is true, as has been before observed, that facts, too stubborn to be resisted, have produced a species of general assent to the abstract proposition that there exist material defects in our national system; but the usefulness of the concession, on the part of the old adversaries of federal measures, is destroyed by a strenuous opposition to a remedy, upon the only principles that can give it a chance of success. While they admit that the government of the United States is destitute of energy, they contend against conferring upon it those powers which are requisite to supply that energy. They seem still to aim at things repugnant and irreconcilable: at an augmentation of federal authority, without a diminution of State authority; at sovereignty in the Union, and complete independence in the members. They still, in fine, seem to cherish with blind devotion the political monster of an *imperium in imperio*. This renders a full display of the principal defects of the Confederation necessary, in order to show that the evils we experience do not proceed from minute or partial imperfections, but from fundamental errors in the structure of the building, which cannot be amended otherwise than by an alteration in the first principles and main pillars of the fabric.

The great and radical vice in the construction of the existing Confederation is in the principle of LEGISLATION for STATES or GOVERNMENTS, in their CORPORATE or COLLECTIVE CAPACITIES, and as contradistinguished from the INDIVIDUALS of which they consist. Though this principle does not run through all the powers delegated to the Union, yet it pervades and governs those on which the efficacy of the rest depends. Except as to the rule of apportionment, the United States has an indefinite discretion to make requisitions for men and money; but they have no authority to raise either, by regulations extending to the individual citizens of America. The consequence of this is, that though in theory their resolutions concerning those objects are laws, constitutionally binding on the members of the Union, yet in practice they are mere recommendations which the States observe or disregard at their option.

It is a singular instance of the capriciousness of the human mind, that, after all the admonitions we have had from experience on this head, there should still be found men who object to the new Constitution for deviating from a principle which has been found the bane of the old, and which is in itself evidently incompatible with the idea of GOVERNMENT; a principle, in short, which, if it is to be executed at all, must substitute the violent and sanguinary agency of the sword to the mild influence of the magistracy.

There is nothing absurd or impracticable in the idea of a league or alliance between independent nations for certain defined purposes precisely stated in a treaty regulating all the details of time, place, circumstance, and quantity; leaving nothing to future discretion; and depending for its execution on the good faith of the parties. Compacts of this kind exist among all civilised nations, subject to the usual vicissitudes of peace and war, of observance and non-observance, as the interests or passions of the contracting powers dictate. In the early part of the present century there was an epidemical rage in Europe for this species of compacts, from which the politicians of the times fondly hoped for benefits which were never realised. With a view to establishing the equilibrium of power and the peace of that part of the world, all the resources of negotiation were exhausted, and triple and quadruple alliances were formed; but they were scarcely formed before they were broken, giving an instructive but afflicting lesson to mankind, how little dependence is to be placed on treaties which have no other sanction than the obligations of good faith, and which oppose general considerations of peace and justice to the impulse of any immediate interest or passion.

If the particular States in this country are disposed to stand in a similar relation to each other, and to drop the project of a general DIS-CRETIONARY SUPERINTENDENCE, the scheme would indeed be pernicious, and would entail upon us all the mischiefs which have been enumerated under the first head; but it would have the merit of being, at least, consistent and practicable. Abandoning all views towards a confederate government, this would bring us to simple alliance offensive and defensive; and would place us in a situation to be alternate friends and enemies of each other, as our mutual jealousies and rivalships, nourished by the intrigues of foreign nations, should prescribe to us.

But if we are unwilling to be placed in this perilous situation; if we still will adhere to the design of a national government, or, which is the same thing, of a superintending power, under the direction of a common council, we must resolve to incorporate into our plan those ingredients which may be considered as forming the characteristic difference between a league and a government; we must extend the authority of the Union to the persons of the citizens—the only proper objects of government.

Government implies the power of making laws. It is essential to the idea of a law, that it be attended with a sanction; or, in other words, a penalty or punishment for disobedience. If there be no penalty annexed to disobedience, the resolutions or commands which pretend to be laws will, in fact, amount to nothing more than advice or recommendation. This penalty, whatever it may be, can only be inflicted in two ways: by the agency of the courts and ministers of justice, or by military force; by the COERCION of the magistracy, or by the COERCION of arms.

The first kind can evidently apply only to men; the last kind must of necessity be employed against bodies politic, or communities, or States. It is evident that there is no process of a court by which the observance of the laws can, in the last resort, be enforced. Sentences may be denounced against them for violations of their duty; but these sentences can only be carried into execution by the sword. In an association where the general authority is confined to the collective bodies of the communities that compose it, every breach of the laws must involve a state of war; and military execution must become the only instrument of civil obedience. Such a state of things can certainly not deserve the name of government, nor would any prudent man choose to commit his happiness to it.

There was a time when we were told that breaches, by the States, of the regulations of the federal authority were not to be expected; that a sense of common interest would preside over the conduct of the respective members, and would beget a full compliance with all the constitutional requisitions of the Union. This language, at the present day, would appear as wild as a great part of what we now hear from the same quarter will be thought, when we shall have received further lessons from that best oracle of wisdom, experience. It at all times betrayed an ignorance of the true springs by which human conduct is actuated, and belied the original inducements to the establishment of civil power. Why has government been instituted at all? Because the passions of men will not conform to the dictates of reason and justice, without constraint. Has it been found that bodies of men act with more rectitude or greater disinterestedness than individuals? The contrary of this has been inferred by all accurate observers of the conduct of mankind; and the inference is founded upon obvious reasons. Regard to reputation has a less active influence, when the infamy of a bad action is to be divided among a number, than when it is to fall singly upon one. A spirit of faction, which is apt to mingle its poison in the deliberations of all bodies of men, will often hurry the persons of whom they are composed into improprieties and excesses, for which they would blush in a private capacity.

In addition to all this, there is, in the nature of sovereign power, an impatience of control, that disposes those who are invested with the exercise of it, to look with an evil eye upon all external attempts to restrain or direct its operations. From this spirit it happens, that in every political association which is formed upon the principle of uniting in a common interest a number of lesser sovereignties, there will be found a kind of eccentric tendency in the subordinate or inferior orbs, by the operation of which there will be a perpetual effort in each to fly off from the common centre. This tendency is not difficult to be accounted for. It has its origin in the love of power. Power controlled or abridged is almost always the rival and enemy of that power by which it is controlled or abridged. This simple proposition will teach us how little reason there is to expect that the persons intrusted with the administration of the affairs of the particular members of a confederacy will at all times be ready, with perfect good humour, and an unbiased regard to the public weal, to execute the resolutions or decrees of the general authority. The reverse of this results from the constitution of human nature.

If, therefore, the measures of the Confederacy cannot be executed without the intervention of the particular administrations, there will be little prospect of their being executed at all. The rulers of the respective members, whether they have a constitutional right to do it or not, will undertake to judge of the propriety of the measures themselves. They will consider the conformity of the thing proposed or required to their immediate interests or aims; the momentary conveniences or inconveniences that would attend its adoption. All this will be done; and in a spirit of interest and suspicious scrutiny, without that knowledge of national circumstances and reasons of state, which is essential to a right judgment, and with that strong predilection in favour of local objects, which can hardly fail to mislead the decision. The same process must be repeated in every member of which the body is constituted; and the execution of the plans, framed by the councils of the whole, will always fluctuate on the discretion of the ill-informed and prejudiced opinion of every part. Those who have been conversant in the proceedings of popular assemblies; who have seen how difficult it often is, where there is no exterior pressure of circumstances, to bring them to harmonious resolutions on important points, will readily conceive how impossible it must be to induce a number of such assemblies, deliberating at a distance from each other, at different times, and under different impressions, long to co-operate in the same views and pursuits.

In our case, the concurrence of thirteen distinct sovereign wills is requisite, under the Confederation, to the complete execution of every important measure that proceeds from the Union. It has happened as was to have been foreseen. The measures of the Union have not been executed; the delinquencies of the States have, step by step, matured themselves to an extreme, which has, at length, arrested all the wheels of the national government, and brought them to an awful stand. Congress at this time scarcely possess the means of keeping up the forms of administration, till the States can have time to agree upon a more substantial substitute for the present shadow of a federal government. Things did not come to this desperate extremity at once. The causes which have been specified produced at first only unequal and disproportionate degrees of compliance with the requisitions of the Union. The greater deficiencies of some States furnished the pretext of example and the temptation of interest to the complying, or to the least delinquent States. Why should we do more in proportion than those who are embarked with us in the same political voyage? Why should we consent to bear more than our proper share of the common burden? These were suggestions which human selfishness could not withstand, and which even speculative men, who looked forward to remote consequences, could not, without hesitation, combat. Each State, yielding to the persuasive voice of immediate interest or convenience, has successively withdrawn its support, till the frail and tottering edifice seems ready to fall upon our heads, and to crush us beneath its ruins.

JAMES MADISON

James Madison (1751–1836), fourth President of the United States, was born in Virginia. After graduating from the College of New Jersey (Princeton), he became politically active. He was a delegate to the 1776 Virginia Convention which asked the Continental Congress to assert colonial independence. Madison's ideas, accepted as the basis of a federal constitution, included the division of the national government into an executive, a two-house legislative, and a judicial branch, leading to his being called "the father of the Constitution." A member of Congress and then Secretary of State under Jefferson, he assumed the Presidency in 1809 and was reelected in 1812. The following selection is his *Federalist* article number 10, appearing originally in the New York *Daily Advertiser*, November 23, 1787. It describes how "factions" originate out of conflicting property interests and how the effects of factions require political regulation, proposing the "checks and balances" concept which is basic in the American political tradition. *The Federalist* articles were a series of letters written by Madison, Hamilton, and Jay to the New York press urging the ratification of the proposed Federal Constitution.

The Wisdom of the Whole

To the People of the State of New York:

Among the numerous advantages promised by a well-constructed union, none deserves to be more accurately developed than its tendency to break and control the violence of faction. The friend of popular governments never finds himself so much alarmed for their character and fate as when he contemplates their propensity to this dangerous vice. He will not fail, therefore, to set a due value on any plan which, without violating the principles to which he is attached, provides a proper cure for it. The instability, injustice, and confusion introduced into the public councils have, in truth, been the mortal diseases under which popular governments have everywhere perished; as they continue to be the favorite and fruitful topics from which the adversaries to liberty derive their most specious declamations. The valuable improvements made by the American constitutions on the popular models, both ancient and modern, cannot certainly be too much admired; but it would be an unwarrantable partiality, to contend that they have as effectually obviated the danger on this side as was wished and expected.

Complaints are everywhere heard from our most considerate and virtuous citizens, equally the friends of public and private faith and of public and personal liberty, that our governments are too unstable; that the public good is disregarded in the conflicts of rival parties; and that measures are too often decided, not according to the rules of justice, and the rights of the minor party, but by the superior force of an interested and overbearing majority. However anxiously we may wish that these complaints had no foundation, the evidence of known facts will not permit us to deny that they are in some degree true. It will be found, indeed, on a candid review of our situation, that some of the distresses under which we labor have been erroneously charged on the operation of our governments; but it will be found, at the same time, that other causes will not alone account for many of our heaviest misfortunes; and, particularly, for that prevailing and increasing distrust of public engagements, and alarm for private rights, which are echoed from one end of the continent to the other. These must be chiefly, if not wholly, effects of the unsteadiness and injustice with which a factious spirit has tainted our public administrations.

By a faction, I understand a number of citizens, whether amounting to a majority or minority of the whole, who are united and actuated by some common impulse of passion, or of interest, adverse to the rights of other citizens or to the permanent and aggregate interests of the community.

There are two methods of curing the mischiefs of faction: the one, by removing its causes; the other, by controlling its effects.

There are again two methods of removing the causes of faction: the one, by destroying the liberty which is essential to its existence; the other, by giving to every citizen the same opinions, the same passions, and the same interests.

It could never be more truly said than of the first remedy, that it was worse than the disease. Liberty is to faction what air is to fire, an ailment without which it instantly expires. But it could not be less folly to abolish liberty, which is essential to political life, because it nourishes faction, than it would be to wish the annihilation of air, which is essential to animal life, because it imports to fire its destructive agency.

The second expedient is as impracticable as the first would be unwise. As long as the reason of man continues fallible, and he is at liberty to exercise it, different opinions will be formed. As long as the connection subsists between his reason and his self-love, his opinions and his passions will have a reciprocal influence on each other; and the former will be objects to which the latter will attach themselves. The diversity in the faculties of men, from which the rights of property originate, is not less an insuperable obstacle to a uniformity of interests. The protection of these faculties is the first object of government. From the protection of different and unequal faculties of acquiring property, the possession of different degrees and kinds of property immediately results; and from the influence of these on the sentiments and views of the respective proprietors ensues a division of the society into different interests and parties.

The latent causes of faction are thus sown in the nature of man; and we see them everywhere brought into different degrees of activity, according to the different circumstances of civil society. A zeal for different opinions concerning religion, concerning government and many other points, as well of speculation as of practice; an attachment to different leaders ambitiously contending for pre-eminence and power, or to persons of other descriptions whose fortunes have been interesting to the human passions, have, in turn, divided mankind into parties, inflamed them with mutual animosity, and rendered them much more disposed to vex and oppress each other, than to co-operate for their common good. So strong is this propensity of mankind to fall into mutual animosities, that where no substantial occasion presents itself, the most frivolous and fanciful distinctions have been sufficient to kindle their unfriendly passions and excite their most violent conflicts. But the most common and durable source of factions has been the various and unequal distribution of property. Those who hold and those who are without property have ever formed distinct interests in society. Those who are creditors and those who are debtors fall under a like discrimination. A landed interest, a manufacturing interest, a mercantile interest, a moneyed interest, with many lesser interests, grow up of necessity in civilized nations, and divide them into different classes, actuated by different sentiments and views. The regulation of these various and interfering interests forms the principal task of modern legislation, and involves the spirit of party and faction in the necessary and ordinary operations of the government.

No man is allowed to be a judge in his own cause; because his interest would certainly bias his judgment and, not improbably, corrupt his integrity. With equal, nay, with greater reason, a body of men are unfit to be both judges and parties at the same time; yet what are many of the most important acts of legislation, but so many judicial determinations, not indeed concerning the rights of single persons, but concerning the rights of large bodies of citizens? and what are the different classes of legislators, but advocates and parties to the causes which they determine? Is a law proposed concerning private debts?—it is a question to which the creditors are parties on one side, and the debtors on the other. Justice ought to hold the balance between them. Yet the parties are, and must be, themselves the judges; and the most numerous party, or, in other words, the most powerful faction, must be expected to prevail. Shall domestic manufactures be encouraged, and in what degree by restrictions on foreign manufactures? are questions which would be differently decided by the landed and the manufacturing classes, and probably by neither with a sole regard to justice and the public good. The apportionment of taxes on the various descriptions of property is an act which seems to require the most exact impartiality; yet there is, perhaps, no legislative act in which greater opportunity and temptation are given to a predominant party, to trample on the rules of justice. Every shilling with which they overburden the inferior number is a shilling saved to their own pockets.

It is in vain to say that enlightened statesmen will be able to adjust these clashing interests and render them all subservient to the public good. Enlightened statesmen will not always be at the helm; nor, in many cases, can such an adjustment be made at all, without taking into view indirect and remote considerations, which will rarely prevail over the immediate interest which one party may find in disregarding the rights of another or the good of the whole.

The inference to which we are brought is that the causes of faction cannot be removed and that relief is only to be sought in the means of controlling its effects.

If a faction consists of less than a majority, relief is supplied by the republican principle, which enables the majority to defeat its sinister views by regular vote. It may clog the administration, it may convulse the society; but it will be unable to execute and mask its violence under the forms of the Constitution. When a majority is included in a faction, the form of popular government, on the other hand, enables it to sacrifice to its ruling passion or interest both the public good and the rights of other citizens. To secure the public good, and private rights, against the danger of such a faction, and at the same time to preserve the spirit and the form of popular government, is then the great object to which our inquiries are directed. Let me add that it is the great *desideratum*, by which alone this form of government can be rescued from the opprobrium under which it has so long labored, and be recommended to the esteem and adoption of mankind.

By what means is this object attainable? Evidently by one of two only. Either the existence of the same passion or interest in a majority, at the same time, must be prevented; or the majority, having such co-existent passion or interest, must be rendered, by their number and local situation, unable to concert and carry into effect schemes of oppression. If the impulse and the opportunity be suffered to coincide, we well know that neither moral nor religious motives can be relied on as an adequate control. They are not found to be such on the injustice and violence of individuals, and lose their efficacy in proportion to the number combined together; that is, in proportion as their efficacy becomes needful.

From this view of the subject it may be concluded that a pure democracy, by which I mean a society consisting of a small number of citizens, who assemble and administer the government in person, can admit of no cure for the mischiefs of faction. A common passion or interest will, in almost every case, be felt by a majority of the whole; a communication and concert results from the form of government itself; and there is nothing to check the inducements to sacrifice the weaker party or an obnoxious individual. Hence it is that such democracies have ever been spectacles of turbulence and contention; have ever been found incompatible with personal security, or the rights of property, and have in general been as short in their lives as they have been violent in their deaths. Theoretic politicians, who have patronized this species of government, have erroneously supposed that by reducing mankind to a perfect equality in their political rights, they would at the same time be perfectly equalized and assimilated in their possessions, their opinions, and their passions.

A republic, by which I mean a government in which the scheme of representation takes place, opens a different prospect, and promises the cure for which we are seeking. Let us examine the points in which it varies from pure democracy, and we shall comprehend both the nature of the cure and the efficacy which it must derive from the union.

The two great points of difference between a democracy and a republic are: First, the delegation of the government, in the latter, to a small number of citizens elected by the rest; secondly, the greater number of citizens, and greater sphere of country, over which the latter may be extended.

The effect of the first difference is, on the one hand, to refine and enlarge the public views, by passing them through the medium of a chosen body of citizens, whose wisdom may best discern the true interest of their country, and whose patriotism and love of justice will be least likely to sacrifice it to temporary or partial considerations. Under such a regulation, it may well happen that the public voice, pronounced by the representatives of the people, will be more consonant to the public good than if pronounced by the people themselves, convened for the purpose. On the other hand, the effect may be inverted. Men of factious tempers, of local prejudices, or of sinister designs, may by intrigue, by corruption, or by other means, first obtain the suffrages, and then betray the interests of the people. The question resulting is, whether small or extensive republics are most favorable to the election of proper guardians of the public weal; and it is clearly decided in favor of the latter by two obvious considerations.

In the first place, it is to be remarked that, however small the republic may be, the representatives must be raised to a certain number, in order to guard against the cabals of a few; and that, however large it may be, they must be limited to a certain number, in order to guard against the confusion of a multitude. Hence, the number of representatives in the two cases not being in proportion to that of the constituents, and being proportionally greatest in the small republic, it follows that if the proportion of fit characters be not less in the large than in the small republic, the former will present a greater option, and consequently a greater probability of a fit choice.

In the next place, as each representative will be chosen by a greater number of citizens in the large than in the small republic, it will be more difficult for unworthy candidates to practise with success the vicious arts, by which elections are too often carried; and the suffrages of the people, being more free, will be more likely to centre in men who possess the most attractive merit and the most diffusive and established characters.

It must be confessed that in this as in most other cases, there is a mean, on both sides of which inconveniences will be found to lie. By enlarging too much the number of electors, you render the representative too little acquainted with all their local circumstances and lesser interests; as by reducing it too much, you render him unduly attached to these, and too little fit to comprehend and pursue great and national objects. The federal Constitution forms a happy combination in this respect; the great and aggregate interests being referred to the national, the local and particular to the State, legislatures.

The other point of difference is, the greater number of citizens and extent of territory which may be brought within the compass of republican than of democratic government; and it is this circumstance principally which renders factious combinations less to be dreaded in the former, than in the latter. The smaller the society, the fewer probably will be the distinct parties and interests composing it; the fewer the distinct parties and interests, the more frequently will a majority be found of the same party; and the smaller the number of individuals composing a majority, and the smaller the compass within which they are placed, the more easily will they concert and execute their plans of oppression. Extend the sphere, and you take in a greater variety of parties and interests; you make it less probable that a majority of the whole will have a common motive to invade the rights of other citizens; or if such a common motive exists, it will be more difficult for all who feel it to discover their own strength, and to act in unison with each other. Besides other impediments, it may be remarked that where there is a consciousness of unjust or dishonorable purposes, communication is always checked by distrust, in proportion to the number whose concurrence is necessary.

Hence it clearly appears that the same advantage which a republic has over a democracy, in controlling the effects of faction, is enjoyed by a large over a small republic—is enjoyed by the Union over the States composing it. Does the advantage consist in the substitution of representatives, whose enlightened views and virtuous sentiments render them superior to local prejudices, and to schemes of injustice? It will not be denied that the representation of the Union will be most likely to possess these requisite endowments. Does it consist in the greater security afforded by a greater variety of parties, against the event of any one party being able to outnumber and oppress the rest? In an equal degree does the increased variety of parties, comprised within the Union, increase this security. Does it, in fine, consist in the greater obstacles opposed to the concert and accomplishment of the secret wishes of an unjust and interested majority? Here, again, the extent of the Union gives it the most palpable advantages.

The influence of factious leaders may kindle a flame within their particular States, but will be unable to spread a general conflagration through the other States. A religious sect may degenerate into a political faction in a part of the confederacy; but the variety of sects dispersed over the entire face of it must secure the national councils against any danger from that source. A rage for paper money, for an abolition of debts, for an equal division of property, or for any other improper and wicked project will be less apt to pervade the whole body of the Union than a particular member of it; in the same proportion as such a malady is more likely to taint a particular county or district than an entire State.

In the extent and proper structure of the Union, therefore, we behold a republican remedy for the diseases most incident to republican government. And according to the degree of pleasure and pride we feel in being republicans, ought to be our zeal in cherishing the spirit and supporting the character of federalists.

PUBLIUS [James Madison]

ABRAHAM LINCOLN

Abraham Lincoln (1809–65), sixteenth President of the United States, was born in Kentucky. He grew up in very humble circumstances, had virtually no formal education, but was encouraged in his self-education by his stepmother. He lived successively in Indiana and Illinois, and often worked as a manual laborer. Lincoln began his political career in the village of New Salem, Illinois, as a Whig and follower of Henry Clay. He later moved to Springfield and established an important law practice. Lincoln went to Congress in 1846 as a Whig but, with the decline of that party, supported the new Republican Party in the Presidential campaign of 1856. His famous debates with Stephen Douglas in 1858 brought him national attention, preparing the way for his election in 1860. Reelected in 1864, he was assassinated April 14, 1865, by the actor John Wilkes Booth. The selection below, Lincoln's First Inaugural Address, is a plea for an alternative to the threat of civil war and for the preservation of the Union. It contains significant interpretations of the American system of government and is a permanent contribution to political philosophy. It is to be found in James D. Richardson, *A Compilation of The Messages and Papers of the Presidents, 1789–1907*, Vol. VI, Washington, D.C., 1908.

The People and the Union

Fellow-citizens of the United States:

In compliance with a custom as old as the government itself, I appear before you to address you briefly, and to take in your presence the oath prescribed by the Constitution of the United States to be taken by the President "before he enters on the execution of his office."

I do not consider it necessary at present for me to discuss those matters of administration about which there is no special anxiety or excitement.

Apprehension seems to exist among the people of the Southern States that by the accession of a Republican administration their property and their peace and personal security are to be endangered. There has never been any reasonable cause for such apprehension. Indeed, the most ample evidence to the contrary has all the while existed and been open to their inspection. It is found in nearly all the published speeches of him who now address you. I do but quote from one of those speeches when I declare that "I have no purpose, directly or indirectly, to interfere with the institution of slavery in the States where it exists. I believe that I have no lawful right to do so, and I have no inclination to do so." Those who nominated and elected me did so with full knowledge that I had made this and many similar declarations, and had never recanted them. And, more than this, they placed in the platform for my acceptance, and as a law to themselves and to me, the clear and emphatic resolution which I now read:

Resolved, That the maintenance inviolate of the rights of the States, and especially the right of each State to order and control its own domestic institutions according to its own judgment exclusively, is essential to that balance of power on which the perfection and endurance of our political fabric depend; and we denounce the lawless invasion by armed force of the soil of any State or Territory, no matter under what pretext, as among the gravest of crimes.

I now reiterate these sentiments; and, in doing so, I only press upon the public attention the most conclusive evidence of which the case is susceptible, that the property, peace, and security of no section are to be in any wise endangered by the now incoming administration. I add, too, that all the protection which, consistently with the Constitution and the laws, can be given, will be cheerfully given to all the States when lawfully demanded, for whatever cause—as cheerfully to one section as to another.

There is much controversy about the delivering up of fugitives from service or labor. The clause I now read is as plainly written in the Constitution as any other of its provisions:

No person held to service or labor in one State, under the laws thereof, escaping into another, shall in consequence of any law or regulation therein be discharged from such service or labor, but shall be delivered up on claim of the party to whom such service or labor may be due.

It is scarcely questioned that this provision was intended by those who made it for the reclaiming of what we call fugitive slaves; and the intention of the lawgiver is the law. All members of Congress swear their support to the whole Constitution—to this provision as much as to any other. To the proposition, then, that slaves whose cases come within the terms of this clause "shall be delivered up," their oaths are unanimous. Now, if they would make the effort in good temper, could they not with nearly equal unanimity frame and pass a law by means of which to keep good that unanimous oath?

There is some difference of opinion whether this clause should be enforced by national or State authority; but surely that difference is not a very material one. If the slave is to be surrendered, it can be of but little consequence to him or to others by which authority it is done. And should anyone in any case be content that his oath shall go unkept on a merely unsubstantial controversy as to how it shall be kept?

Again, in any law upon this subject, ought not all the safeguards of liberty known in civilized and humane jurisprudence to be introduced, so that a free man be not, in any case, surrendered as a slave? And might it not be well at the same time to provide by law for the enforcement of that clause in the Constitution which guarantees that "the citizens of each State shall be entitled to all privileges and immunities of citizens in the several States"?

I take official oath today with no mental reservations, and with no purpose to construe the Constitution or laws by any hypercritical rules. And while I do not choose now to specify particular acts of Congress as proper to be enforced, I do suggest that it will be much safer for all, both in official and private stations, to conform to and abide by all those acts which stand unrepealed, than to violate any of them, trusting to find impunity in having them held to be unconstitutional.

It is seventy-two years since the first inauguration of a President under our National Constitution. During that period fifteen different and greatly distinguished citizens have, in succession, administered the executive branch of the government. They have conducted it through many perils, and generally with great success. Yet, with all this scope of precedent, I now enter upon the same task for the brief constitutional term of four years under great and peculiar difficulty. A disruption of the Federal Union, heretofore only menaced, is now formidably attempted.

I hold that, in contemplation of universal law and of the Constitution, the Union of these States is perpetual. Perpetuity is implied, if not expressed in the fundamental law of all national governments. It is safe to assert that no government proper ever had a provision in its organic law for its own termination. Continue to execute all the express provisions of our National Constitution, and the Union will endure forever—it being impossible to destroy it except by some action not provided for in the instrument itself.

Again, if the United States be not a government proper, but an association of States, in the nature of contract merely, can it, as a contract, be peaceably unmade by less than all the parties who made it?

One party to a contract may violate it—break it, so to speak—but does it not require all to lawfully rescind it?

Descending from these general principles, we find the proposition that in legal contemplation the Union is perpetual confirmed by the history of the Union itself. The Union is much older than the Constitution. It was formed, in fact, by the Articles of Association in 1774. It was matured and continued by the Declaration of Independence in 1776. It was further matured, and the faith of all the then thirteen states expressly plighted and engaged that it should be perpetual, by the Articles of Confederation in 1778. And finally, in 1787, one of the declared objects for ordaining and establishing the Constitution was "to form a more perfect Union."

But if destruction of the Union by one or by a part only of the states be lawfully possible, the Union is *less* perfect than before the Constitution, having lost the vital element of perpetuity.

It follows from these views that no state upon its own mere motion can lawfully get out of the Union; that resolves and ordinances to that effect are legally void, and that acts of violence within any state or states against the authority of the United States are insurrectionary or revolutionary, according to circumstances.

I therefore consider that in view of the Constitution and the laws the Union is unbroken, and to the extent of my ability I shall take care, as the Constitution itself expressly enjoins upon me, that the laws of the Union be faithfully executed in all the states. Doing this I deem to be only a simple duty on my part; and I shall perform it so far as practicable unless my rightful masters, the American people, shall withhold the requisite means or in some authoritative manner direct the contrary. I trust this will not be regarded as a menace, but only as the declared purpose of the Union that it *will* constitutionally defend and maintain itself.

In doing this, there needs to be no bloodshed or violence, and there shall be none unless it be forced upon the national authority. The power confided to me will be used to hold, occupy, and possess the property and places belonging to the government and to collect the duties and imposts; but, beyond what may be necessary for these objects, there will be no invasion, no using of force against or among the people anywhere. Where hostility to the United States in any interior locality, shall be so great and so universal as to prevent competent resident citizens from holding the federal offices, there will be no attempt to force obnoxious strangers among the people for that object. While the strict legal right may exist in the government to enforce the exercise of these offices, the attempt to do so would be so irritating and so nearly impracticable withal, that I deem it better to forgo for the time the uses of such offices.

The mails, unless repelled, will continue to be furnished in all parts of the Union. So far as possible the people everywhere shall have that sense of perfect security which is most favorable to calm thought and reflection. The course here indicated will be followed unless current events and experience shall show a modification or change to be proper, and in every case and exigency my best discretion will be exercised according to cirumstances actually existing, and with a view and a hope of a peaceful solution of the national troubles and the restoration of fraternal sympathies and affections.

That there are persons in one section or another who seek to destroy the Union at all events, and are glad of any pretext to do it, I will neither affirm nor deny; but if there be such, I need address no word to them. To those, however, who really love the Union may I not speak?

Before entering upon so grave a matter as the destruction of our national fabric, with all its benefits, its memories, and its hopes, would it not be wise to ascertain precisely why we do it? Will you hazard so desperate a step while there is any possibility that any portion of the ills you fly from have no real existence? Will you, while the certain ills you fly to are greater than all the real ones you fly from—will you risk the commission of so fearful a mistake?

All profess to be content in the Union if all constitutional rights can be maintained. Is it true, then, that any right, plainly written in the Constitution, has been denied? I think not. Happily the human mind is so constituted that no party can reach to the audacity of doing this. Think, if you can, of a single instance in which a plainly written provision of the Constitution has ever been denied. If by the mere force of numbers a majority should deprive a minority of any clearly written constitutional right, it might, in a moral point of view, justify revolution—certainly would if such a right were a vital one. But such is not our case. All the vital rights of minorities and of individuals are so plainly assured to them by affirmations and negations, guarantees and prohibitions, in the Constitution, that controversies never arise concerning them. But no organic law can ever be framed with a provision specifically applicable to every question which may occur in practical administration. No foresight can anticipate, nor any document of reasonable length contain, express provisions for all possible questions.

Shall fugitives from labor be surrendered by national or by state authority? The Constitution does not expressly say. *May* Congress prohibit slavery in the territories? The Constitution does not expressly say. *Must* Congress protect slavery in the territories? The Constitution does not expressly say.

From questions of this class spring all our constitutional controversies, and we divide upon them into majorities and minorities. If the minority will not acquiesce, the majority must, or the government must cease. There is no other alternative, for continuing the government is acquiescence on one side or the other. If a minority in such case will secede rather than acquiesce, they make a precedent which in turn will divide and ruin them, for a minority of their own will secede from them whenever a majority refuses to be controlled by such minority. For instance, why may not any portion of a new confederacy a year or two hence arbitrarily secede again, precisely as portions of the present Union now claim to secede from it? All who cherish disunion sentiments are now being educated to the exact temper of doing this.

Is there such perfect identity of interests among the states to compose a new union as to produce harmony only and prevent renewed secession?

Plainly the central idea of secession is the essence of anarchy. A majority held in restraint by constitutional checks and limitations, and always changing easily with deliberate changes of popular opinions and sentiments, is the only true sovereign of a free people. Whoever rejects it does of necessity fly to anarchy or to despotism. Unanimity is impossible. The rule of a minority, as a permanent arrangement, is wholly inadmissible; so that, rejecting the majority principle, anarchy, or despotism in some form is all that is left.

I do not forget the position assumed by some that constitutional questions are to be decided by the Supreme Court, nor do I deny that such decisions must be binding in any case upon the parties to a suit as to the object of that suit, while they are also entitled to very high respect and consideration in all parallel cases by all other departments of the government. And while it is obviously possible that such decision may be erroneous in any given case, still the evil effect following it, being limited to that particular case, with the chance that it may be over-ruled and never become a precedent for other cases, can better be borne than could the evils of a different practice. At the same time the candid citizen must confess that if the policy of the government, upon vital questions affecting the whole people, is to be irrevocably fixed by decisions of the Supreme Court, the instant they are made, in ordinary litigation between parties in personal actions, the people will have ceased to be their own rulers, having to that extent practically resigned their government into the hands of that eminent tribunal. Nor is there in this view any assault upon the court or the judges. It is a duty from which they may not shrink to decide cases properly brought before them, and it is no fault of theirs if others seek to turn their decisions to political purposes.

One section of our country believes slavery is right, and ought to be extended, while the other believes it is wrong, and ought not to be extended. This is the only substantial dispute. The fugitive-slave clause of the Constitution, and the law for the suppression of the foreign slave-trade, are each as well enforced, perhaps, as any law can ever be in a community where the moral sense of the people imperfectly supports the law itself. The great body of the people abide by the dry legal obligation in both cases, and a few break over in each. This, I think, cannot be perfectly cured; and it would be worse in both cases after the separation of the sections than before. The foreign slave-trade, now imperfectly suppressed, would be ultimately revived, without restriction, in one section, while fugitive slaves, now only partially surrendered, would not be surrendered at all by the other.

Physically speaking, we cannot separate. We cannot remove our respective sections from each other, nor build an impassable wall between them. A husband and wife may be divorced, and go out of the presence and beyond the reach of each other; but the different parts of our country cannot do this. They cannot but remain face to face, and intercourse, either amicable or hostile, must continue between them. Is it possible, then, to make that intercourse more advantageous or more satisfactory after separation than before? Can aliens make treaties easier than friends can make laws? Can treaties be more faithfully enforced between aliens than laws can among friends? Suppose you go to war, you cannot fight always; and when, after much loss on both sides, and no gain on either, you cease fighting, the identical old questions as to terms of intercourse, are again upon you.

This country, with its institutions, belongs to the people who inhabit it. Whenever they shall grow weary of the existing government, they can exercise their constitutional right of amending it, or their revolutionary right to dismember or overthrow it. I cannot be ignorant of the fact that many worthy and patriotic citizens are desirous of having the National Constitution amended. While I make no recommendation of amendments, I fully recognize the rightful authority of the people over the whole subject, to be exercised in either of the modes prescribed in the instrument itself; and I should, under existing circumstances, favor rather than oppose a fair opportunity being afforded the people to act upon it. I will venture to add that to me the convention mode seems preferable, in that it allows amendments to originate with the people themselves, instead of only permitting them to take or reject propositions originated by others not especially chosen for the purpose, and which might not be precisely such as they would wish to either accept or refuse. I understand a proposed amendment to the Constitution—which amendment, however, I have not seen—has passed Congress, to the effect that the Federal Government shall never interfere with the domestic institutions of the States, including that of persons held to service. To avoid misconstruction of what I have said, I depart from my purpose not to speak of particular amendments so far as to say that, holding such a provision to now be implied constitutional law, I have no objection to its being made express and irrevocable.

The chief magistrate derives all his authority from the people, and they have conferred none upon him to fix terms for the separation of the States. The people themselves can do this also if they choose; but the executive, as such, has nothing to do with it. His duty is to administer the present government, as it came to his hands, and to transmit it, unimpaired by him, to his successor.

Why should there not be a patient confidence in the ultimate justice of the people? Is there any better or equal hope in the world? In our present differences is either party without faith of being in the right? If the Almighty Ruler of Nations, with his eternal truth and justice, be on your side of the North, or on yours of the South, that truth and that justice will surely prevail by the judgment of this great tribunal of the American people.

By the frame of the government under which we live, this same people have wisely given their public servants but little power for mischief; and have, with equal wisdom, provided for the return of that little to their own hands at very short intervals. While the people retain their virtue and vigilance, no administration, by any extreme of wickedness or folly, can very seriously injure the government in the short space of four years.

My countrymen, one and all, think calmly and well upon this whole subject. Nothing valuable can be lost by taking time. If there be an object to hurry any of you in hot haste to a step which you would never take deliberately, that object will be frustrated by taking time; but no good object can be frustrated by it. Such of you as are now dissatisfied, still have the old Constitution unimpaired, and, on the sensitive point, the laws of your own framing under it; while the new administration will have no immediate power, if it would, to change either. If it were admitted that you who are dissatisfied hold the right side in the dispute, there still is no single good reason for precipitate action. Intelligence, patriotism, Christianity, and a firm reliance on Him who has never yet forsaken this favored land, are still competent to adjust in the best way all our present difficulty.

In your hands, my dissatisfied fellow-countrymen, and not in mine, is the momentous issue of civil war. The government will not assail you. You can have no conflict without being yourselves the aggressors. You have no oath registered in heaven to destroy the government, while I shall have the most solemn one to "preserve, protect, and defend it."

I am loath to close. We are not enemies, but friends. We must not be enemies. Though passion may have strained, it must not break our bonds of affection. The mystic chords of memory, stretching from every battlefield and patriot grave to every living heart and hearthstone all over this broad land, will yet swell the chorus of the Union when again touched, as surely they will be, by the better angels of our nature.

HENRY DAVID THOREAU

Henry David Thoreau (1817–62) was born in Concord, Massachusetts, and graduated from Harvard in 1837. Due to the
depressed economic conditions, he was forced to work at a series
of odd jobs. He lived at his famous Walden Pond cabin for two
years, writing his story of the experience in *Walden, or Life in the
Woods*. Much of his writing was about nature, and his philosophy
he considered to be in the spirit of recent Transcendentalism. He
always championed the causes of radical individualism and
philosophical anarchism. Thoreau was once jailed for refusing to
pay taxes to a town which supported the Mexican War efforts.
The following selection is from one of the best statements of
Thoreau's attitude toward the relation of the individual citizen to
government. It also illustrates his attitude toward slavery, and
the defense of civil disobedience as a means for securing civil
liberties. It was first published as "Resistance to Civil Government" in an anthology, *Aesthetic Essays* (1849), edited by
Elizabeth Peabody; and as "Civil Disobedience" it was included
in the posthumous collection, *A Yankee in Canada* (1866).

The Right to Disobey

I heartily accept the motto, "That government is best which governs
least"; and I should like to see it acted up to more rapidly and systematically. Carried out, it finally amounts to this, which also I believe—
"That government is best which governs not at all"; and when men are
prepared for it, that will be the kind of government which they will
have. Government is at best but an expedient; but most governments
are usually, and all governments are sometimes, unexpedient. The
objections which have been brought against a standing army, and they
are many and weighty, and deserve to prevail, may also at last be
brought against a standing government. The standing army is only an
arm of the standing government. The government itself, which is only
the mode which the people have chosen to execute their will, is equally
liable to be abused and perverted before the people can act through it.
Witness the present Mexican war, the work of comparatively a few
individuals using the standing government as their tool; for, in the
outset, the people would not have consented to this measure.

This American government—what is it but a tradition, though a
recent one, endeavoring to transmit itself unimpaired to posterity, but

each instant losing some of its integrity? It has not the vitality and force of a single living man; for a single man can bend it to his will. It is a sort of wooden gun to the people themselves. But it is not the less necessary for this; for the people must have some complicated machinery or other, and hear its din, to satisfy that idea of government which they have. Governments show thus how successfully men can be imposed on, even impose on themselves, for their own advantage. It is excellent, we must all allow. Yet this government never of itself furthered any enterprise, but by the alacrity with which it got out of its way. *It* does not keep the country free. *It* does not settle the West. *It* does not educate. The character inherent in the American people has done all that has been accomplished; and it would have done somewhat more, if the government had not sometimes got in its way. For government is an expedient by which men would fain succeed in letting one another alone; and, as has been said, when it is most expedient, the governed are most let alone by it. Trade and commerce, if they were not made of india-rubber, would never manage to bounce over the obstacles which legislators are continually putting in their way; and, if one were to judge these men wholly by the effects of their actions and not partly by their intentions, they would deserve to be classed and punished with those mischievous persons who put obstructions on the railroads.

But, to speak practically and as a citizen, unlike those who call themselves no-government men, I ask for, not at once no government, but *at once* a better government. Let every man make known what kind of government would command his respect, and that will be one step toward obtaining it.

* * *

I do not hesitate to say, that those who call themselves Abolitionists should at once effectually withdraw their support, both in person and property, from the government of Massachusetts, and not wait till they constitute a majority of one, before they suffer the right to prevail through them. I think that it is enough if they have God on their side, without waiting for that other one. Moreover, any man more right than his neighbors constitutes a majority of one already.

I meet this American government, or its representative, the State government, directly, and face to face, once a year—no more—in the person of its tax-gatherer; this is the only mode in which a man situated as I am necessarily meets it; and it then says distinctly, Recognize me; and the simplest, the most effectual, and, in the present posture of affairs, the indispensablest mode of treating with it on this head, of expressing your little satisfaction with and love for it, is to deny it then. My civil neighbor, the tax-gatherer, is the very man I have to deal with— for it is, after all, with men and not with parchment that I quarrel— and he has voluntarily chosen to be an agent of the government. How shall he ever know well what he is and does as an officer of the government, or as a man, until he is obliged to consider whether he shall treat me, his neighbor, for whom he has respect, as a neighbor and well-disposed man, or as a maniac and disturber of the peace, and see if he can get over this obstruction to his neighborliness without a ruder and more impetuous thought or speech corresponding with his action. I know this well, that if one thousand, if one hundred, if ten men whom I could name—if ten *honest* men only—ay, if *one* HONEST man, in this State of Massachusetts, *ceasing to hold slaves*, were actually to withdraw from this copartnership, and be locked up in the county jail therefor, it would be the abolition of slavery in America. For it matters not how small the beginning may seem to be: what is once well done is done forever. But we love better to talk about it: that we say is our mission. Reform keeps many scores of newspapers in its service, but not one man. If my esteemed neighbor, the State's ambassador, who will devote his days to the settlement of the question of human rights in the Council Chamber, instead of being threatened with the prisons of Carolina, were to sit down the prisoner of Massachusetts, that State which is so anxious to foist the sin of slavery upon her sister—though at present she can discover only an act of inhospitality to be the ground of a quarrel with her—the Legislature would not wholly waive the subject the following winter.

Under a government which imprisons any unjustly, the true place for a just man is also a prison. The proper place today, the only place which Massachusetts has provided for her freer and less desponding spirits, is in her prisons, to be put out and locked out of the State by her own act, as they have already put themselves out by their principles. It is there that the fugitive slave, and the Mexican prisoner on parole, and the Indian come to plead the wrongs of his race should find them; on that separate, but more free and honorable, ground, where the State places those who are not *with* her, but *against* her—the only house in a slave State in which a free man can abide with honor. If any think that their influence would be lost there, and their voices no longer afflict the ear of the State, that they would not be as an enemy within its walls, they do not know by how much truth is stronger than error, nor how much more eloquently and effectively he can combat injustice who has experienced a little in his own person. Cast your whole vote, not a strip of paper merely, but your whole influence. A minority is powerless while it conforms to the majority; it is not even a minority then; but it is irresistible when it clogs by its whole weight. If the alternative is to keep all just men in prison, or give up war and slavery, the State will not hesitate which to choose. If a thousand men were not to pay their tax-bills this year, that would not be a violent and bloody measure, as it would be to pay them, and enable the State to commit violence and shed innocent blood. This is, in fact, the definition of a peaceable revolution, if any such is possible. If the tax-gatherer, or any other public officer, asks me, as one has done, "But what shall I do?" my answer is, "If you really wish to do anything, resign your office." When the subject has refused allegiance, and the officer has resigned his office, then the revolution is accomplished. But even suppose blood should flow. Is there not a sort of blood shed when the conscience is wounded? Through this wound a man's real manhood and immortality flow out, and he bleeds to an everlasting death. I see this blood flowing now.

*   *   *

I have paid no poll-tax for six years. I was put into a jail once on this account, for one night; and, as I stood considering the walls of solid stone, two or three feet thick, the door of wood and iron, a foot thick, and the iron grating which strained the light, I could not help being struck with the foolishness of that institution which treated me as if I were mere flesh and blood and bones, to be locked up. I wondered that it should have concluded at length that this was the best use it could put me to, and had never thought to avail itself of my services in some way. I saw that, if there was a wall of stone between me and my towns-men, there was a still more difficult one to climb or break through before they could get to be as free as I was. I did not for a moment feel con-fined, and the walls seemed a great waste of stone and mortar. I felt as if I alone of all my townsmen had paid my tax. They plainly did not know how to treat me, but behaved like persons who are underbred. In every threat and in every compliment there was a blunder; for they thought that my chief desire was to stand the other side of that stone wall. I could not but smile to see how industriously they locked the door on my meditations, which followed them out again without let or hindrance, and *they* were really all that was dangerous. As they could not reach me, they had resolved to punish my body; just as boys, if they cannot come at some person against whom they have a spite, will abuse his dog. I saw that the State was half-witted, that it was timid as a lone woman with her silver spoons, and that it did not know its friends from its foes, and I lost all my remaining respect for it, and pitied it.

Thus the State never intentionally confronts a man's sense, intellectual or moral, but only his body, his senses. It is not armed with superior wit or honesty, but with superior physical strength. I was not born to be forced. I will breathe after my own fashion. Let us see who is the strongest. What force has a multitude? They only can force me who obey a higher law than I. They force me to become like themselves. I do not hear of *men* being *forced* to live this way or that by masses of men. What sort of life were that to live? When I meet a government which says to me, "Your money or your life," why should I be in haste to give it my money? It may be in a great strait, and not know what to do: I cannot help that. It must help itself; do as I do. It is not worth the while to snivel about it. I am not responsible for the successful working of the machinery of society. I am not the son of the engineer. I perceive that, when an acorn and a chestnut fall side by side, the one does not remain inert to make way for the other, but both obey their own laws, and spring and grow and flourish as best they can, till one, perchance, overshadows and destroys the other. If a plant cannot live according to its nature, it dies; and so a man.

The night in prison was novel and interesting enough. The prisoners in their shirtsleeves were enjoying a chat and the evening air in the doorway, when I entered. But the jailer said, "Come, boys, it is time to lock up"; and so they dispersed, and I heard the sound of their steps returning into the hollow apartments. My room-mate was introduced to me by the jailer as "a first-rate fellow and a clever man." When the door was locked, he showed me where to hang my hat, and how he managed matters there. The rooms were whitewashed once a month; and this one, at least, was the whitest, most simply furnished, and probably the neatest apartment in the town. He naturally wanted to know where I came from, and what brought me there; and, when I had told him, I asked him in my turn how he came there, presuming him to be an honest man, of course; and, as the world goes, I believe he was. "Why," said he, "they accuse me of burning a barn; but I never did it." As near as I could discover, he had probably gone to bed in a barn when drunk, and smoked his pipe there; and so a barn was burnt. He had the reputation of being a clever man, had been there some three months waiting for his trial to come on, and would have to wait as much longer; but he was quite domesticated and contented, since he got his board for nothing, and thought that he was well treated.

He occupied one window, and I the other; and I saw that if one stayed there long, his principal business would be to look out the window. I had soon read all the tracts that were left there, and examined where former prisoners had broken out, and where a grate had been sawed off, and heard the history of the various occupants of that room; for I found that even here there was a history and a gossip which never circulated beyond the walls of the jail. Probably this is the only house in the town where verses are composed, which are afterward printed in a circular form, but not published. I was shown quite a long list of verses which were composed by some young men who had been detected in an attempt to escape, who avenged themselves by singing them.

I pumped my fellow-prisoner as dry as I could, for fear I should never see him again; but at length he showed me which was my bed, and left me to blow out the lamp.

It was like traveling into a far country, such as I had never expected to behold, to lie there for one night. It seemed to me that I never had heard the town clock strike before, nor the evening sounds of the village; for we slept with the windows open, which were inside the grating. It was to see my native village in the light of the Middle Ages, and our Concord was turned into a Rhine stream, and visions of knights and castles passed before me. They were the voices of old burghers that I heard in the streets. I was an involuntary spectator and auditor of whatever was done and said in the kitchen of the adjacent village inn—a wholly new and rare experience to me. It was a closer view of my native town. I was fairly inside of it. I never had seen its institutions before. This is one of its peculiar institutions; for it is a shire town. I began to comprehend what its inhabitants were about.

In the morning, our breakfasts were put through the hole in the door, in small oblong-square tin pans, made to fit, and holding a pint of chocolate, with brown bread, and an iron spoon. When they called for the vessels again, I was green enough to return what bread I had left; but my comrade seized it, and said that I should lay that up for lunch or dinner. Soon after he was let out to work at haying in a neighboring field, whither he went every day, and would not be back till noon; so he bade me good-day, saying that he doubted if he should see me again.

When I came out of prison—for some one interfered, and paid that tax—I did not perceive that great changes had taken place on the common, such as he observed who went in a youth and emerged a tottering and grayheaded man; and yet a change had to my eyes come over the scene—the town, and State, and country—greater than any that mere time could effect. I saw yet more distinctly the State in which I lived. I saw to what extent the people among whom I lived could be trusted as good neighbors and friends; that their friendship was for summer weather only; that they did not greatly propose to do right; that they were a distinct race from me by their prejudices and super-stitions, as the Chinamen and Malays are; that in their sacrifices to humanity they ran no risks, not even to their property; that after all they were not so noble but they treated the thief as he had treated them, and hoped, by a certain outward observance and a few prayers, and by walking in a particular straight though useless path from time to time, to save their souls. This may be to judge my neighbors harshly; for I believe that many of them are not aware that they have such an insti-tution as the jail in their village.

It was formerly the custom in our village, when a poor debtor came out of jail, for his acquaintances to salute him, looking through their fingers, which were crossed to represent the grating of a jail window, "How do ye do?" My neighbors did not thus salute me, but first looked at me, and then at one another, as if I had returned from a long journey. I was put into jail as I was going to the shoemaker's to get a shoe which was mended. When I was let out the next morning, I proceeded to finish my errand, and, having put on my mended shoe, joined a huckleberry party, who were impatient to put themselves under my conduct; and in half an hour—for the horse was soon tackled—was in the midst of a huckleberry field, on one of our highest hills, two miles off, and then the State was nowhere to be seen.

This is the whole history of "My Prisons."

OLIVER WENDELL HOLMES, JR.

Oliver Wendell Holmes, Jr. (1841–1935), son of the distinguished author and physician, was born in Boston. After graduating from Harvard in 1861, he entered the Union Army and was wounded several times during the Civil War. Admitted to the bar in 1867, Holmes began a distinguished career, writing an important work, *The Common Law*, in 1881. He became Chief Justice of the Supreme Judicial Court of Massachusetts, and three years later, in 1902, he began thirty years as an Associate Justice of the United States Supreme Court. The following selection is his minority report, *Dissent in the Abrams Case*, 1919; in *Abrams et al. v. United States*, 250 U.S. (1919), 616 ff. It is a significant treatment of the limitation which ought and ought not to be placed upon the freedom of speech under the First Amendment.

The Law and Free Speech

This indictment is founded wholly upon the publication of two leaflets which I shall describe in a moment. The first count charges a conspiracy pending the war with Germany to publish abusive language about the form of government of the United States, laying the preparation and publishing of the first leaflet as overt acts. The second count charges a conspiracy pending the war to publish language intended to bring the form of government into contempt, laying the preparation and publishing of the two leaflets as overt acts. The third count alleges a conspiracy to encourage resistance to the United States in the same war and to attempt to effectuate the purpose by publishing the same leaflets. The fourth count lays a conspiracy to incite curtailment of production of things necessary to the prosecution of the war and to attempt to accomplish it by publishing the second leaflet to which I have referred.

The other leaflet, headed "Workers—Wake Up," with abusive language says that America together with the Allies will march for Russia to help the Czecho-Slovaks in their struggle against the Bolsheviki, and that this time the hypocrites shall not fool the Russian emigrants and friends of Russia in America. It tells the Russian emigrants that they now must spit in the face of false military propaganda by which their sympathy and help to the prosecution of the war have been called forth and says that with the money they have lent or are going to lend "they will make bullets not only for the Germans but also for the Workers' Soviets of Russia," and further, "Workers in the ammunition factories, you are producing bullets, bayonets, cannon, to murder not only the Germans but also your dearest, best, who are in Russia fighting for freedom." It then appeals to the same Russian emigrants at some length not to consent to the "inquisitionary expedition to Russia," and says that the destruction of the Russian revolution is "the politics of the march on Russia." The leaflet winds up by saying "Workers, our reply to this barbaric intervention has to be a general strike!" and after a few words on the spirit of revolution, exhortations not to be afraid, and some usual tall talk, ends "Woe unto those who will be in the way of progress. Let solidarity live! The Rebels."

No argument seems to me necessary to show that these pronunciamentos in no way attack the form of government of the United States, or that they do not support either of the first two counts. What little I have to say about the third count may be postponed until I have considered the fourth. With regard to that it seems too plain to be denied that the suggestion to workers in ammunition factories that they are producing bullets to murder their dearest, and the further advocacy of a general strike, both in the second leaflet, do urge curtailment of production of things necessary to the prosecution of the war within the meaning of the Act of May 16, 1918 . . . amending Section 3 of the earlier Act of 1917. But to make the conduct criminal that statute requires that it should be "with intent by such curtailment to cripple or hinder the United States in the prosecution of the war." It seems to me that no such intent is proved.

I am aware of course that the word intent as vaguely used in ordinary legal discussion means no more than knowledge at the time of the act that the consequences said to be intended will ensue. Even less than that will satisfy the general principle of civil and criminal liability. A man may have to pay damages, may be sent to prison, at common law might be hanged, if at the time of his act he knew facts from which common experience showed that the consequences would follow, whether he individually could foresee them or not. But, when words are used exactly, a deed is not done with intent to produce a consequence unless that consequence is the aim of the deed. It may be obvious, and obvious to the actor, that the consequence will follow, and he may be liable for it even if he forgets it, but he does not do the act with intent to produce it unless the aim to produce it is the proximate motive of the specific act, although there may be some deeper motive behind.

It seems to me that this statute must be taken to use its words in a strict and accurate sense. They would be absurd in any other. A patriot might think that we were wasting money on aeroplanes, or making more cannon of a certain kind than we needed, and might advocate curtailment with success, yet even if it turned out that the curtailment hindered and was thought by other minds to have been obviously likely to hinder the United States in the prosecution of the war, no one would hold such conduct a crime. I admit that my illustration does not answer all that might be said but it is enough to show what I think and to let me pass to a more important aspect of the case. I refer to the First Amendment to the Constitution that Congress shall make no law abridging the freedom of speech.

I never have seen any reason to doubt that the questions of law that alone were before this Court in the cases of *Schenck*, *Frohwerk* and *Debs*, were rightly decided. I do not doubt for a moment that by the same reasoning that would justify punishing persuasion to murder, the United States constitutionally may punish speech that produces or is intended to produce a clear and imminent danger that it will bring about forthwith certain substantive evils that the United States constitutionally may seek to prevent. The power undoubtedly is greater in time of war than in time of peace because war opens dangers that do not exist at other times.

But as against dangers peculiar to war, as against others, the principle of the right to free speech is always the same. It is only the present danger of immediate evil or an intent to bring it about that warrants Congress in setting a limit to the expression of opinion where private rights are not concerned. Congress certainly cannot forbid all effort to change the mind of the country. Now nobody can suppose that the surreptitious publishing of a silly leaflet by an unknown man, without more, would present any immediate danger that its opinions would hinder the success of the Government arms or have any appreciable tendency to do so. Publishing these opinions for the very purpose of obstructing, however, might indicate a greater danger and at any rate would have the quality of an attempt. So I assume that the second leaflet, if published for the purpose alleged in the fourth count, might be punishable. But it seems pretty clear to me that nothing less than that would bring these papers within the scope of this law.

An actual intent in the sense that I have explained is necessary to constitute an attempt, where a further act of the same individual is required to complete the substantive crime, for reasons given in *Swift & Co. v. United States*, 196 U.S. 375, 396. It is necessary where the success of the attempt depends upon others, because if that intent is not present the actor's aim may be accomplished without bringing about the evils sought to be checked. An intent to prevent interference with the revolution in Russia might have been satisfied without any hindrance to carrying on the war in which we were engaged.

I do not see how anyone can find the intent required by the statute in any of the defendants' words. The second leaflet is the only one that affords even a foundation for the charge, and there, without invoking the hatred of German militarism expressed in the former one, it is evident from the beginning to the end that the only object of the paper is to help Russia and stop American intervention there against the popular government—not to impede the United States in the war that it was carrying on. To say that two phrases taken literally might import a suggestion of conduct that would have interference with the war as an indirect and probably undesired effect seems to me by no means enough to show an attempt to produce that effect.

I return for a moment to the third count. That charges an intent to provoke resistance to the United States in its war with Germany. Taking the clause in the statute that deals with that in connection with the other elaborate provisions of the Act, I think that resistance to the United States means some forcible act of opposition to some proceeding of the United States in pursuance of the war. I think the intent must be the specific intent that I have described and for the reasons that I have given. I think that no such intent was proved or existed in fact. I also think that there is no hint at resistance to the United States as I construe the phrase.

In this case sentences of twenty years' imprisonment have been imposed for the publishing of two leaflets that I believe the defendants had as much right to publish as the Government has to publish the Constitution of the United States now vainly invoked by them. Even if I am technically wrong and enough can be squeezed from these poor and puny anonymities to turn the color of legal litmus paper; I will add, even if what I think the necessary intent were shown; the most nominal punishment seems to me all that possibly could be inflicted, unless the defendants are to be made to suffer not for what the indictment alleges but for the creed that they avow—a creed that I believe to be the creed of ignorance and immaturity when honestly held, as I see no reason to doubt that it was held here, but which, although made the subject of examination at the trial, no one has a right even to consider in dealing with the charges before the Court.

Persecution for the expression of opinions seems to me perfectly logical. If you have no doubt of your premises or your power and want a certain result with all your heart you naturally express your wishes in law and sweep away all opposition. To allow opposition by speech seems to indicate that you think speech impotent, as when a man says that he has squared the circle, or that you do not care wholeheartedly for the result, or that you doubt either your power or your premises.

But when men have realized that time has upset many fighting faiths, they may come to believe even more than they believe the very foundations of their own conduct that the ultimate good desired is better reached by free trade in ideas—that the best test of truth is the power of the thought to get itself accepted in the competition of the market, and that truth is the only ground upon which their wishes safely can be carried out. That, at any rate, is the theory of our Constitution. It is an experiment, as all life is an experiment. Every year if not every day we have to wager our salvation upon some prophecy based upon imperfect knowledge. While that experiment is part of our system I think that we should be eternally vigilant against attempts to check the expression of opinions that we loathe and believe to be fraught with death, unless they so imminently threaten immediate interference with the lawful and pressing purposes of the law that an immediate check is required to save the country.

I wholly disagree with the argument of the Government that the First Amendment left the common law as to seditious libel in force. History seems to me against the notion. I had conceived that the United States through many years has shown its repentance for the Sedition Act of 1798 by repaying fines that it imposed. Only the emergency that makes it immediately dangerous to leave the correction of evil counsels to time warrants making any exception to the sweeping command, "Congress shall make no law . . . abridging the freedom of speech." Of course I am speaking only of expressions of opinion and exhortations, which were all that were uttered here, but I regret that I cannot put into more impressive words my belief that in their conviction upon this indictment the defendants were deprived of their rights under the Constitution of the United States.

JOHN DEWEY

John Dewey (1859–1952) was born in Burlington, Vermont, and graduated from the University of Vermont in 1879. He obtained his PhD from Johns Hopkins in 1884, after which he taught at the University of Minnesota, the University of Michigan, the University of Chicago and, for twenty-six years, at Columbia University. He retired as professor emeritus in 1930, but his literary output continued at its prolific pace. Dewey's philosophy, known as Pragmatism and Instrumentalism, extended into a variety of areas, including social psychology and education as well as the traditional branches of philosophy. Dewey remains one of the most distinguished names in the history of modern as well as American philosophy. This selection* is an excellent formulation of Dewey's enduring concern for the ways in which society and the individual constantly modify each other, and in this case his concern for the possible effects of an increasingly "corporate" America upon the individual citizen.

The United States, Incorporated

It was not long ago that it was fashionable for both American and foreign observers of our national scene to sum up the phenomena of our social life under the title of "individualism." Some treated this alleged individualism as our distinctive achievement; some critics held that it was the source of our backwardness, the mark of a relatively uncivilized state. Today both interpretations seem equally inept and outmoded. Individualism is still carried on our banners and attempts are made to use it as a war cry, especially when it is desired to defeat governmental regulation of any form of industry previously exempt from legal control. Even in high quarters, rugged individualism is praised as the glory of American life. But such words have little relation to the moving facts of that life.

There is no word which adequately expresses what is taking place. "Socialism" has too specific political and economic associations to be appropriate. "Collectivism" is more neutral, but it, too, is a party-word rather than a descriptive term. Perhaps the constantly increasing rôle of corporations in our economic life gives a clue to a fitting name. The word may be used in a wider sense than is conveyed by its technical

* From *Individualism Old and New*, Chapter III (New York: Minton, Balch & Co., 1930). Used by permission from G. P. Putnam's Sons.

legal meaning. We may then say that the United States has steadily moved from an earlier pioneer individualism to a condition of dominant corporateness. The influence business corporations exercise in determining present industrial and economic activities is both a cause and a symbol of the tendency to combination in all phases of life. Associations tightly or loosely organized more and more define the opportunities, the choices and the actions of individuals.

I have said that the growth of legal corporations in manufacturing, transportation, distribution and finance is symbolic of the development of corporateness in all phases of life. The era of trust-busting is an almost forgotten age. Not only are big mergers the order of the day, but popular sentiment now looks upon them with pride rather than with fear. Size is our current measure of greatness in this as in other matters. It is not necessary to ask whether the opportunity for speculative manipulation for the sake of private gain, or increased public service at a lower cost, is the dominant motive. Personal motives hardly count as productive causes in comparison with impersonal forces. Mass production and mass distribution inevitably follow in the wake of an epoch of steam and electricity. These have created a common market, the parts of which are held together by intercommunication and interdependence; distance is eliminated and the tempo of action enormously accelerated. Aggregated capital and concentrated control are the contemporary responses.

Political control is needed, but the movement cannot be arrested by legislation. Witness the condition of nearly innocuous desuetude of the Sherman Anti-Trust Act. Newspapers, manufacturing plants, utilities supplying light, power and local transportation, banks, retail stores, theaters and the movies, have all joined in the movement toward integration. General Motors, the American Telegraph and Telephone Company, United States Steel, the rapid growth of chain-store systems, combinations of radio companies with companies controlling theaters all over the country, are familiar facts. Railway consolidations have been slowed up by politics and internal difficulties, but few persons doubt that they, too, are coming. The political control of the future to be effective must take a positive instead of negative form.

For the forces at work in this movement are too vast and complex to cease operation at the behest of legislation. Aside from direct evasions of laws, there are many legal methods of carrying the movement forward. Interlocking directorates, interpurchase of stocks by individuals and corporations, grouping into holding companies, investing companies with enough holdings to sway policies, effect the same end as do direct mergers. It was stated at a recent convention of bankers that eighty per cent of the capitalization of all the banks of the country is now in the hands of twelve financial concerns. It is evident that virtual control of the other twenty per cent, except for negligible institutions having only local importance, automatically ensues.

An economist could multiply instances and give them a more precise form. But I am not an economist, and the facts in any case are too well known to need detailed rehearsal. For my purpose is only to indicate the bearing of the development of these corporations upon the change of social life from an individual to a corporate affair. Reactions to the change are psychological, professional, political; they affect the working ideas, beliefs and conduct of all of us.

The sad decline of the farmer cannot be understood except in the light of the industrialization of the country which is coincident with its "corporization." The government is now going to try to do for the collectivizing of the agriculturists the sort of thing that business acumen has already done—temporarily against the desire of the government—for manufactures and transportation. The plight of the uncombined and unintegrated is proof of the extent to which the country is controlled by the corporate idea. Sociologists who concern themselves with rural life are now chiefly occupied with pointing out the influence of urban districts—that is, of those where industrial organization predominates—upon the determination of conditions in country districts.

There are other decays which tell the same story. The old-type artisan, trained by individual apprenticeship for skilled individual work, is disappearing. Mass production by men massed together to operate machines with their minute divisions of labor, is putting him out of business. In many cases, a few weeks at a machine give about all the education—or rather training—that is needed. Mass production causes a kind of mass education in which individual capacity and skill are submerged. While the artisan becomes more of a mechanic and less of an artist, those who are still called artists either put themselves, as writers and designers, at the disposal of organized business, or are pushed out to the edge as eccentric bohemians. The artist remains, one may say, as a surviving individual force, but the esteem in which the calling is socially held in this country measures the degree of his force. The status of the artist in any form of social life affords a fair measure of the state of its culture. The inorganic position of the artist in

American life today is convincing evidence of what happens to the isolated individual who lives in a society growing corporate.

* * *

These things are not said to be deplored, nor even in order to weigh their merits and demerits. They are merely reported as indications of the nature of our social scene, of the extent to which it is formed and directed by corporate and collective factors toward collective ends. Coincident with these changes in mentality and prestige are basic, if hardly acknowledged, changes in the ideas by which life is interpreted. Industry, again, provides the striking symbols.

What has become of the old-fashioned ideal of thrift? Societies for the promotion of savings among the young were much hurt in their feelings when Henry Ford urged a free scale of expenditures instead of a close scale of personal savings. But his recommendation was in line with all the economic tendencies of the day. Speeded-up mass production demands increased buying. It is promoted by advertising on a vast scale, by instalment selling, by agents skilled in breaking down sales resistance. Hence buying becomes an economic "duty" which is as consonant with the present epoch as thrift was with the period of individualism. For the industrial mechanism depends upon maintaining some kind of an equilibrium between production and consumption. If the equilibrium is disturbed, the whole social structure is affected and prosperity ceases to have a meaning. Replacement and extension of capital are indeed more required than they ever were. But the savings of individuals, as such, are petty and inadequate to the task. New capital is chiefly supplied by the surplus earnings of big corporate organizations, and it becomes meaningless to tell individual buyers that industry can be kept going only by their abstinence from the enjoyments of consumption. The old plea for "sacrifice" loses its force. In effect, the individual is told that by indulging in the enjoyment of free purchasing he performs his economic duty, transferring his surplus income to the corporate store where it can be most effectively used. Virtue departs from mere thrift.

* * *

I have said that the instances cited of the reaction of the growing corporateness of society upon social mind and habit were not given in order to be either deplored or approved. They are set forth only to call out the picture of the decline of an individualistic philosophy of life, and the formation of a collectivistic scheme of interdependence, which finds its way into every cranny of life, personal, intellectual, emotional, affecting leisure as well as work, morals as well as economics. But because the purpose was to indicate the decay of the older conceptions, although they are still those that are most loudly and vocally professed, the illustrations given inevitably emphasize those features of growing standardization and mass uniformity which critics justly deplore. It would be unfair, accordingly, to leave the impression that these traits are the whole of the story of the "corporization" of American life.

The things which are criticized are the outward signs of an inner movement toward integration on a scale never known before. "Socialization" is not wholly a eulogistic term nor a desirable process. It involves danger to some precious values; it involves a threat of danger to some things which we should not readily lose. But in spite of much cant which is talked about "service" and "social responsibility," it marks the beginning of a new era of integration. What its ultimate possibilities are, and to what extent these possibilities will be realized, is for the future to tell. The need of the present is to apprehend the fact that, for better or worse, we are living in a corporate age.

It is of the nature of society as of life to contain a balance of opposed forces. Actions and reactions are ultimately equal and counterpart. At present the "socialization" is largely mechanical and quantitative. The system is kept in a kind of precarious balance by the movement toward lawless and reckless overstimulation among individuals. If the chaos and the mechanism are to generate a mind and soul, an integrated personality, it will have to be an intelligence, a sentiment and an individuality of a new type.

Meanwhile, the lawlessness and irregularity (and I have in mind not so much outward criminality as emotional instability and intellectual confusion) and the uniform standardization are two sides of the same emerging corporate society. Hence only in an external sense does society maintain a balance. When the corporateness becomes internal, when, that is, it is realized in thought and purpose, it will become qualitative. In this change, law will be realized not as a rule arbitrarily imposed from without but as the relations which hold individuals together. The balance of the individual and the social will be organic. The emotions will be aroused and satisfied in the course of normal living, not in abrupt deviations to secure the fulfillment which is denied them in a situation which is so incomplete that it cannot be admitted into the affections and yet is so pervasive that it cannot be escaped: a situation which defines an individual divided within himself.

III. *Morality*

INTRODUCTION

The most important fact about American morality has been its continuing allegiance to an official and national moral *spirit* or *schema* while also diligently rejecting an official and national moral *system*. A schema formulates only very general guidelines, whereas a system names the specifics. The American tradition has remained flexible in its encounters with moral systems but dogmatic in its defense of the "official" moral schema. The statement of the spirit of American morality is found in the Declaration of Independence:

> We hold these rights to be self-evident—that all men are created equal; that they are endowed by their Creator with certain unalienable rights; that among these are life, liberty, and the pursuit of happiness; that, to secure these rights, governments are instituted among men, deriving their just powers from the consent of the governed; that, whenever any form of government becomes destructive of these ends, it is the right of the people to alter or to abolish it, and to institute a new government, laying its foundations on such principles, and organizing its powers in such form, as shall seem to them most likely to effect their safety and happiness.

The Declaration of Independence is a Declaration of Individuality as well; it declares the worth of the *individual as such*, the intrinsic value of a person just because he *is*, not because he belongs to a certain group, not because his is a special talent or contribution. This is more than a mere expression of humaneness and enlightenment. It is the ultimate moral *commitment*, an assertion of faith, whose implications, however temporarily awkward or unwanted, must be embraced.

Aristotle was, for his time, an enlightened and humane person in many respects, but he could also encourage his former pupil, Alexander the Great, to treat the barbarians, whom Alexander was overpowering in his military expeditions, *as barbarians*. Aristotle did not question the institution of slavery or the distinction between being a "civilized" member of a Greek city-state and being a "barbarian" outsider. In America the sentiments of humaneness and enlightenment could also justify slavery; what became gradually evident was that the spirit of American morality, as formulated by Thomas Jefferson and his colleagues in the Declaration of Independence, was wholly incompatible with the institution of slavery. A simple *logical* inconsistency required either the abandoning of the Declaration's moral commitment or renouncing slavery, and the result shows that, when critical decisions must be reached, the head often has stronger reasons than the heart, possibly even reasons unknown to it. Also revealed is the power that a moral schema, as an ultimate commitment, can be in a nation's affairs; its efficacy is often due, in part, to its being a schema rather than a system. In the same vein, though it is true that a religious reason was given for the worth of individuality, it was at best a religious schema, not even hinting a systematic theology.[1]

The decline of New England theocracy testified to the need for Puritans and Quakers to manage coexistence, to acknowledge the rights of competing moralities and theologies. The prevailing concept of morality has since been *Pragmatic;* it has required moral theses, which may occasionally ask for a greater public honor than is permitted by the ethnic minority or the special sect to which they originally belonged, to prove themselves compatible with democratic tradition and palatable to a substantial cross section of the heterogeneous character of American citizenry.

In his essay "The Moral Philosopher and the Moral Life," William James expressed the Pragmatic concept of morality. He urged that a moral system, like a scientific system, must be tested against the complexities of lengthy experience with full expectation that substantial revisions in the system will be required. The laws and mores of a society which tell the individual how he *ought* to behave are, according to James, the results of generations of moral experimentation; although themselves certainly liable to future modification, they deserve the respect that accrues to something long-in-the-making. But the main point of his Pragmatic notion of morality is that *systems* of morality, as reflected in a nation's mores, laws, education, government, and politics, are experimentally established. In a democratic culture,

[1] This discussion accents what has been emphasized by Arthur M. Schlesinger, Jr., in *Paths of American Thought*, Morton G. White and Arthur M. Schlesinger, Jr., ed. (Boston: Houghton Mifflin Co., 1963), p. 532. Schlesinger's distinction between "ideal" and "ideology" is generally echoed in mine between "schema" and "system."

morality is to be viewed by the individual affected by it as the culmination of experiment and not of dogma. Thus an experimental moral system is always subject to further testing and amplification in the fresh circumstances ahead.[2]

A morality declares what one ought to do, what is forbidden, what values are worth striving for, and what means are apt to realize those values. America has represented, of course, a bewildering congeries of moralities, from those of the Shakers to the preachings of circus performers. The heterogeneity of the culture has been so vast, so perplexing to minds obsessed with unitary formulas, that it is hardly surprising that a main feature of the culture is, in matters of morals, to live and let live. Nevertheless, something approaching a "folk morality" has developed throughout the country, an ethical outlook involving the concept of the self-made man and the hyperbolic concern for individual success.

Scholars disagree about who the *real* Benjamin Franklin was—whether he was Kindly Old Ben or rather the Cunning Opportunist.[3] To what extent Franklin's own morality coincided with the rural philosophy of Poor Richard, the persona created in the Almanacs published by Franklin, is still debated.[4] But all agree that the sayings of Poor Richard became the sagacious proverbs of an American folk morality. Perhaps the essence of Franklinian wisdom, as expressed in Poor Richard's aphorisms, was Franklin's dedication to the Calvinist work-ethic.[5]

In any event, sayings like these became the expression of an American morality: "Men and melons are hard to know"; "Fish and visitors

[2] "These empirical instincts of American liberalism, the preference for fact over logic, for deed over dogma, have found their most brilliant expression in the writings of William James . . . James stood for what he called the unfinished universe . . . a universe where free men may find partial truths, but where no mortal man will ever get an absolute grip on Absolute Truth, a universe where social progress depends not on capitulation to a single, all-consuming body of doctrine, but on the uncoerced intercourse of unconstrained minds." *Ibid.*, p. 535.

[3] *See* Paul W. Conner, *Poor Richard's Politicks; Benjamin Franklin and His New American Order* (New York: Oxford University Press, 1965), p. 6.

[4] *See*, for instance, Carl Van Doren, *Benjamin Franklin* (New York: The Viking Press, 1938), pp. 107–15; Bruce Granger, *Benjamin Franklin: An American Man of Letters* (Ithaca, New York: Cornell University Press, 1964), pp. 57–8, 212–3; Alfred Owen Aldridge, *Franklin and His French Contemporaries* (New York: New York University Press, 1956), p. 53.

[5] Conner, *Ibid.*, p. 41, notes that this was Max Weber's assumption in his *The Protestant Ethic and the Spirit of Capitalism.* Conner then observes that none of Franklin's aphorisms explain why toil is valuable *qua* toil.

smell in three days"; "A country man between two lawyers is like a fish between two cats"; "God helps them that help themselves"; "Early to bed and early to rise makes a man healthy, wealthy, and wise"; "The used key is always bright"; "The sleeping fox catches no poultry. Up! Up!"; "Three may keep a secret if two of them are dead"; "Creditors have better memories than debtors"; "An empty bag cannot stand upright." Franklin was one of the most remarkable men ever produced by America. Given the reputation of the man and the style of his writing, it was only natural that the philosophy of Poor Richard became America's cracker-barrel morality, very fetching in the eyes of Europeans as well as Americans.[6]

A folk morality is highly important, creating, as Franklin thought, a "happy mediocrity," and the morality of prudence, work, self-help, and success was never merely a Protestant ethic; it made perfect sense to successive generations born or naturalized in the Land of Opportunity. An ethic capable of carrying individuals through their daily routine must not be, even slightly, belittled, especially when its contribution to the growth of the democracy is indubitable.

But a folk morality is not expected, of course, to resolve momentous issues in law, international diplomacy, and national government. It did not and could not decide, even in an essentially agrarian economy, between a Hamiltonian aggressive government and a Jeffersonian retiring national administration; it could not pronounce upon the same issue as it festered during the industrialization and the big-business economy of America subsequent to the Civil War. One of the most significant statements of the *moral* obligation of government to its citizens is John Quincy Adams' first message to Congress in 1825. The task of the state is to *improve* the lot of its citizens, and the debate on this thesis took the mind necessarily beyond what Poor Richard could teach. Adams' main argument was this: The Constitution specifies such governmental powers as laying and collecting taxes, reimbursing debts and providing for the national defense, regulating commerce with other nations, establishing post offices and post roads,

---

[6] Aldridge, *op. cit.*, p. 59, says that eighteenth-century France regarded *The Way to Wealth* as a work of "sublime morality." Conner, *Ibid.*, p. 98, quotes a letter to Franklin from David Hume: "America has sent us many good things, gold, silver, sugar, tobacco, indigo. But you are the first philosopher and indeed the first great man of letters for whom we are beholden to her." Doubtlessly, Hume's regard for Franklin was based on his accomplishments beyond the creation of Poor Richard. That Hume also had a less favorable opinion of Franklin is noted by Conner, *Ibid.*, p. 151.

declaring war, and enacting such legislation as is necessary for executing these and other prescribed powers. Thus,

> . . . if these powers and others enumerated in the Constitution may be effectually brought into action by laws promoting the improvement of agriculture, commerce, and manufacturers, the cultivation and encouragement of the mechanic and the elegant arts, the advancement of literature, and the progress of the sciences, ornamental and profound, to refrain from exercising them for the benefit of the people themselves would be to hide in the earth the talent committed to our charge—would be treachery to the most sacred of trusts.[7]

But American fear of governmental encroachment on individual freedom has matched the American desire for economic and social improvement. The tension between the two intensified in the second half of the nineteenth century, which was the great period of *laissez faire* in American economic expansion, the era of Carnegie, Morgan, Rockefeller, Frick, Phipps, and Harriman. The spirit of John Quincy Adams was overshadowed by the spirit of Poor Richard, transmuted through Emerson's concept of self-reliance and the newly dramatized notion of rugged individualism.[8] The person accepted as the spokesman of the spirit of the age, of Social Darwinism, was Herbert Spencer; this British philosopher seemed to have anticipated what many took to be the message of Darwin's *Origin of Species* (1859) and *The Descent of Man* (1871). Spencer celebrated the freedom of the individual and the value of a free society in which survival of the fittest is insured. Both Spencer and Darwin suspected that welfare programs and assistance to the unfortunate are really debilitating, preventing the process of natural selection of the fittest to survive. Spencer's philosophy of evolution also implied the notion of inevitable progress which coincided with the "general optimism of American life, the sanguine views of a

[7] Arthur Schlesinger, Jr., in Schlesinger and White, *op. cit.*, p. 113, writes: "The project of national economic expansion, based on the United States Bank, the tariff, internal improvements, and the national debt, soon acquired a name—the American System. Henry Clay was its most thrilling spokesman and John Quincy Adams its most far-seeing and philosophical advocate."

[8] *See* Donald Fleming, "Social Darwinism" in Schlesinger and White, *op. cit.*, pp. 123–46. Fleming observes that the only known American influence upon Herbert Spencer, the philosopher of Social Darwinism, was Emerson (p. 124). (Despite this influence it would be inaccurate, of course, to describe Emerson as a social Darwinist). "In all but name 'Social Darwinism' antedated Darwinism," since Spencer had already published his ideas in *Social Statics* in 1850 (p. 123).

people who had won their independence and spread to the Pacific."[9] Thus a free society unencumbered by a meddling government was seen by some to be, in every important respect, the most hygienic.

An American Spencerian was William Graham Sumner, Yale professor of political and social science, whose blunt lectures and writings earned him the reputation of being the foremost philosopher of American individualism. Sumner's enemy was government which, in the role of benevolent parent, interfered with the self-regulating social and economic processes of the society. Like his German contemporary, Friedrich Nietzsche, who once characterized democracy as "that mania for counting noses," Sumner blasted the philosophy of equality which merely encourages mediocrity. He saw it as causing potentially superior men to sink passively into the uninspired ethos of the dull multitude. Like Nietzsche and contemporary existentialists, he preached the severity of freedom, the demands it makes upon us such that the feeble of heart seeks to escape it. He also preached the value of suffering. These observations he saw as leading to the conclusion that a government, bent on giving handouts to the poor and the miserable, interferes with the harsh but hygienic and natural process which produces the noblest individuals and societies. In *What Social Classes Owe to Each Other* (1883), Sumner stated his fundamental idea: "Every man and woman in society has one big duty . . . to take care of his or her own self." He warned against the dangers of minding other people's business: "To mind one's own business is a purely negative and unproductive injunction, but, taking social matters as they are just now, it is a sociological principle of the first importance. There might be developed a grand philosophy on the basis of minding one's own business." Such a philosophy had been developed, in Plato's *Republic* where civil justice was defined precisely as the minding of one's own business, of simply doing one's own job; the implications of this classical view have been criticized by political and moral philosophers ever since.

But the Gilded Age evoked an entirely different response in Henry George, an amateur economist whose controversial recommendations for reform brought him to national attention. It appears that George had read John Stuart Mill's *Principles of Political Economy* (1848) as stating the principles of *moral* economy. George echoed the reaction

---

[9] *Ibid.*, p. 126.

of the British Utilitarians to the Industrial Revolution.[10] Although some economists considered economics an objective amoral science, George's assumption, in *Progress and Poverty* (1879) and his other works, was that economic thinking must start from moral considerations. As he put it in "The Rights of Man," economics must be based upon the natural rights of man as formulated in the American Declaration of Independence. There is a moral obligation upon the individual citizen to encourage his government to exercise *its* moral onus, as John Quincy Adams had expressed it, to alleviate the condition of the poor and unfortunate.

In George's view, the nation's institutions had failed to insure the rights of men to their labor and the fruits of their labor, the cause of this being the grossly unequal distribution of wealth. In both England and America too many men were in the position of peasants and slaves, compelled to work, not for themselves, but for the profit of others. It is, says Henry George, the moral duty of the citizen to urge his government to recognize anew its responsibilities for guaranteeing the *natural rights* of human beings. The basic corruption is that the land which commands labor has capitalized value rather than labor itself. American citizenship ought to confer a right to American soil, but it doesn't. In his time what had especially to be fought were the new business monopolies that characterized the post-Civil War era—often referred to as the Gilded Age with its Captains of Industry and Robber Barons.

George's famous proposal was the single-tax. The term "single-tax," however, did not appear in *Progress and Poverty;* it did not come into vogue until years later, and even then it owed its name to the eighteenth-century French physiocrats. The proposal was to abolish all taxes except those upon land; the goal was to insure equal rights to land for all and thus to raise wages. What had to be corrected was the monopoly of land by a very few and to eliminate land speculation, the major cause of depression. Land rent should be obtained through taxation; it should be understood as a *social* asset and, therefore, a legitimate means of public income. *Earned* income, on the other hand, ought not to be taxed, it being a personal rather than a social value. It appears that George's economic theories are largely obsolete. But his great contribution was not his economic proposal but rather "his vivid

---

[10] For accounts of George's relation to Mill, *see* Charles Albro Barker, *Henry George* (New York: Oxford University Press, 1955). For an interesting account of his relation to Herbert Spencer, *see* Anna George de Mille, *Henry George, Citizen of the World* (Chapel Hill: The University of North Carolina Press, 1950).

presentation of his belief that the material progress of society was the outcome of the growth of society, that the greatest gains had come to the possessors of strategic resources, rendered valuable by the progress of society, not by the contributions of the possessors."[11]

The diverse reactions of the Sumners and Georges to the economic changes in the America headed toward the twentieth century, testify to the increasing difficulties encountered by the thoughtful individual trying to locate his moral obligations, trying to define his larger moral context. The individualistic but benevolent folk morality of Poor Richard was in danger of reacting schizophrenically to the moral issues posed by the new and ever-expanding economic America. The nature and scope of one's moral responsibilities were more difficult to comprehend; as one formerly had cocked an ear to theological discussions in order to discern one's moral commitments from the religious perspective as one sat in on learned exchanges about the merits and defects of the Federal Constitution in order to discover one's moral commitments under the law, so now the labyrinthine intricacies of economic theory, especially in its relation to the operations of government, had to be explored before one could ascertain one's moral role as a participant in a productive economy.

Thorstein Veblen, an elusive, fascinating professor of economics and social science, was one of the thoughtful men who truly appreciated the complexities introduced into morality by the new economics of the United States. Early in his intellectual career, Veblen was attracted to the philosophy of Immanuel Kant because of Kant's emphasis upon rationality, the human subject, and morality. For Veblen, as for Kant, philosophy originated in morality, understood as the responsibility for action.[12] Other influences included such conflicting types as William Graham Sumner, Veblen's teacher at Yale, President Noah Porter of Yale, who feuded with Sumner about Spencerian philosophy, Charles S. Peirce, to whom he had been exposed during a stay of study at Johns Hopkins University, John Dewey, and William James. Veblen thus began his career as a philosopher of moral economics, as a "Kantian Pragmatist," a label probably only understood—within the Pragmatic triumverate of Peirce, James, and Dewey—by Peirce; for Peirce admired Kant as the others did not.

[11] Joseph Dorfman, *The Economic Mind in American Civilization*, Vol. 3 (New York: The Viking Press, 1949).

[12] For Veblen's indebtedness to Kant, *see* Joseph Dorfman, *Ibid.*, pp. 433–7, and Dorfman, *Thorstein Veblen and His America* (New York: 1934).

But, despite his genuine fondness for philosophy, Veblen found it more prudent to devote himself professionally to political economy. His aim was to understand modern economy in terms of human nature and its historical development. Some economists considered *laissez-faire* capitalism and the prevailing techniques of competition and business to have evolved naturally to meet the demands of a new social order; Veblen criticized the economic system for being wasteful, exploitative, and emulative. Among his famous concepts are "conspicuous consumption" and "conspicuous waste." His *Theory of the Leisure Class* (1899) was a bitter criticism of the capitalist system, charging men of leisure, in control of the finance which funded industry, with unlimited pecuniary exploitation. It was his view that modern economy exhibited a basic conflict between *industry*, which is productive and useful, and *business*, which is unproductive and wasteful. Businessmen derive their "unearned profit," not through any positive contribution to material and technological progress, but through their command of the money needed for acquiring capital goods; such is the nature of "absentee ownership." Business, in fact, is opposed to industry and society. It is forced to limit productivity by maintaining a condition of restricted supply and high prices. Like George, Veblen sought out the source of business depressions, and found it in the logical structure of corporation finance itself. When loan credit is expanded, because interest rates then escalate, the capitalized value of enterprises fall; higher prices then cause higher costs and dimished demand and profit, causing a business panic culminating in depression.[13]

The implication of Veblen's economic theories is that an economic system is not rooted in nature but is just another human "institution" requiring controls upon it if it is not to destroy industrial and technological progress along with itself. In contrast to George, Veblen, in his writings, does not generally exhibit the spirit of the reformer outraged by the immorality of the great inequality in the distribution

[13] For a lucid, compact treatment of Veblen's economic theories, *see* Max Lerner's Introduction to his *The Portable Veblen* (New York: The Viking Press, 1948). Also Joseph Dorfman, *The Economic Mind in American Civilization*, Vol. 3 (New York: The Viking Press, 1949), pp. 434–47. For a criticism of Veblen's attack on businessmen's alleged greediness, *see* David Riesman, *Thorstein Veblen: A Critical Interpretation* (New York: Charles Scribner's Sons, 1953), p. 190. Riesman observes that the view of businessmen being motivated only by greed and desire for conspicuous display is obtuse; "communal serviceability" also has its place in the businessman's soul. Riesman writes: "In my opinion, much of American individualism and egoism has been big talk, not different in import from Veblen's protestations of cold scientific objectivity."

of wealth. Yet the implication, even if expressed obliquely and ironically, is there. In "Christian Morals and the Competitive System," Veblen asked whether Christianity and modern capitalism were really compatible with each other. In giving his answer, he appealed to his theory that modern man is descended from the primitive "peaceable savage" of ancient times, and has thus inherited that instinct to "brotherly love" which is a distinctive feature of Christian morality. Insofar as pecuniary competition respected the principle of fair play and was such that the workman had an intimate relation with his product, a business economy kept some rapport with the "brotherly love" tenet of Christian morals. But the situation deteriorated when Big Business took on "the character of an impersonal, dispassionate, not to say graceless, investment for profit," creating a serious conflict between the business and the religious cultures. Veblen hoped to resolve the conflict by trying to capture the moral allegiance of Western society; to this end he emphasized the continuing strength of the peaceable impulse inherited from that ancient peaceable savage. "Except for a possible reversion to a cultural situation strongly characterized by ideals of emulation and status, the ancient racial bias embodied in the Christian principle of brotherhood should logically continue to gain ground at the expense of the pecuniary morals of competitive business."

It is generally assumed that what is at issue in American debates between conservative and liberal reformers is the moral philosophy of Utilitarianism.[14] That doctrine maintains that what is *right* and *ought* to be done is whatever produces the best for the greatest number. Advocates of this view would urge that insofar as the liberal cause has triumphed, American morality is Utilitarian. It is certainly true that legislation and governmental policy are often justified by Utilitarian reasons, but this is only a very small part of the story about our moral thinking. Especially overplayed is the theme that Pragmatism and Utilitarianism are natural allies.

The fact is, however, that Utilitarianism is too vague for an honest Pragmatist. It fails to explain how one ought to distribute benefits throughout the population, and too often fails to guide action. All too often, although one acts in the vague hope that his actions will benefit the greatest number, this is usually impossible to anticipate. One's real reasons for action are rarely Utilitarian. More important, it is impossible for most sensitive people to be consistent Utilitarians. The problem was recognized by Dostoyevsky in *The Brothers Karamazov*,

[14] *See* the John Stuart Mill selection in Vol. VI, *Romanticism and Evolution*.

where Ivan asks his saintly brother, Alyosha, if he would sanction the torture of one tiny baby, if this would insure the eternal happiness of all mankind. "No, I wouldn't consent," said Alyosha softly," thereby denying Utilitarianism. The same response was made by William James in "The Moral Philosopher and the Moral Life" (the only essay he ever devoted to theoretical ethics), where this is said:

> Or if the hypothesis were offered us of a world in which Messrs. Fourier's and Bellamy's and Morris's utopias should all be outdone, and millions kept permanently happy on the one simple condition that a certain lost soul on the far-off edge of things should lead a life of lonely torture, what except a specifical and independent sort of emotion can it be which would make us immediately feel, even though an impulse arose within us to clutch at the happiness so offered, how hideous a thing would be its enjoyment when deliberately accepted as the fruit of such a bargain?

In morality, as in government, the American tradition has been the sort of regard for individuality that fears the tyranny of the majority faction. This tradition has judged an espousal of Utilitarianism as too simple for meeting the complexities of concrete moral experience. At best, only a very flexible Utilitarianism can serve the Pragmatist. Pragmatism sees moral systems as *experiments in living* rather than as strict recipes. Pragmatism appears in morality as the motive to meet real needs wherever they occur, to respond to the full detail of a situation *together with* a respect for the principles which are usually relevant to that kind of occasion—but with the willingness to bend the principles a little here and there.

The moral issue of the nature of one's duty to one's fellowman has never really been argued here in Utilitarian terms. The setting of debates has been provided by the Puritan inheritance. What has been at issue is not one's obligation to *most* men but to *any* man. The ultimate importance of *each* individual has been accorded full precedence over the advantage of a mere majority. James thought that one's *sentiment* could decide one's judgment here, and Veblen believed that *instinct* could exercise the decisive vote. They both anticipated Existentialism by seeing that the issue was fundamentally a matter of commitment rather than argument, that, at the very least, any argument had to penetrate to that deeper level from which basic sentiments and instincts make their own baffling demands. It is understandable that a culture, which so effectively supports the Society for the Prevention of Cruelty to Animals, has tended to agree.

BENJAMIN FRANKLIN

Benjamin Franklin (1706–90) was born in Boston, son of a candlemaker, and became one of America's most illustrious names. He established a reputation in Philadelphia as publisher of a newspaper and the famous *Poor Richard's Almanac*, and went on to found the American Philosophical Society and to play an active role in civic affairs. Franklin's investigations into the nature of electricity and his numerous inventions displayed his scientific talents. Active in politics, he formulated the "Articles of Confederation" and was a member of the committee that drafted the Declaration of Independence. He represented America's interests in Europe, his reputation being, as John Adams said, "more universal" than that of Leibniz, Newton, or Voltaire. The following selection is from the celebrated preface to the 1758 *Almanac*, having been reprinted repeatedly under the title "Father Abraham's Speech" as well as "The Way to Wealth."

"*The Way to Wealth*"

Courteous Reader,

I have heard that nothing gives an Author so great Pleasure, as to find his Works respectfully quoted by other learned Authors. This Pleasure I have seldom enjoyed; for tho' I have been, if I may say it without Vanity, an *eminent Author* of Almanacks annually now a full Quarter of a Century, my Brother Authors in the same Way, for what Reason I know not, have ever been very sparing in their Applauses; and no other Author has taken the least Notice of me, so that did not my Writings produce me some *solid Pudding*, the great Deficiency of *Praise* would have quite discouraged me.

I concluded at length, that the People were the best Judges of my Merit; for they buy my Works; and besides, in my Rambles, where I am not personally known, I have frequently heard one or other of my Adages repeated, with, *as Poor Richard says*, at the End on't; this gave me some Satisfaction, as it showed not only that my Instructions were regarded, but discovered likewise some Respect for my Authority; and I own, that to encourage the Practice of remembering and repeating those wise Sentences, I have sometimes *quoted* myself with great Gravity.

Judge then how much I must have been gratified by an Incident I am going to relate to you. I stopt my Horse lately where a great Number of People were collected at a Vendue of Merchant Goods. The Hour of Sale not being come, they were conversing on the Badness of the Times, and one of the Company call'd to a plain clean old Man, with white Locks, *Pray, Father* Abraham, *what think you of the Times? Won't these heavy Taxes quite ruin the Country? How shall we ever be able to pay them? What would you advise us to?*—Father *Abraham* stood up, and reply'd, If you'd have my Advice, I'll give it you in short, for a *Word to the Wise is enough*, and *many Words won't fill a Bushel*, as *Poor Richard* says. They join'd in desiring him to speak his Mind, and gathering round him, he proceeded as follows:

"Friends, says he, and Neighbours, the Taxes are indeed very heavy, and if those laid on by the Government were the only Ones we had to pay, we might more easily discharge them; but we have many others, and much more grievous to some of us. We are taxed twice as much by our *Idleness*, three times as much by our *Pride*, and four times as much by our *Folly*, and from these Taxes the Commissioners cannot ease or deliver us by allowing an Abatement. However let us hearken to good Advice, and something may be done for us; *God helps them that help themselves*, as *Poor Richard* says, in his Almanack of 1733.

It would be thought a hard Government that should tax its People one tenth Part of their *Time*, to be employed in its Service. But *Idleness* taxes many of us much more, if we reckon all that is spent in absolute *Sloth*, or doing of nothing, with that which is spent in idle Employments or Amusements, that amount to nothing. *Sloth* by bringing on Diseases, absolutely shortens Life. *Sloth, like Rust, consumes faster than Labour wears, while the used Key is always bright*, as *Poor Richard* says. But *dost thou love Life, then do not squander Time, for that's the Stuff Life is made of*, as *Poor Richard* says.—How much more than is necessary do we spend in Sleep! forgetting that *The sleeping Fox catches no Poultry*, and that *there will be sleeping enough in the Grave*, as *Poor Richard* says. If Time be of all Things the most precious, *wasting Time* must be, as *Poor Richard* says, *the greatest Prodigality*, since, as he elsewhere tells us, *Lost Time is never found again;* and what we call *Time-enough, always proves little enough:* Let us then up and be doing, and doing to the Purpose; so by Diligence shall we do more with less Perplexity. *Sloth makes all Things difficult, but Industry all easy*, as *Poor Richard* says; and *He that riseth late, must trot all Day, and shall scarce overtake his Business at Night*. While *Laziness travels so slowly, that Poverty soon overtakes him*, as we read in *Poor Richard*, who adds,

Drive thy Business, let not that drive thee; and *Early to Bed, and early to rise, makes a Man healthy, wealthy and wise.*

So what signifies *wishing* and *hoping* for better Times. We may make these Times better if we bestir ourselves. *Industry need not wish*, as *Poor Richard* says, and *He that lives upon Hope, will die fasting. There are no Gains, without Pains;* then *Help Hands, for I have no Lands*, or if I have, they are smartly taxed. And, as *Poor Richard* likewise observes, *He that hath a Trade hath an Estate*, and *He that hath a Calling, hath an Office of Profit and Honour;* but then the *Trade* must be worked at, and the *Calling* well followed, or neither the *Estate*, nor the *Office*, will enable us to pay our Taxes.—If we are industrious we shall never starve; for, as *Poor Richard* says, *At the working Man's House* Hunger *looks in, but dares not enter.* Nor will the Bailiff or the Constable enter, for *Industry pays Debts, while Despair encreaseth them*, says *Poor Richard.*—What though you have found no Treasure, nor has any rich Relation left you a Legacy, *Diligence is the Mother of Good luck*, as *Poor Richard* says, *and God gives all Things to Industry.* Then *plough deep, while Sluggards sleep, and you shall have Corn to sell and to keep*, says *Poor Dick.* Work while it is called To-day, for you know not how much you may be hindered To-morrow, which makes *Poor Richard* say, *One To-day is worth two To-morrows;* and farther, *Have you somewhat to do To-morrow, do it To-day.* If you were a Servant, would you not be ashamed that a good Master should catch you idle? Are you then your own Master, *be ashamed to catch yourself idle*, as *Poor Dick* says. When there is so much to be done for yourself, your Family, your Country, and your gracious King, be up by Peep of Day; *Let not the Sun look down and say, Inglorious here he lies.* Handle your Tools without Mittens; remember that *the Cat in Gloves catches no Mice*, as *Poor Richard* says. 'Tis true there is much to be done, and perhaps you are weak handed, but stick to it steadily, and you will see great Effects, for *constant Dropping wears away Stones*, and by *Diligence and Patience the Mouse ate in two the Cable;* and *little Strokes fell great Oaks*, as *Poor Richard* says in his Almanack, the Year I cannot just now remember.

Methinks I hear some of you say, *Must a Man afford himself no Leisure?*—I will tell thee, my Friend, what *Poor Richard* says, *Employ thy Time well if thou meanest to gain Leisure;* and *since thou art not sure of a Minute, throw not away an Hour.* Leisure, is Time for doing something useful; this Leisure the diligent Man will obtain, but the lazy Man never; so that, as *Poor Richard* says, a *Life of Leisure and a*

Life of Laziness are two Things. Do you imagine that Sloth will afford you more Comfort than Labour? No, for as *Poor Richard* says, *Trouble springs from Idleness, and grievous Toil from needless Ease. Many without Labour, would live by their* WITS *only, but they break for want of Stock.* Whereas Industry gives Comfort, and Plenty, and Respect: *Fly Pleasures, and they'll follow you. The diligent Spinner has a large Shift;* and *now I have a Sheep and a Cow, every Body bids me Good morrow;* all of which is well said by *Poor Richard.*

But with our Industry, we must likewise be *steady, settled* and *careful,* and oversee our own Affairs *with our own Eyes,* and not trust too much to others; for, as *Poor Richard* says,

> *I never saw an oft removed Tree,*
> *Nor yet an oft removed Family,*
> *That throve so well as those that settled be.*

And again, *Three Removes is as bad as a Fire;* and again, *Keep thy Shop, and thy Shop will keep thee;* and again, *If you would have your Business done, go; If not, send.* And again,

> *He that by the Plough would thrive,*
> *Himself must either hold or drive.*

And again, *The Eye of a Master will do more Work than both His Hands;* and again, *Want of Care does us more Damage than Want of Knowledge;* and again, *Not to oversee Workmen, is to leave them your Purse open.* Trusting too much to others Care is the Ruin of many; for, as the *Almanack* says, *In the Affairs of this World, Men are saved, not by Faith, but by the Want of it;* but a Man's own Care is profitable; for, saith *Poor Dick, Learning is to the Studious,* and *Riches to the Careful,* as well as *Power to the Bold,* and *Heaven to the Virtuous.* And farther, *If you would have a faithful Servant, and one that you like, serve yourself.* And again, he adviseth to Circumspection and Care, even in the smallest Matters, because sometimes *a little Neglect may breed great Mischief;* adding, *For want of a Nail the Shoe was lost; for want of a Shoe the Horse was lost; and for want of a Horse the Rider was lost,* being overtaken and slain by the Enemy, all for want of Care about a Horse shoe Nail.

So much for Industry, my Friends, and Attention to one's own Business; but to these we must add *Frugality,* if we would make our *Industry* more certainly successful. A Man may, if he knows not how to save as he gets, *keep his Nose all his life to the Grindstone,* and die not worth a *Groat* at last. *A fat Kitchen makes a lean Will*, as *Poor Richard* says; and,

> *Many Estates are spent in the Getting,*
> *Since Women for Tea forsook Spinning and Knitting,*
> *And Men for Punch forsook Hewing and Splitting.*

If you would be wealthy, says he, in another Almanack, *think of Saving as well as of Getting: The* Indies *have not made* Spain *rich, because her* Outgoes *are greater than her* Incomes. Away then with your expensive Follies, and you will not have so much Cause to complain of hard Times, heavy Taxes, and chargeable Families; for, as *Poor Dick* says,

> *Women and Wine, Game and Deceit,*
> *Make the Wealth small, and the Wants great.*

And farther, *What maintains one Vice, would bring up two Children.* You may think perhaps, That a *little* Tea, or a *little* Punch now and then, Diet a *little* more costly, Clothes a *little* finer, and a *little* Entertainment now and then, can be no *great* Matter; but remember what *Poor Richard* says, *Many* a Little *makes a Mickle; and farther, Beware of* little *Expences; a small Leak will sink a great Ship; and again, Who Dainties love, shall Beggars prove; and moreover Fools make Feasts, and wise Men eat them.*

Here you are all got together at this Vendue of *Fineries* and *Knicknacks.* You call them *Goods,* but if you do not take Care, they will prove *Evils* to some of you. You expect they will be sold *cheap,* and perhaps they may for less than they cost; but if you have no Occasion for them, they must be *dear* to you. Remember what *Poor Richard* says, *Buy what thou hast no Need of, and ere long thou shalt sell thy Necessaries.* And again, *At a great Pennyworth pause a while:* He means, that perhaps the Cheapness is *apparent* only, and not *real;* or the Bargain, by straitning thee in thy Business, may do thee more Harm than Good. For in another place he says, *Many have been ruined by buying good Pennyworths.* Again, *Poor Richard* says, *'Tis foolish to lay out Money in a Purchase of Repentance;* and yet this Folly is practised every Day at Vendues, for want of minding the Almanack. *Wise Men,* as *Poor Dick* says, *learn by others Harms, Fools scarcely by their own;* but *Felix quem faciunt aliena Pericula cautum.** Many a one, for the Sake of Finery on the Back, have gone with a hungry Belly, and half starved their Families; *Silks and Sattins, Scarlet and Velvets,* as *Poor*

* He is fortunate who is made cautious by the misfortunes of another.

Richard says, *put out the Kitchen Fire*. These are not the *Necessaries* of Life; they can scarcely be called the *Conveniences*, and yet only because they look pretty, how many *want* to *have* them. The *artificial* Wants of Mankind thus become more numerous than the *natural;* and, as *Poor Dick* says, *For one* poor *Person, there are an hundred* indigent. By these, and other Extravagancies, the Genteel are reduced to Poverty, and forced to borrow of those whom they formerly despised, but who through *Industry* and *Frugality* have maintained their Standing; in which Case it appears plainly, that a *Ploughman on his Legs is higher than a Gentleman on his Knees*, as *Poor Richard* says. Perhaps they have had a small Estate left them which they knew not the Getting of; they think '*tis Day, and will never be Night;* that a little to be spent out of *so much*, is not worth minding; (*a Child and a Fool*, as *Poor Richard* says, *imagine* Twenty Shillings *and Twenty Years can never be spent*) but, *always taking out of, the Mealtub, and never putting in, soon comes to the Bottom;* then, as *Poor Dick* says, *When the Well's dry, they know the Worth of Water*. But this they might have known before, if they had taken his Advice; *If you would know the Value of Money, go and try to borrow some;* for, *he that goes a borrowing goes a sorrowing;* and indeed so does he that lends to such People, when he goes *to get it in again.—Poor Dick* farther advises, and says,

> *Fond* Pride of Dress *is sure a very Curse;*
> *E'er* Fancy *you consult, consult your Purse.*

And again, *Pride is as loud a Beggar as Want, and a great deal more saucy*. When you have bought one fine Thing you must buy ten more, that your Appearance may be all of a Piece; but *Poor Dick* says, *'Tis easier to* suppress *the first Desire, than to satisfy all that follow it.* And 'tis as truly Folly for the Poor to ape the Rich, as for the Frog to swell, in order to equal the Ox.

> *Great Estates may venture more,*
> *But little Boats should keep near Shore.*

'Tis however a Folly soon punished; for *Pride that dines on Vanity sups on Contempt*, as *Poor Richard* says. And in another Place, *Pride breakfasted with Plenty, dined with Poverty, and supped with Infamy*. And after all, of what Use is this *Pride of Appearance*, for which so much is risked, so much is suffered? It cannot promote Health, or ease Pain;

it makes no Increase of Merit in the Person, it creates Envy, it hastens
Misfortune.

> *What is a Butterfly? At best*
> *He's but a Caterpillar drest.*
> *The gaudy Fop's his Picture just,*

as *Poor Richard* says.

But what Madness must it be to *run in Debt* for these Superfluities!
We are offered, by the Terms of this Vendue, *Six Months Credit;* and
that perhaps has induced some of us to attend it, because we cannot
spare the ready Money, and hope now to be fine without it. But, ah,
think what you do when you run in Debt; *You give to another, Power
over your Liberty*. If you cannot pay at the Time, you will be ashamed
to see your Creditor; you will be in Fear when you speak to him;
you will make poor pitiful sneaking Excuses, and by Degrees come to
lose your Veracity, and sink into base downright lying; for as *Poor
Richard* says, *The second Vice is Lying, the first is running in Debt*.
And again, to the same Purpose, *Lying rides upon Debt's Back*. Whereas
a freeborn *Englishman* ought not to be ashamed or afraid to see or
speak to any Man living. But Poverty often deprives a Man of all
Spirit and Virtue: *'Tis hard for an empty Bag to stand upright*, as *Poor
Richard* truly says. What would you think of that Prince, or that
Government, who should issue an Edict forbidding you to dress like a
Gentleman or a Gentlewoman, on Pain of Imprisonment or Servitude?
Would you not say, that you are free, have a Right to dress as you
please, and that such an Edict would be a Breach of your Privileges,
and such a Government tyrannical? And yet you are about to put
yourself under that Tyranny when you run in Debt for such Dress!
Your Creditor has Authority at his Pleasure to deprive you of your
Liberty, by confining you in Goal [*sic*] for Life, or to sell you for a
Servant, if you should not be able to pay him! When you have got
your Bargain, you may, perhaps, think little of Payment; but *Creditors,
Poor Richard* tells us, *have better Memories than Debtors;* and in
another Place says, *Creditors are a superstitious Sect, great Observers
of set Days and Times*. The Day comes round before you are aware,
and the Demand is made before you are prepared to satisfy it. Or if
you bear your Debt in Mind, the Term which at first seemed so long,
will, as it lessens, appear extreamly short. *Time* will seem to have added
Wings to Heels as well as Shoulders. *Those have a short Lent*, saith
Poor Richard, who owe Money to be paid at Easter. Then since, as he

says, *The Borrower is a Slave to the Lender, and the Debtor to the Creditor*, disdain the Chain, preserve your Freedom; and maintain your Independency: Be *industrious* and *free;* be *frugal* and *free*. At present, perhaps, you may think yourself in thriving Circumstances, and that you can bear a little Extravangance [*sic*] without Injury;

> *For Age and Want, save while you may;*
> *No Morning Sun lasts a whole Day,*

as *Poor Richard* says—Gain may be temporary and uncertain, but ever while you live, Expence is constant and certain; and *'tis easier to build two Chimnies than to keep one in Fuel*, as *Poor Richard* says. So *rather go to Bed supperless than rise in Debt.*

> *Get what you can, and what you get hold;*
> *'Tis the Stone that will turn all your Lead into Gold,*

as *Poor Richard* says. And when you have got the Philosopher's Stone, sure you will no longer complain of bad Times, or the Difficulty of paying Taxes.

This Doctrine, my Friends, is *Reason* and *Wisdom;* but after all, do not depend too much upon your own *Industry*, and *Frugality*, and *Prudence*, though excellent Things, for they may all be blasted without the Blessing of Heaven; and therefore ask that Blessing humbly, and be not uncharitable to those that at present seem to want it, but comfort and help them. Remember *Job* suffered, and was afterwards prosperous.

And now to conclude, *Experience keeps a dear School, but Fools will learn in no other, and scarce in that;* for it is true, *we may give Advice, but we cannot give Conduct*, as *Poor Richard* says: However, remember this, *They that won't be counselled, can't be helped*, as *Poor Richard* says: And farther, That *if you will not hear Reason, she'll surely rap your Knuckles.*

Thus the old Gentleman ended his Harangue. The People heard it, and approved the Doctrine and immediately practised the contrary, just as if it had been a common Sermon; for the Vendue opened, and they began to buy extravagantly, notwithstanding all his Cautions, and their own Fear of Taxes.—I found the good Man had thoroughly studied my Almanacks, and digested all I had dropt on those Topicks during the Course of Five-and-twenty Years. The frequent Mention he made of me must have tired any one else, but my Vanity was wonderfully delighted with it, though I was conscious that not a tenth Part of the Wisdom was my own which he ascribed to me, but rather the *Gleanings* I had made of the Sense of all Ages and Nations. However, I resolved to be the better for the Echo of it; and though I had at first determined to buy Stuff for a new Coat, I went away resolved to wear my old One a little longer. *Reader*, if thou wilt do the same, thy Profit will be as great as mine.

I am, as ever,

Thine to serve thee,

July 7, 1757.   RICHARD SAUNDERS.

JOHN QUINCY ADAMS

John Quincy Adams (1767–1848), sixth President of the United States, son of John Adams, was born in Massachusetts. After graduating from Harvard, he practiced law. Minister to the Netherlands and later to Russia, he became Secretary of State under President James Monroe. Adams was an important architect of American foreign policy, being mainly responsible for the Monroe Doctrine. His most notable achievement was the Transcontinental Treaty with Spain in 1819. Elected President in 1824, he was defeated for reelection in 1828 by Andrew Jackson. From 1830 until his death, Adams represented Massachusetts in Congress. His Message to Congress in 1825* is a memorable statement of the moral obligations of government.

Morality and the Constitution

The great object of the institution of civil government is the improvement of the condition of those who are parties to the social compact, and no government, in whatever form constituted, can accomplish the lawful ends of its institution but in proportion as it improves the condition of those over whom it is established. Roads and canals, by multiplying and facilitating the communications and intercourse between distant regions and multitudes of men, are among the most important means of improvement. But moral, political, intellectual improvement are duties assigned by the Author of Our Existence to social no less than to individual man. For the fulfillment of those duties governments are invested with power, and to the attainment of the end—the progressive improvement of the condition of the governed —the exercise of delegated powers is a duty as sacred and indispensable as the usurpation of powers not granted is criminal and odious. Among the first, perhaps the very first, instrument for the improvement of the conditions of men is knowledge, and to the acquisition of much of the knowledge adapted to the wants, the comforts, and enjoyments of human life public institutions and seminaries of learning are essential. So convinced of this was the first of my predecessors in this office, now first in the memory, as, living, he was first in the hearts, of our countrymen, that once and again in his addresses to the Congresses with whom he cooperated in the public service he earnestly recom-

* Taken from Richardson, *Messages and Papers*, II, pp. 311–14.

mended the establishment of seminaries of learning, to prepare for all the emergencies of peace and war—a national university and a military academy. With respect to the latter, had he lived to the present day, in turning his eyes to the institution at West Point he would have enjoyed the gratification of his most earnest wishes; but in surveying the city which has been honored with his name he would have seen the spot of earth which he had destined and bequeathed to the use and benefit of his country as the site for an university still bare and barren.

In assuming her station among the civilized nations of the earth it would seem that our country had contracted the engagement to contribute her share of mind, of labor, and of expense to the improvement of those parts of knowledge which lie beyond the reach of individual acquisition, and particularly to geographical and astronomical science. Looking back to the history only of the half century since the declaration of our independence, and observing the generous emulation with which the Governments of France, Great Britain, and Russia have devoted the genius, the intelligence, the treasures of their respective nations to the common improvement of the species in these branches of science, is it not incumbent upon us to inquire whether we are not bound by obligations of a high and honorable character to contribute our portion of energy and exertion to the common stock? The voyages of discovery prosecuted in the course of that time at the expense of those nations have not only redounded to their glory, but to the improvement of human knowledge. We have been partakers of that improvement and owe for it a sacred debt, not only of gratitude, but of equal or proportional exertion in the same common cause. Of the cost of these undertakings, if the mere expenditures of outfit, equipment, and completion of the expeditions were to be considered the only charges, it would be unworthy of a great and generous nation to take a second thought. One hundred expeditions of circumnavigation like those of Cook and La Pérouse would not burden the exchequer of the nation fitting them out so much as the ways and means of defraying a single campaign in war. But if we take into the account the lives of those benefactors of mankind of which their services in the cause of their species were the purchase, how shall the cost of those heroic enterprises be estimated, and what compensation can be made to them or to their countries for them? Is it not by bearing them in affectionate remembrance? Is it not still more by imitating their example—by enabling countrymen of our own to pursue the same career and to hazard their lives in the same cause?

In inviting the attention of Congress to the subject of internal improvements upon a view thus enlarged it is not my design to recommend the equipment of an expedition for circumnavigating the globe for purposes of scientific research and inquiry. We have objects of useful investigation nearer home, and to which our cares may be more beneficially applied. The interior of our own territories has yet been very imperfectly explored. Our coasts along many degrees of latitude upon the shores of the Pacific Ocean, though much frequented by our spirited commercial navigators, have been barely visited by our public ships. The River of the West, first fully discovered and navigated by a countryman of our own, still bears the name of the ship in which he ascended its waters, and claims the protection of our armed national flag at its mouth. With the establishment of a military post there or at some other point of that coast, recommended by my predecessor and already matured in the deliberations of the last Congress, I would suggest the expediency of connecting the equipment of a public ship for the exploration of the whole northwest coast of this continent.

The establishment of an uniform standard of weights and measures was one of the specific objects contemplated in the formation of our Constitution, and to fix that standard was one of the powers delegated by express terms in that instrument to Congress. The Governments of Great Britain and France have scarcely ceased to be occupied with inquiries and speculations on the same subject since the existence of our Constitution, and with them it has expanded into profound, laborious, and expensive researches into the figure of the earth and the comparative length of the pendulum vibrating seconds in various latitudes from the equator to the pole. These researches have resulted in the composition and publication of several works highly interesting to the cause of science. The experiments are yet in the process of performance. Some of them have recently been made on our own shores, within the walls of one of our own colleges, and partly by one of our own fellow-citizens. It would be honorable to our country if the sequel of the same experiments should be countenanced by the patronage of our Government, as they have hitherto been by those of France and Britain.

Connected with the establishment of an university, or separate from it, might be undertaken the erection of an astronomical observatory, with provision for the support of an astronomer, to be in constant attendance of observation upon the phenomena of the heavens, and for the periodical publication of his observations. It is with no feeling of pride as an American that the remark may be made that on the comparatively small territorial surface of Europe there are existing upward of 130 of these light-houses of the skies, while throughout the whole American hemisphere there is not one. If we reflect a moment upon the discoveries which in the last four centuries have been made in the physical contribution of the universe by the means of these buildings and of observers stationed in them, shall we doubt of their usefulness to every nation? And while scarcely a year passes over our heads without bringing some new astronomical discovery to light, which we must fain receive at second hand from Europe, are we not cutting ourselves off from the means of returning light for light while we have neither observatory nor observer upon our half of the globe and the earth revolves in perpetual darkness to our unsearching eyes?

When, on the 25th of October, 1791, the first President of the United States announced to Congress the result of the first enumeration of the inhabitants of this Union, he informed them that the returns gave the pleasing assurance that the population of the United States bordered on 4,000,000 persons. At the distance of thirty years from that time the last enumeration, five years since completed, presented a population bordering upon 10,000,000. Perhaps of all the evidences of a prosperous and happy condition of human society the rapidity of the increase of population is the most unequivocal. But the demonstration of our prosperity rests not alone upon this indication. Our commerce, our wealth, and the extent of our territories have increased in corresponding proportions, and the number of independent communities associated in our Federal Union has since that time nearly doubled. The legislative representation of the States and people in the two Houses of Congress has grown with the growth of their constituent bodies. The House, which then consisted of 65 members, now numbers upward of 200. The Senate, which consisted of 26 members, has now 48. But the executive and, still more, the judiciary departments are yet in a great measure confined to their primitive organization, and are now not adequate to the urgent wants of a still growing community.

The naval armaments, which at an early period forced themselves upon the necessities of the Union, soon led to the establishment of a Department of the Navy. But the Departments of Foreign Affairs and of the Interior, which early after the formation of the Government had been united in one, continue so united to this time, to the unquestionable detriment of the public service. The multiplication of our relations with the nations and Governments of the Old World has kept pace with that of our population and commerce, while within the last ten years a new family of nations in our own hemisphere has arisen among the inhabitants of the earth, with whom our intercourse, commercial and political, would of itself furnish occupation to an active and industrious department. The constitution of the judiciary, experimental and imperfect as it was even in the infancy of our existing Government, is yet more inadequate to the administration of national justice at our present maturity. . . .

The laws relating to the administration of the Patent Office are deserving of much consideration and perhaps susceptible of some improvement. The grant of power to regulate the action of Congress upon this subject has specified both the end to be obtained and the means by which it is to be effected, "to promote the progress of science and useful arts by securing for limited times to authors and inventors the exclusive right to their respective writings and discoveries." If an honest pride might be indulged in the reflection that on the records of that office are already found inventions the usefulness of which has scarcely been transcended in the annals of human ingenuity, would not its exultation be allayed by the inquiry whether the laws effectively insured to the inventors the reward destined to them by the Constitution —even a limited term of exclusive right to their discoveries?

On the 24th of December, 1799, it was resolved by Congress that a marble monument should be erected by the United States in the Capitol at the City of Washington; that the family of General Washington should be requested to permit his body to be deposited under it, and that the monument be so designed as to commemorate the great events of his military and political life. In reminding Congress of this resolution and that the monument contemplated by it remains yet without execution, I shall indulge only the remarks that the works at the Capitol are approaching completion; that the consent of the family, desired by the resolution, was requested and obtained; that a monument has been recently erected in this city over the remains of another distinguished patriot of the Revolution, and that a spot has been reserved within the walls where you are deliberating for the benefit of this and future ages, in which the mortal remains may be deposited of him whose spirit hovers over you and listens with delight to every act of the representatives of his nation which can tend to exalt and adorn his and their country.

The Constitution under which you are assembled is a charter of limited powers. After full and solemn deliberation upon all or any of the objects which, urged by an irresistible sense of my own duty, I have recommended to your attention should you come to the conclusion that, however desirable in themselves, the enactment of laws for effecting them would transcend the powers committed to you by that venerable instrument which we are all bound to support, let no consideration induce you to assume the exercise of powers not granted to you by the people. But if the power to exercise exclusive legislation in all cases whatsoever over the district of Columbia; if the power to lay and collect taxes, duties, imposts, and excises, to pay the debts and provide for the common defense and general welfare of the United States; if the power to regulate commerce with foreign nations and among the several States and with the Indian tribes, to fix the standard of weights and measures, to establish post-offices and post-roads, to declare war, to raise and support armies, to provide and maintain a navy, to dispose of and make all needful rules and regulations respecting the territory of other property belonging to the United States, and to make all laws which shall be necessary and proper for carrying these powers into execution—if these powers and others enumerated in the Constitution may be effectually brought into action by laws promoting the improvement of agriculture, commerce, and manufactures, the cultivation and encouragement of the mechanic and of the elegant arts, the advancement of literature, and the progress of the sciences, ornamental and profound, to refrain from exercising them for the benefit of the people themselves would be to hide in the earth the talent committed to our charge—would be treachery to the most sacred of trusts.

The spirit of improvement is abroad upon the earth. It stimulates the hearts and sharpens the faculties not of our fellow-citizens alone, but of the nations of Europe and of their rulers. While dwelling with pleasing satisfaction upon the superior excellence of our political institutions, let us not be unmindful that liberty is power; that the nation blessed with the largest portion of liberty must in proportion to its numbers be the most powerful nation upon earth, and that the tenure of power by man is, in the moral purposes of his Creator, upon condition that it shall be exercised to ends of beneficence, to improve the condition of himself and his fellowmen. While foreign nations less blessed with that freedom which is power than ourselves are advancing with gigantic strides in the career of public improvement, were we to slumber in indolence or fold up our arms and proclaim to the world that we are palsied by the will of our constituents, would it not be to cast away the bounties of Providence and doom ourselves to perpetual inferiority? In the course of the year now drawing to its close we have beheld, under the auspices and at the expense of one State of this Union, a new university unfolding its portals to the sons of science and holding up the torch of human improvement to eyes that seek the light. We have seen under the persevering and enlightened enterprise of another State the waters of our Western lakes mingle with those of the ocean. If undertakings like these have been accomplished in the compass of a few years by the authority of single members of our Confederation, can we, the representative authorities of the whole Union, fall behind our fellow-servants in the exercise of the trust committed to us for the benefit of our common sovereign by the accomplishment of works important to the whole and to which neither the authority nor the resources of any one State can be adequate?

Finally, fellow-citizens, I shall wait with cheering hope and faithful cooperation the result of your deliberations, assured that, without encroaching upon the powers reserved to the authorities of the respective States or to the people, you will, with a due sense of your obligations to your country and of the high responsibilities weighing upon yourselves, give efficacy to the means committed to you for the common good. And may He who searches the hearts of the children of men prosper your exertions to secure the blessings of peace and promote the highest welfare of our country.

WILLIAM GRAHAM SUMNER

William Graham Sumner (1840–1910), educator and sociologist, was born in New Jersey, the son of an uneducated English railroad worker. He graduated from Yale, became an Episcopal rector, and returned to Yale in 1872 as professor of political and social science. A brilliant lecturer, he was a highly influential university figure. His *Folkways* (1907) attracted considerable attention. Sumner's defense of "rugged individualism" and distrust of governmental interference in social and economic affairs, which follows, is taken from his *What Social Classes Owe Each Other* (1883).

The Man of Virtue

The passion for dealing with social questions is one of the marks of our time. Every man gets some experience of, and makes some observations on social affairs. Except matters of health, probably none have such general interest as matters of society. Except matters of health, none are so much afflicted by dogmatism and crude speculation as those which appertain to society. The amateurs in social science always ask: What shall we do? What shall we do with Neighbor A? What shall we do for Neighbor B? What shall we make Neighbor A do for Neighbor B? It is a fine thing to be planning and discussing broad and general theories of wide application. The amateurs always plan to use the individual for some constructive and inferential social purpose, or to use the society for some constructive and inferential individual purpose. For A to sit down and think, What shall I do? is commonplace; but to think what B ought to do is interesting, romantic, moral, self-flattering, and public-spirited all at once. It satisfies a great number of human weaknesses at once. To go on and plan what a whole class of people ought to do is to feel one's self a power on earth, to win a public position, to clothe one's self in dignity. Hence we have an unlimited supply of reformers, philanthropists, humanitarians, and would-be managers-in-general of society.

Every man and woman in society has one big duty. That is, to take care of his or her own self. This is a social duty. For, fortunately, the matter stands so that the duty of making the best of one's self individually is not a separate thing from the duty of filling one's place in society, but the two are one, and the latter is accomplished when the former is done. The common notion, however, seems to be that one has a duty to society, as a special and separate thing, and that this duty consists in considering and deciding what other people ought to do. Now, the man who can do anything for or about anybody else than himself is fit to be head of a family; and when he becomes head of a family he has duties to his wife and his children, in addition to the former big duty. Then, again, any man who can take care of himself and his family is in a very exceptional position, if he does not find in his immediate surroundings people who need his care and have some sort of a personal claim upon him. If, now, he is able to fulfil all this, and to take care of anybody outside his family and his dependents, he must have a surplus of energy, wisdom, and moral virtue beyond what he needs for his own business. No man has this; for a family is a charge which is capable of infinite development, and no man could suffice to the full measure of duty for which a family may draw upon him. Neither can a man give to society so advantageous an employment of his services, whatever they are, in any other way as by spending them on his family. Upon this, however, I will not insist. I recur to the observation that a man who proposes to take care of other people must have himself and his family taken care of, after some sort of a fashion, and must have an as yet unexhausted store of energy.

The danger of minding other people's business is twofold. First, there is the danger that a man may leave his own business unattended to; and, second, there is the danger of an impertinent interference with another's affairs. The "friends of humanity" almost always run into both dangers. I am one of humanity, and I do not want any volunteer friends. I regard friendship as mutual, and I want to have my say about it. I suppose that other components of humanity feel in the same way about it. If so, they must regard any one who assumes the *rôle* of a friend of humanity as impertinent. The reference of the friend of humanity back to his own business is obviously the next step.

Yet we are constantly annoyed, and the legislatures are kept constantly busy, by the people who have made up their minds that it is wise and conducive to happiness to live in a certain way, and who want to compel everybody else to live in their way. Some people have decided to spend Sunday in a certain way, and they want laws passed to make other people spend Sunday in the same way. Some people have resolved to be teetotalers, and they want a law passed to make everybody else a teetotaler. Some people have resolved to eschew luxury, and they want taxes laid to make others eschew luxury. The taxing power is especially something after which the reformer's fingers always itches.

Sometimes there is an element of self-interest in the proposed reformation, as when a publisher wanted a duty imposed on books, to keep Americans from reading books, which would unsettle their Americanism: and when artists wanted a tax laid on pictures, to save Americans from buying bad paintings.

*   *   *

The social doctors enjoy the satisfaction of feeling themselves to be more moral or more enlightened than their fellow-men. They are able to see what other men ought to do when the other men do not see it. An examination of the work of the social doctors, however, shows that they are only more ignorant and more presumptuous than other people. We have a great many social difficulties and hardships to contend with. Poverty, pain, disease, and misfortune surround our existence. We fight against them all the time. The individual is a centre of hopes, affections, desires, and sufferings. When he dies, life changes its form, but does not cease. That means that the person—the centre of all the hopes, affections, etc.—after struggling as long as he can, is sure to succumb at last. We would, therefore, as far as the hardships of the human lot are concerned, go on struggling to the best of our ability against them but for the social doctors, and we would endure what we could not cure. But we have inherited a vast number of social ills which never came from Nature. They are the complicated products of all the tinkering, muddling, and blundering of social doctors in the past. These products of social quackery are now buttressed by habit, fashion, prejudice, platitudinarian thinking, and new quackery in political economy and social science. It is a fact worth noticing, just when there seems to be a revival of faith in legislative agencies, that our States are generally providing against the experienced evils of over-legislation by ordering that the Legislature shall sit only every other year. During the hard times, when Congress had a real chance to make or mar the public welfare, the final adjournment of that body was hailed year after year with cries of relief from a great anxiety. The greatest reforms which could now be accomplished would consist in undoing the work of statesmen in the past, and the greatest difficulty in the way of reform is to find out how to undo their work without injury to what is natural and sound. All this mischief has been done by men who sat down to consider the problem (as I heard an apprentice of theirs once express it). What kind of a society do we want to make?

When they had settled this question *a priori* to their satisfaction, they set to work to make their ideal society, and to-day we suffer the consequences. Human society tries hard to adapt itself to any conditions in which it finds itself, and we have been warped and distorted until we have got used to it, as the foot adapts itself to an ill-made boot. Next, we have come to think that that is the right way for things to be; and it is true that a change to a sound and normal condition would for a time hurt us, as a man whose foot has been distorted would suffer if he tried to wear a well-shaped boot. Finally, we have produced a lot of economists and social philosophers who have invented sophisms for fitting our thinking to the distorted facts.

Society, therefore, does not need any care or supervision. If we can acquire a science of society, based on observation of phenomena and study of forces, we may hope to gain some ground slowly toward the elimination of old errors and the re-establishment of a sound and natural social order. Whatever we gain that way will be by growth, never in the world by any reconstruction of society on the plan of some enthusiastic social architect. The latter is only repeating the old error over again, and postponing all our chances of real improvement. Society needs first of all to be freed from these meddlers—that is, to be let alone. Here we are, then, once more back at the old doctrine—*Laissez faire*. Let us translate it into blunt English, and it will read, Mind your own business. It is nothing but the doctrine of liberty. Let every man be happy in his own way. If his sphere of action and interest impinges on that of any other man, there will have to be compromise and adjustment. Wait for the occasion. Do not attempt to generalize those interferences or to plan for them *a priori*. We have a body of laws and institutions which have grown up as occasion has occurred for adjusting rights. Let the same process go on. Practise the utmost reserve possible in your interferences even of this kind, and by no means seize occasion for interfering with natural adjustments. Try first long and patiently whether the natural adjustment will not come about through the play of interests and the voluntary concessions of the parties.

I have said that we have an empirical political economy and social science to fit the distortions of our society. The test of empiricism in this matter is the attitude which one takes up toward *laissez faire*. It no doubt wounds the vanity of a philosopher who is just ready with a new solution of the universe to be told to mind his own business. So he goes on to tell us that if we think that we shall, by being let alone, attain to perfect happiness on earth, we are mistaken. The half-way men—the professional socialists—join him. They solemnly shake their heads, and tell us that he is right—that letting us alone will never secure us perfect happiness. Under all this lies the familiar logical fallacy, never expressed, but really the point of the whole, that we *shall* get perfect happiness if we put ourselves in the hands of the world-reformer. We never supposed that *laissez faire* would give us perfect happiness. We have left perfect happiness entirely out of our account. If the social doctors will mind their own business, we shall have no troubles but what belong to Nature. Those we will endure or combat as we can. What we desire is, that the friends of humanity should cease to add to them. Our disposition toward the ills which our fellow-man inflicts on us through malice or meddling is quite different from our disposition toward the ills which are inherent in the conditions of human life.

To mind one's own business is a purely negative and unproductive injunction, but, taking social matters as they are just now, it is a sociological principle of the first importance. There might be developed a grand philosophy on the basis of minding one's own business.

HENRY GEORGE

Henry George (1839–97), born in Philadelphia, was for a time a seafarer, then a printer in San Francisco, and later an editor of the San Francisco *Times*. His most famous work as an amateur economist is *Progress and Poverty* (1879), in which he attempted a diagnosis of the nature of business depressions. He is remembered for initiating the "single-tax" movement. An ardent reformer, whose spirit was conveyed through his considerable literary talent, he moved to New York City in 1880, writing and working for the single-tax movement. He was defeated as a candidate for mayor in 1886. George's eloquent expression of his attitude toward poverty and the natural rights of the individual, which follows,* was written a year after his return from a visit to England and Ireland.

"The Rights of Man"

There are those who, when it suits their purpose, say that there are no natural rights, but that all rights spring from the grant of the sovereign political power. It were waste of time to argue with such persons. There are some facts so obvious as to be beyond the necessity of argument. And one of these facts, attested by universal consciousness, is that there are rights as between man and man which existed before the formation of government, and which continue to exist in spite of the abuse of government; that there is a higher law than any human law—to wit, the law of the Creator, impressed upon and revealed through nature, which is before and above human laws, and upon conformity to which all human laws must depend for their validity. To deny this is to assert that there is no standard whatever by which the rightfulness or wrongfulness of laws and institutions can be measured; to assert that there can be no actions in themselves right and none in themselves wrong; to assert that an edict which commanded mothers to kill their children should receive the same respect as a law prohibiting infanticide.

These natural rights, this higher law, form the only true and sure basis for social organization. Just as, if we would construct a successful machine, we must conform to physical laws, such as the law of gravitation, the law of combustion, the law of expansion, etc.; just as, if we

* From Vol. II, *Social Problems*, of the *Complete Works of Henry George* (Fels Fund Library Edition, 1883).

would maintain bodily health, we must conform to the laws of physiology; so, if we would have a peaceful and healthful social state, we must conform our institutions to the great moral laws—laws to which we are absolutely subject, and which are as much above our control as are the laws of matter and of motion. And as, when we find that a machine will not work, we infer that in its construction some law of physics has been ignored or defied, so when we find social disease and political evils may we infer that in the organization of society moral law has been defied and the natural rights of man have been ignored.

These natural rights of man are thus set forth in the American Declaration of Independence as the basis upon which alone legitimate government can rest:

> We hold these truths to be self-evident—that all men are created equal; that they are endowed by their Creator with certain unalienable rights; that among these are life, liberty, and the pursuit of happiness; that, to secure these rights, governments are instituted among men, deriving their just powers from the consent of the governed; that, whenever any form of government becomes destructive of these ends, it is the right of the people to alter or to abolish it, and to institute a new government, laying its foundations on such principles, and organizing its powers in such form, as shall seem to them most likely to effect their safety and happiness.

So does the preamble to the Constitution of the United States appeal to the same principles:

> We, the people of the United States, in order to form a more perfect union, *establish justice*, insure domestic tranquillity, provide for the common defense, promote the general welfare, and *secure the blessings of liberty to ourselves and our posterity*, do ordain and establish this Constitution for the United States of America.

And so, too, is the same fundamental and self-evident truth set forth in that grand Declaration of the Rights of Man and of Citizens, issued by the National Assembly of France in 1789:

> The representatives of the people of France, formed into a National Assembly, *considering that ignorance, neglect, or contempt of human rights are the sole causes of public misfortunes and corruptions of government*, have resolved to set forth, in a solemn declaration, those natural, imprescriptible and inalienable rights, [and do] recognize and declare, in the presence of the Supreme Being, and with the hope of His blessing and favor, the following *sacred* rights of men and of citizens:

I. Men are born and always continue free and equal in respect of their rights. Civil distinctions, therefore, can only be founded on public utility.

II. The end of all political associations is the preservation of the natural and imprescriptible rights of man, and these rights are liberty, property, security, and resistance of oppression.

It is one thing to assert the eternal principles, as they are asserted in times of upheaval, when men of convictions and of the courage of their convictions come to the front, and another thing for a people just emerging from the night of ignorance and superstition, and enslaved by habits of thought formed by injustice and oppression, to adhere to and carry them out. The French people have not been true to these principles, nor yet, with far greater advantages, have we. And so, though the ancient *régime*, with its blasphemy of "right divine," its Bastille and its *lettres-de-cachet*, has been abolished in France; there have come red terror and white terror, Anarchy masquerading as Freedom, and Imperialism deriving its sanction from universal suffrage, culminating in such a poor thing as the French Republic of to-day. And here, with our virgin soil, with our exemption from foreign complications, and our freedom from powerful and hostile neighbors, all we can show is another poor thing of a Republic, with its rings and its bosses, its railroad kings controlling sovereign states, its gangrene of corruption eating steadily toward the political heart, its tramps and its strikes, its ostentation of ill-gotten wealth, its children toiling in factories, and its women working out their lives for bread!

It is possible for men to see the truth, and assert the truth, and to hear and repeat, again and again, formulas embodying the truth, without realizing all that that truth involves. Men who signed the Declaration of Independence, or applauded the Declaration of Independence, men who year after year read it, and heard it, and honored it, did so without thinking that the eternal principles of right which it invoked condemned the existence of negro slavery as well as the tyranny of George III. And many who, awakening to the fuller truth, asserted the unalienable rights of man against chattel slavery, did not see that these rights involved far more than the denial of property in human flesh and blood; and as vainly imagined that they had fully asserted them when chattel slaves had been emancipated and given suffrage, as their fathers vainly imagined they had fully asserted them, when they threw off allegiance to the English king and established here a democratic republic.

The common belief of Americans of to-day is that among us the equal and unalienable rights of man are now all acknowledged, while as for poverty, crime, low wages, "over-production," political corruption, and so on, they are to be referred to the nature of things—that is to say, if any one presses for a more definite answer, they exist because it is the will of God, the Creator, that they should exist. Yet I believe that these evils are demonstrably due to our failure fully to acknowledge the equal and unalienable rights with which, as asserted as a self-evident truth by the Declaration of Independence, all men have been endowed by God, their Creator. I believe the National Assembly of France were right when, a century ago, inspired by the same spirit that gave us political freedom, they declared that the great cause of public misfortunes and corruptions of government is ignorance, neglect or contempt of human rights. And just as the famine which was then decimating France, the bankruptcy and corruption of her government, the brutish degradation of her working-classes, and the demoralization of her aristocracy, were directly traceable to the denial of the equal, natural and imprescriptible rights of men, so now the social and political problems which menace the American Republic, in common with the whole civilized world, spring from the same cause.

Let us consider the matter. The equal, natural and unalienable right to life, liberty and the pursuit of happiness, does it not involve the right of each to the free use of his powers in making a living for himself and his family, limited only by the equal right of all others? Does it not require that each shall be free to make, to save and to enjoy what wealth he may, without interference with the equal rights of others; that no one shall be compelled to give forced labor to another, or to yield up his earnings to another; that no one shall be permitted to extort from another labor or earnings? All this goes without the saying. Any recognition of the equal right to life and liberty which would deny the right to property—the right of a man to his labor and to the full fruits of his labor—would be mockery.

But that is just what we do. Our so-called recognition of the equal and natural rights of man is to large classes of our people nothing but a mockery, and as social pressure increases, is becoming a more bitter mockery to larger classes, because our institutions fail to secure the rights of men to their labor and the fruits of their labor.

That this denial of a primary human right is the cause of poverty on the one side and of overgrown fortunes on the other, and of all the waste and demoralization and corruption that flow from the grossly unequal distribution of wealth, may be easily seen.

As I am speaking of conditions general over the whole civilized world, let us first take the case of another country, for we can sometimes see the faults of our neighbors more clearly than our own. England, the country from which we derive our language and institutions, is behind us in the formal recognition of political liberty; but there is as much industrial liberty there as here—and in some respects more, for England, though she has not yet reached free trade, has got rid of the "protective" swindle, which we still hug. And the English people—poor things—are, as a whole, satisfied with their freedom, and boast of it. They think, for it has been so long preached to them that most of them honestly believe it, that Englishmen are the freest people in the world, and they sing "Britons never shall be slaves," as though it were indeed true that slaves could not breathe British air.

Let us take a man of the masses of this people—a "free-born Englishman," coming of long generations of "free-born Englishmen," in Wiltshire or Devonshire or Somersetshire, on soil which, if you could trace his genealogy, you would find his fathers have been tilling from early Saxon times. He grows to manhood, we will not stop to inquire how, and, as is the natural order, he takes himself a wife. Here he stands, a man among his fellows, in a world in which the Creator has ordained that he should get a living by his labor. He has wants, and as, in the natural order, children come to him, he will have more; but he has in brain and muscle the natural power to satisfy these wants from the storehouse of nature. He knows how to dig and plow, to sow and to reap, and there is the rich soil, ready now, as it was thousands of years ago, to give back wealth to labor. The rain falls and the sun shines, and as the planet circles around her orbit, spring follows winter, and summer succeeds spring. It is this man's first and clearest right to earn his living, to transmute his labor into wealth, and to possess and enjoy that wealth for his own sustenance and benefit, and for the sustenance and benefit of those whom nature places in dependence on him. He has no right to demand any one else's earnings, nor has any one else a right to demand any portion of his earnings. He has no right to compel any one else to work for his benefit; nor have others a right to demand that he shall work for their benefit. This right to himself, to the use of his own powers and the results of his own exertions, is a natural, self-evident right, which, as a matter of principle, no one can dispute, save upon the blasphemous contention that some men were created to work for other men. And this primary, natural right to his own labor, and to the fruits of his own labor, accorded, this man can abundantly provide for his own needs and for the needs of his family. His labor will, in the natural order, produce wealth, which, exchanged in accordance with mutual desires for wealth which others have produced, will supply his family with all the material comforts of life, and in the absence of serious accident, enable him to bring up his children, and lay by such a surplus that he and his wife may take their rest, and enjoy their sunset hour in the declining years when strength shall fail, without asking any one's alms or being beholden to any bounty save that of "Our Father which art in heaven."

But what is the fact? The fact is, that the right of this "free-born Englishman" to his own labor and the fruits of his labor is denied as fully and completely as though he were made by law a slave; that he is compelled to work for the enrichment of others as truly as though English law had made him the property of an owner. The law of the land does not declare that he is a slave: on the contrary, it formally declares that he is a free man—free to work for himself, and free to enjoy the fruits of his labor. But a man cannot labor without something to labor on, any more than he can eat without having something to eat. It is not in human powers to make something out of nothing. This is not contemplated in the creative scheme. Nature tells us that if we will not work we must starve; but at the same time supplies us with everything necessary to work. Food, clothing, shelter, all the articles that minister to desire and that we call wealth, can be produced by labor, but only when the raw material of which they must be composed is drawn from the land.

* * *

In what is the condition of such a "free-born Englishman" as this, better than that of a slave? Yet if this is not a fair picture of the condition of the English agricultural laborers, it is only because I have not dwelt upon the darkest shades—the sodden ignorance and brutality, the low morality of these degraded and debased classes. In quantity and quality of food, in clothing and housing, in ease and recreation, and in morality, there can be no doubt that the Southern slave was better off than the average agricultural laborer is in England to-day— that his life was healthier and happier and fuller. So long as a plump, well-kept, hearty negro was worth £1000, no slave-owner, selfish or cold-blooded as he might be, would keep his negroes as great classes of "free-born Englishmen" must live. But these white slaves have no money value. It is not the labor, it is the land that commands the labor, that has a capitalized value. You can get the labor of men for from nine to twelve shillings a week—less than it would cost to keep a slave in good marketable condition; and of children for sixpence a week, and when they are worked out they can be left to die or "go on the parish."

The negroes, some say, are an inferior race. But these white slaves of England are of the stock that has given England her scholars and her poets, her philosophers and statesmen, her merchants and inventors, who have formed the bulwark of the sea-girt isle, and have carried the meteor flag around the world. They are ignorant, and degraded, and debased; they live the life of slaves and die the death of paupers, simply because they are robbed of their natural rights.

In the same neighborhood in which you may find such people as these, in which you may see squalid laborers' cottages where human beings huddle together like swine, you may also see grand mansions set in great, velvety, oak-graced parks, the habitations of local "God Almighties," as the Laureate styles them, and as these brutalized English people seem almost to take them to be. They never do any work—they pride themselves upon the fact that for hundreds of years their ancestors have never done any work; they look with the utmost contempt not merely upon the man who works, but even upon the man whose grandfather had to work. Yet they live in the utmost luxury. They have town houses and country houses, horses, carriages, liveried servants, yachts, packs of hounds; they have all that wealth can command in the way of literature and education and the culture of travel. And they have wealth to spare, which they can invest in railway shares, or public debts, or in buying up land in the United States. But not an iota of this wealth do they produce. They get it because, it being conceded that they own the land, the people who do produce wealth must hand their earnings over to them.

Here, clear and plain, is the beginning and primary cause of that inequality in the distribution of wealth which, in England, produces such dire, soul-destroying poverty, side by side with such wantonness of luxury, and which is to be seen in the cities even more glaringly than in the country. Here, clear and plain, is the reason why labor seems a drug, and why, in all occupations in which mere laborers can engage, wages tend to the merest pittance on which life can be maintained. Deprived of their natural rights to land, treated as intruders upon

God's earth, men are compelled to an unnatural competition for the privilege of mere animal existence, that in manufacturing towns and city slums reduces humanity to a depth of misery and debasement in which beings, created in the image of God, sink below the level of the brutes.

And the same inequality of conditions which we see beginning here, is it not due to the same primary cause? American citizenship confers no right to American soil. The first and most essential rights of man— the rights to life, liberty and the pursuit of happiness—are denied here as completely as in England. And the same results must follow.

THORSTEIN B. VEBLEN

Thorstein B. Veblen (1857–1929), born in Wisconsin, the son of Norwegian parents, and reared in the farming area of Wisconsin and Minnesota, studied at Carltoen College and Johns Hopkins University and received his PhD at Yale. He was a professor of economics and political economy at the University of Chicago, Stanford University, the University of Missouri, and the New School for Social Research, and, for a while, managing editor of the *Journal of Political Economy*. His writings, including *The Theory of the Leisure Class* (1899), were influential among liberal thinkers. Veblen's views on the possible conflict between Christianity and capitalism were forcefully expressed in his "Christian Morals and the Competitive System," which follows, included in *Essays of Our Changing Order* (1934), edited by Leon Ardzrooni after Veblen's death.*

Christianity and Capitalism

In the light of the current materialistic outlook and the current skepticism touching supernatural matters, some question may fairly be entertained as to the religious cult of Christianity. Its fortunes in the proximate future, as well as its intrinsic value for the current scheme of civilisation, may be subject to doubt. But a similar doubt is not readily entertained as regards the morals of Christianity. In some of its elements this morality is so intimately and organically connected with the scheme of western civilisation that its elimination would signify a cultural revolution whereby occidental culture would lose its occidental characteristics and fall into the ranks of ethnic civilisations at large. Much the same may be said of that pecuniary competition which today rules the economic life of Christendom and in large measure guides western civilisation in much else than the economic respect.

Both are institutional factors of first-rate importance in this culture, and as such it might be difficult or impracticable to assign the primacy to the one or the other, since each appears to be in a dominant position. Western civilisation is both Christian and competitive (pecuniary); and it seems bootless to ask whether its course is more substantially under the guidance of the one than of the other of these two institutional

---

norms. Hence, if it should appear, as is sometimes contended, that there is an irreconcilable discrepancy between the two, the student of this culture might have to face the question: Will western civilisation dwindle and decay if one or the other, the morals of competition or the morals of Christianity, definitively fall into abeyance?

In a question between the two codes, or systems of conduct, each must be taken at its best and simplest. That is to say, it is a question of agreement or discrepancy in the larger elementary principles of each, not a question of the variegated details, nor the practice of the common run of Christians, on the one hand, and of competitive business men, on the other. The variety of detailed elaboration and sophistication is fairly endless in both codes; at the same time many Christians are engaged in competitive business, and conversely. Under the diversified exigencies of daily life neither the accepted principles of morality nor those of business competition work out in an untroubled or untempered course of conduct. Circumstances constrain men unremittingly to shrewd adaptations, if not to some degree of compromise, in their endeavors to live up to their accustomed principles of conduct. Yet both of these principles, or codes of conduct, are actively present throughout life in any modern community. For all the shrewd adaptation to which they may be subject in the casuistry of individual practice, they will not have fallen into abeyance so long as the current scheme of life is not radically altered. Both the Christian morality and the morality of pecuniary competition are intimately involved in this occidental scheme of life; for it is out of these and the like habits of thought that the scheme of life is made up. Taken at their best, do the two further and fortify one another? do they work together without mutual help or hindrance? or do they mutually inhibit and defeat each other?

In the light of modern science the principles of Christian morality or of pecuniary competition must, like any other principles of conduct, be taken simply as prevalent habits of thought. And in this light no question can be entertained as to the intrinsic merit, the eternal validity, of either. They are, humanly speaking, institutions which have arisen in the growth of the western civilisation. Their genesis and growth are incidents, or possibly episodes, in the life-history of this culture—habits of thought induced by the discipline of life in the course of this culture's growth, and more or less intrinsic and essential to its character as a phase of civilisation. Therefore, the question of their consistency with one another, or with the cultural scheme in which they are involved, turns into a question as to the conditions to which they owe their rise and continued force as institutions—as to the discipline of experience in the past, out of which each of them has come and to which, therefore, each is (presumably) suited. The exigencies of life and the discipline of experience in a complex cultural situation are many and diverse, and it is always possible that any given phase of culture may give rise to divergent lines of institutional growth, to habits of conduct which are mutually incompatible, and which may at the same time be incompatible with the continued life of that cultural situation which has brought them to pass. The dead civilisations of history, particularly the greater ones, seem commonly to have died of some such malady. If Christian morality and pecuniary competition are the outgrowth of the same or similar lines of habituation, there should presumably be no incompatibility or discrepancy between them; otherwise it is an open question.

Leaving on one side, then, all question of its divine or supernatural origin, force, and warrant, as well as of its truth and its intrinsic merit or demerit, it may be feasible to trace the human line of derivation of this spirit of Christianity, considered as a spiritual attitude habitual to civilised mankind. . . . Certain elemental features of this Christian animus stand forth obtrusively in its beginnings, and have, with varying fortunes of dominance and decay, persisted or survived unbroken, on the whole, to the present day. These are non-resistance (humility) and brotherly love. Something further might be added, perhaps, but this much is common, in some degree, to the several variants of Christianity, late or early; and the inclusion of other common principles besides these would be debatable and precarious, except in case of such moral principles as are also common to certain of the ethnic cults as well as to Christianity. Even with respect to the two principles named, there might be some debate as to their belonging peculiarly and characteristically to the Christian spirit, exclusive of all other spiritual habits of mind. But it is at least a tenable position that these principles are intrinsic to the Christian spirit, and that they habitually serve as competent marks of identification. With the exclusion or final obsolescence of either of these, the cult would no longer be Christian, in the current acceptation of the term; though much else, chiefly not of an ethical character, would have to be added to make up a passably complete characterisation of the Christian system, as, *e.g.*, monotheism, sin and atonement, eschatological retribution, and the like. But the two principles named bear immediately on the morals of Christianity;

they are, indeed, the spiritual capital with which the Christian movement started out, and they are still the characteristics by force of
which it survives.

*   *   *

It appears, then, that these two codes of conduct, Christian morals
and business principles, are the institutional by-products of two different
cultural situations. The former, in so far as they are typically Christian,
arose out of the abjectly and precariously servile relations in which the
populace stood to their masters in late Roman times, as also, in a great,
though perhaps less, degree, during the "Dark" and the Middle Ages.
The latter, the morals of pecuniary competition, on the other hand,
are habits of thought induced by the exigencies of vulgar life under the
rule of handicraft and petty trade, out of which has come the peculiar
system of rights and duties characteristic of modern Christendom.
Yet there is something in common between the two. The Christian
principles inculcate brotherly love, mutual succor: Love thy neighbor
as thyself; *Mutuum date, nihil inde sperantes*. This principle seems, in
its elements at least, to be a culturally atavistic trait, belonging to the
ancient, not to say primordial, peaceable culture of the lower savagery.
The natural-rights analogue of this principle of solidarity and mutual
succor is the principle of fair play, which appears to be the nearest
approach to the golden rule that the pecuniary civilisation will admit.
There is no reach of ingenuity or of ingenuousness by which the one
of these may be converted into the other; nor does the régime of fair
play—essentially a régime of emulation—conduce to the reinforcement
of the golden rule. Yet throughout all the vicissitudes of cultural
change, the golden rule of the peaceable savage has never lost the
respect of occidental mankind, and its hold on men's convictions is,
perhaps, stronger now than at any earlier period of the modern time.
It seems incompatible with business principles, but appreciably less so
than with the principles of conduct that ruled the western world in the
days before the Grace of God was supplanted by the Rights of Man.
The distaste for the spectacle of contemporary life seldom rises to the
pitch of "renunciation of the world" under the new dispensation.
While one half of the Christian moral code, that pious principle which
inculcates humility, submission to irresponsible authority, found easier
lodgment in the mediaeval culture, the more humane moral element of
mutual succor seems less alien to the modern culture of pecuniary
self-help.

The presumptive degree of compatibility between the two codes of
morality may be shown by a comparison of the cultural setting, out of

which each has arisen and in which each should be at home. In the most general outline, and neglecting details as far as may be, we may describe the upshot of this growth of occidental principles as follows: The ancient Christian principle of humility, renunciation, abnegation, or non-resistance has been virtually eliminated from the moral scheme of Christendom; nothing better than a sophisticated affectation of it has any extensive currency in modern life. The conditions to which it owes its rise—bare-handed despotism and servile helplessness—are, for the immediate present and the recent past, no longer effectual elements in the cultural situation; and it is, of course, in the recent past that the conditions must be sought which have shaped the habits of thought of the immediate present. Its companion principle, brotherly love or mutual service, appears, in its elements at least, to be a very deeprooted and ancient cultural trait, due to an extremely protracted experience of the race in the early stages of human culture, reinforced and defined by the social conditions prevalent in the early days of Christianity. In the naïve and particular formulation given it by the early Christians, this habit of thought has also lost much of its force, or has fallen somewhat into abeyance; being currently represented by a thrifty charity, and, perhaps, by the negative principle of fair play, neither of which can fairly be rated as a competent expression of the Christian spirit. Yet this principle is forever reasserting itself in economic matters, in the impulsive approval of whatever conduct is serviceable to the common good and in the disapproval of disserviceable conduct even within the limits of legality and natural right. It seems, indeed, to be nothing else than a somewhat specialised manifestation of the instinct of workmanship, and as such it has the indefeasible vitality that belongs to the hereditary traits of human nature.

The pecuniary scheme of right conduct is of recent growth, but it is an outcome of a recently past phase of modern culture rather than of the immediate present. This system of natural rights, including the right of ownership and the principles of pecuniary good and evil that go with it, no longer has the consistent support of current events. Under the conditions prevalent in the era of handicraft, the rights of ownership made for equality rather than the reverse, so that their exercise was in effect not notably inconsistent with the ancient bias in favor of mutual aid and human brotherhood. This is more particularly apparent if the particular form of organisation and the spirit of the regulations then ruling in vulgar life be kept in mind. The technology of handicraft, as well as the market relations of the system of petty trade, pushed the individual workman into the foreground and led men to think of economic interests in terms of this workman and his work; the situation emphasised his creative relation to his product, as well as his responsibility for this product and for its serviceability to the common welfare. It was a situation in which the acquisition of property depended, in the main, on the workmanlike serviceability of the man who acquired it, and in which, on the whole, honesty was the best policy. Under such conditions the principles of fair play and the inviolability of ownership would be somewhat closely in touch with the ancient human instinct of workmanship, which approves mutual aid and serviceability to the common good. On the other hand, the current experience of men in the communities of Christendom, now no longer acts to reinforce these habits of thought embodied in the system of natural rights; and it is scarcely conceivable that a conviction of the goodness, sufficiency, and inviolability of the rights of ownership could arise out of such a condition of things, technological and pecuniary, as now prevails.

Hence there are indications in current events that these principles—habits of thought—are in process of disintegration rather than otherwise. With the revolutionary changes that have supervened in technology and in pecuniary relations, there is no longer such a close and visible touch between the workman and his product as would persuade men that the product belongs to him by force of an extension of his personality; nor is there a visible relation between serviceability and acquisition; nor between the discretionary use of wealth and the common welfare. The principles of fair play and pecuniary discretion have, in great measure, lost the sanction once afforded them by the human propensity for serviceability to the common good, neutral as that sanction has been at its best. Particularly is this true since business has taken on the character of an impersonal, dispassionate, not to say graceless, investment for profit. There is little in the current situation to keep the natural right of pecuniary discretion in touch with the impulsive bias of brotherly love, and there is in the spiritual discipline of this situation much that makes for an effectual discrepancy between the two. Except for a possible reversion to a cultural situation strongly characterised by ideals of emulation and status, the ancient racial bias embodied in the Christian principle of brotherhood should logically continue to gain ground at the expense of the pecuniary morals of competitive business.

WILLIAM JAMES

William James (1842–1910), older brother of the novelist Henry James, was born in New York City and received his MD degree in 1869 at Harvard. He taught anatomy and physiology at Harvard, then psychology, establishing the first psychology laboratory in America. His book *The Principles of Psychology* (1890) earned him an international reputation. Subsequently, his interests moved toward philosophy, and he contributed to the development of Pragmatism, psychical research, and religious experience. With the possible exception of John Dewey, James is the most influential philosopher produced in America. "The Moral Philosopher and the Moral Life," which follows, was originally delivered as an address to the Yale philosophy club in 1891, and is included in *The Will to Believe, and Other Essays in Popular Philosophy*, New York, 1897. It is the best statement of James's moral theory and its implied relation to his pragmatism.

A Morality for Americans

The main purpose of this paper is to show that there is no such thing possible as an ethical philosophy dogmatically made up in advance. We all help to determine the content of ethical philosophy so far as we contribute to the race's moral life. In other words, there can be no final truth in ethics any more than in physics, until the last man has had his experience and said his say. In the one case as in the other, however, the hypotheses which we now make while waiting, and the acts to which they prompt us, are among the indispensable conditions which determine what that "say" shall be.

First of all, what is the position of him who seeks an ethical philosophy? To begin with, he must be distinguished from all those who are satisfied to be ethical sceptics. He *will* not be a sceptic; therefore so far from ethical scepticism being one possible fruit of ethical philosophizing, it can only be regarded as that residual alternative to all philosophy which from the outset menaces every would-be philosopher who may give up the quest discouraged, and renounce his original aim. That aim is to find an account of the moral relations that obtain among things, which will weave them into the unity of a stable system, and make of the world what one may call a genuine universe from the ethical point of view. So far as the world resists reduction to the form of unity, so far as ethical propositions seem unstable, so far does the philosopher fail of his ideal. The subject-matter of his study is the ideals he finds existing in the world; the purpose which guides him is this ideal of his own, of getting them into a certain form. This ideal is thus a factor in ethical philosophy whose legitimate presence must never be overlooked; it is a positive contribution which the philosopher himself necessarily makes to the problem. But it is his only positive contribution. At the outset of his inquiry he ought to have no other ideals. Were he interested peculiarly in the triumph of any one kind of good, he would *pro tanto* cease to be a judicial investigator, and become an advocate for some limited element of the case.

*   *   *

. . . the Benthams, the Mills, and the Bains have done a lasting service in taking so many of our human ideals and showing how they must have arisen from the association with acts of simple bodily pleasures and reliefs from pain. Association with many remote pleasures will unquestionably make a thing significant of goodness in our minds; and the more vaguely the goodness is conceived of, the more mysterious will its source appear to be. But it is surely impossible to explain all our sentiments and preferences in this simple way. The more minutely psychology studies human nature, the more clearly it finds there traces of secondary affections, relating the impressions of the environment with one another and with our impulses in quite different ways from those mere associations of coexistence and succession which are practically all that pure empiricism can admit. Take the love of drunkenness; take bashfulness, the terror of high places, the tendency to sea-sickness, to faint at the sight of blood, the susceptibility to musical sounds; take the emotion of the comical, the passion for poetry, for mathematics, or for metaphysics—no one of these things can be wholly explained by either association or utility. They go with other things that can be so explained, no doubt; and some of them are prophetic of future utilities, since there is nothing in us for which some use may not be found. But their origin is in incidental complications to our cerebral structure, a structure whose original features arose with no reference to the perception of such discords and harmonies as these.

Well, a vast number of our moral perceptions also are certainly of this secondary and brain-born kind. They deal with directly felt fitnesses between things, and often fly in the teeth of all the prepossessions of habit and presumptions of utility. The moment you get beyond the coarser and more commonplace moral maxims, the Decalogues and Poor Richard's Almanacs, you fall into schemes and positions which to the eye of common-sense are fantastic and overstrained. The sense for abstract justice which some persons have is as eccentric a variation, from the natural-history point of view, as is the passion for music or for the higher philosophical consistencies which consumes the soul of others. The feeling of the inward dignity of certain spiritual attitudes, as peace, serenity, simplicity, veracity; and of the essential vulgarity of others, as querulousness, anxiety, egoistic fussiness, etc.—are quite inexplicable except by an innate preference of the more ideal attitude for its own pure sake. The nobler thing *tastes* better, and that is all that we can say. "Experience" of consequences may truly teach us what things are *wicked*, but what have consequences to do with what is *mean* and *vulgar?* If a man has shot his wife's paramour, by reason of what subtle repugnancy in things is it that we are so disgusted when we hear that the wife and the husband have made it up and are living comfortably together again? Or if the hypothesis were offered us of a world in which Messrs. Fourier's and Bellamy's and Morris's utopias should all be outdone, and millions kept permanently happy on the one simple condition that a certain lost soul on the far-off edge of things should lead a life of lonely torture, what except a specifical and independent sort of emotion can it be which would make us immediately feel, even though an impulse arose within us to clutch at the happiness so offered, how hideous a thing would be its enjoyment when deliberately accepted as the fruit of such a bargain? To what, once more, but subtle brain-born feelings of discord can be due all these recent protests against the entire race-tradition of retributive justice?—I refer to Tolstoï with his ideas of nonresistance, to Mr. Bellamy with his substitution of oblivion for repentance (in his novel of Dr. Heidenhain's Process), to M. Guyau with his radical condemnation of the punitive ideal. All these subtileties of the moral sensibility go as much beyond what can be ciphered out from the "laws of association" as the delicacies of sentiment possible between a pair of young lovers go beyond such precepts of the "etiquette to be observed during engagement" as are printed in manuals of social form

No! Purely inward forces are certainly at work here. All the higher, more penetrating ideals are revolutionary. They present themselves far less in the guise of effects of past experience than in that of probable causes of future experience, factors to which the environment and the lessons it has so far taught us must learn to bend.

. . . Since everything which is demanded is by that fact a good, must not the guiding principle for ethical philosophy (since all demands conjointly cannot be satisfied in this poor world) be simply to satisfy at all times *as many demands as we can?* That act must be the best act accordingly, which makes for the *best whole*, in the sense of awakening the least sum of dissatisfactions. In the casuistic scale, therefore, those ideals must be written highest which *prevail at the least cost*, or by whose realization the least possible number of other ideals are destroyed. Since victory and defeat there must be, the victory to be philosophically prayed for is that of the more inclusive side, of the side which even in the hour of triumph will to some degree do justice to the ideals in which the vanquished party's interests lay. The course of history is nothing but the story of men's struggles from generation to generation to find the more and more inclusive order. *Invent some manner* of realizing your own ideals which will also satisfy the alien demands— that and that only is the path of peace! Following this path, society has shaken itself into one sort of relative equilibrium after another by a series of social discoveries quite analogous to those of science. Polyandry and polygamy and slavery, private warfare and liberty to kill, judicial torture and arbitrary royal power have slowly succumbed to actually aroused complaints; and though some one's ideals are unquestionably the worse off for each improvement, yet a vastly greater total number of them find shelter in our civilized society than in the older savage ways. So far then, and up to date, the casuistic scale is made for the philosopher already far better than he can ever make it for himself. An experiment of the most searching kind has proved that the laws and usages of the land are what yield the maximum of satisfaction to the thinkers taken all together. The presumption in cases of conflict must always be in favor of the conventionally recognized good. The philosopher must be a conservative, and in the construction of his casuistic scale must put the things most in accordance with the customs of the community on top.

And yet if he be a true philosopher he must see that there is nothing final in any actually given equilibrium of human ideals, but that, as our present laws and customs have fought and conquered other past ones, so they will in their turn be overthrown by any newly discovered order which will hush up the complaints that they still give rise to, without producing others louder still. "Rules are made for man, not man for rules,"—that one sentence is enough to immortalize Green's Prolegomena to Ethics. And although a man always risks much when he breaks away from established rules and strives to realize a larger ideal whole than they permit, yet the philosopher must allow that it is at all times open to any one to make the experiment, provided he fear not to stake his life and character upon the throw. The pinch is always here. Pent in under every system of moral rules are innumerable persons whom it weighs upon, and goods which it represses; and these are always rumbling and grumbling in the background, and ready for any issue by which they may get free. See the abuses which the institution of private property covers, so that even to-day it is shamelessly asserted among us that one of the prime functions of the national government is to help the adroiter citizens to grow rich. See the unnamed and unnamable sorrows which the tyranny, on the whole so beneficent, of the marriage-institution brings to so many, both of the married and the unwed. See the wholesale loss of opportunity under our *régime* of so-called equality and industrialism, with the drummer and the counter-jumper in the saddle, for so many faculties and graces which could flourish in the feudal world. See our kindliness for the humble and the outcast, how it wars with that stern weeding-out which until now has been the condition of every perfection in the breed. See everywhere the struggle and the squeeze; and everlastingly the problem how to make them less. The anarchists, nihilists, and free-lovers; the free-silverites, socialists, and single-tax men; the free-traders and civil-service reformers; the prohibitionists and anti-vivisectionists; the radical darwinians with their idea of the suppression of the weak—these and all the conservative sentiments of society arrayed against them, are simply deciding through actual experiment by what sort of conduct the maximum amount of good can be gained and kept in this world. These experiments are to be judged, not *a priori*, but by actual finding, after the fact of their making, how much more outcry or how much appeasement comes about. What closet-solutions can possibly anticipate the result of trials made on such a scale? Or what can any superficial theorist's judgment be worth, in a world where every one of hundreds of ideals has its special champion already provided in the shape of some genius expressly born to feel it, and to fight to death in its behalf? The pure philosopher can only follow the windings of the spectacle, confident that the line of least resistance will always be towards the richer and the more inclusive arrangement, and that by one tack after another some approach to the kingdom of heaven is incessantly made.

IV

All this amounts to saying that, so far as the casuistic question goes, ethical science is just like physical science, and instead of being deducible all at once from abstract principles, must simply bide its time, and be ready to revise its conclusions from day to day. The presumption of course, in both sciences, always is that the vulgarly accepted opinions are true, and the right casuistic order that which public opinion believes in; and surely it would be folly quite as great, in most of us, to strike out independently and to aim at originality in ethics as in physics. Every now and then, however, some one is born with the right to be original, and his revolutionary thought or action may bear prosperous fruit. He may replace old "laws of nature" by better ones; he may, by breaking old moral rules in a certain place, bring in a total condition of things more ideal than would have followed had the rules been kept.

On the whole, then, we must conclude that no philosophy of ethics is possible in the old-fashioned absolute sense of the term. Everywhere the ethical philosopher must wait on facts. The thinkers who create the ideals come he knows not whence, their sensibilities are evolved he knows not how; and the question as to which of two conflicting ideals will give the best universe then and there, can be answered by him only through the aid of the experience of other men. I said some time ago, in treating of the "first" question, that the intuitional moralists deserve credit for keeping most clearly to the psychological facts. They do much to spoil this merit on the whole, however, by mixing with it that dogmatic temper which, by absolute distinctions and unconditional "thou shalt nots," changes a growing, elastic, and continuous life into a superstitious system of relics and dead bones. In point of fact, there are no absolute evils, and there are no non-moral goods; and the *highest* ethical life—however few may be called to bear its burdens—consists at all times in the breaking of rules which have grown too narrow for the actual case. There is but one unconditional commandment, which is that we should seek incessantly, with fear and trembling, so to vote and to act as to bring about the very largest total universe of good which we can see. Abstract rules indeed can help; but they help the less in proportion as our intuitions are more piercing, and our vocation is the stronger for the moral life. For every real dilemma is in literal strictness a unique situation; and the exact combination of ideals realized and ideals disappointed which each decision creates is always a universe without a precedent, and for which no adequate previous rule exists. The philosopher, then, *quâ* philosopher, is no better able to determine the best universe in the concrete emergency than other men. He sees, indeed, somewhat better than most men what the question always is, not a question of this good or that good simply taken, but of the two total universes with which these goods respectively belong. He knows that he must vote always for the richer universe, for the good which seems most organizable, most fit to enter into complex combinations, most apt to be a member of a more inclusive whole. But which particular universe this is he cannot know for certain in advance; he only knows that if he makes a bad mistake the cries of the wounded will soon inform him of the fact. In all this the philosopher is just like the rest of us non-philosophers, so far as we are just and sympathetic instinctively, and so far as we are open to the voice of complaint. His function is in fact indistinguishable from that of the best kind of statesman at the present day. His books upon ethics, therefore, so far as they truly touch the moral life, must more and more ally themselves with a literature which is confessedly tentative and suggestive rather than dogmatic, I mean with novels and dramas of the deeper sort, with sermons, with books on statecraft and philanthropy and social and economical reform. Treated in this way ethical treatises may be voluminous and luminous as well; but they never can be *final*, except in their abstractest and vaguest features; and they must more and more abandon the old-fashioned, clear-cut, and would-be "scientific" form.

V

The chief of all the reasons why concrete ethics cannot be final is that they have to wait on metaphysical and theological beliefs. I said some time back that real ethical relations existed in a purely human world. They would exist even in what we called a moral solitude if the thinker had various ideals which took hold of him in turn. His self of one day would make demands on his self of another; and some of the demands might be urgent and tyrannical, while others were gentle and easily put aside. We call the tyrannical demands *imperatives*. If we ignore these we do not hear the last of it. The good which we have wounded returns to plague us with interminable crops of consequential damages, compunctions and regrets. Obligation can thus exist inside a single thinker's consciousness; and perfect peace can abide with him only so far as he lives according to some sort of a casuistic scale which keeps his more imperative goods on top. It is the nature of these goods to be cruel to their rivals. Nothing shall avail when weighed in the balance against them. They call out all the mercilessness in our disposition, and do not easily forgive us if we are so soft-hearted as to shrink from sacrifice in their behalf.

The deepest difference, practically, in the moral life of man is the difference between the easy-going and the strenuous mood. When in the easy-going mood the shrinkage from present ill is our ruling consideration. The strenuous mood, on the contrary, makes us quite indifferent to present ill, if only the greater ideal be attained. The capacity for the strenuous mood probably lies slumbering in every man, but it has more difficulty in some than in others in waking up. It needs the wilder passions to arouse it, the big fears, loves, and indignations; or else the deeply penetrating appeal of some one of the higher fidelities, like justice, truth, or freedom. Strong relief is a necessity of its vision; and a world where all the mountains are brought down and all the valleys are exalted is no congenial place for its habitation. This is why in a solitary thinker this mood might slumber on forever without waking. His various ideals, known to him to be mere preferences of his own, are too nearly of the same denominational value: he can play fast or loose with them at will. This too is why, in a merely human world without a God, the appeal to our moral energy falls short of its maximal stimulating power. Life, to be sure, is even in such a world a genuinely ethical symphony; but it is played in the compass of a couple of poor octaves, and the infinite scale of values fails to open up. Many of us, indeed, like Sir James Stephen in those eloquent *Essays by a Barrister*, would openly laugh at the very idea of the strenuous mood being awakened in us by those claims of remote posterity which constitute the last appeal of the religion of humanity. We do not love these men of the future keenly enough; and we love them perhaps the less the more we hear of their evolutionized perfection, their high average longevity and education, their freedom from war and crime, their relative immunity from pain and zymotic disease, and all their other negative superiorities. This is all too finite, we say; we see too well the vacuum beyond. It lacks the note of infinitude and mystery, and may all be dealt with in the don't-care mood. No need of agonizing ourselves or making others agonize for these good creatures just at present.

When, however, we believe that a God is there, and that he is one of the claimants, the infinite perspective opens out. The scale of the symphony is incalculably prolonged. The more imperative ideals now begin to speak with an altogether new objectivity and significance, and to utter the penetrating, shattering, tragically challenging note of appeal. They ring out like the call of Victor Hugo's alpine eagle, "*qui parle au précipice et que le gouffre entend,*" and the strenuous mood awakens at the sound. It saith among the trumpets, ha, ha! it smelleth the battle afar off, the thunder of the captains and the shouting. Its blood is up; and cruelty to the lesser claims, so far from being a deterrent element, does not add to the stern joy with which it leaps to answer to the greater. All through history, in the periodical conflicts of puritanism with the don't-care temper, we see the antagonism of the strenuous and genial moods, and the contrast between the ethics of infinite and mysterious obligation from on high, and those of prudence and the satisfaction of merely finite need.

The capacity of the strenuous mood lies so deep down among our natural human possibilities that even if there were no metaphysical or traditional grounds for believing in a God, men would postulate one simply as a pretext for living hard, and getting out of the game of existence its keenest possibilities of zest. Our attitude towards concrete evils is entirely different in a world where we believe there are none but finite demanders, from what it is in one where we joyously face tragedy for an infinite demander's sake. Every sort of energy and endurance, of courage and capacity for handling life's evils, is set free in those who have religious faith. For this reason the strenuous type of character will on the battlefield of human history always outwear the easy-going type, and religion will drive irreligion to the wall.

It would seem, too—and this is my final conclusion—that the stable and systematic moral universe for which the ethical philosopher asks is fully possible only in a world where there is a divine thinker with all-enveloping demands. If such a thinker existed, his way of subordinating the demands to one another would be the finally valid casuistic scale; his claims would be the most appealing; his ideal universe would be the most inclusive realizable whole. If he now exist, then actualized in his thought already must be that ethical philosophy which we seek as the pattern which our own must evermore approach. In the interests of our own ideal of systematically unified moral truth, therefore, we, as would-be philosophers, must postulate a divine thinker, and pray for the victory of the religious cause. Meanwhile, exactly what the thought of the infinite thinker may be is hidden from us even were we sure of his existence; so that our postulation of him after all serves only to let loose in us the strenuous mood. But this is what it does in all men, even those who have no interest in philosophy. The ethical philosopher, therefore, whenever he ventures to say which course of action is the best, is on no essentially different level from the common man. "See, I have set before thee this day life and good, and death and evil; therefore, choose life that thou and thy seed may live"— when this challenge comes to us, it is simply our total character and personal genius that are on trial; and if we invoke any so-called philosophy, our choice and use of that also are but revelations of our personal aptitude or incapacity for moral life. From this unsparing practical ordeal no professor's lectures and no array of books can save us. The solving word, for the learned and the unlearned man alike, lies in the last resort in the dumb willingnesses and unwillingnesses of their interior characters, and nowhere else. It is not in heaven, neither is it beyond the sea; but the word is very nigh unto three, in thy mouth and in thy heart, that thou mayest do it.

IV. *Reason*

INTRODUCTION

George Santayana in *The Idea of Christ in the Gospels* pondered the nature of Christ's life between the Resurrection and the Ascension, when "he had one foot on earth and the other in heaven," and concluded that this was a state truly fit for man and god alike.[1] The attitude of sensitive Americans has mirrored Santayana's picture of the transfigured Savior, one foot squarely on earth and the other suspended on the ethereal level of a precious ideal; this has been the spiritual climate of the pious blacksmith, the worshiping farmer, or the Quaker mystic in his Philadelphia office.

Much has been said about the American reverence for Yankee prudence, for imported Scottish common sense, for pragmatic or realistic appraisals of alternatives, for practical checks on lofty abstractions and ideals. But the ideal has been as important as the practical success, which serves for most Americans as the confirmation of some ideal; the American deprived either of his ideal or his actuality feels only half-dressed, but more, deeply bereft.

The worth of individuality *as such* has been the central ideal, periodically requiring new defenses in new quarters. Profound respect for the intrinsic value of individuality naturally confers upon the individual the responsibility to *show* his worth. Echoing the Puritan inheritance, the individual has had to define for himself a context in which religious, governmental, legal, moral, and economic concerns figure in his thinking as ideals. Especially since the development of the physical, biological, engineering, and the social sciences, he has been compelled to define the context in which individuality can flourish in terms of a *rational ideal*. The individual, by recognizing the need to check his aspiration and beliefs against what rational insight recognizes, has helped to create a tradition in our culture of respect for reason.

[1] Cited by Herbert W. Schneider, *A History of American Philosophy*, second edition (New York & London: Columbia University Press, 1963), p. 509. Schneider remarks: "In America, too, there is a wide response to a saintly appeal of this kind, but we are far from the spirit of American realism when we yield to such enticements."

Remembered for his contribution to that tradition is Thomas Paine. Praised by Washington, Jefferson, and Franklin, a friend of Monroe, Paine was a master of the incendiary word and a symbol of the American revolutionary spirit. He carried it to France where a period in prison ensued. Apparently as intemperate as he was intense, Paine has been a puzzle for historians.[2] But he emerges clearly as a reflection of the Enlightenment, when science and human reason made dramatic efforts to emancipate themselves from traditional dogma and authority. Like Franklin and Jefferson, he combined interests in politics and science, in the nature of man and human destiny. Like them, he reached heterodox religious conclusions known as Deism. Paine's career and true convictions have been obscured by the furor resulting from the publication of his *The Age of Reason* (1794) and the subsequent but mistaken charges of atheism; it was "the most calumniated book of the epoch."[3] Paine said that his motive in writing the book was to persuade the French not to embrace atheism after having abolished the national order of priesthood, compulsive systems of religion, and compulsive articles of faith. Given his own religious background and the favorable references made by him to it, it is a safe assumption that Paine was wholly sincere in his own declaration of belief in a single Deity.

The most significant assertion in the book is this: "Infidelity does not consist in believing, or in disbelieving; it consists in professing to believe what he does not believe." Though *The Age of Reason* was an attack against institutionalized religion of any kind, but especially against traditional Christianity, its author disclaimed any right to condemn those believing otherwise. His point was that one cannot be faithful to ideas which one's reason has disclosed to be inadequate, and that one can denounce such notions without necessarily condemning their individual supporters. Paine criticized Christianity for claiming to be a "revealed" religion since it is contradictory to call a second-hand report a revelation; in Part Two of *The Age of Reason* he gave his arguments for considering the Bible as confused, contradictory, and even immoral.

For his own, Paine declared, "It is only by the exercise of reason, that man can discover God." Nature, the work of the Deity, is evidence

[2] Besides the standard study, M. D. Conway's *Life of Thomas Paine* (1892), *see* Alfred Owen Aldridge, *Man of Reason: The Life of Thomas Paine* (Philadelphia and New York: J. B. Lippincott, 1959); the present account is indebted to this work.

[3] Aldridge, *Ibid.*, p. 8.

enough for man's reason to see that it is the manifestation of a supreme creator. This Deistic belief that God is everywhere testified to by natural phenomena, also known as *natural religion*, was thought by Paine to be more deeply religious than Christianity since the latter "professes to believe in a man rather than in God. It is a compound made up chiefly of manism with but little deism, and is as near to atheism as twilight is to darkness." He argued that true religion is capable of rational demonstration, that revelation, sacred Scriptures, and ecclesiastical authority are antirational. Paine spoke in the spirit of the Enlightenment in warning against Mystery, Miracle, and Prophesy; what cannot be brought into the clear light of reason must be suspected: "Man does not learn religion as he learns the secrets and mysteries of a trade. He learns the theory of religion by reflection. It arises out of the action of his own mind upon the things which he sees, or upon what he may happen to hear or to read, and the practice joins itself thereto." With his defense of reason Paine kept one foot on the ground, and another foot higher up with his Deism. In this posture the eighteenth-century Enlightenment entered America.

As the need increased to interpret life rationally, so did the need for a basic education—the ability to read and write, to own the minimal information utilized by the sophisticated in their discussions of religion, morality, government, law, economics. The crucial role of widespread popular education was recognized as necessary to sustain the deepening democratic process. On this last issue Thomas Jefferson's views were, as in other areas, enduringly important. In a letter in 1816 he had pointed up the importance of a stipulation of the Spanish constitution making literacy requisite to citizenship:

> It is impossible sufficiently to estimate the wisdom of this provision. Of all those which have been thought of for securing fidelity in the administration of the government, constant reliance to the principles of the constitution, and progressive amendments with the progressive advances of the human mind, or changes in human affairs, it is the most effectual. Enlighten the people generally, and tyranny and oppressions of mind and body will vanish like evil spirits at the dawn of day. Although I do not with some enthusiasts, believe that the human condition will ever advance to such a state of perfection as that there shall no longer be pain or vice in the world, yet I believe it susceptible of much improvement, and most of all, in matters of government and religion; and that the diffusion of knowledge among the people is to be the instrument by which it is to be effected.

Jefferson recognized that education was necessary to preserve freedom and happiness, to maintain peace and order. Consequently, it was the responsibility of the government to insure the education of the people. It was his conviction that, once enlightened, the people would readily comprehend their own interest as requiring the maintenance of a harmonious democracy.[4] In his later years Jefferson became increasingly preoccupied with the cause of widespread education. His efforts culminated in founding the University of Virginia, the first American university without any official church affiliation. When the university opened in 1825, it represented a personal realization of Jefferson's hope for a more intensive process of education throughout the country. In his Sixth Annual Message as President, he had recommended a national establishment to make education a matter of public care. In 1779, as Governor, he had already submitted a plan for Virginia, *A Bill for the More General Diffusion of Knowledge*. The bill provided for an elementary education for the poor as well as the wealthy. Although the bill did not propose to extend the advantages of advanced education to the majority, Jefferson's views were ahead of his time. His recommendations were by no means always adopted, and not until 1846, for example, did Virginia initiate free primary schools.[5] But a gradual respect for Jefferson's faith in education developed in America, and though it took time, something close to his conception of a general public school system eventually materialized.[6]

The remarkable achievement of the Puritans in establishing a Latin grammar school in 1635 and a year later Harvard College, within six years of the founding of Boston colony, is significant, of course, for it made formal education an historic part of the nation's birth. This precedent is not easy to forget. The Puritan educational goal had been to inspire in youth a habit of discipline and virtue, without which salvation was impossible. In 1642 and 1647 two laws were passed in Massachusetts which "stand second to none in significance for American

[4] Letter to Madison, Dec. 20, 1787, *Writings*, VI, 392, quoted by Charles M. Wiltse, *The Jeffersonian Tradition in American Democracy* (New York: Hill and Wang), p. 140.

[5] "Jefferson believed in an aristocracy of intellectual talent, and on this he was far more selective than almost any modern advocate of rigorous standards in schools." Edward A. Krug, *Salient Dates in American Education: 1635–1964* (New York: Harper & Row, 1966), p. 23.

[6] Cf. Wiltse, *op. cit.*, p. 144.

education."[7] In 1642 town officials became obligated to ascertain whether parents were teaching their children to read, delinquent parents being liable to fines. In 1647 the famous Old Deluder Law was enacted, which read:

> It being one of the chief projects of that old deluder Satan to keep men from the knowledge of the Scriptures, as in former times by keeping them in an unknown tongue, that so in these latter times by persuading from the use of tongues so at least the true sense and meaning of the original might be clouded by false gloss of saint-seeming deceivers, that learning not be buried in the grave of our fathers in the church and commonwealth, the Lord assisting our endeavors:
>
> *It is therefore ordered*, That every township in this jurisdiction, after the Lord hath increased them to the number of fifty householders, shall then henceforth appoint one within their town to teach such children as shall resort to him to write and read, whose wages shall be paid either by the parents or masters of such children, or by the inhabitants in general, by way of supply, as the major part of those that order the prudentials of the town shall appoint: *Provided*, those that send their children be not oppressed by paying much more than they can have them taught for in other towns; and
>
> *It is further ordered*, that where any town shall increase to the number of one hundred families or householders; they shall set up a grammar school, the master thereof being able to instruct youth, so far as they may be fitted, for the university: *Provided*, that if any town neglect the performance hereof above one year, that every such town shall pay five pounds of the next school until they shall perform this order.[8]

Compulsory school attendance was not required by law in Massachusetts until 1852. But the principle of compulsory schooling, under the direction of the state and supported by public funds, had been determined by the Massachusetts laws of 1642 and 1647, and the other New England colonies followed the precedent. Yet, as is well known, the cause of education always has to be redefended, especially when its objectives are not described in simple moral and religious terms. Because the cause itself has often been regarded with suspicion, or its cost in dollars may have seemed unjustified, the course of education and

---

[7] Ernest E. Bayles and Bruce L. Hood, *Growth of American Educational Thought and Practice* (New York: Harper & Row, 1966), p. 10.

[8] Massachusetts Bay Law of November 11, 1647. Krug, *op. cit.*, p. 10, notes that Clifford K. Shipton and Samuel Eliot Morison have argued that the religious references were included to make the law more acceptable, not that the law was passed for primarily religious ends.

its contribution to furthering the ideal of rationality for the individual has had its ups and downs.

In 1647, the Massachusetts Bay Colony had almost 20,000 people in more than thirty towns, with seven grammar schools and Harvard College. But two hundred years later, Horace Mann, in the same state of Massachusetts, felt the need to promote anew the cause of public education. Sacrificing a successful legal practice, Mann, as secretary to the newly established State Board of Education, fought for a program of training elementary schoolteachers and a public school system. Horace Mann and Henry Barnard were leaders of our Great Educational Awakening from 1825 to 1860.[9]

It was Mann's purpose in his *Democracy and Education* (1846) to persuade the dubious of the principle that there is a public obligation to educate the children of the community as a whole. His argument was a masterpiece of the American genius for blending the ideal and the pragmatic. Since every man is indebted to his community, being no island unto himself, and since the communities of men have already appropriated the world's property, such that no "islands" remain for future generations, any present generation must acknowledge the claim of the next one, not only to affection and care, but to the *property* which it commands. "The claim of a child, then, to a portion of preexistent property begins with the first breath he draws." This ought to convince any reluctant rich farmer, opulent manufacturer, or capitalist, Mann declared, of his obligation to be taxed on behalf of public education. Since the state must provide for the mind as well as the body of the child, to keep it from drifting into vice, the choice is drastic—either "every State is bound to enact a code of laws legalizing and enforcing Infanticide, or a code of laws establishing Free Schools."[10]

As "The Case for Public High Schools" in an 1857 issue of the *American Journal of Education* testifies, there was not a single public high school beyond Massachusetts in 1838, and the situation was not greatly improved twenty years later. The article pleaded for schools which would be both inexpensive and good, supported by public taxes

[9] Bayles and Hood, *op. cit.*, pp. 16, 79–80.

[10] It had always been a greater problem to win support for the merits of higher education. American colleges and universities did not really come into their own until after the Civil War; until then a college degree was regarded as largely superfluous and the quality of instruction was not impressive. For instance, *see* Richard M. Hofstadter, "The Revolution in Higher Education," in M. White and A. Scheslinger, Jr., *Paths of American Thought* (Boston: Houghton Mifflin Company, 1963).

and equal in caliber to any private academy. Besides preparing young men for business and college, such schools would "give to every young woman a well disciplined mind, high moral aims, refined tastes, gentle and graceful manners, practical views of her own duties, and those resources of health, thought, conversation, and occupation, which bless alike the highest and lowest station in life." Since, in addition, the public high school would mix the heterogeneous elements of the community in the same classroom, thus serving as a "bond of union, a channel of sympathy, a spring-head of healthy influence, a stimulus to the whole community," the rational ideal appeared, in this instance, to have ample pragmatic justification.

Develop a habit and it becomes a philosophy. The American habit of admitting only those ideals pragmatically supportable, eventually crystallized in the truly indigenous philosophy of Pragmatism. It was an outlook with extensive ramifications for science, religion, morality, society, and education. Its aim was to formulate a workable *rational ideal* for the individual in any context. Charles Sanders Peirce, an eccentric genius, whose temperament was so uncongenial to academic appointments that he spent many years with the Geodetic Survey instead, was credited at the insistence of William James with initiating the Pragmatic movement. According to James, ideas presented by Peirce in discussions in the early 1870's, and in a *Popular Science Monthly* article in 1878, originated Pragmatism. Its popular impact did not come for some twenty years when James, crediting Peirce, announced it as his own philosophical creed.

Peirce's intellect dealt perceptively with an astonishing range of subjects. His goal was to emulate that other encyclopedic mind, Aristotle, in developing such a comprehensive philosophic outlook that it would include appropriate application to every branch of human knowledge. He began with logic to which he made important contributions, and the methodological lessons learned from the natural sciences. He ended with a complex, imaginative, and startling blend of ideas which only he could have connected in such fashion. For Peirce, as well as for William James and John Dewey, Pragmatism was as visionary as it was practical. The practical side of Peirce was manifested in his insistence that philosophy ought to be scientific in attitude, the alleged demonstrations of traditional metaphysicians being regarded as "moonshine." Only hypotheses capable of verification or refutation by future teams of investigators using the self-correcting techniques of science, deserve respect.

Peirce's technical discussions of the concepts of meaning, truth and belief had the larger intention of producing more enlightened individuals. He realized that every man has at least an implicit metaphysics. These deeper philosophical assumptions with which we operate in both everyday common sense and the special sciences must be explicitly examined in the scientific spirit rather than being merely adhered to dogmatically. In his *Minute Logic* (1902), for example, he declared that the truth sought by the logician "is nothing but a phase of the *summum bonum* which forms the subject of pure ethics," and inquiry into the *summum bonum*, or highest good, includes "the true life-germ of all the truths I have to unfold."[11] Peirce's thesis here as elsewhere was that the purpose of philosophy, like that of science, is to remove doubts and to settle beliefs. For our beliefs are not mere intellectual abstractions; they are, in fact, rules of action, guides for conduct, which we employ.

The Pragmatists argued that some ideas can powerfully and beneficially influence men's lives. Other ideas, when examined, are disclosed to have no relevance whatever and therefore serve to stupefy the mind and paralyze the will. Accordingly, they looked for a means of distinguishing useful from pointless ideas.

William James, like Peirce, believed that the truth laboriously sought by scientist and philosopher alike is a *species of good;* thus truth is essentially an ethical concept. They likewise urged that any idea worth giving time to ought to be relevant to human conduct. But James widened the "practical significance" of ideas to include their effect, not only upon one's future actions, but upon one's *experiences* and *attitudes*. Although much European philosophy of the nineteenth century was impatiently dismissed by James as nonsense disguised in glittering abstractions, his own broadened notion of "practical significance" salvaged as respectable many metaphysical and religious ideas. (This contrasted with followers of Peirce who sought to make the Pragmatist principle more strictly scientific, and dismissed much metaphysical and religious thought as pointless.) James's dictum was that a distinction in ideas must *make* a difference somewhere; thus, if a religious idea makes a difference in a person's attitude or emotion, then that idea possesses for that person significance of its own.

A major division between the Pragmatism of Pierce and that of James is that, whereas the former made the *consensus of a scientific*

---

[11] Quoted, with interesting comments, by Manley Thompson, *The Pragmatic Philosophy of C. S. Peirce* (Chicago: The University of Chicago Press, 1953), pp. 194 *ff.*

community the standard of what it is rational to believe, the latter permitted the individual to consult *his own individual experience* in deciding which ideas to trust. It is a fact—and no professor of philosophy, however gnawing his qualms, can indefinitely refrain from saying it at least once in his life—that the spirit of American culture is essentially Pragmatic. But, since it clearly incorporates in its attitudes the division between Peircean and Jamesian Pragmatism, the culture continues to be of two minds in its Pragmatism, and Pragmatism itself can offer no resolution.

In John Dewey, the third major representative of American Pragmatism, the results of technical, philosophical studies are applied more specifically to social and educational issues. He was much more the active reformist, wanting to take a hand himself in the translation of ideas into practice. Like his fellow Pragmatists, Dewey reflected the influence of Darwin. He attacked traditional theories which failed to emphasize the evolutionary nature of life, of change and novelty. He worked out the implications of the biological understanding of man as an organism in an endless process of interaction with the environment. He stressed the practical or "instrumental" function of mind or intelligence in effecting a more harmonious adaptation to the environment. Since everything we know and value is disclosed as lessons learned from the accumulation of experience rather than as lightning bolts originating outside our experience, the most important philosophical concept is the concept of *experience*.

Dewey said as much in his discussion of education. Dewey's deep influence on the rise of progressive education is generally acknowledged; he is also often blamed for all its shortcomings. The record is set straight, however, in his essay "A Contrast Between Traditional and Progressive Education," where he cautioned against the exaggerations of the reaction away from traditional education. Dewey summarized the distinctions between progressive and traditional education in this way: Progressive education emphasizes expression and cultivation of individuality, free and spontaneous activity, learning through experience, learning in order to achieve attractive goals, enjoying the present, coming to know a changing world; in contrast, the traditional approach emphasized "imposition from above," by teacher and school, external discipline, learning from teachers and texts, learning through drill and recitation, preparing for a remote future, and generally seeing the world in terms of static aims. Because of the organic relation between education and experience, a theory of education necessitates an explanation of the nature of experience; much of Dewey's philosophy was an attempt to provide one.

It is sometimes forgotten that Dewey was no less interested than James in phenomenological descriptions of experience, in trying to bring neglected aspects of our experiences into view.[12] Experiences are occurrences having continuity, in response to the constant influence of the environment. Within that continuity are moments or phases, which may either coalesce and mature into a progression toward a kind of consummation, or they may occur disconnectedly in what could be described as an inchoate experience. Each experience has its own distinctive quality, marking its peculiar individuality. The different moments in an experience retain their self-identity while passing into successive phases. Experience is characterized by thrust or resistance, struggle and conflict, or by smooth progression toward some maturation or culmination, and when this occurs, one feels the delight of having an integrated, harmonious experience; this may happen in watching a ballet or listening to Bach.

The function of education is to promote the capacity to have a fuller experience, to create more integrated individuals enjoying more integrated experiences. But Dewey also seemed to intimate on occasion that everything, including experience itself, was in the service of education, as if education were the end rather than the means.[13] Since Dewey thought the usual means-ends distinction to be a confusion, he probably meant simply that education and experience are just made *for* each other, that they form what he called a "continuum of ends and means." The rational ideal for the traditional individual, according to this Pragmatic philosopher, it would appear, is to appreciate, despite dissenting theologies and philosophies, that life is what you should treasure, that the world is your oyster, and you can help in making it ever more succulent. To any man he would say: "You are your experience; experience is all."

[12] The chapter "Having an Experience" in *Art as Experience* is an example in point. It compares very favorably, for phenomenological ingenuity, with the relevant passages in James's *Principles of Psychology*.

[13] I am indebted for this observation to Schneider, *op. cit.*, p. 498.

THOMAS PAINE

Thomas Paine (1737–1809) was born in England, the son of a Quaker staymaker. In London he met Benjamin Franklin, who was partially responsible for his going to Philadelphia in 1774. Two years later he wrote *Common Sense*, urging separation of the colonies from England, and shortly thereafter the patriotic and popular *Crisis*. In danger of being prosecuted while on a trip to England (for the views expressed in *The Rights of Man*), he fled to France where, when he refused to endorse the death sentence imposed on Louis XVI, he was imprisoned. After Robespierre's fall, he was released and returned to America, but was ostracized because of his radicalism. Formerly a friend of the great, he died in comparative oblivion. This selection, from *The Age of Reason* (1794), contains Paine's famous statement of Deism and his declaration of the relation between reason and religion.

The Rational Way to God

It has been my intention, for several years past, to publish my thoughts upon religion; I am well aware of the difficulties that attend the subject, and, from that consideration, had reserved it to a more advanced period of life. I intended it to be the last offering I should make to my fellow-citizens of all nations, and that at a time when the purity of the motive that induced me to it, could not admit of a question, even by those who might disapprove the work.

The circumstance that has now taken place in France of the total abolition of the whole national order of priesthood, and of everything appertaining to compulsive systems of religion, and compulsive articles of faith, has not only precipitated my intention, but rendered a work of this kind exceedingly necessary, lest, in the general wreck of superstition, of false systems of government, and false theology, we lose sight of morality, of humanity, and of the theology that is true.

*   *   *

I do not mean by this declaration to condemn those who believe otherwise; they have the same right to their belief as I have to mine. But it is necessary to the happiness of man, that he be mentally faithful to himself. Infidelity does not consist in believing, or in disbelieving; it consists in professing to believe what he does not believe.

It is impossible to calculate the moral mischief, if I may so express it, that mental lying has produced in society. When a man has so far corrupted and prostituted the chastity of his mind, as to subscribe his professional belief to things he does not believe, he has prepared himself for the commission of every other crime. He takes up the trade of a priest for the sake of gain, and, in order to qualify himself for that trade, he begins with a perjury. Can we conceive any thing more destructive to morality than this?

* * *

It is only by the exercise of reason, that man can discover God. Take away that reason, and he would be incapable of understanding any thing; and, in this case it would be just as consistent to read even the book called the Bible to a horse as to a man. How then is it that those people pretend to reject reason?

Almost the only parts in the book called the Bible, that convey to us any idea of God, are some chapters in Job, and the 19th Psalm; I recollect no other. Those parts are true *deistical* compositions; for they treat of the *Deity* through his works. They take the book of Creation as the word of God, they refer to no other book, and all the inferences they make are drawn from that volume.

* * *

The allusions in Job have all of them the same tendency with the Psalm; that of deducing or proving a truth that would be otherwise unknown, from truths already known.

I recollect not enough of the passages in Job, to insert them correctly: but there is one occurs to me that is applicable to the subject I am speaking upon. "Canst thou by searching find out God? Canst thou find out the Almighty to perfection?"

I know not how the printers have pointed this passage, for I keep no Bible; but it contains two distinct questions, that admit of distinct answers.

First—Canst thou by searching find out God? Yes; because in the first place, I know I did not make myself, and yet I have existence; and by *searching* into the nature of other things find that no other thing could make itself; and yet millions of other things exist; therefore it is, that I know, by positive conclusion resulting from this search, that there is a power superior to all those things and that power is God.

Secondly—Canst thou find out the Almighty to *perfection?* No; not only because the power and wisdom He has manifested in the structure of the Creation that I behold is to me incomprehensible, but because even this manifestation, great as it is, is probably but a small display of that immensity of power and wisdom, by which millions of other worlds, to me invisible by their distance, were created and continue to exist.

It is evident that both of these questions are put to the reason of the person to whom they are supposed to have been addressed; and it is only by admitting the first question to be answered affirmatively, that the second could follow. It would have been unnecessary, and even absurd, to have put a second question more difficult than the first, if the first question had been answered negatively. The two questions have different objects; the first refers to the existence of God, the second to his attributes; reason can discover the one, but it falls infinitely short in discovering the whole of the other.

I recollect not a single passage in all the writings ascribed to the men called apostles, that convey any idea of what God is. Those writings are chiefly controversial; and the subject they dwell upon, that of a man dying in agony on a cross, is better suited to the gloomy genius of a monk in a cell, by whom it is not impossible they were written, than to any man breathing the open air of the Creation. The only passage that occurs to me, that has any reference to the works of God, by which only his power and wisdom can be known, is related to have been spoken by Jesus Christ, as a remedy against distrustful care. "Behold the lilies of the field, they toil not, neither do they spin." This, however, is far inferior to the allusions in Job and in the 19th Psalm; but it is similar in idea, and the modesty of the imagery is correspondent to the modesty of the man.

As to the Christian system of faith, it appears to me as a species of atheism—a sort of religious denial of God. It professes to believe in a man rather than in God. It is a compound made up chiefly of manism with but little deism, and is as near to atheism as twilight is to darkness. It introduces between man and his Maker an opaque body, which it calls a Redeemer, as the moon introduces her opaque self between the earth and the sun, and it produces by this means a religious or an irreligious eclipse of light. It has put the whole orbit of reason into shade.

The effect of this obscurity has been that of turning every thing upside down, and representing it in reverse; and among the revolutions it has thus magically produced, it has made a revolution in Theology.

That which is now called natural philosophy, embracing the whole circle of science, of which Astronomy occupies the chief place, is the study of the works of God, and of the power and wisdom of God in his works, and is the true theology.

As to the theology that is now studied in its place, it is the study of human opinions, and of human fancies *concerning* God. It is not the study of God himself in the works that he has made, but in the works or writings that man has made; and it is not among the least of the mischiefs that the Christian system has done to the world, that it has abandoned the original and beautiful system of theology, like a beautiful innocent, to distress and reproach, to make room for the hag of superstition.

*   *   *

From the time I was capable of conceiving an idea, and acting upon it by reflection, I either doubted the truth of the Christian system, or thought it to be a strange affair; I scarcely knew which it was: but I well remember, when about seven or eight years of age, hearing a sermon read by a relation of mine, who was a great devotee of the church, upon the subject of what is called *redemption by the death of the Son of God.* After the sermon was ended, I went into the garden, and as I was going down the garden steps (for I perfectly recollect the spot) I revolted at the recollection of what I had heard, and thought to myself that it was making God Almighty act like a passionate man, that killed his son, when he could not revenge himself any other way; and as I was sure a man would be hanged that did such a thing, I could not see for what purpose they preached such sermons. This was not one of those kind of thoughts that had anything in it of childish levity; it was to me a serious reflection, arising from the idea I had, that God was too good to do such an action, and also too almighty to be under any necessity of doing it. I believe in the same manner at this moment; and I moreover believe, that any system of religion that has anything in it that shocks the mind of a child, cannot be a true system.

It seems as if parents of the Christian profession were ashamed to tell their children anything about the principles of their religion. They sometimes instruct them in morals, and talk to them of the goodness of what they call Providence; for the Christian mythology has five deities—there is God the Father, God the Son, God the Holy Ghost, the God Providence, and the Goddess Nature. But the Christian story of God the Father putting his son to death, or employing people to do it, (for that is the plain language of the story) cannot be told by a parent to a child; and to tell him that it was done to make mankind happier and better, is making the story still worse, as if mankind could be improved by the example of murder; and to tell him that all this is a mystery, is only making an excuse for the incredibility of it.

How different is this to the pure and simple profession of Deism! The true Deist has but one Deity; and his religion consists in contemplating the power, wisdom, and benignity of the Deity in his works, and in endeavouring to imitate him in every thing moral, scientifical, and mechanical.

The religion that approaches the nearest of all others to true Deism, in the moral and benign part thereof, is that professed by the Quakers: but they have contracted themselves too much, by leaving the works of God out of their system. Though I reverence their philanthropy, I cannot help smiling at the conceit, that if the taste of a Quaker could have been consulted at the creation, what a silent and drab-colored creation it would have been! Not a flower would have blossomed its gaieties, nor a bird been permitted to sing.

*   *   *

As, therefore, the Creator made nothing in vain, so also must it be believed that He organized the structure of the universe in the most advantageous manner for the benefit of man; and as we see, and from experience feel, the benefits we derive from the structure of the universe, formed as it is, which benefits we should not have had the opportunity of enjoying, if the structure, so far as relates to our system, had been a solitary globe—we can discover at least one reason why a *plurality* of worlds has been made, and that reason calls for the devotional gratitude of man, as well as his admiration.

But it is not to us, the inhabitants of this globe, only, that the benefits arising from a plurality of worlds are limited. The inhabitants of each of the worlds of which our system is composed, enjoy the same opportunities of knowledge as we do. They behold the revolutionary motions of our earth, as we behold theirs. All the planets revolve in sight of each other; and, therefore, the same universal school of science presents itself to all.

Neither does the knowledge stop here. The system of worlds next to us exhibits, in its revolutions, the same principles and school of science, to the inhabitants of their system, as our system does to us, and in like manner throughout the immensity of space.

Our ideas, not only of the almightiness of the Creator, but of his wisdom and his beneficence, become enlarged in proportion as we contemplate the extent and the structure of the universe. The solitary idea of a solitary world, rolling or at rest in the immense ocean of space, gives place to the cheerful idea of a society or worlds, so happily contrived as to administer, even by their motion, instruction to man. We see our earth filled with abundance; but we forget to consider how much of that abundance is owing to the scientific knowledge the vast machinery of the universe has unfolded.

But, in the midst of those reflections, what are we to think of the Christian system of faith, that forms itself upon the idea of only one world, and that of no greater extent, as is before shown, than twenty-five thousand miles? An extent which a man, walking at the rate of three miles an hour, for twelve hours in the day, could he keep on in a circular direction, would walk entirely round in less than two years. Alas! what is this to the mighty ocean of space, and the almighty power of the Creator!

From whence then could arise the solitary and strange conceit, that the Almighty, who had millions of worlds equally dependent on his protection, should quit the care of all the rest, and come to die in our world, because, they say, one man and one woman had eaten an apple! And, on the other hand, are we to suppose that every world in the boundless creation, had an Eve, an apple, a serpent and a redeemer? In this case, the person who is irreverently called the Son of God, and sometimes God himself, would have nothing else to do than to travel from world to world, in an endless succession of death, with scarcely a momentary interval of life.

It has been rejecting the evidence, that the word or works of God in the creation affords to our senses, and the action of our reason upon that evidence, that so many wild and whimsical systems of faith, and of religion, have been fabricated and set up. There may be many systems of religion, that so far from being morally bad, are in many respects morally good; but there can be but ONE that is true; and that one necessarily must, as it ever will, be in all things consistent with the ever existing word of God that we behold in his works. But such is the strange construction of the Christian system of faith, that every evidence the Heavens afford to man, either directly contradicts it, or renders it absurd.

It is possible to believe, and I always feel pleasure in encouraging myself to believe it, that there have been men in the world, who persuade themselves that, what is called a *pious fraud*, might at least under particular circumstances, be productive of some good. But the fraud being once established, could not afterwards be explained; for it is with a pious fraud as with a bad action, it begets a calamitous necessity of going on.

The persons who first preached the Christian system of faith, and in some measure combined it with the morality preached by Jesus Christ, might persuade themselves that it was better than the heathen mythology that then prevailed. From the first preachers the fraud went on to the second, and to the third, till the idea of its being a pious fraud became lost in the belief of its being true; and that belief became again encouraged by the interests of those who made a livelihood by preaching it.

But though such a belief might, by such means, be rendered almost general among the laity, it is next to impossible to account for the continual persecution carried on by the church, for several hundred years, against the sciences, and against the professors of sciences, if the church had not some record or tradition, that it was originally no other than a pious fraud, or did not foresee, that it could not be maintained against the evidence that the structure of the universe afforded.

Having thus shown the irreconcilable inconsistencies between the real word of God existing in the universe and that which is called *the word of God*, as shown to us in a printed book that any man might make, I proceed to speak of the three principal means that have been employed in all ages, and perhaps in all countries, to impose upon mankind.

Those three means are Mystery, Miracle, and Prophesy. The two first are incompatible with true religion, and the third ought always to be suspected.

With respect to mystery, everything we behold is, in one sense, a mystery; the whole vegetable world is a mystery. We cannot account how it is that an acorn, when put into the ground, is made to develop itself, and become an oak. We know not how it is that the seed we sow unfolds and multiplies itself, and returns to us such an abundant interest for so small a capital.

The fact, however, as distinct from the operating cause, is not a mystery, because we see it; and we know also the means we are to use, which is no other than putting seed in the ground. We know, therefore, as much as is necessary for us to know; and that part of the operation that we do not know, and which if we did we could not perform, the Creator takes upon himself and performs it for us. We are, therefore, better off than if we had been let into the secret, and left to do it for ourselves.

But though every created thing is, in this sense, a mystery, the word mystery cannot be applied to *moral truth*, any more than obscurity can be applied to light. The God in whom we believe is a God of moral truth, and not a God of mystery or obscurity. Mystery is the antagonist of truth. It is a fog of human invention, that obscures truth, and represents it in distortion. Truth never envelopes *itself* in mystery; and the mystery in which it is at any time enveloped, is the work of its antagonist, and never of itself.

Religion, therefore, being the belief of a God, and the practice of moral truth, cannot have connection with mystery. The belief of a God so far from having anything of mystery in it, is of all beliefs the most easy, because it arises to us, as is before observed, out of necessity. And the practice of moral truth, or, in other words, a practical imitation of the moral goodness of God, is no other than our acting towards each other as he acts benignly towards all. We *cannot* serve God in the manner we serve those who cannot do without such service; and, therefore, the only idea we can have of serving God, is that of contributing to the happiness of the living creation that God has made. This cannot be done by retiring ourselves from the society of the world, and spending a recluse life in selfish devotion.

The very nature and design of religion, if I may so express it, prove, even to demonstration, that it must be free from everything of mystery and unencumbered with everything that is mysterious. Religion, considered as a duty, is incumbent upon every living soul alike, and, therefore, must be on a level to the understanding and comprehension of all. Man does not learn religion as he learns the secrets and mysteries of a trade. He learns the theory of religion by reflection. It arises out of the action of his own mind upon the things which he sees, or upon what he may happen to hear or to read, and the practice joins itself thereto.

THOMAS JEFFERSON

Thomas Jefferson (1743–1826), the third President of the United States, was born in Virginia to an aristocratic family. As a young man, he was interested in science but elected law as a career. Active in local government, he became distinguished in politics and drafted the Declaration of Independence in 1776. He was Governor of Virginia, 1779–1781; succeeded Franklin as minister to France; served as Secretary of State, 1790–1793; and was elected President in 1800 and reelected four years later. His last years were spent at his self-designed home, Monticello, many of them devoted to the eventual founding of the University of Virginia, chartered in 1819. This selection,* a letter (April 24, 1816) to Dupont de Nemours, is a succinct statement of Jefferson's great regard for education.

The Importance of Being Literate

Poplar Forest, April 24, 1816. I received, my dear friend, your letter covering the constitution for your equinoctial republics, just as I was setting out for this place. I brought it with me, and have read it with great satisfaction. I suppose it well formed for those for whom it was intended, and the excellence of every government is its adaptation to the state of those to be governed by it. For us it would not do. Distinguishing between the structure of the government and the moral principles on which you prescribe its administration, with the latter we concur cordially, with the former we should not. We of the United States, you know, are constitutionally and conscientiously, democrats. We consider society as one of the natural wants with which man has been created; that he has been endowed with faculties and qualities to effect its satisfaction by concurrence of others having the same want; that when, by the exercise of these faculties, he has procured a state of society, it is one of his acquisitions which he has a right to regulate and control, jointly indeed with all those who have concurred in the procurement, whom he cannot exclude from its use or direction more than they him. We think experience has proved it safer, for the mass of individuals composing the society, to reserve to themselves personally the

* In Saul K. Padover, *A Jefferson Profile* (New York: John Day Company, 1956), pp. 271–5.

exercise of all rightful powers to which they are competent, and to delegate those to which they are not competent to deputies named, and
removable for unfaithful conduct, by themselves immediately. Hence,
with us, the people (by which is meant the mass of individuals composing
the society) being competent to judge of the facts occurring in ordinary
life, they have retained the functions of judges of facts, under the name
of jurors; but being unqualified for the management of affairs requiring
intelligence above the common level, yet competent judges of human
character, they chose, for their management, representatives, some by
themselves immediately, others by electors chosen by themselves. Thus
our President is chosen by ourselves, directly in *practice*, for we vote
for A as elector only on the condition he will vote for B, our representatives by ourselves immediately, our Senate and judges of law through
electors chosen by ourselves. And we believe that this proximate choice
and power of removal is the best security which experience has sanc-
tioned for ensuring an honest conduct in the functionaries of society.
Your three or four alembications have indeed a seducing appearance.
We should conceive, *primâ facie*, that the last extract would be the pure
alcohol of the substance, three or four times rectified. But in proportion
as they are more and more sublimated, they are also farther and farther
removed from the control of the society; and the human character, we
believe, requires in general constant and immediate control, to prevent
its being biased from right by the seductions of self-love. Your process
produces therefore a structure of government from which the fundamental principle of ours is excluded. You first set down as zeros all
individuals not having lands, which are the greater number in every
society of long standing. Those holding lands are permitted to manage
in person the small affairs of their commune or corporation, and to
elect a deputy for the canton; in which election, too, every one's vote
is to be a unit, a plurality, or a fraction, in proportion to his landed
possessions. The assemblies of cantons, then, elect for the districts; those
of districts for circles; and those of circles for the national assemblies.
Some of these highest councils, too, are in a considerable degree self-
elected, the regency partially, the judiciary entirely, and some are for
life. Whenever, therefore, an *esprit de corps*, or of party, gets possession
of them, which experience shows to be inevitable, there are no means of
breaking it up, for they will never elect but those of their own spirit.
Juries are allowed in criminal cases only. I acknowledge myself strong
in affection to our own form, yet both of us act and think from the same
motive, we both consider the people as our children, and love them with

parental affection. But you love them as infants whom you are afraid to trust without nurses; and I as adults whom I freely leave to self-government. And you are right in the case referred to you; my criticism being built on a state of society not under your contemplation. It is, in fact, like a critic on Homer by the laws of the drama.

But when we come to the moral principles on which the government is to be administered, we come to what is proper for all conditions of society. I meet you there in all the benevolence and rectitude of your native character; and I love myself always most where I concur most with you. Liberty, truth, probity, honor, are declared to be the four cardinal principles of your society. I believe with you that morality, compassion, generosity, are innate elements of the human constitution; that there exists a right independent of force; that a right to property is founded in our natural wants, in the means with which we are endowed to satisfy these wants, and the right to what we acquire by those means without violating the similar rights of other sensible beings; that no one has a right to obstruct another, exercising his faculties innocently for the relief of sensibilities made a part of his nature; that justice is the fundamental law of society; that the majority, oppressing an individual, is guilty of a crime, abuses its strength, and by acting on the law of the strongest breaks up the foundations of society; that action by the citizens in person, in affairs within their reach and competence, and in all others by representatives, chosen immediately, and removable by themselves, constitutes the essence of a republic; that all governments are more or less republican in proportion as this principle enters more or less into their composition; and that a government by representation is capable of extension over a greater surface of country than one of any other form. These, my friend, are the essentials in which you and I agree; however, in our zeal for their maintenance, we may be perplexed and divaricate as to the structure of society most likely to secure them.

In the constitution of Spain, as proposed by the late Cortes, there was a principle entirely new to me, and not noticed in yours, that no person, born after that day, should ever acquire the rights of citizenship until he could read and write. It is impossible sufficiently to estimate the wisdom of this provision. Of all those which have been thought of for securing fidelity in the administration of the government, constant ralliance to the principles of the constitution, and progressive amendments with the progressive advances of the human mind, or changes in human affairs, it is the most effectual. Enlighten the people generally, and tyranny and oppressions of body and mind will vanish like evil spirits at the dawn of day. Although I do not, with some enthusiasts, believe that the human condition will ever advance to such a state of perfection as that there shall no longer be pain or vice in the world, yet I believe it susceptible of much improvement, and most of all, in matters of government and religion; and that the diffusion of knowledge among the people is to be the instrument by which it is to be effected. The constitution of the Cortes had defects enough; but when I saw in it this amendatory provision, I was satisfied all would come right in time, under its salutary operation. No people have more need of a similar provision than those for whom you have felt so much interest. No mortal wishes them more success than I do. But if what I have heard of the ignorance and bigotry of the mass be true, I doubt their capacity to understand and to support a free government; and fear that their emancipation from the foreign tyranny of Spain, will result in a military despotism at home. Palacios may be great; others may be great; but it is the multitude which possesses force; and wisdom must yield to that. For such a condition of society, the constitution you have devised is probably the best imaginable. It is certainly calculated to elicit the best talents; although perhaps not well guarded against the egoism of its functionaries. But that egoism will be light in comparison with the pressure of a military despot, and his army of janissaries. Like Solon to the Athenians, you have given to your Columbians, not the best possible government, but the best they can bear. By-the-bye, I wish you had called them the Columbian republics, to distinguish them from our American republics. Theirs would be the most honorable name, and they best entitled to it; for Columbus discovered their continent, but never saw ours.

To them liberty and happiness; to you the meed of wisdom and goodness in teaching them how to attain them, with the affectionate respect and friendship of,

TH: JEFFERSON

HORACE MANN

Horace Mann (1796–1859) was born in Massachusetts. A graduate of Brown University in 1819, he became a successful Massachusetts lawyer. His career in education began in 1837, almost accidentally, when he was appointed secretary to the State Board of Education to revise and reorganize public schools in Massachusetts. The schools were in lamentable condition, and Mann is remembered for his effective propagandizing on behalf of reforms in public education. There was considerable controversy over the question whether taxes ought to be used in financing the public schools, and the following selection,* from his Tenth Annual Report (1846), is a forceful statement of Mann's views on the issue. In 1848 Mann returned to politics, being elected to Congress as an antislavery Whig. He declined the nomination for Governor of Massachusetts in 1852 but did accept the offer to become President of Antioch College in Ohio.

The Right to Education

But sometimes, the rich farmer, the opulent manufacturer, or the capitalist, when sorely pressed with his legal and moral obligation, to contribute a portion of his means for the education of the young, replies,—either in form or in spirit;—"My lands, my machinery, my gold and my silver, are mine; may not I do what I will with my own?" There is one supposable case, and only one, where this argument would have plausibility. If it were made by an isolated, solitary being,—a being having no relations to a community around him, having no ancestors to whom he had been indebted for ninety-nine parts in every hundred of all he possesses, and expecting to leave no posterity after him,—it might not be easy to answer it. If there were but one family in this western hemisphere, and one only in the eastern hemisphere, and these two families bore no civil and social relations to each other, and were to be the first and last of the whole race, it might be difficult, except on very high and almost transcendental grounds, for either one of them to show good cause why the other should contribute to help to educate children not his own. And perhaps the force of such an appeal would be still further diminished, if the nearest neighbor of a single family upon our

* From *The Republic and The School*. Reprinted with the permission of Lawrence A. Cremin, editor for Teachers College Press (Teachers College: Columbia University), copyright 1957.

planet were as far from the earth as Uranus or Sirius. In self-defence, or in selfishness, one might say to the other, "What are your fortunes to me? You can neither benefit nor molest me. Let us each keep to our own side of the planetary spaces." But is this the relation which any man amongst us sustains to his fellows? In the midst of a populous community to which he is bound by innumerable ties, having had his own fortune and condition almost predetermined and foreordained by his predecessors, and being about to exert upon his successors as commanding an influence as has been exerted upon himself, the objector can no longer shrink into his individuality, and disclaim connection and relationship with the world. He cannot deny that there are thousands around him on whom he acts, and who are continually reacting upon him. The earth is much too small, or the race is far too numerous, to allow us to be hermits, and therefore we cannot adopt either the philosophy or the morals of hermits. All have derived benefits from their ancestors, and all are bound, as by an oath, to transmit those benefits, even in an improved condition, to posterity. We may as well attempt to escape from our own personal identity, as to shake off the three-fold relation which we bear to others,—the relation of an associate with our contemporaries; of a beneficiary of our ancestors; of a guardian to those who, in the sublime order of Providence, are to follow us. Out of these relations, manifest duties are evolved. The society of which we necessarily constitute a part, must be preserved; and, in order to preserve it, we must not look merely to what one individual or family needs, but to what the whole community needs; not merely to what one generation needs, but to the wants of a succession of generations. To draw conclusions without considering these facts, is to leave out the most important part of the premises.

A powerfully corroborating fact remains untouched. Though the earth and the beneficent capabilities with which it is endued, belong in common to the race; yet we find that previous and present possessors have laid their hands upon the whole of it;—have left no part of it unclaimed and unappropriated. They have circumnavigated the globe; they have drawn lines across every habitable portion of it, and have partitioned amongst themselves, not only its whole area, or superficial contents, but have claimed it down to the centre, and up to the concave;—a great inverted pyramid for each proprietor,—so that not an unclaimed rood is left, either in the caverns below, or in the aërial spaces above, where a new adventurer upon existence can take unresisted possession. They have entered into a solemn compact with each other for mutual protection of their respective parts. They have created legislators and judges and executive officers, who denounce and inflict penalties even to the taking of life; and they have organized armed bands to repel aggression upon their claims. Indeed, so grasping and rapacious have mankind been, in this particular, that they have taken more than they could use, more than they could perambulate and survey, more than they could see from the top of the mast-head, or from the highest peak of the mountain. There was some limit to their physical power of taking possession, but none to the exorbitancy of their desires. Like robbers, who divide their spoils, before they know whether they shall find a victim, men have claimed a continent while still doubtful of its existence, and spread out their title from ocean to ocean, before their most adventurous pioneers had ever seen a shore of the realms they coveted. The whole planet, then, having been appropriated; there being no waste or open lands, from which the new generations may be supplied as they come into existence, have not those generations the strongest conceivable claim upon the present occupants, for that which is indispensable to their well-being? They have more than a preëmptive, they have a possessory right to some portion of the issues and profits of that, all of which has been taken up and appropriated. A denial of this right by the present possessors, is a breach of trust,—a fraudulent misuse of power given, and of confidence reposed. On mere principles of political economy, it is folly; on the broader principles of duty and morality, it is embezzlement.

It is not at all in contravention of this view of the subject, that the adult portion of society does take, and must take, upon itself, the control and management of all existing property, until the rising generation has arrived at the age of majority. Nay, one of the objects of their so doing is to preserve the rights of the generation which is still in its minority. Society, to this extent, is only a trustee managing an estate for the benefit of a part-owner, or of one who has a reversionary interest in it. This civil regulation, therefore, made necessary even for the benefit of both present and future possessors, is only in furtherance of the great law under consideration.

Coincident, too, with this great law, but in no manner superseding or invalidating it, is that wonderful provision which the Creator has made for the care of offspring, in the affection of their parents. Heaven did not rely merely upon our perceptions of duty towards our children, and our fidelity in its performance. A powerful, all-mastering instinct of love was therefore implanted in the parental, and especially in the maternal breast, to anticipate the idea of duty, and to make duty delightful. Yet the great doctrine, founded upon the will of God, as made known to us in the natural order and relation of things, would still remain the same, though all that beautiful portion of our moral being, whence parental affection springs, were a void and a non-entity. Emphatically would the obligations of society remain the same for all those children who have been bereaved of parents; or who, worse than bereavement, have only monster-parents of intemperance, or cupidity, or of any other of those forms of vice, that seem to suspend or to obliterate the law of love in the parental breast. For these, society is doubly bound to be a parent, and to exercise all that rational care and providence which a wise father would exercise for his own children.

If the previous argument began with sound premises and has been logically conducted, then it has established this position;—that a vast portion of the present wealth of the world either consists in, or has been immediately derived from, those great natural substances and powers of the earth, which were bestowed by the Creator, alike on all mankind; or from the discoveries, inventions, labors and improvements of our ancestors, which were alike designed for the common benefit of all their descendants. The question now arises, *at what time*, is this wealth to be transferred from a preceding to a succeeding generation? At what point, are the latter to take possession of, or to derive benefit from it, or at what time, are the former to surrender it in their behalf? Is each existing generation, and each individual of an existing generation, to hold fast to his possessions until death relaxes his grasp; or is something of the right to be acknowledged, and something of the benefit to be yielded, beforehand? It seems too obvious for argument, that the latter is the only alternative. If the incoming generation have no rights until the outgoing generation have actually retired, then is every individual that enters the world liable to perish on the day he is born. According to the very constitution of things, each individual must obtain sustenance and succor, as soon as his eyes open to the light, or his lungs are inflated by the air. His wants cannot be delayed until he himself can supply them. If the demands of his nature are ever to be answered, they must be answered years before he can make any personal provision for them, either by the performance of labor, or by any exploits of skill. The infant must be fed, before he can earn his bread; he must be clothed before he can prepare garments; he must be protected from the elements before he can erect a dwelling; and it is just as clear that he must be instructed before he can engage a tutor. A course contrary to this, would be the destruction of the young, that we might withhold their rightful inheritance. Carried to its extreme, it would be the act of Herod, seeking, in a general massacre, the life of one who was supposed to endanger his power. Here, then, the claims of the succeeding generation, not only upon the affection and the care, but upon the *property* of the preceding one, attach. God having given to the second generation as full and complete a right to the incomes and profits of the world, as he has given to the first; and to the third generation as full and complete a right as he has given to the second, and so on while the world stands; it necessarily follows that children must come into a partial and qualified possession of these rights, by the paramount law of nature, as soon as they are born. No human enactments can abolish or countervail this paramount and supreme law; and all those positive, and often arbitrary enactments of the civil code, by which, for the encouragement of industry and frugality, the possessor of property is permitted to control it for a limited period after his decease, must be construed and executed in subservience to this sovereign and irrepealable ordinance of nature.

Nor is this transfer always, or even generally, to be made *in kind;* but according to the needs of the recipient. The recognition of this principle is universal. A guardian or trustee may possess lands, while the ward, or owner under the trust, may need money; or the former may have money, while the latter need raiment or shelter. The form of the estate must be changed, if need be, and adapted to the wants of the receiver.

The claim of a child, then, to a portion of preëxistent property begins with the first breath he draws. The new-born infant must have sustenance and shelter and care. If the natural parents are removed, or parental ability fails,—in a word, if parents either cannot or will not supply the infant's wants, then society at large,—the government,—having assumed to itself the ultimate control of all property,—is bound to step in and fill the parents' place. To deny this to any child would be equivalent to a sentence of death,—a capital execution of the innocent, —at which every soul shudders! It would be a more cruel form of infanticide than any which is practised in China or in Africa.

But to preserve the animal life of a child only, and there to stop, would be,—not the bestowment of a blessing or the performance of a duty,—but the infliction of a fearful curse. A child has interests far higher than those of mere physical existence. Better that the wants of the natural life should be disregarded, than that the higher interests of the character should be neglected. If a child has any claim to bread to keep him from perishing, he has a far higher claim to knowledge to preserve him from error and its fearful retinue of calamities. If a child has any claim to shelter to protect him from the destroying elements, he has a far higher claim to be rescued from the infamy and perdition of vice and crime.

All moralists agree, nay, all moralists maintain, that a man is as responsible for his omissions as for his commissions;—that he is as guilty of the wrong which he could have prevented, but did not, as for that which his own hand has perpetrated. They then, who knowingly withhold sustenance from a newly-born child, and he dies, are guilty of infanticide. And, by the same reasoning, they who refuse to enlighten the intellect of the rising generation, are guilty of degrading the human race! They who refuse to train up children in the way they should go, are training up incendiaries and madmen to destroy property and life, and to invade and pollute the sanctuaries of society! In a word, if the mind is as real and substantive a part of human existence as the body, then mental attributes during the periods of childhood, demand provision at least as imperatively as bodily appetites. The time when these respective obligations attach, corresponds with the periods when the nurture, whether physical or mental, is needed. As the right of sustenance is of equal date with birth, so the right to intellectual and moral training begins, at least as early as when children are ordinarily sent to school. At that time, then, by the irrepealable law of nature, every child succeeds to so much more of the property of the community as is necessary for his education. He is to receive this, not in the form of lands, or of gold and silver, but in the form of knowledge and a training to good habits. This is one of the steps in the transfer of the property of the present to a succeeding generation. Human sagacity may be at fault in fixing the amount of property to be transferred, or the time when the transfer should be made, to a dollar or to an hour; but certainly, in a republican government, the obligation of the predecessors, and the right of the successors, extend to and embrace the means of such an amount of education as will prepare each individual to perform all the duties which devolve upon him as a man and a citizen. It may go further than this point; certainly, it cannot fall short of it.

Under our political organization, the places and the processes where this transfer is to be provided for, and its amount determined, are the district school meeting, the town meeting, legislative halls, and conventions for establishing or revising the fundamental laws of the State.

If it be not done there, society is false to its high trusts; and any community, whether national or state, that ventures to organize a government, or to administer a government already organized, without making provision for the free education of all its children, dares the certain vengeance of Heaven; and, in the squalid forms of poverty and destitution, in the scourges of violence and misrule, in the heart-destroying corruptions of licentiousness and debauchery, and in political profligacy and legalized perfidy,—in all the blended and mutually aggravated crimes of civilization and of barbarism, will be sure to feel the terrible retributions of its delinquency.

I bring my argument on this point, then, to a close; and I present a test of its validity, which, as it seems to me, defies denial or evasion.

In obedience to the laws of God and to the laws of all civilized communities, society is bound to protect the natural life; and the natural life cannot be protected without the appropriation and use of a portion of the property which society possesses. We prohibit infanticide under penalty of death. We practise a refinement in this particular. The life of an infant is inviolable even before he is born; and he who feloniously takes it, even before birth, is as subject to the extreme penalty of the law, as though he had struck down manhood in its vigor, or taken away a mother by violence from the sanctuary of home, where she blesses her offspring. But why preserve the natural life of a child, why preserve unborn embryos of life, if we do not intend to watch over and to protect them, and to expand their subsequent existence into usefulness and happiness? As individuals, or as an organized community, we have no natural right; we can derive no authority or countenance from reason; we can cite no attribute or purpose of the divine nature, for giving birth to any human being, and then inflicting upon that being the curse of ignorance, of poverty and of vice, with all their attendant calamities. We are brought then to this startling but inevitable alternative. The natural life of an infant should be extinguished as soon as it is born, or the means should be provided to save that life from being a curse to its possessor; and therefore every State is bound to enact a code of laws legalizing and enforcing Infanticide, or a code of laws establishing Free Schools!

The three following propositions, then, describe the broad and ever-enduring foundation on which the Common School system of Massachusetts reposes:

The successive generations of men, taken collectively, constitute one great Commonwealth.

The property of this Commonwealth is pledged for the education of all its youth, up to such a point as will save them from poverty and vice, and prepare them for the adequate performance of their social and civil duties.

The successive holders of this property are trustees, bound to the faithful execution of their trust, by the most sacred obligations; because embezzlement and pillage from children and descendants are as criminal as the same offences when perpetrated against contemporaries.

AMERICAN JOURNAL OF EDUCATION

The selection, originally entitled "The Case for the Public High Schools," is reprinted from *American Journal of Education*, Volume 3, Number 8, March, 1857, pp. 185–9. Anonymously written, it shows how the cause of public high schools was argued in the middle of the nineteenth century.

Defense of Public Education

[The following considerations respecting the character and advantages of a school of the highest grade in a system of public instruction in cities and large villages, were first presented to the public in 1838, when there was not a single institution of the kind out of Massachusetts. They are still widely applicable in every State.]

By a Public or Common High School, is intended a public or common school for the older and more advanced scholars of the community in which the same is located, in a course of instruction adapted to their age, and intellectual and moral wants, and, to some extent, to their future pursuits in life. It is common or public in the same sense in which the district school, or any lower grade of school established and supported under a general law and for the public benefit, is common or public. It is open to all the children of the community to which the school belongs, under such regulations as to age, attainments, &c., as the good of the institution may require, or the community may adopt. A Public High School is not necessarily a free school. It may be supported by a fund, a public tax, or an assessment or rate of tuition per scholar, or by a combination of all, or any two of these modes. Much less is it a public or common school in the sense of being cheap, inferior, ordinary. To be truly a public school, a High School must embrace in its course of instruction studies which can be more profitably pursued there than in public schools of a lower grade, or which gather their pupils from a more circumscribed territory, and as profitably as in any private school of the same pretensions. It must make a good education common in the highest and best sense of the word common—common because it is good enough for the best, and cheap enough for the poorest family in the community. It would be a mockery of the idea of such a school, to call it a Public High School, if the course of instruction pursued in it is not higher and better than can be got in public schools of a lower grade, or if it does not meet the wants of the wealthiest and best educated families, or, if the course of instruction is liberal and thorough, and at the same time the worthy and talented child of a poor family is shut out from its privileges by a high rate of tuition. The school, to be common practically, must be both cheap and good. To be cheap, its support must be provided for wholly or mainly out of a fund, or by public tax. And to justify the imposition of a public tax, the advantages of such a school must accrue to the whole community. It must be shown to be a common benefit, a common interest, which cannot be secured so well, or at all, except through the medium of taxation. What, then, are the advantages which may reasonably be anticipated from the establishment of a Public High School, properly organized, instructed, and supervised?

First. Everything which is now done in the several district schools, and schools of lower grade, can be better done, and in a shorter time, because the teachers will be relieved from the necessity of devoting the time and attention now required by few of the older and more advanced pupils, and can bestow all their time and attention upon the preparatory studies and younger children. These studies will be taught in methods suited to the age and attainments of the pupils. A right beginning can thus be made in the lower schools, in giving a thorough practical knowledge of elementary principles, and in the formation of correct mental and moral habits, which are indispensable to all sound education. All this will be done under the additional stimulus of being early and thoroughly fitted for the High School.

Second. A High School will give completeness to the system of public instruction which may be in operation. It will make suitable provision for the older and more advanced pupils of both sexes, and will admit of the methods of instruction and discipline which cannot be profitably introduced into the schools below. The lower grade of schools—those which are established for young children,—require a large use of oral and simultaneous methods, and a frequent change of place and position on the part of the pupils. The higher branches, especially all mathematical subjects, require patient application and habits of abstraction on the part of the older pupils, which can with difficulty, if at all, be attained by many pupils amid a multiplicity of distracting exercises, movements, and sounds. The recitations of this class of pupils, to be profitable and satisfactory, must be conducted in a manner which requires time, discussion, and explanation, and the undivided attention both of pupils and teacher. The course of instruction provided in the High School will be equal in extent and value to that which may be given in any private school, academy, or female seminary in the place, and which is now virtually denied to the great mass of the children by the burdensome charge of tuition.

As has been already implied, the advantages of a High School should not be confined to the male sex. The great influence of the female sex, as daughters, sisters, wives, mothers, companions, and teachers, in determining the manners, morals, and intelligence of the whole community, leaves no room to question the necessity of providing for the girls the best means of intellectual and moral culture. The course of instruction should embrace the first principles of natural and mechanical philosophy, by which inventive genius and practical skill in the useful arts can be fostered; such studies as navigation, book-keeping, surveying, botany, chemistry, and kindred studies, which are directly connected with success in the varied departments of domestic and inland trade, with foreign commerce, with gardening, agriculture, the manufacturing and domestic arts; such studies as astronomy, physiology, the history of our own state and nation, the principles of our state and national constitutions, political economy, and moral science; in fine, such a course of study as is now given in more than fifty towns and cities in New England, and which shall prepare every young man, whose parents may desire it, for business, or for college, and give to every young woman a well disciplined mind, high moral aims, refined tastes, gentle and graceful manners, practical views of her own duties, and those resources of health, thought, conversation, and occupation, which bless alike the highest and lowest station in life. When such a course is provided and carried out, the true idea of the High School will be realized.

Third. It will equalize the opportunities of a good education, and exert a happy, social influence throughout the whole community from which it gathers its scholars. From the want of a public school of this character, the children of such families as rely exclusively on the district school are isolated, and are condemned to an inferior education, both in quality and quantity; they are cut off from the stimulus and sympathy which the mingling of children of the same age from different parts of the same community would impart. The benefits, direct and indirect, which will result to the country districts, or poor families who live in the outskirts of the city, from the establishment of a school of this class, cannot easily be overestimated. The number of young men and young women who will receive a thorough education, qualifying them for business, and to be teachers, will increase from year to year; and the number who will press up to the front ranks of scholarship in the school, bearing away the palm of excellence by the vigor of sound minds in sound bodies, of minds and bodies made vigorous by long walks and muscular labor in the open air, will be greater in proportion to their number than from the city districts. It will do both classes good, the children of the city, and the children of the country districts, to measure themselves intellectually in the same fields of study, and to subject the peculiarities of their respective manners, the roughness and awkwardness sometimes characteristic of the one, and the artificiality and flippancy of the other, to the harmonizing influence of reciprocal action and reaction. The isolation and estrangement which now divide and subdivide the community into country and city clans, which, if not hostile, are strangers to each other, will give place to the frequent intercourse and esteem of individual and family friendship, commenced in the school-room, and on the play-ground of the school. The school will thus become a bond of union, a channel of sympathy, a spring-head of healthy influence, and stimulus to the whole community.

Fourth. The privileges of a good school will be brought within the reach of all classes of the community, and will actually be enjoyed by children of the same age from families of the most diverse circumstances as to wealth, education, and occupation. Side by side in the same recitations, heart and hand in the same sports, pressing up together to the same high attainments in knowledge and character, will be found the children of the rich and poor, the more and the less favored in outward circumstances, without knowing or caring to know how far their families are separated by the arbitrary distinctions which divide and distract society. With nearly equal opportunities of education in childhood and youth, the prizes of life, its best fields of usefulness, and sources of happiness will be open to all, whatever may have been their accidents of birth and fortune. From many obscure and humble homes in the city and in the country, will be called forth and trained inventive talent, productive skill, intellectual taste, and Godlike benevolence, which will add to the general wealth, multiply workshops, increase the value of farms, and carry forward every moral and religious enterprise which aims to bless, purify, and elevate society.

Fifth. The influence of the annual or semi-annual examination of candidates for admission into the High School, will operate as a powerful and abiding stimulus to exertion throughout all the lower schools.

The privileges of the High School will be held forth as the reward of exertion in the lower grade of schools; and promotion to it, based on the result of an impartial examination, will form an unobjectional standard by which the relative standing of the different schools can be ascertained, and will also indicate the studies and departments of education to which the teachers in particular schools should devote special attention. This influence upon the lower schools, upon scholars and teachers, upon those who reach, and those who do not reach the High School, will be worth more than all it costs, independent of the advantages received by its pupils.

Sixth. While the expenses of public or common schools will necessarily be increased by the establishment of a school of this class, in addition to those already supported, the aggregate expenditures for education, including public and private schools, will be diminished. Private schools of the same relative standing will be discontinued for want of patronage, while those of a higher grade, if really called for by the educational wants of the community, will be improved. A healthy competition will necessarily exist between the public and private schools of the highest grade, and the school or schools which do not come up to the highest mark, must go down in public estimation. Other things being equal, viz., school-houses, teachers, classification, and the means and appliances of instruction, the public school is always better than the private. From the uniform experience of those places where a High School has been established, it may be safely stated, that there will be an annual saving in the expenses of education to any community, equal to one half the amount paid for tuition in private schools, and, with this saving of expense, there will be a better state of education.

Seventh. The successful establishment of a High School, by improving the whole system of common schools, and interesting a larger number of families in the prosperity of the schools, will create a better public sentiment on the subject than has heretofore existed, and the schools will be regarded as the common property, the common glory, the common security of the whole community. The wealthy will feel that the small additional tax required to establish and sustain this school, if not saved to them in the diminished tuition for the education of their own children in private schools, at home and abroad, is returned to them a hundred fold in the enterprise which it will quicken, in the increased value given to property, and in the number of families which will resort to the place where it is located, as a desirable residence, because of the facilities enjoyed for a good education. The poor will feel that, whatever may betide them, their children are born to an inheritance more valuable than lands or shops, in the free access to institutions where as good an education can be had as money can buy at home or abroad. The stranger will be invited to visit not only the institutions which public or individual benevolence has provided for the poor, the orphan, the deaf mute, and the criminal, but schools where the children and youth of the community are trained to inventive and creative habits of mind, to a practical knowledge of the fundamental principles of business, to sound moral habits, refined tastes, and respectful manners. And in what balance, it has well been asked in reference to the cost of good public schools, as compared with these advantages, shall we weigh the value of cultivated, intelligent, energetic, polished, and virtuous citizens? How much would a community be justified in paying for a physician who should discover or practice some mode of treatment through which many lives should be preserved? How much for a judge, who, in the able administration of the laws, should secure many fortunes, or rights more precious than fortunes, that might else be lost? How much for a minister of religion who should be the instrument of saving hundreds from vice and crime, and persuading them to the exertion of their best powers for the common good? How much for the ingenious inventor, who, proceeding from the first principles of science onward, should produce some improvement that should enlarge all the comforts of society, not to say a steam-engine or a magnetic telegraph? How much for the patriotic statesman, who, in difficult times, becomes the savior of his country? How much for the well-instructed and enterprising merchant who should suggest and commence the branches of business that should bring in a vast accession of wealth and strength? One such person as any of these might repay what a High School would cost for centuries. Whether, in the course of centuries, every High School would produce one such person, it would be useless to prophesy. But it is certain that it would produce many intelligent citizens, intelligent men of business, intelligent servants of the state, intelligent teachers, intelligent wives and daughters, who, in their several spheres, would repay to any community much more than they and all their associates had received. The very taxes of a town, in twenty years, will be lessened by the existence of a school which will continually have sent forth those who were so educated as to become not burdens but benefactors.

These results have been realized wherever a Public High School has been opened under circumstances favorable to the success of a private school of the same grade,—wherever a good school-house, good regulations, (for admission, attendance, studies, and books,) good teachers, and good supervision have been provided.

CHARLES SANDERS PEIRCE

Charles Sanders Peirce (1839–1914) was born in Massachusetts, son of the distinguished Harvard mathematician Benjamin Peirce. He himself graduated from that institution in 1859. A student of many disciplines, he wrote articles on logic, psychology, metaphysics, mathematics, engineering, chemistry, and optics. Peirce taught at Johns Hopkins University, and for many years was with the Geodetic Survey. He is generally credited with being the initiator of American Pragmatism, and is considered by many scholars the most brilliant and original of American philosophers. The following selections* are taken from "Preface to Principles of Philosophy" and "Notes on Scientific Philosophy."

Science and Metaphysics

1.   To erect a philosophical edifice that shall outlast the vicissitudes of time, my care must be, not so much to set each brick with nicest accuracy, as to lay the foundations deep and massive. Aristotle built upon a few deliberately chosen concepts—such as matter and form, act and power—very broad, and in their outlines vague and rough, but solid, unshakable, and not easily undermined; and thence it has come to pass that Aristotelianism is babbled in every nursery, that "English Common Sense," for example, is thoroughly peripatetic, and that ordinary men live so completely within the house of the Stagyrite that whatever they see out of the windows appears to them incomprehensible and metaphysical. Long it has been only too manifest that, fondly habituated though we be to it, the old structure will not do for modern needs; and accordingly, under Descartes, Hobbes, Kant, and others, repairs, alterations, and partial demolitions have been carried on for the last three centuries. One system, also, stands upon its own ground; I mean the new Schelling-Hegel mansion, lately run up in the German taste, but with such oversights in its construction that, although brand new, it is already pronounced uninhabitable. The undertaking which this volume inaugurates is to make a philosophy like that of Aristotle, that is to say, to outline a theory so comprehensive that, for a long time to come, the entire work of human reason, in philosophy of every school and kind, in mathematics, in psychology, in physical science,

* From *Collected Papers*, Vol. I, edited by Charles Hartshorne and Paul Weiss (Cambridge: Harvard University Press, 1931). Used by permission.

in history, in sociology, and in whatever other department there may be, shall appear as the filling up of its details. The first step toward this is to find simple concepts applicable to every subject.

2.   But before all else, let me make the acquaintance of my reader, and express my sincere esteem for him and the deep pleasure it is to me to address one so wise and so patient. I know his character pretty well, for both the subject and the style of this book ensure his being one out of millions. He will comprehend that it has not been written for the purpose of confirming him in his preconceived opinions, and he would not take the trouble to read it if it had. He is prepared to meet with propositions that he is inclined at first to dissent from; and looks to being convinced that some of them are true, after all. He will reflect, too, that the thinking and writing of this book has taken, I won't say how long, quite certainly more than a quarter of an hour, and consequently fundamental objections of so obvious a nature that they must strike everyone instantaneously will have occurred to the author, although the replies to them may not be of that kind whose full force can be instantly apprehended.

3.   The reader has a right to know how the author's opinions were formed. Not, of course, that he is expected to accept any conclusions which are not borne out by argument. But in discussions of extreme difficulty, like these, when good judgment is a factor, and pure ratiocination is not everything, it is prudent to take every element into consideration. From the moment when I could think at all, until now, about forty years, I have been diligently and incessantly occupied with the study of methods [of] inquiry, both those which have been and are pursued and those which ought to be pursued. For ten years before this study began, I had been in training in the chemical laboratory. I was thoroughly grounded not only in all that was then known of physics and chemistry, but also in the way in which those who were successfully advancing knowledge proceeded. I have paid the most attention to the methods of the most exact sciences, have intimately communed with some of the greatest minds of our times in physical science, and have myself made positive contributions—none of them of any very great importance, perhaps—in mathematics, gravitation, optics, chemistry, astronomy, etc. I am saturated, through and through, with the spirit of the physical sciences. I have been a great student of logic, having read everything of any importance on the subject, devoting a great deal of time to medieval thought, without neglecting the works of the Greeks, the English, the Germans, the French, etc., and have

produced systems of my own both in deductive and in inductive logic. In metaphysics, my training has been less systematic; yet I have read and deeply pondered upon all the main systems, never being satisfied until I was able to think about them as their own advocates thought.

4. The first strictly philosophical books that I read were of the classical German schools; and I became so deeply imbued with many of their ways of thinking that I have never been able to disabuse myself of them. Yet my attitude was always that of a dweller in a laboratory, eager only to learn what I did not yet know, and not that of philosophers bred in theological seminaries, whose ruling impulse is to teach what they hold to be infallibly true. I devoted two hours a day to the study of Kant's *Critic of the Pure Reason* for more than three years, until I almost knew the whole book by heart, and had critically examined every section of it. For about two years, I had long and almost daily discussions with Chauncey Wright, one of the most acute of the followers of J. S. Mill.

5. The effect of these studies was that I came to hold the classical German philosophy to be, upon its argumentative side, of little weight; although I esteem it, perhaps am too partial to it, as a rich mine of philosophical suggestions. The English philosophy, meagre and crude, as it is, in its conceptions, proceeds by surer methods and more accurate logic. The doctrine of the association of ideas is, to my thinking, the finest piece of philosophical work of the prescientific ages. Yet I can but pronounce English sensationalism to be entirely destitute of any solid bottom. From the evolutionary philosophers, I have learned little although I admit that, however hurriedly their theories have been knocked together, and however antiquated and ignorant Spencer's *First Principles* and general doctrines, yet they are under the guidance of a great and true idea, and are developing it by methods that are in their main features sound and scientific.

6. The works of Duns Scotus have strongly influenced me. If his logic and metaphysics, not slavishly worshipped, but torn away from its medievalism, be adapted to modern culture, under continual wholesome reminders of nominalistic criticisms, I am convinced that it will go far toward supplying the philosophy which is best to harmonize with physical science. But other conceptions have to be drawn from the history of science and from mathematics.

7. Thus, in brief, my philosophy may be described as the attempt of a physicist to make such conjecture as to the constitution of the universe as the methods of science may permit, with the aid of all that

has been done by previous philosophers. I shall support my propositions by such arguments as I can. Demonstrative proof is not to be thought of. The demonstrations of the metaphysicians are all moonshine. The best that can be done is to supply a hypothesis, not devoid of all likelihood, in the general line of growth of scientific ideas, and capable of being verified or refuted by future observers.

Scientific Philosophy

Laboratory and Seminary Philosophies

126. The kind of philosophy which interests me and must, I think, interest everybody is that philosophy which uses the most rational methods it can devise, for finding out the little that can as yet be found out about the universe of mind and matter from those observations which every person can make in every hour of his waking life. It will not include matters which are more conveniently studied by students of special sciences, such as psychology. Thus, everybody has remarked that there are four prominent qualities of the sense of taste, sweet, sour, salt, and bitter. But there may be other tastes, not so readily made out without special study; and in any case tastes are conveniently studied in connection with flavors and odors, which make a difficult experimental inquiry. Besides, the four tastes are altogether special and throw no light on the problems which, on account of their extreme generality, will naturally be examined by a class of researchers of entirely different aptitudes from those which adapt men to the discovery of recondite facts.

127. If anybody asks what there is in the study of obvious phenomena to make it particularly interesting, I will give two answers. The first is the one which seems to me the strongest; the other is that which nobody can fail to feel the force of. The first answer is that the spirit in which, as it seems to me, philosophy ought to be studied is the spirit in which every branch of science ought to be studied; namely, the spirit of joy in learning ourselves and in making others acquainted with the glories of God. Each person will feel this joy most in the particular branch of science to which his faculties are best adapted. It is not a sin to have no taste for philosophy as I define philosophy. As a matter of fact, however, almost everybody does feel an interest in philosophical problems, especially at that time of life at which he is spoiling for an intellectual tussle.

128. It is true that philosophy is in a lamentably crude condition at present; that very little is really established about it; while most philosophers set up a pretension of knowing all there is to know—a pretension calculated to disgust anybody who is at home in any real science. But all we have to do is to turn our backs upon all such truly vicious conduct, and we shall find ourselves enjoying the advantages of having an almost virgin soil to till, where a given amount of really scientific work will bring in an extraordinary harvest, and that a harvest of very fundamental truth of exceptional value from every point of view.

129. This consideration touches upon the second reason for studying laboratory-philosophy (as contradistinguished from seminary-philosophy). It is that the special sciences are obliged to take for granted a number of most important propositions, because their ways of working afford no means of bringing these propositions to the test. In short, they always rest upon metaphysics. At one time, for example, we find physicists, Kelvin, Maxwell and others, assuming that a body cannot act where it is not, meaning by "where it is not" where its lines of force do not centre. At another time, we find them assuming that the laws of mechanics (including the principles of metric geometry) hold good for the smallest corpuscles. Now, it is one thing to infer from the laws of little things how great things, that consist of little things, will act; but it is quite a different thing to infer from the phenomena presented by great things how single things billions of times smaller will act. It is like inferring that because in any country one man in so many will commit suicide, therefore, every individual, once in such a period of time, will make an attempt at suicide. The psychical sciences, especially psychology, are, if possible, even more necessitated to assume general principles that cannot be proved or disproved by their ordinary methods of work. The philosopher alone is equipped with the facilities for examining such "axioms" and for determining the degree to which confidence may safely be reposed in them. Find a scientific man who proposes to get along without any metaphysics—not by any means every man who holds the ordinary reasonings of metaphysicians in scorn—and you have found one whose doctrines are thoroughly vitiated by the crude and uncriticized metaphysics with which they are packed. We must philosophize, said the great naturalist Aristotle—if only to avoid philosophizing. Every man of us has a metaphysics, and has to have one; and it will influence his life greatly. Far better, then, that that metaphysics should be criticized and not be allowed to run loose. A man may say, "I will content myself with common sense." I, for one,

am with him there, in the main. I shall show why I do not think there can be any *direct* profit in going behind common sense—meaning by common sense those ideas and beliefs that man's situation absolutely forces upon him. We shall later see more definitely what is meant. I agree, for example, that it is better to recognize that some things are red and some others blue, in the teeth of what optical philosophers say, that it is merely that some things are resonant to shorter ether waves and some to longer ones. But the difficulty is to determine what really is and what is not the authoritative decision of common sense and what is merely *obiter dictum*. In short, there is no escape from the need of a critical examination of "first principles."

WILLIAM JAMES

William James is, of course, the foremost spokesman for American Pragmatism. It was only after James had brought Peirce's work to public attention that the word "pragmatism" came into widespread use and became something of a household word. This selection is from James's *Pragmatism* (New York & London: Longmans, Green & Company, 1907).* It is an excellent, detailed formulation of the essence of Pragmatism as James explained it.

The Meaning of Pragmatism

Some years ago, being with a camping party in the mountains, I returned from a solitary ramble to find every one engaged in a ferocious metaphysical dispute. The *corpus* of the dispute was a squirrel—a live squirrel supposed to be clinging to one side of a tree-trunk; while over against the tree's opposite side a human being was imagined to stand. This human witness tries to get sight of the squirrel by moving rapidly round the tree, but no mattter how fast he goes, the squirrel moves as fast in the opposite direction, and always keeps the tree between himself and the man, so that never a glimpse of him is caught. The resultant metaphysical problem now is this: *Does the man go round the squirrel or not?* He goes round the tree, sure enough, and the squirrel is on the tree; but does he go round the squirrel? In the unlimited leisure of the wilderness, discussion had been worn threadbare. Everyone had taken sides, and was obstinate; and the numbers on both sides were even. Each side, when I appeared therefore appealed to me to make it a majority. Mindful of the scholastic adage that whenever you meet a contradiction you must make a distinction, I immediately sought and found one, as follows: "Which party is right," I said, "depends on what you *practically mean* by 'going round' the squirrel. If you mean passing from the north of him to the east, then to the south, then to the west, and then to the north of him again, obviously the man does go round him, for he occupies these successive positions. But if on the contrary you mean being first in front of him, then on the right of him, then behind him, then on his left, and finally in front again, it is quite as obvious that the man fails to go round him, for by the compensating

* Reprinted by permission of G. P. Putnam's Sons.

movements the squirrel makes, he keeps his belly turned towards the man all the time, and his back turned away. Make the distinction, and there is no occasion for any farther dispute. You are both right and both wrong according as you conceive the verb 'to go round' in one practical fashion or the other."

Although one or two of the hotter disputants called my speech a shuffling evasion, saying they wanted no quibbling or scholastic hair-splitting, but meant just plain honest English "round," the majority seemed to think that the distinction had assuaged the dispute.

I tell this trivial anecdote because it is a peculiarly simple example of what I wish now to speak of as *the pragmatic method*. The pragmatic method is primarily a method of settling metaphysical disputes that otherwise might be interminable. Is the world one or many?—fated or free?—material or spiritual?—here are notions either of which may or may not hold good of the world; and disputes over such notions are unending. The pragmatic method in such cases is to try to interpret each notion by tracing its respective practical consequences. What difference would it practically make to any one if this notion rather than that notion were true? If no practical difference whatever can be traced, then the alternatives mean practically the same thing, and all dispute is idle. Whenever a dispute is serious, we ought to be able to show some practical difference that must follow from one side or the other's being right.

A glance at the history of the idea will show you still better what pragmatism means. The term is derived from the same Greek word πραγμα, meaning action, from which our words "practice" and "practical" come. It was first introduced into philosophy by Mr. Charles Peirce in 1878. In an article entitled "How to Make Our Ideas Clear," in the *Popular Science Monthly* for January of that year, Mr. Peirce, after pointing out that our beliefs are really rules for action, said that, to develop a thought's meaning, we need only determine what conduct it is fitted to produce: that conduct is for us its sole significance. And the tangible fact at the root of all our thought-distinctions, however subtle, is that there is no one of them so fine as to consist in anything but a possible difference of practice. To attain perfect clearness in our thoughts of an object, then, we need only consider what conceivable effects of a practical kind the object may involve—what sensations we are to expect from it, and what reactions we must prepare. Our conception of these effects, whether immediate or remote, is then for us the whole of our conception of the object, so far as that conception has positive significance at all.

This is the principle of Peirce, the principle of pragmatism. It lay entirely unnoticed by any one for twenty years, until I, in an address before Professor Howison's philosophical union at the University of California, brought it forward again and made a special application of it to religion. By that date (1898) the times seemed ripe for its reception. The word "pragmatism" spread, and at present it fairly spots the pages of the philosophic journals. On all hands we find the "pragmatic movement" spoken of, sometimes with respect, sometimes with contumely, seldom with clear understanding. It is evident that the term applies itself conveniently to a number of tendencies that hitherto have lacked a collective name, and that it has "come to stay."

To take in the importance of Peirce's principle, one must get accustomed to applying it to concrete cases. I found a few years ago that Ostwald, the illustrious Leipzig chemist, had been making perfectly distinct use of the principle of pragmatism in his lectures on the philosophy of science, though he had not called it by that name.

"All realities influence our practice," he wrote me, "and that influence is their meaning for us. I am accustomed to put questions to my classes in this way: In what respects would the world be different if this alternative or that were true? If I can find nothing that would become different, then the alternative has no sense."

That is, the rival views mean practically the same thing, and meaning, other than the practical, there is for us none. Ostwald in a published lecture gives this example of what he means. Chemists have long wrangled over the inner constitution of certain bodies called "tautomerous." Their properties seemed equally consistent with the notion that an instable hydrogen atom oscillates inside of them, or that they are instable mixtures of two bodies. Controversy raged, but never was decided. "It would never have begun," says Ostwald, "if the combatants had asked themselves what particular experimental fact could have been made different by one or the other view being correct. For it would then have appeared that no difference of fact could possibly ensue; and the quarrel was as unreal as if, theorizing in primitive times about the raising of dough by yeast, one party should have invoked a 'brownie,' while another insisted on an 'elf' as the true cause of the phenomenon."

It is astonishing to see how many philosophical disputes collapse into insignificance the moment you subject them to this simple test of tracing a concrete consequence. There can *be* no difference anywhere that doesn't *make* a difference elsewhere—no difference in abstract truth that doesn't express itself in a difference in concrete fact and in conduct consequent upon that fact, imposed on somebody, somehow, somewhere, and somewhen. The whole function of philosophy ought to be to find out what definite difference it will make to you and me, at definite instants of our life, if this world-formula or that world-formula be the true one.

There is absolutely nothing new in the pragmatic method. Socrates was an adept at it. Aristotle used it methodically. Locke, Berkeley, and Hume made momentous contributions to truth by its means. Shadworth Hodgson keeps insisting that realities are only what they are "known as." But these forerunners of pragmatism used it in fragments: they were preluders only. Not until in our time has it generalized itself, become conscious of a universal mission, pretended to a conquering destiny. I believe in that destiny, and I hope I may end by inspiring you with my belief.

Pragmatism represents a perfectly familiar attitude in philosophy, the empiricist attitude, but it represents it, as it seems to me, both in a more radical and in a less objectionable form than it has ever yet assumed. A pragmatist turns his back resolutely and once for all upon a lot of inveterate habits dear to professional philosophers. He turns away from abstraction and insufficiency, from verbal solutions, from bad *a priori* reasons, from fixed principles, closed systems, and pretended absolutes and origins. He turns towards concreteness and adequacy, towards facts, towards action and towards power. That means the empiricist temper regnant and the rationalist temper sincerely given up. It means the open air and possibilities of nature, as against dogma, artificiality, and the pretence of finality in truth.

At the same time it does not stand for any special results. It is a method only. But the general triumph of that method would mean an enormous change in what I called in my last lecture the "temperament" of philosophy. Teachers of the ultra-rationalistic type would be frozen out, much as the courtier type is frozen out in republics, as the ultramontane type of priest is frozen out in protestant lands. Science and metaphysics would come much nearer together, would in fact work absolutely hand in hand.

Metaphysics has usually followed a very primitive kind of quest. You know how men have always hankered after unlawful magic, and you know what a great part in magic *words* have always played. If you have his name, or the formula of incantation that binds him, you can control the spirit, genie, afrite, or whatever the power may be. Solomon knew the names of all the spirits, and having their names, he held them subject to his will. So the universe has always appeared to the natural mind as a kind of enigma, of which the key must be sought in the shape of some illuminating or power-bringing word or name. That word names the universe's *principle*, and to possess it is after a fashion to possess the universe itself. "God," "Matter," "Reason," "the Absolute," "Energy," are so many solving names. You can rest when you have them. You are at the end of your metaphysical quest.

But if you follow the pragmatic method, you cannot look on any such word as closing your quest. You must bring out of each word its practical cash-value, set it at work within the stream of your experience. It appears less as a solution, then, than as a program for more work, and more particularly as an indication of the ways in which existing realities may be *changed*.

Theories thus become instruments, not answers to enigmas, in which we can rest. We don't lie back upon them, we move forward, and, on occasion, make nature over again by their aid. Pragmatism unstiffens all our theories, limbers them up and sets each one at work. Being nothing essentially new, it harmonizes with many ancient philosophic tendencies. It agrees with nominalism for instance, in always appealing to particulars; with utilitarianism in emphasizing practical aspects; with positivism in its disdain for verbal solutions, useless questions and metaphysical abstractions.

All these, you see, are *anti-intellectualist* tendencies. Against rationalism as a pretension and a method pragmatism is fully armed and militant. But, at the outset, at least, it stands for no particular results. It has no dogmas, and no doctrines save its method. As the young Italian pragmatist Papini has well said, it lies in the midst of our theories, like a corridor in a hotel. Innumerable chambers open out of it. In one you may find a man writing an atheistic volume; in the next some one on his knees praying for faith and strength; in a third a chemist investigating a body's properties. In a fourth a system of idealistic metaphysics is being excogitated; in a fifth the impossibility of metaphysics is being shown. But they all own the corridor, and all must pass through it if they want a practicable way of getting into or out of their respective rooms.

No particular results then, so far, but only an attitude of orientation, is what the pragmatic method means. *The attitude of looking away from*

*first things, principles, "categories," supposed necessities; and of looking
towards last things, fruits, consequences, facts.*

So much for the pragmatic method! You may say that I have been
praising it rather than explaining it to you, but I shall presently explain
it abundantly enough by showing how it works on some familiar
problems. Meanwhile the word pragmatism has come to be used in a
still wider sense, as meaning also a certain *theory of truth.* I mean to
give a whole lecture to the statement of that theory, after first paving
the way, so I can be very brief now. But brevity is hard to follow, so
I ask for your redoubled attention for a quarter of an hour. If much
remains obscure, I hope to make it clearer in the later lectures.

One of the most successfully cultivated branches of philosophy in
our time is what is called inductive logic, the study of the conditions
under which our sciences have evolved. Writers on this subject have
begun to show a singular unanimity as to what the laws of nature and
elements of fact mean, when formulated by mathematicians, physicists
and chemists. When the first mathematical, logical, and natural uni-
formities, the first *laws*, were discovered, men were so carried away by
the clearness, beauty and simplification that resulted, that they believed
themselves to have deciphered authentically the eternal thoughts of the
Almighty. His mind also thundered and reverberated in syllogisms. He
also thought in conic sections, squares and roots and ratios, and
geometrized like Euclid. He made Kepler's laws for the planets to
follow; he made velocity increase proportionally to the time in falling
bodies; he made the law of the sines for light to obey when refracted;
he established the classes, orders, families and genera of plants and
animals, and fixed the distances between them. He thought the arche-
types of all things, and devised their variations; and when we rediscover
any one of these his wondrous institutions, we seize his mind in its very
literal intention.

But as the sciences have developed farther the notion has gained
ground that most, perhaps all, of our laws are only approximations.
The laws themselves, moreover, have grown so numerous that there is
no counting them; and so many rival formulations are proposed in all
the branches of science that investigators have become accustomed to
the notion that no theory is absolutely a transcript of reality, but that
any one of them may from some point of view be useful. Their great
use is to summarize old facts and to lead to new ones. They are only a
man-made language, a conceptual shorthand, as some one calls them,

in which we write our reports of nature; and languages, as is well known, tolerate much choice of expression and many dialects.

* * *

. . . The individual has a stock of old opinions already, but he meets a new experience that puts them to a strain. Somebody contradicts them; or in a reflective moment he discovers that they contradict each other; or he hears of facts with which they are incompatible; or desires arise in him which they cease to satisfy. The result is an inward trouble to which his mind till then had been a stranger, and from which he seeks to escape by modifying his previous mass of opinions. He saves as much of it as he can, for in this matter of belief we are all extreme conservatives. So he tries to change first this opinion, and then that (for they resist change very variously), until at last some new idea comes up which he can graft upon the ancient stock with a minimum of disturbance of the latter, some idea that mediates between the stock and the new experience and runs them into one another most felicitously and expediently.

This new idea is then adopted as the true one. It preserves the older stock of truths with a minimum of modification, stretching them just enough to make them admit the novelty, but conceiving that in ways as familiar as the case leaves possible. An *outrée* explanation, violating all our preconceptions, would never pass for a true account of a novelty. We should scratch round industriously till we found something less eccentric. The most violent revolutions in an individual's beliefs leaves most of his old order standing. Time and space, cause and effect, nature and history, and one's own biography remain untouched. New truth is always a go-between, a smoother-over of transitions. It marries old opinion to new fact so as ever to show a minimum of jolt, a maximum of continuity. We hold a theory true just in proportion to its success in solving this "problem of maxima and minima." But success in solving this problem is eminently a matter of approximation. We say this theory solves it on the whole more satisfactorily than that theory; but that means more satisfactorily to ourselves, and individuals will emphasize their points of satisfaction differently. To a certain degree, therefore, everything here is plastic.

* * *

. . . A new opinion counts as "true" just in proportion as it gratifies the individual's desire to assimilate the novel in his experience to his beliefs in stock. It must both lean on old truth and grasp new fact; and its success (as I said a moment ago) in doing this, is a matter for the individual's appreciation. When old truth grows, then, by new truth's addition, it is for subjective reasons. We are in the process and obey the reasons. That new idea is truest which performs most felicitously its function of satisfying our double urgency. It makes itself true, gets itself classed as true, by the way it works; grafting itself then upon the ancient body of truth, which thus grows much as a tree grows by the activity of a new layer of cambium.

*　　*　　*

Now pragmatism, devoted though she be to facts, has no such materialistic bias as ordinary empiricism labors under. Moreover, she has no objection whatever to the realizing of abstractions, so long as you get about among particulars with their aid and they actually carry you somewhere. Interested in no conclusions but those which our minds and our experiences work out together, she has no *a priori* prejudices against theology. *If theological ideas prove to have a value for concrete life, they will be true, for pragmatism, in the sense of being good for so much. For how much more they are true, will depend entirely on their relations to the other truths that also have to be acknowledged.*

What I said just now about the Absolute, of transcendental idealism, is a case in point. First, I called it majestic and said it yielded religious comfort to a class of minds, and then I accused it of remoteness and sterility. But so far as it affords such comfort, it surely is not sterile; it has that amount of value; it performs a concrete function. As a good pragmatist, I myself ought to call the Absolute true "in so far forth," then; and I unhesitatingly now do so.

But what does *true in so far forth* mean in this case? To answer, we need only apply the pragmatic method. What do believers in the Absolute mean by saying that their belief affords them comfort? They mean that since, in the Absolute finite evil is "overruled" already, we may, therefore, whenever we wish, treat the temporal as if it were potentially the eternal, be sure that we can trust its outcome, and, without sin, dismiss our fear and drop the worry of our finite responsibility. In short, they mean that we have a right ever and anon to take a moral holiday, to let the world wag in its own way, feeling that its issues are in better hands than ours and are none of our business.

The universe is a system of which the individual members may relax their anxieties occasionally, in which the don't-care mood is also right for men, and moral holidays in order—that, if I mistake not, is part, at least, of what the Absolute is "known-as," that is the great difference in our particular experiences which his being true makes, for us, that is his cash-value when he is pragmatically interpreted. Farther than that the ordinary lay-reader in philosophy who thinks favorably of absolute idealism does not venture to sharpen his conceptions. He can use the Absolute for so much, and so much is very precious. He is pained at hearing you speak incredulously of the Absolute, therefore, and disregards your criticisms because they deal with aspects of the conception that he fails to follow.

If the Absolute means this, and means no more than this, who can possibly deny the truth of it? To deny it would be to insist that men should never relax, and that holidays are never in order.

I am well aware how odd it must seem to some of you to hear me say that an idea is "true" so long as to believe it is profitable to our lives. That it is *good*, for as much as it profits, you will gladly admit. If what we do by its aid is good, you will allow the idea itself to be good in so far forth, for we are the better for possessing it. But is it not a strange misuse of the word "truth," you will say, to call ideas also "true" for this reason?

To answer this difficulty fully is impossible at this stage of my account. You touch here upon the very central point of Messrs. Schiller's, Dewey's and my own doctrine of truth, which I can not discuss with detail until my sixth lecture. Let me now say only this, that truth is *one species of good*, and not, as is usually supposed, a category distinct from good, and coordinate with it. *The true is the name of whatever proves itself to be good in the way of belief, and good, too, for definite, assignable reasons.* Surely you must admit this, that if there were *no* good for life in true ideas, or if the knowledge of them were positively disadvantageous and false ideas the only useful ones, then the current notion that truth is divine and precious, and its pursuit a duty, could never have grown up or become a dogma. In a world like that, our duty would be to *shun* truth, rather. But in this world, just as certain foods are not only agreeable to our taste, but good for our teeth, our stomach, and our tissues; so certain ideas are not only agreeable to think about, or agreeable as supporting other ideas that we are fond of, but they are also helpful in life's practical struggles. If there be any life that it is really better we should lead, and if there be any idea which, if believed in, would help us to lead that life, then it would be really *better for us* to believe in that idea, *unless, indeed, belief in it incidentally clashed with other greater vital benefits.*

"What would be better for us to believe"! This sounds very like a definition of truth. It comes very near to saying "what we *ought* to believe": and in *that* definition none of you would find any oddity. Ought we ever not to believe what it is *better for us* to believe? And can we then keep the notion of what is better for us, and what is true for us, permanently apart?

Pragmatism says no, and I fully agree with her. Probably you also agree, so far as the abstract statement goes, but with a suspicion that if we practically did believe everything that made for good in our own personal lives, we should be found indulging all kinds of fancies about this world's affairs, and all kinds of sentimental superstitions about a world hereafter. Your suspicion here is undoubtedly well founded, and it is evident that something happens when you pass from the abstract to the concrete that complicates the situation.

I said just now that what is better for us to believe is true *unless the belief incidentally clashes with some other vital benefit.* Now in real life what vital benefits is any particular belief of ours most liable to clash with? What indeed except the vital benefits yielded by *other beliefs* when these prove incompatible with the first ones? In other words, the greatest enemy of any one of our truths may be the rest of our truths. Truths have once for all this desperate instinct of self-preservation and of desire to extinguish whatever contradicts them. My belief in the Absolute, based on the good it does me, must run the gauntlet of all my other beliefs. Grant that it may be true in giving me a moral holiday. Nevertheless, as I conceive it—and let me speak now confidentially, as it were, and merely in my own private person—it clashes with other truths of mine whose benefits I hate to give up on its account. It happens to be associated with a kind of logic of which I am the enemy, I find that it entangles me in metaphysical paradoxes that are inacceptable, etc., etc. But as I have enough trouble in life already without adding the trouble of carrying these intellectual inconsistencies, I personally just give up the Absolute. I just *take* my moral holidays; or else as a professional philosopher, I try to justify them by some other principle.

If I could restrict my notion of the Absolute to its bare holiday-giving value, it wouldn't clash with any other truths. But we can not easily thus restrict our hypotheses. They carry supernumerary features, and these it is that clash so. My disbelief in the Absolute means then disbelief in those other supernumerary features, for I fully believe in the legitimacy of taking moral holidays.

You see by this what I meant when I called pragmatism a mediator and reconciler and said, borrowing the word from Papini, that she "unstiffens" our theories. She has in fact no prejudices whatever, no obstructive dogmas, no rigid canons of what shall count as proof. She is completely genial. She will entertain any hypothesis, she will consider any evidence. It follows that in the religious field she is at a great advantage both over positivistic empiricism, with its anti-theological bias and over religious rationalism, with its exclusive interest in the remote, the noble, the simple, and the abstract in the way of conception.

In short, she widens the field of search for God. Rationalism sticks to logic and the empyrean. Empiricism sticks to the external senses. Pragmatism is willing to take anything, to follow either logic or the senses and to count the humblest and most personal experiences. She will count mystical experiences if they have practical consequences. She will take a God who lives in the very dirt of private fact—if that should seem a likely place to find him.

Her only test of probable truth is what works best in the way of leading us, what fits every part of life best and combines with the collectivity of experience's demands, nothing being omitted. If theological ideas should do this, if the notion of God, in particular, should prove to do it, how could pragmatism possibly deny God's existence? She could see no meaning in treating as "not true" a notion that was pragmatically so successful. What other kind of truth could there be, for her, than all this agreement with concrete reality?

In my last lecture I shall return again to the relations of pragmatism with religion. But you see already how democratic she is. Her manners are as various and flexible, her resources as rich and endless, and her conclusions as friendly as those of mother nature.

JOHN DEWEY

Dewey applied Pragmatism to theories of education and his writing resulted in the birth of "progressive" education. In urging suggested revisions in traditional educational theories, Dewey pointed out the need for clarification of the concept of experience itself. Education, after all, must grow out of a person's experience as well as contribute to the future shaping of it. The following selection,* "A Contrast Between Progressive and Traditional Education," is a concise statement of Dewey's theory of progressive education and its relation to a Pragmatic concept of human experience.

Experience and Education

If one attempts to formulate the philosophy of education implicit in the practices of the newer education, we may, I think, discover certain common principles amid the variety of progressive schools now existing. To imposition from above is opposed expression and cultivation of individuality; to external discipline is opposed free activity; to learning from texts and teachers, learning through experience; to acquisition of isolated skills and techniques by drill, is opposed acquisition of them as means of attaining ends which make direct vital appeal; to preparation for a more or less remote future is opposed making the most of the opportunities of present life; to static aims and materials is opposed acquaintance with a changing world.

Now, all principles by themselves are abstract. They become concrete only in the consequences which result from their application. Just because the principles set forth are so fundamental and far-reaching, everything depends upon the interpretation given them as they are put into practice in the school and the home. It is at this point that the reference made earlier to *Either-Or* philosophies becomes peculiarly pertinent. The general philosophy of the new education may be sound, and yet the difference in abstract principles will not decide the way in which the moral and intellectual preference involved shall be worked out in practice. There is always the danger in a new movement that in rejecting the aims and methods of that which it would supplant, it may develop its principles negatively rather than positively and construc-

* From *Experience and Education.* Used by permission.

tively. Then it takes its clew in practice from that which is rejected instead of from the constructive development of its own philosophy.

I take it that the fundamental unity of the newer philosophy is found in the idea that there is an intimate and necessary relation between the processes of actual experience and education. If this be true, then a positive and constructive development of its own basic idea depends upon having a correct idea of experience. Take, for example, the question of organized subject-matter—which will be discussed in some detail later. The problem for progressive education is: What is the place and meaning of subject-matter and of organization *within* experience? How does subject-matter function? Is there anything inherent in experience which tends towards progressive organization of its contents? What results follow when the materials of experience are not progressively organized? A philosophy which proceeds on the basis of rejection, of sheer opposition, will neglect these questions. It will tend to suppose that because the old education was based on ready-made organization, therefore it suffices to reject the principle of organization *in toto*, instead of striving to discover what it means and how it is to be attained on the basis of experience. We might go through all the points of difference between the new and the old education and reach similar conclusions. When external control is rejected, the problem becomes that of finding the factors of control that are inherent within experience. When external authority is rejected, it does not follow that all authority should be rejected, but rather that there is need to search for a more effective source of authority. Because the older education imposed the knowledge, methods, and the rules of conduct of the mature person upon the young, it does not follow, except upon the basis of the extreme *Either-Or* philosophy, that the knowledge and skill of the mature person has no directive value for the experience of the immature. On the contrary, basing education upon personal experience may mean more multiplied and more intimate contacts between the mature and the immature than ever existed in the traditional school, and consequently more, rather than less, guidance by others. The problem, then, is: how these contacts can be established without violating the principle of learning through personal experience. The solution of this problem requires a well thought-out philosophy of the social factors that operate in the constitution of individual experience.

What is indicated in the foregoing remarks is that the general principles of the new education do not of themselves solve any of the problems of the actual or practical conduct and management of progressive schools. Rather, they set new problems which have to be worked out on the basis of a new philosophy of experience. The problems are not even recognized, to say nothing of being solved, when it is assumed that it suffices to reject the ideas and practices of the old education and then go to the opposite extreme. Yet I am sure that you will appreciate what is meant when I say that many of the newer schools tend to make little or nothing of organized subject-matter of study; to proceed as if any form of direction and guidance by adults were an invasion of individual freedom, and as if the idea that education should be concerned with the present and future meant that acquaintance with the past has little or no role to play in education. Without pressing these defects to the point of exaggeration, they at least illustrate what is meant by a theory and practice of education which proceeds negatively or by reaction against what has been current in education rather than by a positive and constructive development of purposes, methods, and subject-matter on the foundation of a theory of experience and its educational potentialities.

It is not too much to say that an educational philosophy which professes to be based on the idea of freedom may become as dogmatic as ever was the traditional education which is reacted against. For any theory and set of practices is dogmatic which is not based upon critical examination of its own underlying principles. Let us say that the new education emphasizes the freedom of the learner. Very well. A problem is now set. What does freedom mean and what are the conditions under which it is capable of realization? Let us say that the kind of external imposition which was so common in the traditional school limited rather than promoted the intellectual and moral development of the young. Again, very well. Recognition of this serious defect sets a problem. Just what is the role of the teacher and of books in promoting the educational development of the immature? Admit that traditional education employed as the subject-matter for study facts and ideas so bound up with the past as to give little help in dealing with the issues of the present and future. Very well. Now we have the problem of discovering the connection which actually exists *within* experience between the achievements of the past and the issues of the present. We have the problem of ascertaining how acquaintance with the past may be translated into a potent instrumentality for dealing effectively with the future. We may reject knowledge of the past as the *end* of education and thereby only emphasize its importance as a *means*. When we do that we have a problem that is new in the story of education: How shall the young become acquainted with the past in such a way that the acquaintance is a potent agent in appreciation of the living present?

The Need of a Theory of Experience

In short, the point I am making is that rejection of the philosophy and practice of traditional education sets a new type of difficult education problem for those who believe in the new type of education. We shall operate blindly and in confusion until we recognize this fact; until we thoroughly appreciate that departure from the old solves no problems. What is said in the following pages is, accordingly, intended to indicate some of the main problems with which the newer education is confronted and to suggest the main lines along which their solution is to be sought. I assume that amid all uncertainties there is one permanent frame of reference: namely, the organic connection between education and personal experience; or, that the new philosophy of education is committed to some kind of empirical and experimental philosophy. But experience and experiment are not self-explanatory ideas. Rather, their meaning is part of the problem to be explored. To know the meaning of empiricism we need to understand what experience is.

The belief that all genuine education comes about through experience does not mean that all experiences are genuinely or equally educative. Experience and education cannot be directly equated to each other. For some experiences are mis-educative. Any experience is mis-educative that has the effect of arresting or distorting the growth of further experience. An experience may be such as to engender callousness; it may produce lack of sensitivity and of responsiveness. Then the possibilities of having richer experience in the future are restricted. Again, a given experience may increase a person's automatic skill in a particular direction and yet tend to land him in a groove or rut; the effect again is to narrow the field of further experience. An experience may be immediately enjoyable and yet promote the formation of a slack and careless attitude; this attitude then operates to modify the quality of subsequent experiences so as to prevent a person from getting out of them what they have to give. Again, experiences may be so disconnected from one another that, while each is agreeable or even exciting in itself, they are not linked cumulatively to one another. Energy is then dissipated and a person becomes scatter-brained. Each experience may be lively, vivid, and "interesting," and yet their disconnectedness may artificially generate dispersive, disintegrated, centrifugal habits. The consequence of formation of such habits is inability to control future experiences. They are then taken, either by way of enjoyment or of discontent and revolt, just as they come. Under such circumstances, it is idle to talk of self-control.

Traditional education offers a plethora of examples of experiences of the kinds just mentioned. It is a great mistake to suppose, even tacitly, that the traditional schoolroom was not a place in which pupils had experiences. Yet this is tacitly assumed when progressive education as a plan of learning by experience is placed in sharp opposition to the old. The proper line of attack is that the experiences which were had, by pupils and teachers alike, were largely of a wrong kind. How many students, for example, were rendered callous to ideas, and how many lost the impetus to learn because of the way in which learning was experienced by them? How many acquired special skills by means of automatic drill so that their power of judgment and capacity to act intelligently in new situations was limited? How many came to associate the learning process with ennui and boredom? How many found what they did learn so foreign to the situations of life outside the school as to give them no power of control over the latter? How many came to associate books with dull drudgery, so that they were "conditioned" to all but flashy reading matter?

If I ask these questions, it is not for the sake of wholesale condemnation of the old education. It is for quite another purpose. It is to emphasize the fact, first, that young people in traditional schools do have experiences; and, secondly, that the trouble is not the absence of experiences, but their defective and wrong character—wrong and defective from the standpoint of connection with further experiences. The positive side of this point is even more important in connection with progressive education. It is not enough to insist upon the necessity of experience, nor even of activity in experience. Everything depends upon the *quality* of the experience which is had. The quality of any experience has two aspects. There is an immediate aspect of agreeableness or disagreeableness, and there is its influence upon later experiences. The first is obvious and easy to judge. The *effect* of an experience is not borne on its face. It sets a problem to the educator. It is his business to arrange for the kind of experiences which, while they do not repel the student, but rather engage his activities are, nevertheless, more than immediately enjoyable since they promote having desirable future experiences. Just as no man lives or dies to himself, so no experience lives and dies to itself. Wholly independent of desire or intent, every experience lives on in further experiences. Hence the central problem of an education based upon experience is to select the kind of present experiences that live fruitfully and creatively in subsequent experiences.

Later, I shall discuss in more detail the principle of the continuity of experience or what may be called the experiential continuum. Here I wish simply to emphasize the importance of this principle for the philosophy of educative experience. A philosophy of education, like any theory, has to be stated in words, in symbols. But so far as it is more than verbal it is a plan for conducting education. Like any plan, it must be framed with reference to what is to be done and how it is to be done. The more definitely and sincerely it is held that education is a development within, by, and for experience, the more important it is that there shall be clear conceptions of what experience is. Unless experience is so conceived that the result is a plan for deciding upon subject-matter, upon methods of instruction and discipline, and upon material equipment and social organization of the school, it is wholly in the air. It is reduced to a form of words which may be emotionally stirring but for which any other set of words might equally well be substituted unless they indicate operations to be initiated and executed. Just because traditional education was a matter of routine in which the plans and programs were handed down from the past, it does not follow that progressive education is a matter of planless improvisation.

The traditional school could get along without any consistently developed philosophy of education. About all it required in that line was a set of abstract words like culture, discipline, our great cultural heritage, etc., actual guidance being derived not from them but from custom and established routines. Just because progressive schools cannot rely upon established traditions and institutional habits, they must either proceed more or less haphazardly or be directed by ideas which, when they are made articulate and coherent, form a philosophy of education. Revolt against the kind of organization characteristic of the traditional school constitutes a demand for a kind of organization based upon ideas. I think that only slight acquaintance with the history of education is needed to prove that educational reformers and innovators alone have felt the need for a philosophy of education. Those who adhered to the established system needed merely a few fine-sounding words to justify existing practices. The real work was done by habits which were so fixed as to be institutional. The lesson for progressive education is that it requires in an urgent degree, a degree more pressing than was incumbent upon former innovators, a philosophy of education based upon a philosophy of experience.

I remarked incidentally that the philosophy in question is, to para-
phrase the saying of Lincoln about democracy, one of education of, by,
and for experience. No one of these words, *of, by,* or *for,* names anything which is self-evident. Each of them is a challenge to discover and
put into operation a principle of order and organization which follows
from understanding what educative experience signifies.

It is, accordingly, a much more difficult task to work out the kinds
of materials, of methods, and of social relationships that are appropriate to the new education than is the case with traditional education.
I think many of the difficulties experienced in the conduct of progressive
schools and many of the criticisms leveled against them arise from this
source. The difficulties are aggravated and the criticisms are increased
when it is supposed that the new education is somehow easier than
the old. This belief is, I imagine, more or less current. Perhaps it illustrates again the *Either-Or* philosophy, springing from the idea that
about all which is required is *not* to do what is done in traditional
schools.

V. *Metaphysics*

INTRODUCTION

An essentially religious culture, like the American, is naturally disposed to respect metaphysics, at least to make a home for it. Metaphysics is many things. It is speculation about that which, for lack of evidence, science and common sense must be mostly reticent; it is sometimes sheer defiance of the offered evidence, declaring, for instance, that every man is selfish or that no person voluntarily does evil; it may be an argument to prove the existence of unseen realities, ranging from God and the soul to the abstract entities composing logic and mathematics; it is occasionally the dogmatic assertion that, in certain respects, the world is too much for the human intellect, and therefore some important belief must always rest on faith; it may be the attitude which gropes for a defense of the conviction that metaphors are somehow literally true, that history is cyclical, that time is unreal, or that everything is really one. It generally advances the claim that what a thing really is, is not necessarily identical with how it appears; it triggers the suspicion that the world as it appears may not coincide with its true nature; it may even claim that the most important realities do not even appear at all—that, at best, they are only "sensed," or "suggested," for reasons themselves unclear; it may be an unexplained yearning to downgrade the familiar and understood in favor of the strange, the elusive, the uncanny.

Metaphysics may supplement religion by offering special arguments on behalf of supernatural realities originally accepted on the basis of revelation, authority, and faith; it may serve as a consoling substitute when religious disillusionment occurs. Metaphysics, in America as everywhere else, has served the vigorous, and replaced the feeble, religion. Whether in the guise of philosophy, or astrology, the rural almanac, theosophy, ritualistic clubs and cults, fundamentalism, mysticism, or revolutionism, America has always bred metaphysics.

A *religious democracy* teaches simultaneously that, no matter how petty your achievement, it is yet important; that, however grand your success, it is nonetheless insignificant—without ever presuming to deny either pettiness or grandness as mortal happenings. Despite the accomplishments which are habitually credited to Yankee ingenuity, to American realism, to its pragmatism—its devotion to common sense, its healthy skepticism, its concern for economic and material progress, its respect for the concrete in the here-and-now—the remarkable phenomenon is that the culture itself always denigrates the success it simultaneously applauds. Whatever the explanation, whether because repeated success begets contempt for itself or because the experience of success is a lesson in humility which reveals the limits of even a greater talent, this paradox is inherent in American thought. The greater the material success, the greater the faith that the metaphysical will supplement or supplant the religious in showing how such success enjoys even greater significance, which can only be described or hinted at through *unfamiliar* concepts.

Success, in a religious democracy, can make a person feel that this life is now so well understood that he must search for meaning beyond it; he then activates a metaphysical frame of mind that harbors the notion that another life, a deeper reality which dwarfs the apparent present actuality, is dimly seen over the horizon. His search for significance proceeds on the notion that somehow the here-and-now experience is not really all. It can be persuasively argued that this traditional cultural tendency toward metaphysics has been beneficial, promoting a humility and a skepticism which permit respect for, but not adoration of, human achievement, however impressive its proportions. But, of course, by not settling for common sense, there is always the danger of surrender to superstition and wishful thinking.

This strain in American culture is exemplified in Ralph Waldo Emerson; his articulation of his preference for a poetic rather than scientific conception of the world, made his a household name. His spiritual colleagues were the Neoplatonists, Coleridge, Carlyle, Wordsworth, and the Swedish mystic Swedenborg, whose thought also greatly influenced the father of William and Henry James. Emerson's Transcendentalism, the belief in a mystical unity of everything and the immanence of God, all somehow accessible to individual intuition, motivated his famous essay "The Over-Soul." He declared how he was compelled to acknowledge at every moment a divine origin of things, which he described as "that Unity, that Over-Soul, within which every man's particular being is contained and made one with all other." The whole is the soul, and it is immanent in each man; the soul is not an organ or function, "but a light." One's own soul is enveloped by the Over-Soul, the spirit of the whole. Its nature contradicts much that we appear to learn from ordinary experience. Our senses restrict us to a world of illusion, of vulgar reality. "The landscape, the figures, Boston, London, are facts as fugitive as any institution past, or any whiff of mist or smoke, and so is society and so is the world." The higher reality is spiritual and known directly by the soul in its mystical union with the Over-Soul which is beyond the space and time of the everyday world.

For Emerson, Transcendentalism replaced inherited Unitarianism; metaphysics substituted for traditional religion. His glorification of the individual, of the individual's ability to intuit directly the spiritual reality of the Over-Soul and one's participation in it, was simultaneously to define for the individual a *metaphysical context*. The world is more than it seems to ordinary experience; that world in which we move is pervaded by the spiritual unity of the Eternal One. This insight is available to the ordinary man, though not to ordinary perceptual experience; indeed, there is a "certain wisdom of humanity which is common to the greatest men with the lowest, and which our ordinary education often labors to silence and obstruct." Emerson believed, as George Bernard Shaw was to put it for a subsequent generation, that the difference between a genius and the ordinary man is, after all, very slight. "The learned and the studious of thought have no monopoly of wisdom," said Emerson. "The simplest person who in his integrity worships God, becomes God," and if one is to discover what the great God declares, one must " 'go into his closet and shut the door,' as Jesus said." Emerson's celebrated optimism, his defense of the "extraordinary hopes of man" born in mystical or poetic moments, affirmed the individual's right to set his own metaphysical ideal and not to be put off by the appeals of science and common sense to ordinary experience. Individual intuition is always held to be the final court of appeal.

William James was influenced by Emerson, who was a family friend, and even more so by his own father, in trying to find a place for religion in an increasingly scientific era. Much of James's psychology and philosophy was motivated by the desire to construct a metaphysical outlook which would either support a religious outlook or take its place. In the end, he decided for a "metaphysics of experience" which, while not capable of justifying religious beliefs, might yet show how they are *possibly* true. In any experience, he said, there is a "center," in clear focus, surrounded by a "fringe" or "more," which is only dimly or not at all apprehended. Any given experience includes "more" than one can be consciously aware of. One cannot assign a boundary to "an experience" in the same way in which one can describe a specific object in that experience. The question of the scope of one's *experience*, its extent and its content, cannot be answered as one can answer the same question when referring to the extent and content of *consciousness*. This fact suggested the possibility that our experiences radiate beyond the limits of our consciousness, perhaps even merging with other experiences, but especially perhaps with a wider experience or self deserving to be called God.

God, considered as a wider, more inclusive, experience with which individual experiences blend in a way not consciously inspectable, is very similar to Emerson's Over-Soul. James appreciated this, but he noted that Emerson had spoken of the Over-Soul as being "impersonal," and James preferred to think of his Deity as a personal self, sharing concerns with humans. He once observed, "Transcendentalists are fond of the term 'Over-Soul,' but as a rule they use it in an intellectualist sense, as meaning only a medium of communion. 'God' is a causal agent as well as a medium of communion, and that is the aspect which I wish to emphasize."

James came to believe in what he called a "finite" or "limited" god, unlike the traditional God of the Judaic-Christian tradition. Although he believed religion to be a matter of personal experience, he apparently never claimed to have experienced the divine, but he thought some of his experiences might be explained by the divine. These were what he called "saving" or "regenerative" experiences, in which one feels a sudden surge of new vitality and energy, an impressive subjective phenomenon, especially in those moments when one's spirit is so low that life itself seems hopeless. It seemed to James that the origin of this energy and vitality might be the wider self or God—that "more" with which our wider experience is in contact, beyond the limits of what we can consciously register. The wider self is thus the concept of a personal source of concern and assistance.

James, like Emerson, preached a philosophy of individualism. He attempted to show how the individual, understanding the metaphysical character of even ordinary experience, could appreciate its possible religious significance. Religion and a metaphysics interested in the religious are expressions of the emotional yearnings created by poignant experiences. They begin in individual experience and are not essentially social in origin. As James put it, "The pivot round which the religious life, as we have traced it, revolves, is the interest of the individual in his private personal destiny. Religion, in short, is a monumental chapter in the history of human egotism . . . the religious individual tells you that the divine meets him on the basis of his personal concerns."

But it can be argued that the nature of the metaphysical context in which individuals find themselves cannot be determined until the question what *individuality* itself is is answered. Josiah Royce, James's colleague and friend at Harvard, contended that James's theory was exaggeratedly individualistic, its conception of the person's context too atomistic, isolated, fragmentary. The truth is rather that, once individuality is recognized for what it really is, the person's metaphysical situation is seen to be *communal* at the outset.

Ordinary opinion assumes, Royce observed, that each person's experiences are necessarily private; no one can witness the inner experience of another, and this privacy is not an empirical but a logical necessity; to share your headache or nostalgia, I should have to be identical with you. In this view, "Each of us lives within the charmed circle of his own conscious will and meaning—each of us is more or less clearly the object of his own inspection, but is hopelessly beyond the direct observation of his fellows." It is then an easy step to conclude that each person is, in his *choices* too, essentially private and thus *morally* independent of other people; in fact, it might be urged that it is precisely our choices which individuate us.

But this usual account, Royce argued, fails to comprehend the concept of an individual as a full-fledged self or person. A person is not a simple datum given to introspection; a person is not a momentary consciousness. A full-fledged self includes a past, partly remembered, largely interpreted; thus, "my idea of myself is an interpretation of my past—linked also with an interpretation of my hopes and intentions as to my future." One's concept of oneself, then, is mainly an interpretation, ranging beyond one's present private experiences, "an interpretation or the sense, of the tendency of the coherence, and of the value of a life to which belongs the memory of its own past." Community occurs when different individuals connect their private experiences with an identical past, when they share the same interpretation, or *community of memory*, of the past. In this way, one's concept of oneself, which necessarily includes his interpretation of the shared past, includes reference to others who share that interpretation. Community occurs, not on the level of headaches and private sensations, but on the level of interpretation, which connects the present with a *social past* and a *social future*. Consequently, since one's concept of one's *present* self involves that same interpretation, referring to a social past and a social future, one's present self is essentially a social self. The metaphysical context in which the individual lives is not that of private nostalgias but of social conceptions, including the concept of one's own being in a world with others.

Alfred North Whitehead also sought a metaphysics confirming unity rather than individual isolation. Philosophy does society a service in displaying the metaphysics of individuality, particularly how it is in the nature of the individual to be valued insofar as he *transcends* himself. What civilizations need, Whitehead declared, is to exclude the "restless egotism with which they have often in fact been pursued." Society needs a binding principle, which will connect the other necessary features of a good community—Truth, Beauty, Adventure, and Art. That principle of harmony, Whitehead said, is the concept of Peace. A civilized society is one whose people "participate in the five qualities—Truth, Beauty, Adventure, Art, Peace." What he meant by "Peace," he admitted, was hard to define, but what could be said is this:

> It is not a hope for the future, nor is it an interest in present details. It is a broadening of feeling due to the emergence of some deep metaphysical insight, unverbalized and yet momentous in its coordination of values. Its first effect is the removal of the stress of acquisitive feeling arising from the soul's preoccupation with itself. Thus Peace carries with it a surpassing of personality . . . It is a sense that fineness of achievement is as it were a key unlocking treasures that the narrow nature of things would keep remote. There is thus involved a grasp of infinitude, an appeal beyond boundaries. Its emotional effect is the subsidence of turbulence which inhibits. More accurately, it preserves the springs of energy, and at the same time masters them for the avoidance of paralyzing distractions.

If a society were composed of people having experiences and feelings which they were disposed to describe in such fashion, then that society would be dynamically peaceful. Like Royce, Whitehead believed that the individual only comes into possession of the concept of himself as a full-fledged person when he sees himself, beyond the immediate occasion, as a social creature sharing with others an interest in a mutual past and future. What is especially obligatory is the identification of one's purposes with ideals beyond one's own limitations and the appreciation that one's context is a "unity of many occasions with a value beyond that of any individual occasion." One understands his own metaphysical context as something which enlarges the value of being an individual when one's own consciousness is enlarged by one's unity with others; this is to understand the value of belonging, not only to a community, but also to a whole civilization.

Metaphysics includes the attempt to explain, where the answers of science and common sense for some reason do not suffice, discrepancies between appearance and reality and the confusions found in those duped by the discrepancies. George Santayana, in surveying the world as it teetered on the brink of the First World War, saw moral confusion everywhere. This was partly due, he thought, to the fact that Christian civilization was in process of being succeeded by an "emancipated, atheistic, international democracy," which represented the combined assertion of the "unconquerable mind of the East, the pagan past, the industrial socialistic future." It is idle to deprecate or lament this, Santayana noted, because we are already caught up in the vitality, however schizophrenic its consequences, communicated by the mammoth transition. The change to a new era actually appeals to something deep in our animal nature.

Nevertheless, despite the exhilaration felt when participating in the takeover by a fresh civilization, the price is thorough moral confusion. "Never perhaps were men so like one another and so divided within themselves." In Santayana's judgment, since traditional values had been suspended, individuals were now internally insecure as the twentieth century took off; their insecurity extended to fundamental moral principles, to abstract subjects, and to politics. For example, Liberalism had originated as a defense of liberty but was now proposing controls over every segment of the economy. Quantity counts more than quality, and the principle of the happiness for the greatest number is in danger, as the Founding Fathers had feared, of establishing a tyranny of the majority. Another form in which moral confusion shows itself is in Nationalism. Although the age seemed to be one aimed at linking all men and nations, breaking class, racial, and national barriers, everywhere new patriotisms and nationalisms were erupting. One explanation, according to Santayana, is that man, as an animal needing ideals, reaches out confusedly, in prejudice and ignorance, to Nationalism for support. But, he suggested, there is a metaphysical explanation which provides a deeper understanding of the moral confusion characterizing the new age. People will never understand such anomalies until they

. . . accustom themselves to a theory to which they have always turned a deaf ear, because, though simple and true, it is materialistic: namely, that mind is not the cause of our actions but an effect, collateral with our actions, of bodily growth and organization. It may therefore easily come about that the thoughts of men, tested by the principles that seem to rule their conduct, may be related, or irrelevant, or premonitory. . . .

A materialistic theory of mind shows how man's metaphysical context is calculated to make his ideals belated and premonitory at once, both behind and ahead of his times; moral confusion is thus inevitable.

Santayana thought that the Pragmatism and Radical Empiricism of his Harvard colleague William James, and the Vitalism of Henri Bergson (two philosophies similar enough to make James and Bergson intellectual friends), were further examples of the new confusion. He considered these philosophical innovations merely "romantic anarchy," the logical conclusion of the tradition of Locke, Berkeley, and Hume in relying too exclusively upon subjectivity in the quest for philosophic understanding. The philosophies of James and Bergson reach "the extreme of self-concentration and self-expansion, the perfect identity and involution of everything in oneself. And such indeed is the inevitable goal of the malicious theory of knowledge . . . remote as that goal may be from the boyish naturalism and innocent intent of many of its pupils."

Pragmatism, for Santayana, was but one more symptom of the fact that reason was abdicating in the face of lustier forces. Cruder powers, he claimed, have substituted the ideal of letting life run with the swiftest wind for that of constraint, firm purpose, and rational calm. What can the Materialism and Naturalism of Santayana say, looking at this spectacle, as a forecast? This question raises another: "These are but gusts of doctrine; yet they prove that the spirit is not dead in the lull between its seasons of steady blowing. Who knows which of them may not gather force presently and carry the mind of the coming age steadily before it?"

Santayana's pose as the passive but sensitive spectator of an irrational world creating irrational philosophies had few American imitators. Yet his assessment of Pragmatism was shared by many, who were troubled by James's apparent use of it to justify one's believing whatever he pleased and by James's defense of subjectivity in philosophic method.

John Dewey shared Santayana's Naturalism and, accordingly, was unsympathetic to James's linkage of Pragmatic methodology with religious belief. But Dewey, of course, did not appreciate the negative evaluation offered by Santayana of Pragmatism as such. For Dewey, the important, revolutionary metaphysical implication of Pragmatism was the value it placed upon consequences and the future, no longer upon antecedent circumstances as a dictatorial past. Dewey wrote in *Philosophy and Civilization* (1931): "And this taking into consideration of the future takes us to the conception of a universe whose evolution is not finished, of a universe which is still, in James's term, 'in the making,' 'in the process of becoming,' of a universe up to a certain point still plastic." A universe whose future is truly open, which is undetermined by the past, a universe whose future one's intelligence and deed could shape—this was what Peirce, James, and Dewey emphasized. What was held to be important in Pragmatism was not, as Santayana pictured it, simply a restless delight in change for its own sake but rather its basis for hoping that a better future was within human power to produce. The delight occurred in thinking that one might oneself contribute to that end.

Dewey emphasized the British and European roots of all aspects of American thought, including Pragmatism, but acknowledged that there was yet an American difference:

> One-sided and egoistic individualism in American life has left its imprint on our practices. For better or worse, depending on the point of view, it has transformed the esthetic and fixed individualism of the old European culture into an active individualism. But the idea of a society of individuals is not foreign to American thought; it penetrates even our current individualism which is unreflective and brutal. And the individual which American thought idealized is not an individual *per se*, an individual fixed in isolation and set up for himself, but an individual who develops in a natural and human environment.

Pragmatism, according to Dewey, is distinctively American in its encouragement of a more *active* individualism than was permitted in the European past. The goal of Pragmatism is not egotistic. It is, instead, the simultaneous insistence upon the worth of individuality *per se*, the capacity of the individual to make genuine contributions in fashioning the future, and the recognition of the increasing need for cooperative action between individuals for meeting mounting numbers of social problems.

To say that American culture has gradually adopted the metaphysics of either Pragmatism or of Naturalism, however, would be rash.

Possibly these philosophies have gained ground in the nation's life, especially in developing a frame of mind which is better suited for negotiating portentous disputes, in collective bargaining, in politics, in international diplomacy. Pragmatism may be the word for the American attitude as to how one best threads one's way through the daily disagreements. Possibly Pragmatism and Naturalism (not at all identical, of course) have won more devotees as personal metaphysics.

But the fact is that the metaphysics of religion is, as it was at the beginning, still very much the spirit of American culture. And any increase in the number of Naturalists is probably matched by those consulting astrology magazines. Insofar as Pragmatism has a metaphysics which declares the difference between appearance and reality, suggesting the limitations of human intellect to fathom it all, then the religious and esoteric strains in American life respond; insofar as Pragmatism presents itself as eternally optimistic about an endless future, then the same dominant elements nod their heads.

The individual in this culture does not promise, within the near future, to cease defining his *personal* metaphysical context in terms of either a religious or metaphysical optimism. What has been called the American innocence, persistently undismayed by anything the world shows, remains the most recognizable feature of the American outlook.

RALPH WALDO EMERSON

Ralph Waldo Emerson (1830–82), son of the minister of the First Church of Boston (Unitarian), became one of America's most influential essayists and poets. Graduating from Harvard, he continued his studies at Harvard Divinity School but, because of ill health, was compelled to interrupt his work to recuperate. He assumed the pastorship of the Old North Church in Boston in 1829, but resigned three years later because of his views, which the congregation found too controversial. After meeting Carlyle, Wordsworth, and Coleridge on a trip to Europe, his interest in Transcendentalism became more pronounced. His essays presenting this New England philosophical version of Kantianism brought him into prominence. In addition to his essays, including those pleading for both an independent American culture and an independent American individual, and his popular poems, Emerson's antislavery activities also made him a celebrity. The following selection is taken from the essay "The Over-Soul" (in his *Essays*, first series, 1841), and is an excellent statement of the basic ideas of his Transcendentalism.

The Soul in Man

There is a difference between one and another hour of life in their authority and subsequent effect. Our faith comes in moments; our vice is habitual. Yet there is a depth in those brief moments which constrains us to ascribe more reality to them than to all other experiences. For this reason the argument which is always forthcoming to silence those who conceive extraordinary hopes of man, namely the appeal to experience, is for ever invalid and vain. We give up the past to the objector, and yet we hope. He must explain this hope. We grant that human life is mean, but how did we find out that it was mean? What is the ground of this uneasiness of ours; of this old discontent? What is the universal sense of want and ignorance, but the fine innuendo by which the soul makes its enormous claim? Why do men feel that the natural history of man has never been written, but he is always leaving behind what you have said of him, and it becomes old, and books of metaphysics worthless? The philosophy of six thousand years has not searched the chambers and magazines of the soul. In its experiments there has always remained, in the last analysis, a residuum it could not resolve. Man is a stream whose source is hidden. Our being is descending into us from we know not whence. The most exact calculator has no prescience that somewhat incalculable may not balk the very next moment. I am constrained every moment to acknowledge a higher origin for events than the will I call mine.

As with events, so is it with thoughts. When I watch that flowing river, which, out of regions I see not, pours for a season its streams into me, I see that I am a pensioner; not a cause but a surprised spectator of this ethereal water; that I desire and look up and put myself in the attitude of reception, but from some alien energy the visions come.

The Supreme Critic on the errors of the past and the present, and the only prophet of that which must be, is that great nature in which we rest as the earth lies in the soft arms of the atmosphere; that Unity, that Over-Soul, within which every man's particular being is contained and made one with all other; that common heart of which all sincere conversation is the worship, to which all right action is submission; that over-powering reality which confutes our tricks and talents, and constrains every one to pass for what he is, and to speak from his character and not from his tongue, and which evermore tends to pass into our thought and hand and become wisdom and virtue and power and beauty. We live in succession, in division, in parts, in particles. Meantime within man is the soul of the whole; the wise silence; the universal beauty, to which every part and particle is equally related; the eternal ONE. And this deep power in which we exist and whose beatitude is all accessible to us, is not only self-sufficing and perfect in every hour, but the act of seeing and the thing seen, the seer and the spectacle, the subject and the object, are one. We see the world piece by piece, as the sun, the moon, the animal, the tree; but the whole, of which these are the shining parts, is the soul. Only by the vision of that Wisdom can the horoscope of the ages be read, and by falling back on our better thoughts, by yielding to the spirit of prophecy which is innate in every man, we can know what it saith. Every man's words who speaks from that life must sound vain to those who do not dwell in the same thought on their own part. I dare not speak for it. My words do not carry its august sense; they fall short and cold. Only itself can inspire whom it will, and behold! their speech shall be lyrical, and sweet, and universal as the rising of the wind. Yet I desire, even by profane words, if I may not use sacred, to indicate the heaven of this deity and to report what hints I have collected of the transcendent simplicity and energy of the Highest Law.

If we consider what happens in conversation, in reveries, in remorse, in times of passion, in surprises, in the instructions of dreams, wherein often we see ourselves in masquerade,—the droll disguises only magnifying and enhancing a real element and forcing it on our distant notice,—we shall catch many hints that will broaden and lighten into knowledge of the secret of nature. All goes to show that the soul in man is not an organ, but animates and exercises all the organs; is not a function, like the power of memory, of calculation, of comparison, but uses these as hands and feet; is not a faculty, but a light; is not the intellect or the will, but the master of the intellect and the will; is the background of our being, in which they lie,—an immensity not possessed and that cannot be possessed. From within or from behind, a light shines through us upon things and makes us aware that we are nothing, but the light is all. A man is the façade of a temple wherein all wisdom and all good abide. What we commonly call man, the eating, drinking, planting, counting man, does not, as we know him, represent himself, but misrepresents himself. Him we do not respect, but the soul, whose organ he is, would he let it appear through his action, would make our knees bend. When it breathes through his intellect, it is genius; when it breathes through his will, it is virtue; when it flows through his affection, it is love. And the blindness of the intellect begins when it would be something of itself. The weakness of the will begins when the individual would be something of himself. All reform aims in some one particular to let the soul have its way through us; in other words, to engage us to obey.

Of this pure nature every man is at some time sensible. Language cannot paint it with his colors. It is too subtile. It is undefinable, unmeasurable; but we know that it pervades and contains us. We know that all spiritual being is in man. A wise old proverb says, "God comes to see us without bell;" that is, as there is no screen or ceiling between our heads and the infinite heavens, so is there no bar or wall in the soul, where man, the effect, ceases, and God, the cause, begins. The walls are taken away. We lie open on one side to the deeps of spiritual nature, to the attributes of God. Justice we see and know, Love, Freedom, Power. These natures no man ever got above, but they tower over us, and most in the moment when our interests tempt us to wound them.

The sovereignty of this nature whereof we speak is made known by its independency of those limitations which circumscribe us on every hand. The soul circumscribes all things. As I have said, it contradicts all experience. In like manner it abolishes time and space. The influence of the senses has in most men overpowered the mind to that degree that the walls of time and space have come to look real and insurmountable; and to speak with levity of these limits is, in the world, the sign of insanity. Yet time and space are but inverse measures of the force of the soul. The spirit sports with time,—

> "Can crowd eternity into an hour,
> Or stretch an hour to eternity."

We are often made to feel that there is another youth and age than that which is measured from the year of our natural birth. Some thoughts always find us young, and keep us so. Such a thought is the love of the universal and eternal beauty. Every man parts from that contemplation with the feeling that it rather belongs to ages than to mortal life. The last activity of the intellectual powers redeems us in a degree from the conditions of time. In sickness, in languor, give us a strain of poetry or a profound sentence, and we are refreshed; or produce a volume of Plato or Shakspeare, or remind us of their names, and instantly we come into a feeling of longevity. See how the deep divine thought reduces centuries and millenniums, and makes itself present through all ages. Is the teaching of Christ less effective now than it was when first his mouth was opened? The emphasis of facts and persons in my thought has nothing to do with time. And so always the soul's scale is one, the scale of the senses and the understanding is another. Before the revelations of the soul, Time, Space and Nature shrink away. In common speech we refer all things to time, as we habitually refer the immensely sundered stars to one concave sphere. And so we say that the Judgment is distant or near, that the Millennium approaches, that a day of certain political, moral, social reforms is at hand, and the like, when we mean that in the nature of things one of the facts we contemplate is external and fugitive, and the other is permanent and connate with the soul. The things we now esteem fixed shall, one by one, detach themselves like ripe fruit from our experience, and fall. The wind shall blow them none knows whither. The landscape, the figures, Boston, London, are facts as fugitive as any institution past, or any whiff of mist or smoke, and so is society, and so is the world. The soul looketh steadily forwards, creating a world before her, leaving worlds behind her. She has no dates, nor rites, nor persons, nor specialties nor men. The soul knows only the soul; the web of events is the flowing robe in which she is clothed.

One mode of the divine teaching is the incarnation of the spirit in a form,—in forms, like my own. I live in society; with persons who answer to thoughts in my own mind, or express a certain obedience to the great instincts to which I live. I see its presence to them. I am certified of a common nature; and these other souls, these separated selves, draw me as nothing else can. They stir in me the new emotions we call passion; of love, hatred, fear, admiration, pity; thence come conversation, competition, persuasion, cities and war. Persons are supplementary to the primary teaching of the soul. In youth we are made for persons. Childhood and youth see all the world in them. But the larger experience of man discovers the identical nature appearing through them all. Persons themselves acquaint us with the impersonal. In all conversation between two persons tacit reference is made, as to a third party, to a common nature. That third party or common nature is not social; it is impersonal; is God. And so in groups where debate is earnest, and especially on high questions, the company become aware that the thought rises to an equal level in all bosoms, that all have a spiritual property in what was said, as well as the sayer. They all become wiser than they were. It arches over them like a temple, this unity of thought in which every heart beats with nobler sense of power and duty, and thinks and acts with unusual solemnity. All are conscious of attaining to a higher self-possession. It shines for all. There is a certain wisdom of humanity which is common to the greatest men with the lowest, and which our ordinary education often labors to silence and obstruct. The mind is one, and the best minds, who love truth for its own sake, think much less of property in truth. They accept it thankfully everywhere, and do not label or stamp it with any man's name, for it is theirs long beforehand, and from eternity. The learned and the studious of thought have no monopoly of wisdom. Their violence of direction in some degree disqualifies them to think truly. We owe many valuable observations to people who are not very acute or profound, and who say the thing without effort which we want and have long been hunting in vain. The action of the soul is oftener in that which is felt and left unsaid than in that which is said in any conversation. It broods over every society, and they unconsciously seek for it in each other. We know better than we do. We do not yet possess ourselves, and we know at the same time that we are much more. I feel the same truth how often in my trivial conversation with my neighbors, that somewhat higher in each of us overlooks this by-play, and Jove nods to Jove from behind each of us.

Men descend to meet. In their habitual and mean service to the world, for which they forsake their native nobleness, they resemble those Arabian sheiks who dwell in mean houses and affect an external poverty, to escape the rapacity of the Pacha, and reserve all their display of wealth for their interior and guarded retirements.

*　　*　　*

Ineffable is the union of man and God in every act of the soul. The simplest person who in his integrity worships God, becomes God; yet for ever and ever the influx of this better and universal self is new and unsearchable. It inspires awe and astonishment. How dear, how soothing to man, arises the idea of God, peopling the lonely place, effacing the scars of our mistakes and disappointments! When we have broken our god of tradition and ceased from our god of rhetoric, then may God fire the heart with his presence. It is the doubling of the heart itself, nay, the infinite enlargement of the heart with a power of growth to a new infinity on every side. It inspires in man an infallible trust. He has not the conviction, but the sight, that the best is the true, and may in that thought easily dismiss all particular uncertainties and fears, and adjourn to the sure revelation of time the solution of his private riddles. He is sure that his welfare is dear to the heart of being. In the presence of law to his mind he is overflowed with a reliance so universal that it sweeps away all cherished hopes and the most stable projects of mortal condition in its flood. He believes that he cannot escape from his good. The things that are really for thee gravitate to thee. You are running to seek your friend. Let your feet run, but your mind need not. If you do not find him, will you not acquiesce that it is best you should not find him? for there is a power, which, as it is in you, is in him also, and could therefore very well bring you together, if it were for the best. You are preparing with eagerness to go and render a service to which your talent and your taste invite you, the love of men and the hope of fame. Has it not occurred to you that you have no right to go, unless you are equally willing to be prevented from going? O, believe, as thou livest, that every sound that is spoken over the round world, which thou oughtest to hear, will vibrate on thine ear! Every proverb, every book, every byword that belongs to thee for aid or comfort, shall surely come home through open or winding passages. Every friend whom not thy fantastic will but the great and tender heart in thee craveth, shall lock thee in his embrace. And this because the heart in thee is the heart of all; not a valve, not a wall, not an intersection is there anywhere in nature, but one blood rolls uninterruptedly an endless circulation through all men, as the water of the globe is all one sea, and, truly seen, its tide is one.

Let man then earn the revelation of all nature and all thought to his heart; this, namely: that the Highest dwells with him; that the sources of nature are in his own mind, if the sentiment of duty is there. But if he would know what the great God speaketh, he must "go into his closet and shut the door," as Jesus said. God will not make himself manifest to cowards. He must greatly listen to himself, withdrawing himself from all the accents of other men's devotion. Even their prayers are hurtful to him, until he have made his own. Our religion vulgarly stands on numbers of believers. When ever the appeal is made,—no matter how indirectly,—to numbers, proclamation is then and there made that religion is not. He that finds God a sweet enveloping thought to him never counts his company. When I sit in that presence, who shall dare to come in? When I rest in perfect humility, when I burn with pure love, what can Calvin or Swedenborg say?

It makes no difference whether the appeal is to numbers or to one. The faith that stands on authority is not faith. The reliance on authority measures the decline of religion, the withdrawal of the soul. The position men have given to Jesus, now for many centuries of history, is a position of authority. It characterizes themselves. It cannot alter the eternal facts. Great is the soul, and plain. It is no flatterer, it is no follower; it never appeals from itself. It believes in itself. Before the immense possibilities of man all mere experience, all past biography, however spotless and sainted, shrinks away. Before that heaven which our presentiments foreshow us, we cannot easily praise any form of life we have seen or read of. We not only affirm that we have few great men, but, absolutely speaking, that we have none; that we have no history, no record of any character or mode of living that entirely contents us. The saints and demigods whom history worships we are constrained to accept with a grain of allowance. Though in our lonely hours we draw a new strength out of their memory, yet, pressed on our attention, as they are by the thoughtless and customary, they fatigue and invade. The soul gives itself, alone, original and pure, to the Lonely, Original and Pure, who, on that condition, gladly inhabits, leads and speaks through it. Then is it glad, young and nimble. It is not wise, but it sees through all things. It is not called religious, but it is innocent. It calls the light its own, and feels that the grass grows and the stone falls by a law inferior to, and dependent on, its nature. Behold, it saith, I am born into the great, the universal mind. I, the imperfect, adore my own Perfect. I am somehow receptive of the great soul, and thereby I do overlook the sun and the stars and feel them to be the fair accidents and effects which change and pass. More and more the surges of everlasting nature enter into me, and I become public and human in my regards and actions. So come I to live in thoughts and act with energies which are immortal. Thus revering the soul, and learning, as the ancient said, that "its beauty is immense," man will come to see that the world is the perennial miracle which the soul worketh, and be less astonished at particular wonders; he will learn that there is no profane history; that all history is sacred; that the universe is represented in an atom, in a moment of time. He will weave no longer a spotted life of shreds and patches, but he will live with a divine unity. He will cease from what is base and frivolous in his life and be content with all places and with any service he can render. He will calmly front the morrow in the negligency of that trust which carries God with it and so hath already the whole future in the bottom of the heart.

WILLIAM JAMES

William James inherited from his father, Henry James, Sr., a profound desire to establish the plausibility of religious belief upon what can be found in experience itself, apart from revelation and Scripture. James, at the risk of being considered a crank by his scientific colleagues, was one of the pioneers in the American Society for Psychical Research. Much of his philosophy and psychology was a defense of the religious component of experience. This selection, from Lecture XX and the Postscript in *The Varieties of Religious Experience* (1902), provides one of the clearest explanations of how William James connected his psychology of experience with his philosophy of religion.

Religion Through Experience

Summing up in the broadest possible way the characteristics of the religious life, as we have found them, it includes the following beliefs:—

1.   That the visible world is part of a more spiritual universe from which it draws its chief significance;

2.   That union or harmonious relation with that higher universe is our true end;

3.   That prayer or inner communion with the spirit thereof—be that spirit 'God' or 'law'— is a process wherein work is really done, and spiritual energy flows in and produces effects, psychological or material, within the phenomenal world.

Religion includes also the following psychological characteristics:—

4.   A new zest which adds itself like a gift to life, and takes the form either of lyrical enchantment or of appeal to earnestness and heroism.

5.   An assurance of safety and a temper of peace, and, in relation to others, a preponderance of loving affections.

*   *   *

The pivot round which the religious life, as we have traced it, revolves, is the interest of the individual in his private personal destiny. Religion, in short, is a monumental chapter in the history of human egotism. The gods believed in—whether by crude savages or by men disciplined intellectually—agree with each other in recognizing personal calls. Religious thought is carried on in terms of personality, this being, in the world of religion, the one fundamental fact. Today, quite as much as at any previous age, the religious individual tells you that the divine meets him on the basis of his personal concerns.

Science, on the other hand, has ended by utterly repudiating the personal point of view. She catalogues her elements and records her laws indifferent as to what purpose may be shown forth by them, and constructs her theories quite careless of their bearing on human anxieties and fates. Though the scientist may individually nourish a religion, and be a theist in his irresponsible hours, the days are over when it could be said that for Science herself the heavens declare the glory of God and the firmament showeth his handiwork. Our solar system, with its harmonies, is seen now as but one passing case of a certain sort of moving equilibrium in the heavens, realized by a local accident in an appalling wilderness of worlds where no life can exist. In a span of time which as a cosmic interval will count but as an hour, it will have ceased to be. The Darwinian notion of chance production, and subsequent destruction, speedy or deferred, applies to the largest as well as to the smallest facts. It is impossible, in the present temper of the scientific imagination, to find in the driftings of the cosmic atoms, whether they work on the universal or on the particular scale, anything but a kind of aimless weather, doing and undoing, achieving no proper history, and leaving no result. Nature has no one distinguishable ultimate tendency with which it is possible to feel a sympathy. In the vast rhythm of her processes, as the scientific mind now follows them, she appears to cancel herself.

* * *

. . . The God whom science recognizes must be a God of universal laws exclusively, a God who does a wholesale, not a retail business. He cannot accommodate his processes to the convenience of individuals. The bubbles on the foam which coats a stormy sea are floating episodes, made and unmade by the forces of the wind and water. Our private selves are like those bubbles,—epiphenomena, as Clifford, I believe, ingeniously called them; their destinies weigh nothing and determine nothing in the world's irremediable currents of events.

You see how natural it is, from this point of view, to treat religion as a mere survival, for religion does in fact perpetuate the traditions of the most primeval thought. To coerce the spiritual powers, or to square them and get them on our side, was, during enormous tracts of time, the one great object in our dealings with the natural world. For our ancestors, dreams, hallucinations, revelations, and cock-and-bull stories were inextricably mixed with facts. Up to a comparatively recent date such distinctions as those between what has been verified and what is only conjectured, between the impersonal and the personal aspects of existence, were hardly suspected or conceived. . . .

* * *

The world of our experience consists at all times of two parts, an objective and subjective part, of which the former may be incalculably more extensive than the latter, and yet the latter can never be omitted or suppressed. The objective part is the sum total of whatsoever at any given time we may be thinking of, the subjective part is the inner 'state' in which the thinking comes to pass. What we think of may be enormous,—the cosmic times and spaces, for example,—whereas the inner state may be the most fugitive and paltry activity of mind. Yet the cosmic objects, so far as the experience yields them, are but ideal pictures of something whose existence we do not inwardly possess but only point at outwardly, while the inner state is our very experience itself; its reality and that of our experience are one. A conscious field *plus* its object as felt or thought of *plus* an attitude towards the object *plus* the sense of a self to whom the attitude belongs—such a concrete bit of personal experience may be a small bit, but it is a solid bit as long as it lasts; not hollow, not a mere abstract element of experience, such as the 'object' is when taken all alone. It is a *full* fact, even though it be an insignificant fact; it is of the *kind* to which all realities whatsoever must belong; the motor currents of the world run through the like of it; it is on the line connecting real events with real events. That unsharable feeling which each one of us has of the pinch of his individual destiny as he privately feels it rolling out on fortune's wheel may be disparaged for its egotism, may be sneered at as unscientific, but it is the one thing that fills up the measure of our concrete actuality. . . .

If this be true, it is absurd for science to say that the egotistic elements of experience should be suppressed. The axis of reality runs solely through the egotistic places,—they are strung upon it like so many beads. To describe the world with all the various feelings of the individual pinch of destiny, all the various spiritual attitudes, left out from the description—they being as describable as anything else—would be something like offering a printed bill of fare as the equivalent for a solid meal. Religion makes no such blunder. The individual's religion may be egotistic, and those private realities which it keeps in touch with may be narrow enough; but at any rate it always remains infinitely less hollow and abstract, as far as it goes, than a science which prides itself on taking no account of anything private at all.

*   *   *

You see now why I have been so individualistic throughout these lectures, and why I have seemed so bent on rehabilitating the element of feeling in religion and subordinating its intellectual part. Individuality is founded in feeling; and the recesses of feeling, the darker, blinder strata of character, are the only places in the world in which we catch real fact in the making, and directly perceive how events happen, and how work is actually done. Compared with this world of living individualized feelings, the world of generalized objects which the intellect contemplates is without solidity or life. As in stereoscopic or kinetoscopic pictures seen outside the instrument, the third dimension, the movement, the vital element, are not there. We get a beautiful picture of an express train supposed to be moving, but where in the picture, as I have heard a friend say, is the energy or the fifty miles an hour?

Let us agree, then, that Religion, occupying herself with personal destinies and keeping thus in contact with the only absolute realities which we know, must necessarily play an eternal part in human history. The next thing to decide is what she reveals about those destinies, or whether indeed she reveals anything distinct enough to be considered a general message to mankind. We have done as you see, with our preliminaries, and our final summing up can now begin.

*   *   *

The next step is to characterize the feelings. To what psychological order do they belong?

The resultant outcome of them is in any case what Kant calls a 'sthenic' affection, an excitement of the cheerful, expansive, 'dynamogenic' order which, like any tonic, freshens our vital powers. In almost every lecture, but especially in the lectures on Conversion and on Saintliness, we have seen how this emotion overcomes temperamental melancholy and imparts endurance to the Subject, or a zest, or a meaning or an enchantment and glory to the common objects of life. The name of 'faith-state,' by which Professor Leuba designates it, is a good one. It is a biological as well as a psychological condition, and Tolstoy is absolutely accurate in classing faith among the forces *by which men live*. The total absence of it, anhedonia, means collapse.

The faith-state may hold a very minimum of intellectual content. We saw examples of this in those sudden raptures of the divine presence, or in such mystical seizures as Dr. Bucke described. It may be a mere vague enthusiasm, half spiritual, half vital, a courage, and a feeling that great and wondrous things are in the air.

When, however, a positive intellectual content is associated with a faith-state, it gets invincibly stamped in upon belief, and this explains the passionate loyalty of religious persons everywhere to the minutest details of their so widely differing creeds. Taking creeds and faith-state together, as forming 'religions,' and treating these as purely subjective phenomena, without regard to the question of their 'truth,' we are obliged, on account of their extraordinary influence upon action and endurance, to class them amongst the most important biological functions of mankind. Their stimulant and anæsthetic effect is so great that Professor Leuba, in a recent article, goes so far as to say that so long as men can *use* their God, they care very little who he is, or even whether he is at all. "The truth of the matter can be put," says Leuba, "in this way: *God is not known, he is not understood: he is used*—sometimes as meat-purveyor, sometimes as moral support, sometimes as friend, sometimes as an object of love. If he proves himself useful, the religious consciousness asks for no more than that. Does God really exist? How does he exist? What is he? are so many irrelevant questions. Not God, but life, more life, a larger, richer, more satisfying life is, in the last analysis, the end of religion. The love of life, at any and every level of development, is the religious impulse."

At this purely subjective rating, therefore, Religion must be considered vindicated in a certain way from the attacks of her critics. It would seem that she cannot be a mere anachronism and survival, but must exert a permanent function, whether she be with or without intellectual content, and whether, if she have any, it be true or false.

We must next pass beyond the point of view of merely subjective utility, and make inquiry into the intellectual content itself.

First, is there, under all the discrepancies of the creeds, a common nucleus to which they bear their testimony unanimously?

And second, ought we to consider the testimony true?

I will take up the first question first, and answer it immediately in the affirmative. The warring gods and formulas of the various religions do indeed cancel each other, but there is a certain uniform deliverance in which religions all appear to meet. It consists of two parts:—

1. An uneasiness; and
2. Its solution.

1. The uneasiness, reduced to its simplest terms, is a sense that there is *something wrong about us* as we naturally stand.

2. The solution is a sense that *we are saved from the wrongness* by making proper connection with the higher powers.

In those more developed minds which alone we are studying, the wrongness takes a moral character, and the salvation takes a mystical tinge. I think we shall keep well within the limits of what is common to all such minds if we formulate the essence of their religious experience in terms like these:—

The individual, so far as he suffers from his wrongness and criticises it, is to that extent consciously beyond it, and in at least possible touch with something higher, if anything higher exist. Along with the wrong part there is thus a better part of him, even though it may be but a most helpless germ. With which part he should identify his real being is by no means obvious at this stage; but when stage 2 (the stage of solution or salvation) arrives, the man identifies his real being with the germinal higher part of himself; and does so in the following way. *He becomes conscious that this higher part is conterminous and continuous with a* MORE *of the same quality, which is operative in the universe outside of him, and which he can keep in working touch with, and in a fashion get on board and save himself when all his lower being has gone to pieces in the wreck.*

It seems to me that all the phenomena are accurately describable in these very simple general terms. They allow for the divided self and the struggle; they involve the change of personal centre and the surrender of the lower self; they express the appearance of exteriority of the help- ing power and yet account for our sense of union with it; and they fully justify our feelings of security and joy. There is probably no autobio- graphic document, among all those which I have quoted, to which the description will not well apply. One need only add such specific details as will adapt it to various theologies and various personal tempera- ments, and one will then have the various experiences reconstructed in their individual forms.

So far, however, as this analysis goes, the experiences are only psychological phenomena. They possess, it is true, enormous biological worth. Spiritual strength really increases in the subject when he has them, a new life opens for him, and they seem to him a place of conflux where the forces of two universes meet; and yet this may be nothing but his subjective way of feeling things, a mood of his own fancy, in spite of the effects produced. I now turn to my second question: What is the objective 'truth' of their content?

The part of the content concerning which the question of truth most pertinently arises is that 'MORE of the same quality' with which our own higher self appears in the experience to come into harmonious working relation. Is such a 'more' merely our own notion, or does it really exist? If so, in what shape does it exist? Does it act, as well as exist? And in what form should we conceive of that 'union' with it of which religious geniuses are so convinced?

It is in answering these questions that the various theologies perform their theoretic work, and that their divergencies most come to light. They all agree that the 'more' really exists; though some of them hold it to exist in the shape of a personal god or gods, while others are satisfied to conceive it as a stream of ideal tendency embedded in the eternal structure of the world. They all agree, moreover, that it acts as well as exists, and that something really is effected for the better when you throw your life into its hands. It is when they treat of the experience of 'union' with it that their speculative differences appear most clearly. Over this point pantheism and theism, nature and second birth, works and grace and karma, immortality and reincarnation, rationalism and mysticism, carry on inveterate disputes.

At the end of my lecture on Philosophy I held out the notion that an impartial science of religions might sift out from the midst of their discrepancies a common body of doctrine which she might also formulate in terms to which physical science need not object. This, I said, she might adopt as her own reconciling hypothesis, and recommend it for general belief. I also said that in my last lecture I should have to try my own hand at framing such an hypothesis.

The time has now come for this attempt. Who says 'hypothesis' renounces the ambition to be coercive in his arguments. The most I can do is, accordingly, to offer something that may fit the facts so easily that your scientific logic will find no plausible pretext for vetoing your impulse to welcome it as true.

The 'more,' as we called it, and the meaning of our 'union' with it, form the nucleus of our inquiry. Into what definite description can these words be translated, and for what definite facts do they stand? It would never do for us to place ourselves off hand at the position of a particular theology, the Christian theology, for example, and proceed immediately to define the 'more' as Jehovah, and the 'union' as his imputation to us of the righteousness of Christ. That would be unfair to other religions and, from our present standpoint at least, would be an over-belief.

We must begin by using less particularized terms; and, since one of the duties of the science of religions is to keep religion in connection with the rest of science, we shall do well to seek first of all a way of describing the 'more,' which psychologists may also recognize as real. The *subconscious self* is nowadays a well-accredited psychological entity; and I believe that in it we have exactly the mediating term required. Apart from all religious considerations, there is actually and literally more life in our total soul than we are at any time aware of. The exploration of the transmarginal field has hardly yet been seriously undertaken, but what Mr. Myers said in 1892 in his essay on the Subliminal Consciousness is as true as when it was first written: "Each of us is in reality an abiding psychical entity far more extensive than he knows—an individuality which can never express itself completely through any corporeal manifestation. The Self manifests through the organism; but there is always some part of the Self unmanifested; and always, as it seems, some power of organic expression in abeyance or reserve." Much of the content of this larger background against which our conscious being stands out in relief is insignificant. Imperfect memories, silly jingles, inhibitive timidities, 'dissolutive' phenomena of various sorts, as Myers calls them, enter into it for a large part. But in it many of the performances of genius seem also to have their origin; and in our study of conversion, of mystical experiences, and of prayer, we have seen how striking a part invasions from this region play in the religious life.

Let me then propose, as an hypothesis, that whatever it may be on its *farther* side, the 'more' with which in religious experience we feel ourselves connected is on its *hither* side the subconscious continuation of our conscious life. Starting thus with a recognized psychological fact as our basis, we seem to preserve a contact with 'science' which the ordinary theologian lacks. At the same time the theologian's contention that the religious man is moved by an external power is vindicated, for it is one of the peculiarities of invasions from the subconscious region to take on objective appearances, and to suggest to the Subject an external control. In the religious life the control is felt as 'higher'; but since on our hypothesis it is primarily the higher faculties of our own hidden mind which are controlling, the sense of union with the power beyond us is a sense of something, not merely apparently, but literally true.

This doorway into the subject seems to me the best one for a science of religions, for it mediates between a number of different points of view. Yet it is only a doorway, and difficulties present themselves as soon as we step through it, and ask how far our transmarginal consciousness carries us if we follow it on its remoter side. Here the over-beliefs begin: here mysticism and the conversion-rapture and Vedantism and transcendental idealism bring in their monistic interpretations and tell us that the finite self rejoins the absolute self, for it was always one with God and identical with the soul of the world. Here the prophets of all the different religions come with their visions, voices, raptures, and other openings, supposed by each to authenticate his own peculiar faith.

Those of us who are not personally favored with such specific revelations must stand outside of them altogether and, for the present at least, decide that, since they corroborate incompatible theological doctrines, they neutralize one another and leave no fixed result. If we follow any one of them, or if we follow philosophical theory and embrace monistic pantheism on non-mystical grounds, we do so in the exercise of our individual freedom, and build out our religion in the way most congruous with our personal susceptibilities. Among these susceptibilities intellectual ones play a decisive part. Although the religious question is primarily a question of life, of living or not living in the higher union which opens itself to us as a gift, yet the spiritual excitement in which the gift appears a real one will often fail to be aroused in an individual until certain particular intellectual beliefs or ideas which, as we say, come home to him, are touched. These ideas will thus be essential to that individual's religion;—which is as much as to say that over-beliefs in various directions are absolutely indispensable, and that we should treat them with tenderness and tolerance so long as they are not intolerant themselves. As I have elsewhere written, the most interesting and valuable things about a man are usually his over-beliefs.

Disregarding the over-beliefs, and confining ourselves to what is common and generic, we have in *the fact that the conscious person is continuous with a wider self through which saving experiences come*, a positive content of religious experience which, it seems to me, *is literally and objectively true as far as it goes*. If I now proceed to state my own hypothesis about the farther limits of this extension of our personality, I shall be offering my own over-belief—though I know it will appear a sorry under-belief to some of you—for which I can only bespeak the same indulgence which in a converse case I should accord to yours.

The further limits of our being plunge, it seems to me, into an alto-gether other dimension of existence from the sensible and merely 'understandable' world. Name it the mystical region, or the super-natural region, whichever you choose. So far as our ideal impulses originate in this region (and most of them do originate in it, for we find them possessing us in a way for which we cannot articulately account), we belong to it in a more intimate sense than that in which we belong to the visible world, for we belong in the most intimate sense wherever our ideals belong. Yet the unseen region in question is not merely ideal, for it produces effects in this world. When we com-mune with it, work is actually done upon our finite personality, for we are turned into new men, and consequences in the way of conduct follow in the natural world upon our regenerative change. But that which produces effects within another reality must be termed a reality itself, so I feel as if we had no philosophic excuse for calling the unseen or mystical world unreal.

God is the natural appellation, for us Christians at least, for the supreme reality, so I will call this higher part of the universe by the name of God. We and God have business with each other; and in opening ourselves to his influence our deepest destiny is fulfilled. The universe, at those parts of it which our personal being constitutes, takes a turn genuinely for the worse or for the better in proportion as each one of us fulfills or evades God's demands. As far as this goes I prob-ably have you with me, for I only translate into schematic language what I call the instinctive belief of mankind: God is real since he produces real effects.

The real effects in question, so far as I have as yet admitted them, are exerted on the personal centres of energy of the various subjects but the spontaneous faith of most of the subjects is that they embrace a wider sphere than this. Most religious men believe (or 'know,' if they be mystical) that not only they themselves, but the whole universe of beings to whom the God is present, are secure in his parental hands. There is a sense, a dimension, they are sure, in which we are *all* saved, in spite of the gates of hell and all adverse terrestrial appearances. God's existence is the guarantee of an ideal order that shall be permanently preserved. This world may indeed, as science assures us, some day burn up or freeze; but if it is part of his order, the old ideals are sure to be brought elsewhere to fruition, so that where God is, tragedy is only provisional and partial, and shipwreck and dissolution are not the absolutely final things. Only when this farther step of faith concerning

God is taken, and remote objective consequences are predicted, does religion, as it seems to me, get wholly free from the first immediate subjective experience, and bring a *real hypothesis* into play. A good hypothesis in science must have other properties than those of the phenomenon it is immediately invoked to explain, otherwise it is not prolific enough. God, meaning only what enters into the religious man's experience of union, falls short of being an hypothesis of this more useful order. He needs to enter into wider cosmic relations in order to justify the subject's absolute confidence and peace.

That the God with whom, starting from the hither side of our own extra-marginal self, we come at its remoter margin into commerce should be the absolute world-ruler, is of course a very considerable over-belief. Over-belief as it is, though, it is an article of almost every one's religion. Most of us pretend in some way to prop it upon our philosophy, but the philosophy itself is really propped upon this faith. What is this but to say that Religion, in her fullest exercise of function, is not a mere illumination of facts already elsewhere given, not a mere passion, like love, which views things in a rosier light. It is indeed that, as we have seen abundantly. But it is something more, namely, a postulator of new *facts* as well. The world interpreted religiously is not the materialistic world over again with an altered expression; it must have, over and above the altered expression, *a natural constitution* different at some point from that which a materialistic world would have. It must be such that different events can be expected in it, different conduct must be required.

This thoroughly 'pragmatic' view of religion has usually been taken as a matter of course by common men. They have interpolated divine miracles into the field of nature, they have built a heaven out beyond the grave. It is only transcendentalist metaphysicians who think that, without adding any concrete details to Nature, or subtracting any, but by simply calling it the expression of absolute spirit, you make it more divine just as it stands. I believe the pragmatic way of taking religion to be the deeper way. It gives it body as well as soul, it makes it claim, as everything real must claim, some characteristic realm of fact as its very own. What the more characteristically divine facts are, apart from the actual inflow of energy in the faith-state and the prayer-state, I know not. But the over-belief on which I am ready to make my personal venture is that they exist. The whole drift of my education goes to persuade me that the world of our present consciousness is only one out of many worlds of consciousness that exist, and that those other worlds must contain experiences which have a meaning for our life also; and that although in the main their experiences and those of this world keep discrete, yet the two become continuous at certain points, and higher energies filter in. By being faithful in my poor measure to this over-belief, I seem to myself to keep more sane and true. I *can*, of course, put myself into the sectarian scientist's attitude, and imagine vividly that the world of sensations and of scientific laws and objects may be all. But whenever I do this, I hear that inward monitor of which W. K. Clifford once wrote, whispering the word 'bosh!' Humbug is humbug, even though it bear the scientific name, and the total expression of human experience, as I view it objectively, invincibly urges me beyond the narrow 'scientific' bounds. Assuredly, the real world is of a different temperament,—more intricately built than physical science allows. So my objective and my subjective conscience both hold me to the over-belief which I express. Who knows whether the faithfulness of individuals here below to their own poor over-beliefs may not actually help God in turn to be more effectively faithful to his own greater tasks?

JOSIAH ROYCE

The curious fact has been noted, particularly by Ralph Barton
Perry, that William James came from an affluent, rich New York
family, yet his philosophy stressed individualism, whereas
Josiah Royce was born into humble and lonely circumstances in
California, and his philosophy emphasized the role of the
communal life. Royce's philosophy sought the unity of things;
society, which integrates the individual, was for him an important
aspect of an ever-larger cosmic unity. The following selection*
contains Royce's reasoning for his view that individuality is
incomprehensible without a metaphysical conception of the
community.

Defining the Individual

Motives which are as familiar as they are hard to analyze have convinced us all, before we begin to philosophize, that our human world
contains a variety of individually distinct minds or selves, and that some,
for us decisively authoritative, principle of individuation, keeps these
selves apart, and forbids us to regard their various lives merely as
incidents, or as undivided phases of a common life. This conviction—
the stubborn pluralism of our present and highly cultivated social
consciousness—tends indeed, under criticism, to be subject to various
doubts and modifications—the more so as, in case we are once challenged to explain who we are, none of us find it easy to define the
precise boundaries of the individual self, or to tell wherein it differs
from the rest of the world, and, in particular, from the selves of other
men.

But to all such doubts our social common sense replies by insisting
upon three groups of facts. These facts combine to show that the individual human selves are sundered from one another by gaps which,
as it would seem, are in some sense impassable.

First, in this connection, our common sense insists upon the empirical
sundering of the feelings—that is, of the immediate experiences of
various human individuals. One man does not feel, and, speaking in
terms of direct experience, cannot feel, the physical pains of another
man. Sympathy may try its best to bridge the gulf thus established by

* Josiah Royce, "Lectures IX and X," in *The Problem of Christianity*, Vol. II.
Used by permission.

nature. Love may counsel me to view the pangs of my fellow *as if they were* my own. But, as a fact, my sensory nerves do not end in my fellow's skin, but in mine. And the physical sundering of the organisms corresponds to a persistent sundering of our streams of immediate feeling. Even the most immediate and impressive forms of sympathy with the physical pangs of another human being only serve the more to illustrate how our various conscious lives are thus kept apart by gulfs which we cannot cross. When a pitiful man shrinks, or feels faint, or is otherwise overcome with emotion, at what is called "the sight" of another's suffering—how unlike are the sufferings of the shrinking or terrified or overwhelmed spectator, and the pangs of the one with whom he is said to sympathize. As a fact, the sympathizer does not feel the sufferer's pain. What he feels is his own emotional reverberation at the sight of its symptoms. That is, in general, something very different, both in quality and in intensity, from what the injured man feels.

We appear, then, to be individuated by the diversity and the separateness of our streams of immediate feeling. My toothache cannot directly become an item in my neighbor's mind. Facts of this sort form the first group of evidences upon which common sense depends for its pluralistic view of the world of human selves.

The facts of the second group are closely allied to the former, but lie upon another level of individual life—namely, upon the level of our more organized ideas.

"One man," so says our social common sense, "can only indirectly discover the intentions, the thoughts, the ideas of another man." Direct telepathy, if it ever occurs at all, is a rare and, in most of our practical relations, a wholly negligible fact. By nature, every man's plans, intents, opinions, and range of personal experience are secrets, except in so far as his physical organism indirectly reveals them. His fellows can learn these secrets only through his expressive movements. Control your expression, keep silence, avoid the unguarded look and the telltale gesture; and then nobody can discover what is in your mind. No man can directly read the hearts of his fellows. This seems, for our common sense, to be one of the deepest-seated laws of our social experience. It is often expressed as if it were not merely an empirical law, but a logical necessity. How could I possibly possess or share or become conscious of the thoughts and purposes of another mind, unless I were myself identical with that mind? So says our ordinary common sense. The very supposition that I could be conscious of a thought or of an intent which was all the while actually present to the consciousness of another individual man, is often regarded as a supposition not only contrary to fact, but also contrary to reason. Such a supposition, it is often said, would involve a direct self-contradiction.

Otherwise expressed, the facts of this second group, and the principles which they exemplify, are summed up by asserting, as our social common sense actually asserts: We are individuated by the law that our trains of conscious thought and purpose are mutually inaccessible through any mode of direct intuition. Each of us lives within the charmed circle of his own conscious will and meaning—each of us is more or less clearly the object of his own inspection, but is hopelessly beyond the direct observation of his fellows.

*   *   *

The third group of facts here in question is the group upon which our cultivated social common sense most insists whenever ethical problems are in question; and therefore it is precisely this third group of facts which has most interest in its bearings upon the idea of the community.

"We are all members one of another." So says the doctrine of the community. "On the contrary," so our social common sense insists: "We are beings, each of whom has a soul of his own, a destiny of his own, rights of his own, worth of his own, ideals of his own, and an individual life in which this soul, this destiny, these rights, these ideals, get their expression. No other man can do my deed for me. When I choose, my choice coalesces with the voluntary decision of no other individual." Such, I say, is the characteristic assertion to which this third group of facts leads our ordinary social pluralism.

In brief: We thus seem to be individuated by our deeds. The will whereby I choose my own deed, is not my neighbor's will. My act is my own. Another man can perform an act which repeats the type of my act, or which helps or hinders my act. But if the question arises concerning any one act: Who hath done this?—such a question admits of only one true answer. Deeds and their doers stand in one-one correspondence. Such is the opinion of our cultivated modern ethical common sense . . .

Nevertheless, all these varieties of individual experience, these chasms which at any one present moment seem to sunder mind and mind, and these ethical considerations which have taught us to think of one man as morally independent of another, do not tell us the whole truth about the actual constitution of the social realm. There are facts that seem to show that these many are also one. These, then, are facts which force upon us the problem of the community . . .

We may be aided in making a more decisive advance towards understanding what a community is by emphasizing at this point a motive which we have not before mentioned, and which no doubt plays a great part in the psychology of the social consciousness.

Any notable case wherein we find a social organization which we can call, in the psychological sense, either a highly developed community or the creation or product of such a community, is a case where some process of the nature of a history—that is, of coherent social evolution—has gone on and has gone on for a long time, and is more or less remembered by the community in question. If, ignoring history, you merely take a cross-section of the social order at any one moment; and if you thus deal with social groups that have little or no history, and confine your attention to social processes which occur during a short period of time—for example, during an hour, or a day, or a year—what then is likely to come to your notice takes either the predominantly pluralistic form of the various relatively independent doings of detached individuals, or else the social form of the confused activities of a crowd. A crowd, whether it be a dangerous mob, or an amiably joyous gathering at a picnic, is not a community. It has a mind, but no institutions, no organization, no coherent unity, no history, no traditions. It may be a unit, but is then of the type which suggests James's mere blending of various consciousnesses—a sort of mystical loss of personality on the part of its members. On the other hand, a group of independent buyers at market, or of the passers-by in a city street, is not a community. And it also does not suggest to the onlooker any blending of many selves in one. Each purchaser seeks his own affairs. There may be gossip, but gossip is not a function which establishes the life of a community. For gossip has a short memory. But a true community is essentially a product of a time process. A community has a past and will have a future. Its more or less conscious history, real or ideal, is a part of its very essence. A community requires for its existence a history and is greatly aided in its consciousness by a memory. . . .

*   *   *

At this present moment I am indeed here, as this creature of the moment—sundered from the other selves. But nevertheless, if considered simply in this passing moment of my life, I am hardly a self at all.

I am just a flash of consciousness—the mere gesticulation of a self—not a coherent personality. Yet memory links me with my own past—and not, in the same way, with the past of anyone else. This joining of the present to the past reveals a more or less steady tendency—a sense about the whole process of my remembered life. And this tendency and sense of my individual life agree, on the whole, with the sense and the tendencies that belong to the entire flow of the time-stream, so far as it has sense at all. My individual life, my own more or less well-sundered stream of tendency, not only is shut off at each present moment by various barriers from the lives of other selves—but also constitutes an intelligible sequence in itself, so that, as I look back, I can say: "What I yesterday intended to pursue, that I am today still pursuing." "My present carries farther the plan of my past." Thus, then, I am one more or less coherent plan expressed in a life. "The child is father to the man." My days are "bound each to each by mutual piety."

Since I am this self, not only by reason of what now sunders me from the inner lives of other selves, but by reason of what links me, in significant fashion, to the remembered experiences, deeds, plans, and interests of my former conscious life, I need a somewhat extended and remembered past to furnish the opportunity for my self to find, when it looks back, a long process that possesses sense and coherence. In brief, my idea of myself is an interpretation of my past—linked also with an interpretation of my hopes and intentions as to my future.

Precisely as I thus define myself with reference to my own past, so my fellows also interpret the sense, the value, the qualifications, and the possessions of my present self by virtue of what are sometimes called my antecedents. In the eyes of his fellow-men, the child is less of a self than is the mature man; and he is so not merely because the child just now possesses a less wealthy and efficient conscious life than a mature man possesses, but because the antecedents of his present self are fewer than are the antecedents of the present self of the mature man. The child has little past. He has accomplished little. The mature man bears the credit and the burden of his long life of deeds. He not only possesses, but in great part is, for his fellow-men, a record. . . .

*　　*　　*

Now when many contemporary and distinct individual selves so interpret, each his own personal life, that each says of an individual past or of a determinate future event or deed: "That belongs to my life," "That occurred, or will occur, to me," then these many selves may be defined as hereby constituting, in a perfectly definite and objective, but also in a highly significant, sense, a community. They may be said to constitute a community *with reference* to that particular past or future event, or group of events, which each of them accepts or interprets as belonging to his own personal past or to his own individual future. A community constituted by the fact that each of its members accepts as part of his own individual life and self the same *past* events that each of his fellow-members accepts, may be called a *community of memory*. Such is any group of persons who individually either remember or commemorate the same dead—each one finding, because of personal affection or of reverence for the dead, that those whom he commemorates form for him a part of his own past existence.

A community constituted by the fact that each of its members accepts, as part of his own individual life and self, the same expected *future* events that each of his fellows accepts, may be called a *community of expectation*, or upon occasion, a *community of hope*.

* * *

The *first* condition upon which the existence of a community, in our sense of the word, depends, is the power of an individual self to extend his life, in ideal fashion, so as to regard it as including past and future events which lie far away in time, and which he does not now personally remember. That this power exists, and that man has a self which is thus ideally extensible in time without any definable limit, we all know.

This power itself rests upon the principle that, however a man may come by his idea of himself, the self is no mere datum, but is in its essence a life which is interpreted, and which interprets itself, and which, apart from some sort of ideal interpretation, is a mere flight of ideas, or a meaningless flow of feelings, or a vision that sees nothing, or else a barren abstract conception. How deep the process of interpretation goes in determining the real nature of the self, we shall only later be able to estimate.

There is no doubt that what we usually call our personal memory does indeed give us assurances regarding our own past, so far as memory extends and is trustworthy. But our trust in our memories is itself an interpretation of their data. All of us regard as belonging, even to our recent past life, much that we cannot just now remember. And the future self shrinks and expands with our hopes and our energies. No one can merely, from without, set for us the limits of the life of the self, and say to us: "Thus far and no farther."

In my ideal extensions of the life of the self, I am indeed subject to some sort of control—to what control we need not here attempt to formulate. I must be able to give myself some sort of reason, personal, or social, or moral, or religious, or metaphysical, for taking on or throwing off the burden, the joy, the grief, the guilt, the hope, the glory of past and of future deeds and experiences; but I must also myself personally share in this task of determining how much of the past and the future shall ideally enter into my life, and shall contribute to the value of that life.

And if I choose to say, "There is a sense in which *all* the tragedy and the attainment of an endless past and future of deeds and of fortunes enter into my own life," I say only what saints and sages of the most various creeds and experiences have found their several reasons for saying. The fact and the importance of such ideal extensions of the self must therefore be recognized. Here is the first basis for every clear idea of what constitutes a community. . . .

The *second* condition upon which the existence of a community depends is the fact that there are in the social world a number of distinct selves capable of social communication, and, in general, engaged in communication.

The distinctness of the selves we have illustrated at length in our previous discussion. We need not here dwell upon the matter further, except to say, expressly, that a community does not become one, in the sense of my definition, by virtue of any reduction or melting of these various selves into a single merely present self, or into a mass of passing experience. That mystical phenomena may indeed form part of the life of a community, just as they may also form part of the life of an individual human being, I fully recognize. . . .

The *third* of the conditions for the existence of the community which my definition emphasizes consists in the fact that the ideally extended past and future selves of the members include at least some events which are, for all these selves, identical. This third condition is the one which furnishes both the most exact, the most widely variable, and the most important of the motives which warrant us in calling a community a real unit. The Pauline metaphor of the body and the members finds, in this third condition, its most significant basis—a basis capable of exact description. . . .

Men do not form a community, in our present restricted sense of that word, merely in so far as the men cooperate. They form a community, in our present limited sense, when they not only cooperate, but accompany this cooperation with that ideal extension of the lives of individuals whereby each cooperating member says: "This activity which we perform together, this work of ours, its past, its future, its sequence, its order, its sense,—all these enter into my life, and are the life of my own self writ large."

* * *

When love of the community, nourished by common memories, and common hope, both exists and expresses itself in devoted individual lives, it can constantly tend, despite the complexity of the present social order, to keep the consciousness of the community alive. And when this takes place, the identification of the loyal individual self with the life of the community will tend, both in ideal and in feeling, to identify each self not only with the distant past and future of the community, but with the present activities of the whole social body. . . .

ALFRED NORTH WHITEHEAD

Whitehead, like Royce, constructed a metaphysics which found unity where others found division and distinction. For example, he thought the distinction between fact and value was not ultimate, as others claimed, and philosophy could show how the alleged distinction vanished from a larger, more unified perspective. The same was true, he held, of the putative difference between the value of the individual and that of society. The following selection,* from the final chapter of his *Adventures of Ideas*, is one of Whitehead's best explanations of what civilization means for the individual and why the value of individuality increases with increasing identification of the individual member with his larger cultural community.

Civilizing the Individual

. . . We are in a way seeking for the notion of a Harmony of Harmonies, which shall bind together the other four qualities, so as to exclude from our notion of civilization the restless egotism with which they have often in fact been pursued. 'Impersonality' is too dead a notion, and 'Tenderness' too narrow. I choose the term 'Peace' for that Harmony of Harmonies which calms destructive turbulence and completes civilization. Thus a society is to be termed civilized whose members participate in the five qualities—Truth, Beauty, Adventure, Art, Peace.

. . . The Peace that is here meant is not the negative conception of anaesthesia. It is a positive feeling which crowns the 'life and motion' of the soul. It is hard to define and difficult to speak of. It is not a hope for the future, nor is it an interest in present details. It is a broadening of feeling due to the emergence of some deep metaphysical insight, unverbalized and yet momentous in its coordination of values. Its first effect is the removal of the stress of acquistitive feeling arising from the soul's preoccupation with itself. Thus Peace carries with it a surpassing of personality. There is an inversion of relative values. It is primarily a trust in the efficacy of Beauty. It is a sense that fineness of achievement is as it were a key unlocking treasures that the narrow nature of things would keep remote. There is thus involved a grasp of infinitude, an

* From *Adventures of Ideas* (New York: The Macmillan Company, copyright 1933, renewed 1961 by Evelyn Whitehead). Reprinted with permission of The Macmillan Company.

appeal beyond boundaries. Its emotional effect is the subsidence of turbulence which inhibits. More accurately, it preserves the springs of energy, and at the same time masters them for the avoidance of paralyzing distractions. The trust in the self-justification of Beauty introduces faith, where reason fails to reveal the details.

The experience of Peace is largely beyond the control of purpose. It comes as a gift. The deliberate aim at Peace very easily passes into its bastard substitute, Anaesthesia. In other words, in the place of a quality of 'life and motion,' there is substituted their destruction. Thus Peace is the removal of inhibition and not its introduction. It results in a wider sweep of conscious interest. It enlarges the field of attention. Thus Peace is self-control at its widest—at the width where the 'self' has been lost, and interest has been transferred to coordinations wider than personality. Here the real motive interests of the spirit are meant, and not the superficial play of discursive ideas. Peace is helped by such superficial width, and also promotes it. In fact it is largely for this reason that Peace is so essential for civilization. It is the barrier against narrowness. One of its fruits is that passion whose existence Hume denied the love of mankind as such.

. . . The meaning of Peace is most clearly understood by considering it in its relation to the tragic issues which are essential in the nature of things. Peace is the understanding of tragedy, and at the same time its preservation.

We have seen that there can be no real halt of civilization in the indefinite repetition of a perfected ideal. Staleness sets in. And this fatigue is nothing other than the creeping growth of anaesthesia, whereby that social group is gradually sinking towards nothingness. The defining characteristics are losing their importance. There may be no pain or conscious loss. There is merely a slow paralysis of surprise. And apart from surprise, intensity of feeling collapses.

Decay, Transition, Loss, Displacement belong to the essence of the Creative Advance. The new direction of aim is initiated by Spontaneity, an element of confusion. The enduring Societies with their rise, culmination, and decay, are devices to combine the necessities of Harmony and Freshness. There is the deep underlying Harmony of Nature, as it were a fluid, flexible support; and on its surface the ripples of social efforts, harmonizing and clashing in their aims at ways of satisfaction. The lower types of physical objects can have a vast endurance of inorganic life. The higher types, involving animal life and the dominance of a personality primarily mental, preserve their zest by the quick succession of stages from birth, culmination, to death. As soon as high consciousness is reached, the enjoyment of existence is entwined with pain, frustration, loss, tragedy. Amid the passing of so much beauty, so much heroism, so much daring, Peace is then the intuition of permanence. It keeps vivid the sensitiveness to the tragedy; and it sees the tragedy as a living agent persuading the world to aim at fineness beyond the faded level of surrounding fact. Each tragedy is the disclosure of an ideal—What might have been, and was not: What can be. The tragedy was not in vain. This survival power in motive force, by reason of appeal to reserves of Beauty, marks the difference between the tragic evil and the gross evil. The inner feeling belonging to this grasp of the service of tragedy is Peace—the purification of the emotions.

* * *

. . . The general health of social life is taken care of by formularized moral precepts, and formularized religious beliefs and religious institutions. All of these explicitly express the doctrine that the perfection of life resides in aims beyond the individual person in question.

It is a doctrine of great generality, capable of a large variety of specializations, not all of them mutually consistent. For example, consider the patriotism of the Roman farmers, in the full vigour of the Republic. Certainly Regulus did not return to Carthage, with the certainty of torture ana death, cherishing any mystic notions of another life—either a Christian Heaven or a Buddhist Nirvana. He was a practical man, and his ideal aim was the Roman Republic flourishing in this world. But this aim transcended his individual personality; for this aim he entirely sacrificed every gratification bounded by such limits. For him there was something in the world which could not be expressed as sheer personal gratification—and yet in thus sacrificing himself, his personal existence rose to its full height. He may have been mistaken in his estimate of the worth of the Roman Republic. The point is that with that belief, he achieved magnificence by the sacrifice of himself.

In this estimate, Regulus has not in any way proved himself to be exceptional. His conduct showed heroism that is unusual. But this estimate of the worth of such conduct has evoked widest assent. The Roman farmers agreed; and generation after generation, amid all the changes of history, have agreed by the instinctive pulse of emotions as the tale is handed down.

Moral codes have suffered from the exaggerated claims made for them. The dogmatic fallacy has here done its worst. Each such code has been put out by a God on a mountain top, or by a Saint in a cave, or by a divine Despot on a throne, or, at the lowest, by ancestors with a wisdom beyond later question. In any case, each code is incapable of improvement; and unfortunately in details they fail to agree either with each other or with our existing moral intuitions. The result is that the world is shocked, or amused, by the sight of saintly old people hindering in the name of morality the removal of obvious brutalities from a legal system. Some *Acta Sanctorum* go ill with civilization.

The details of these codes are relative to the social circumstances of the immediate environment—life at a certain date on 'the fertile fringe' of the Arabian desert, life on the lower slopes of the Himalayan Mountains, life on the plains of China, or on the plains of India, life on the delta of some great river. Again the meaning of the critical terms is shifting and ambiguous, for example, the notions of ownership, family, marriage, murder, God. Conduct which in one environment and at one stage produces its measure of harmonious satisfaction, in other surroundings at another stage is destructively degrading. Each society has its own type of perfection, and puts up with certain blots, at that stage inevitable. Thus the notion that there are certain regulative notions, sufficiently precise to prescribe details of conduct, for all reasonable beings on Earth, in every planet, and in every star-system, is at once to be put aside. That is the notion of the one type of perfection at which the Universe aims. All realization of the Good is finite, and necessarily excludes certain other types.

But what these codes do witness to, and what their interpretation by seers of various races throughout history does witness to, is the aim at a social perfection. Such a realized fact is conceived as an abiding perfection in the nature of things, a treasure for all ages. It is not a romance of thought, it is a fact of Nature. For example, in one sense the Roman Republic declined and fell; in another sense, it stands a stubborn fact in the Universe. To perish is to assume a new function in the process of generation. Devotion to the Republic magnified the type of personal satisfactions for those who conformed their purposes to its maintenance. Such conformation of purpose to ideal[s] beyond personal limitations is the conception of that Peace with which the wise man can face his fate, master of his soul.

. . . The wide scope of the notion of 'society' requires attention. Transcendence begins with the leap from the actuality of the immediate occasion to the notion of personal existence, which is a society of occasions. In terms of human life, the soul is a society. Care for the future of personal existence, regret or pride in its past, are alike feelings which leap beyond the bounds of the sheer actuality of the present. It is in the nature of the present that it should thus transcend itself by reason of the immanence in it of the 'other.' But there is no necessity as to the scale of emphasis that this fact of nature should receive. It belongs to the civilization of consciousness to magnify the large sweep of harmony.

Beyond the soul there are other societies, and societies of societies. There is the animal body ministering to the soul; there are families, groups of families, nations, species, groups involving different species associated in the joint enterprise of keeping alive. These various societies, each in its measure, claim loyalties and loves. In human history the various responses to these claims disclose the essential transcendence of each individual actuality beyond itself. The stubborn reality of the absolute self-attainment of each individual is bound up with a relativity which it issues from and issues into. The analysis of the various strands of relativity is the analysis of the social structure of the Universe, as in this epoch.

Although particular codes of morality reflect, more or less imperfectly, the special circumstances of social structure concerned, it is natural to seek for some highly general principles underlying all such codes. Such generalities should reflect the very notions of the harmonizing of harmonies, and of particular individual actualities as the sole authentic reality. These are the principles of the generality of harmony, and of the importance of the individual. The first means 'order,' and the second means 'love.' Between the two there is a suggestion of opposition. For 'order' is impersonal; and love, above all things, is personal. The antithesis is solved by rating types of order in relative importance according to their success in magnifying the individual actualities, that is to say, in promoting strength of experience. Also in rating the individual on the double basis, partly on the intrinsic strength of its own experience, and partly on its influence in the promotion of a high-grade type of order. These two grounds in part coalesce. For a weak individual exerts a weak influence. The essence of Peace is that the individual whose strength of experience is founded upon this ultimate intuition, thereby is extending the influence of the source of all order.

The moral code is the behaviour-patterns which in the environment for which it is designed will promote the evolution of that environment towards its proper perfection.

. . . The attainment of Truth belongs to the essence of Peace. By this it is meant, that the intuition constituting the realization of Peace has as its objective that Harmony whose inter-connections involve Truth. A defect in Truth is a limitation to Harmony. There can be no secure efficacy in the Beauty which hides within itself the dislocations of falsehood.

The truth or falsehood of propositions is not directly to the point in this demand for Truth. Since each proposition is yoked to a contradictory proposition, and since of these one must be true and the other false, there are necessarily as many false as there are true propositions. This bare 'truth or falsehood' of propositions is a comparatively superficial factor affecting the discursive interests of the intellect. The essential truth that Peace demands is the conformation of Appearance to Reality. There is the Reality from which the occasion of experience springs—a Reality of inescapable, stubborn fact; and there is the Appearance with which the occasion attains its final individuality—an Appearance including its adjustment of the Universe by simplification, valuation, transmutation, anticipation. A feeling of dislocation of Appearance from Reality is the final destructive force, robbing life of its zest for adventure. It spells the decadence of civilization, by stripping from it the very reason for its existence.

There can be no necessity governing this conformation. Sense-perception, which dominates the appearance of things, in its own nature re-arranges, and thus in a way distorts. Also there can be no mere blunt truth about the Appearance which it provides. In its own nature Sense-perception is an interpretation, and this interpretation may be completely misleading. If there were a necessary conformation of Appearance to Reality, then Morality would vanish. There is no morality about the multiplication table, whose items are necessarily linked. Art would also be a meaningless term. For it presupposes the efficacy of purpose. Art is an issue of Adventure.

The question for discussion is whether there exists any factor in the Universe constituting a general drive towards the conformation of Appearance to Reality. This drive would then constitute a factor in each occasion persuading an aim at such truth as is proper to the special appearance in question. This concept of truth, proper to each special appearance, would mean that the appearance has not built itself up by the inclusion of elements that are foreign to the reality from which it springs. The appearance will then be a generalization and an adaptation of emphasis; but not an importation of qualities and relations without any corresponding exemplification in the reality. This concept of truth is in fact the denial of the doctrine of Appearance which lies on the surface of Kant's *Critique of Pure Reason.* . . .

. . . The answer to this question must issue from a survey of the factors in terms of which individual experience has been interpreted:— The antecedent World from which each occasion springs, a World of many occasions presenting for the new creature harmonies and discords: the easy road of Anaesthesia by which discordant factors are dismissed into irrelevance: the activity of the mental poles in building conceptual experience into patterns of feeling which rescue discords from loss: the spontaneity of the mental action and its persuasion by a sense of relevance: the selective nature of consciousness and its initial failure to discriminate the deeper sources of feeling: that there is no agency in abstraction from actual occasions, and that existence involves implication in agency: the sense of a unity of many occasions with a value beyond that of any individual occasion; for example, the soul, the complete animal, the social group of animals, the material body, the physical epoch: the aim at immediate individual contentment.

The justification for the suggestion derived from this group of factors must mainly rest upon their direct elucidation of first-hand experience. They are not, and should not be, the result of an argument. For all argument must rest upon premises more fundamental than the conclusions. Discussion of fundamental notions is merely for the purpose of disclosing their coherence, their compatibility, and the specializations which can be derived from their conjunction.

The above set of metaphysical notions rests itself upon the ordinary, average experience of mankind, properly interpreted. But there is a further set for which the appeal lies to occasions and modes of experience which in some degree are exceptional. It must be remembered that the present level of average waking human experience was at one time exceptional among the ancestors of mankind. We are justified therefore in appealing to those modes of experience which in our direct judgment stand above the average level. The gradual emergence of such modes, and their effect on human history, have been among the themes of this book in its appeal to history. We have found the growth of Art: its gradual sublimation into the pursuit of Truth and Beauty: the sublimation of the egoistic aim by its inclusion of the transcendent whole: the youthful zest in the transcendent aim: the sense of tragedy: the sense of evil: the persuasion towards Adventure beyond achieved perfection: the sense of Peace.

. . . The concept of Civilization, as developed up to this stage, remains inherently incomplete. No logical argument can demonstrate this gap. Such arguments are merely subsidiary helps for the conscious realization of metaphysical intuitions.—*Non in dialectica complacuit Deo salvum facere populum suum.* This saying, quoted by Cardinal Newman, should be the motto of every metaphysician. He is seeking, amid the dim recesses of his ape-like consciousness and beyond the reach of dictionary language, for the premises implicit in all reasoning. The speculative methods of metaphysics are dangerous, easily perverted. So is all Adventure; but Adventure belongs to the essence of civilization.

The incompleteness of the concept relates to the notion of Transcendence, the feeling essential for Adventure, Zest, and Peace. This feeling requires for its understanding that we supplement the notion of the Eros by including it in the concept of an Adventure in the Universe as One. This Adventure embraces all particular occasions but as an actual fact stands beyond any one of them. It is, as it were, the complement to Plato's Receptacle, its exact opposite, yet equally required for the unity of all things. In every way, it is contrary to the Receptacle. The Receptacle is bare of all forms: the Unity of Adventure includes the Eros which is the living urge towards all possibilities, claiming the goodness of their realization. The Platonic Receptacle is void, abstract from all individual occasions: The Unity of Adventure includes among its components all individual realities, each with the importance of the personal or social fact to which it belongs. Such individual importance in the components belongs to the essence of Beauty. In this Supreme Adventure, the Reality which the Adventure transmutes into its Unity of Appearance requires the real occasions of the advancing world each claiming its due share of attention. This Appearance, thus enjoyed, is the final Beauty with which the Universe achieves its justification. This Beauty has always within it the renewal derived from the Advance of the Temporal World. It is the immanence of the Great Fact including this initial Eros and this final Beauty which constitutes the zest of self-forgetful transcendence belonging to Civilization at its height.

At the heart of the nature of things, there are always the dream of youth and the harvest of tragedy. The Adventure of the Universe starts with the dream and reaps tragic Beauty. This is the secret of the union of Zest with Peace:—That the suffering attains its end in a Harmony of Harmonies. The immediate experience of this Final Fact, with its union of Youth and Tragedy, is the sense of Peace. In this way the World receives its persuasion towards such perfections as are possible for its diverse individual occasions.

GEORGE SANTAYANA

George Santayana (1863–1952), born in Madrid of a Spanish
father and Bostonian mother, became a distinguished American
philosopher and man of letters. He came to the United States in
1872 and graduated from Harvard in 1886. Santayana, as a
colleague of William James and Josiah Royce, taught philosophy
at Harvard until 1912; he resigned on the grounds that he preferred a solitary life and had never particularly enjoyed either
academic life or American culture. His philosophical writings are
still consulted as distinguished contributions, and his novel, *The
Last Puritan* (1935), is a revealing portrayal of the American
ethos. Santayana, though an avowed materialist, retired to Italy
to a convent and withdrawal. The following selection* is an
interesting description of how he viewed the beginning of the
twentieth century, particularly in America, and its philosophies,
including Pragmatism.

The Pagan Era

The present age is a critical one and interesting to live in. The civilisation characteristic of Christendom has not disappeared, yet another
civilisation has begun to take its place. We still understand the value of
religious faith; we still appreciate the pompous arts of our forefathers;
we are brought up on academic architecture, sculpture, painting, poetry,
and music. We still love monarchy and aristocracy, together with that
picturesque and dutiful order which rested on local institutions, class
privileges, and the authority of the family. We may even feel an organic
need for all these things, cling to them tenaciously, and dream of rejuven-
ating them. On the other hand the shell of Christendom is broken. The
unconquerable mind of the East, the pagan past, the industrial socialistic
future confront it with their equal authority. Our whole life and mind is
saturated with the slow upward filtration of a new spirit—that of an
emancipated, atheistic, international democracy.

These epithets may make us shudder; but what they describe is
something positive and self-justified, something deeply rooted in our
animal nature and inspiring to our hearts, something which, like every
vital impulse, is pregnant with a morality of its own. In vain do we
deprecate it; it has possession of us already through our propensities,

*From *Winds of Doctrine* (London: J. M. Dent & Sons, 1913). Used by permission.

fashions, and language. Our very plutocrats and monarchs are at ease only when they are vulgar. Even prelates and missionaries are hardly sincere or conscious of an honest function, save as they devote themselves to social work; for willy-nilly the new spirit has hold of our consciences as well. This spirit is amiable as well as disquieting, liberating as well as barbaric; and a philosopher in our day, conscious both of the old life and of the new, might repeat what Goethe said of his successive love affairs—that it is sweet to see the moon rise while the sun is still mildly shining.

*   *   *

A chief characteristic of the situation is that moral confusion is not limited to the world at large, always the scene of profound conflicts, but that it has penetrated to the mind and heart of the average individual. Never perhaps were men so like one another and so divided within themselves. In other ages, even more than at present, different classes of men have stood at different levels of culture, with a magnificent readiness to persecute and to be martyred for their respective principles. These militant believers have been keenly conscious that they had enemies; but their enemies were strangers to them, whom they could think of merely as such, regarding them as blank negative forces, hateful black devils, whose existence might make life difficult but could not confuse the ideal of life. No one sought to understand these enemies of his, nor even to conciliate them, unless under compulsion or out of insidious policy, to convert them against their will; he merely pelted them with blind refutations and clumsy blows. Every one sincerely felt that the right was entirely on his side, a proof that such intelligence as he had moved freely and exclusively within the lines of his faith. The result of this was that his faith was intelligent, I mean, that he understood it, and had a clear, almost instinctive perception of what was compatible or incompatible with it. He defended his walls and he cultivated his garden. His position and his possessions were unmistakable.

*   *   *

. . . Nor is this insecurity about first principles limited to abstract subjects. It reigns in politics as well. Liberalism had been supposed to advocate liberty; but what the advanced parties that still call themselves liberal now advocate is control, control over property, trade, wages, hours of work, meat and drink, amusements, and in a truly advanced country like France control over education and religion; and it is only on the subject of marriage (if we ignore eugenics) that liberalism is growing more and more liberal. Those who speak most of progress measure it by quantity and not by quality; how many people read and write, or how many people there are, or what is the annual value of their trade; whereas true progress would rather lie in reading or writing fewer and better things, and being fewer and better men, and enjoying life more. But the philanthropists are now preparing an absolute subjection of the individual, in soul and body, to the instincts of the majority—the most cruel and unprogressive of masters; and I am not sure that the liberal maxim, "the greatest happiness of the greatest number," has not lost whatever was just or generous in its intent and come to mean the greatest idleness of the largest possible population.

Nationality offers another occasion for strange moral confusion. It had seemed that an age that was levelling and connecting all nations, an age whose real achievements were of international application, was destined to establish the solidarity of mankind as a sort of axiom. The idea of solidarity is indeed often invoked in speeches, and there is an extreme socialistic party that—when a wave of national passion does not carry it the other way—believes in international brotherhood. But even here, black men and yellow men are generally excluded; and in higher circles, where history, literature, and political ambition dominate men's minds, nationalism has become of late an omnivorous all-permeating passion. Local parliaments must be everywhere established, extinct or provincial dialects must be galvanised into national languages, philosophy must be made racial, religion must be fostered where it emphasises nationality and denounced where it transcends it. Man is certainly an animal that, when he lives at all, lives for ideals. Something must be found to occupy his imagination, to raise pleasure and pain into love and hatred, and change the prosaic alternative between comfort and discomfort into the tragic one between happiness and sorrow. Now that the hue of daily adventure is so dull, when religion for the most part is so vague and accommodating, when even war is a vast impersonal business, nationality seems to have slipped into the place of honour. It has become the one eloquent, public, intrepid illusion. Illusion, I mean, when it is taken for an ultimate good or a mystical essence, for of course nationality is a fact. People speak some particular language and are very uncomfortable where another is spoken or where their own is spoken differently. They have habits, judgments, assumptions to which they are wedded, and a society where all this is unheard of shocks them and puts them at a galling disadvantage. To ignorant people the foreigner as such is ridiculous, unless he is superior to them in numbers or prestige, when he becomes hateful. It is natural for a man to like to live at home, and to live long elsewhere without a sense of exile is not good for his moral integrity. It is right to feel a greater kinship and affection for what lies nearest to oneself. But this necessary fact and even duty of nationality is accidental; like age or sex it is a physical fatality which can be made the basis of specific and comely virtues; but it is not an end to pursue or a flag to flaunt or a privilege not balanced by a thousand incapacities. Yet of this distinction our contemporaries tend to make an idol, perhaps because it is the only distinction they feel they have left.

Anomalies of this sort will never be properly understood until people accustom themselves to a theory to which they have always turned a deaf ear, because, though simple and true, it is materialistic: namely, that mind is not the cause of our actions but an effect, collateral with our actions, of bodily growth and organisation. It may therefore easily come about that the thoughts of men, tested by the principles that seem to rule their conduct, may be related, or irrelevant, or pre-monitory; for the living organism has many strata, on any of which, at a given moment, activities may exist perfect enough to involve con-sciousness, yet too weak and isolated to control the organs of outer expression; so that (to speak geologically) our practice may be historic, our manners glacial, and our religion palaeozoic. The ideals of the nine-teenth century may be said to have been all belated; the age still yearned with Rousseau or speculated with Kant, while it moved with Darwin, Bismarck, and Nietzsche: and today, in the half-educated classes, among the religious or revolutionary sects, we may observe quite modern methods of work allied with a somewhat antiquated mentality. The whole nineteenth century might well cry with Faust: "Two souls, alas, dwell in my bosom!" The revolutions it witnessed filled it with horror and made it fall in love romantically with the past and dote on ruins, because they were ruins . . . .

* * *

. . . In philosophy, besides the survival of all the official and endowed systems, there has been of late a very interesting fresh movement, largely among the professors themselves, which in its various hues may be called irrationalism, vitalism, pragmatism, or pure empiricism. But this movement, far from being a reawakening of any organising instinct, is simply an extreme expression of romantic anarchy. It is in essence but a franker confession of the principle upon which modern philosophy has been building—or unbuilding—for these three hundred years, I mean the principle of subjectivity. Berkeley and Hume, the first prophets of the school, taught that experience is not a partial discovery of other things but is itself the only possible object of experience. Therefore, said Kant and the second generation of prophets, any world we may seem to live in, even those worlds of theology or of history which Berkeley or Hume had inadvertently left standing, must be an idea which our present experience suggests to us and which we frame as the principles of our mind allow and dictate that we should. But then, say the latest prophets—Avenarius, William James, M. Bergson—these mental principles are no antecedent necessities or duties imposed on our imagination; they are simply parts of flying experience itself, and the ideas—say of God or of matter—which they lead us to frame have nothing compulsory or fixed about them. Their sole authority lies in the fact that they may be more or less congenial or convenient, by enriching the flying moment æsthetically, or helping it to slip prosperously into the next moment. Immediate feeling, pure experience, is the only reality, the only *fact:* if notions which do not reproduce it fully as it flows are still called true (and they evidently ought not to be) it is only in a pragmatic sense of the word, in that while they present a false and heterogeneous image of reality they are not practically misleading; as, for instance, the letters on this page are no true image of the sounds they call up, nor the sounds of the thoughts, yet both may be correct enough if they lead the reader in the end to the things they symbolise. It is M. Bergson, the most circumspect and best equipped thinker of this often scatter-brained school, who has put this view in a frank and tenable form, avoiding the bungling it has sometimes led to about the "meaning of truth." Truth, according to M. Bergson, is given only in intuitions which prolong experience just as it occurs, in its full immediacy; on the other hand, all representation, thought, theory, calculation, or discourse is so much mutilation of the truth, excusable only because imposed upon us by practical exigences. The world, being a feeling, must be felt to be known, and then the world and the knowledge of it are identical; but if it is talked about or thought about it is denaturalised, although convention and utility may compel the poor human being to talk and to think, exiled as he is from reality in his Babylon of abstractions. Life, like the porcupine when not ruffled by practical alarms, can let its fretful quills subside. The mystic can live happy in the droning consciousness of his own heart-beats and those of the universe.

With this we seem to have reached the extreme of self-concentration and self-expansion, the perfect identity and involution of everything in oneself. And such indeed is the inevitable goal of the malicious theory of knowledge, to which this school is committed, remote as that goal may be from the boyish naturalism and innocent intent of many of its pupils. If all knowledge is of experience and experience cannot be knowledge of anything else, knowledge proper is evidently impossible. There can be only feeling; and the least self-transcendence, even in memory, must be an illusion.

*   *   *

. . . Among the pragmatists the worship of power is also optimistic, but it is not to logic that power is attributed. Science, they say, is good as a help to industry, and philosophy is good for correcting whatever in science might disturb religious faith, which in turn is helpful in living. What industry or life are good for it would be unsympathetic to inquire: the stream is mighty, and we must swim with the stream. Concern for survival, however, which seems to be the pragmatic principle in morals, does not afford a remedy for moral anarchy. To take firm hold on life, according to Nietzsche, we should be imperious, poetical, atheistic; but according to William James we should be democratic, concrete, and credulous. It is hard to say whether pragmatism is come to emancipate the individual spirit and make it lord over things, or on the contrary to declare the spirit a mere instrument for the survival of the flesh. In Italy, the mind seems to be raised deliriously into an absolute creator, evoking at will, at each moment, a new past, a new future, a new earth, and a new God. In America, however, the mind is recommended rather as an unpatented device for oiling the engine of the body and making it do double work.

*   *   *

When chaos has penetrated so far into the moral being of nations they can hardly be expected to produce great men. A great man need not be virtuous, nor his opinions right, but he must have a firm mind, a distinctive, luminous character; if he is to dominate things, something must be dominant in him. We feel him to be great in that he clarifies and brings to expression something which was potential in the rest of us, but which with our burden of flesh and circumstance we were too torpid to utter. The great man is a spontaneous variation in humanity; but not in any direction. A spontaneous variation might be a mere madness or mutilation or monstrosity; in finding the variation admirable we evidently invoke some principle of order to which it conforms. Perhaps it makes explicit what was preformed in us also; as when a poet finds the absolutely right phrase for a feeling, or when nature suddenly astonishes us with a form of absolute beauty. Or perhaps it makes an unprecedented harmony out of things existing before, but jangled and detached. The first man was a great man for this latter reason; having been an ape perplexed and corrupted by his multiplying instincts, he suddenly found a new way of being decent, by harnessing all those instincts together, through memory and imagination, and giving each in turn a measure of its due; which is what we call being rational. It is a new road to happiness, if you have strength enough to castigate a little the various impulses that sway you in turn. Why then is the martyr, who sacrifices everything to one attraction, distinguished from the criminal or the fool, who do the same thing? Evidently because the spirit that in the martyr destroys the body is the very spirit which the body is stifling in the rest of us; and although his private inspiration may be irrational, the tendency of it is not, but reduces the public conscience to act before any one else has had the courage to do so. Greatness is spontaneous; simplicity, trust in some one clear instinct, are essential to it; but the spontaneous variation must be in the direction of some possible sort of order; it must exclude and leave behind what is incapable of being moralised. How, then, should there be any great heroes, saints, artists, philosophers, or legislators in an age when nobody trusts himself, or feels any confidence in reason, in an age when the word *dogmatic* is a term of reproach? Greatness has character and severity, it is deep and sane, it is distinct and perfect. For this reason there is none of it today.

* * *

Without great men and without clear convictions this age is nevertheless very active intellectually; it is studious, empirical, inventive, sympathetic. Its wisdom consists in a certain contrite openness of mind; it flounders, but at least in floundering it has gained a sense of possible depths in all directions. Under these circumstances, some triviality and great confusion in its positive achievements are not unpromising things, nor even unamiable. These are the *Wanderjahre* of faith; it looks smilingly at every new face, which might perhaps be that of a predestined friend; it chases after any engaging stranger; it even turns up again from time to time at home, full of a new tenderness for all it had abandoned there. But to settle down would be impossible now. The intellect, the judgment are in abeyance. Life is running turbid and full; and it is no marvel that reason, after vainly supposing that it ruled the world, should abdicate as gracefully as possible, when the world is so obviously the sport of cruder powers—vested interests, tribal passions, stock sentiments, and chance majorities. Having no responsibility laid upon it, reason has become irresponsible. Many critics and philosophers seem to conceive that thinking aloud is itself literature. Sometimes reason tries to lend some moral authority to its present masters, by proving how superior they are to itself; it worships evolution, instinct, novelty, action, as it does in modernism, pragmatism, and the philosophy of M. Bergson. At other times it retires into the freehold of those temperaments whom this world has ostracised, the region of the non-existent, and comforts itself with its indubitable conquests there. This happened earlier to the romanticists . . . although their poetic and political illusions did not suffer them to perceive it. It is happening now, after disillusion, to some radicals and mathematicians like Mr. Bertrand Russell, and to others of us who, perhaps without being mathematicians or even radicals, feel that the sphere of what happens to exist is too alien and accidental to absorb all the play of a free mind, whose function after it has come to clearness and made its peace with things, is to touch them with its own moral and intellectual light, and to exist for its own sake.

These are but gusts of doctrine; yet they prove that the spirit is not dead in the lull between its seasons of steady blowing. Who knows which of them may not gather force presently and carry the mind of the coming age steadily before it?

JOHN DEWEY

It is sometimes assumed that Dewey's Pragmatism was designed to eliminate metaphysics altogether. Certainly, he became
increasingly unsympathetic, in his philosophical development,
with a good deal of traditional metaphysics. But, as this selection*
testifies, Dewey never denounced metaphysics entirely. It is
perhaps Dewey's finest discussion of the development and
significance of American Pragmatism.

Pragmatism in America

Pragmatism ... presents itself as an extension of historical empiricism,
but with this fundamental difference, that it does not insist upon antecedent phenomena but upon consequent phenomena; not upon the
precedents but upon the possibilities of action. And this change in point
of view is almost revolutionary in its consequences. An empiricism
which is content with repeating facts already past has no place for
possibility and for liberty. It cannot find room for general conceptions
or ideas, at least no more than to consider them as summaries or records.
But when we take the point of view of pragmatism we see that general
ideas have a very different rôle to play than that of reporting and registering past experiences. They are the bases of organizing future observations and experiences. Whereas, for empiricism, in a world already
constructed and determined, reason or general thought has no other
meaning than that of summing up particular cases, in a world where
the future is not a mere word, where theories, general notions, rational
ideas have consequences for action, reason necessarily has a constructive function. Nevertheless the conceptions of reasoning have only a
secondary interest in comparison with the reality of facts since they
must be confronted with concrete observations.[1]

* From *Philosophy and Civilization*, "The Development of American Pragmatism"
(New York: Capricorn Books, Copyright 1931). Used by permission.

[1]William James said in a happy metaphor, that they must be "cashed in," by
producing specific consequences. This expression means that they must be able to
lead to concrete facts. But for those who are not familiar with American idioms,
James' formula was taken to mean that the consequences themselves of our rational
conceptions must be narrowly limited by their pecuniary value. Thus Mr. Bertrand
Russell wrote recently that pragmatism is merely a manifestation of American
commercialism.

Pragmatism thus has a metaphysical implication. The doctrine of the value of consequences leads us to take the future into consideration. And this taking into consideration of the future takes us to the conception of a universe whose evolution is not finished, of a universe which is still, in James' term, "in the making," "in the process of becoming," of a universe up to a certain point still plastic.

Consequently reason, or thought, in its more general sense, has a real, though limited, function, a creative, constructive function. If we form general ideas and if we put them in action, consequences are produced which could not be produced otherwise. Under these conditions the world will be different from what it would have been if thought had not intervened. This consideration confirms the human and moral importance of thought and of its reflective operation in experience. It is therefore not true to say that James treated reason, thought, and knowledge with contempt, or that he regarded them as mere means of gaining personal or even social profits. For him reason has a creative function, limited because specific, which helps to make the world other than it would have been without it. It makes the world really more reasonable; it gives to it an intrinsic value. One will understand the philosophy of James better if one considers it in its totality as a revision of English empiricism, a revision which replaces the value of past experience, of what is already given, by the future, by that which is as yet mere possibility.

These considerations naturally bring us to the movement called instrumentalism. The survey which we have just made of James' philosophy shows that he regarded conceptions and theories purely as instruments which can serve to constitute future facts in a specific manner. But James devoted himself primarily to the moral aspects of this theory, to the support which it gave to "meliorism" and moral idealism, and to the consequences which followed from it concerning the sentimental value and the bearing of various philosophical systems, particularly to its destructive implications for monistic rationalism and for absolutism in all its forms. He never attempted to develop a complete theory of the forms or "structures" and of the logical operations which are founded on this conception. Instrumentalism is an attempt to establish a precise logical theory of concepts, of judgments and inferences in their various forms, by considering primarily how thought functions in the experimental determinations of future consequences. That is to say, it attempts to establish universally recognized distinctions and rules of logic by deriving them from the reconstructive or mediative function ascribed to reason. It aims to constitute a theory of the general forms of conception and reasoning, and not of this or that particular judgment or concept related to its own content, or to its particular implications.

As far as the historical antecedents of instrumentalism are concerned, two factors are particularly important, over and above this matter of experimental verification which we have already mentioned in connection with James. The first of these two factors is psychological, and the second is a critique of the theory of knowledge and of logic which has resulted from the theory proposed by neo-kantian idealism and expounded in the logical writings of such philosophers as Lotze, Bosanquet, and F. H. Bradley. As we have already said, neo-kantian influence was very marked in the United States during the last decade of the nineteenth century. I myself, and those who have collaborated with me in the exposition of instrumentalism, began by being neo-kantians, in the same way that Peirce's point of departure was kantianism and that of James was the empiricism of the British School.

The psychological tendencies which have exerted an influence on instrumentalism are of a biological rather than a physiological nature. They are, more or less, closely related to the important movement whose promoter in psychology has been Doctor John Watson and to which he has given the name of Behaviorism. Briefly, the point of departure of this theory is the conception of the brain as an organ for the coordination of sense stimuli (to which one should add modifications caused by habit, unconscious memory, or what are called today "conditioned reflexes") for the purpose of effecting appropriate motor responses. On the basis of the theory of organic evolution it is maintained that the analysis of intelligence and of its operations should be compatible with the order of known biological facts, concerning the intermediate position occupied by the central nervous system in making possible responses to the environment adequate to the needs of the living organism. It is particularly interesting to note that in the *Studies in Logical Theory* (1903), which was their first declaration, the instrumentalists recognized how much they owed to William James for having forged the instruments which they used, while at the same time, in the course of the studies, the authors constantly declared their belief in a close union of the "normative" principles of logic and the real processes of thought, in so far as these are determined by an objective or biological psychology and not by an introspective psychology of states of consciousness. But it is curious to note that the "instruments" to which allusion is made, are not the considerations which were of the greatest service to James. They precede his pragmatism and it is among some of the pages of his *Principles of Psychology* that one must look for them. This important work (1890) really developed two distinct theses.

The one is a re-interpretation of introspective psychology, in which James denies that sensations, images and ideas are discrete and in which he replaces them by a continuous stream which he calls "the stream of consciousness." This conception necessitates a consideration of relations as an immediate part of the field of consciousness, having the same status as qualities. And throughout his *Psychology* James gives a philosophical tinge to this conception by using it in criticizing the atomism of Locke and of Hume as well as the *a-priorism* of the synthesis of rational principles by Kant and his successors, among whom should be mentioned in England, Thomas Hill Green, who was then at the height of his influence.

The other aspect of his *Principles of Psychology* is of a biological nature. It shows itself in its full force in the criterion which James established for discovering the existence of mind. "The pursuance of future ends and the choice of means for their attainment are thus the mark and criterion of the presence of mentality in a phenomenon."[2] The force of this criterion is plainly shown in the chapter on Attention, and its relation to Interest considered as the force which controls it, and its teleological function of selection and integration; in the chapter on Discrimination and Comparison (Analysis and Abstraction), where he discusses the way in which ends to be attained and the means for attaining them evoke and control intellectual analysis; and in the chapter on Conception, where he shows that a general idea is a mode of signifying particular things and not merely an abstraction from particular cases or a super-empirical function—that it is a teleological instrument. James then develops this idea in the chapter on reasoning where he says that "the only meaning of essence is teleological, and that classification and conception are purely teleological weapons of mind."

One might complete this brief enumeration by mentioning also the chapter of James' book in which he discusses the Nature of Necessary Truths and the Rôle of Experience, and affirms in opposition to Herbert Spencer, that many of our most important modes of perception and conception of the world of sensible objects are not the cumulative products of particular experience, but rather original biological sports,

[2]*Psychology*, vol. I, p. 8.

spontaneous variations, which are maintained because of their applicability to concrete experiences after once having been created. Number, space, time, resemblance and other important "categories" could have been brought into existence, he says, as a consequence of some particular cerebral instability, but they could by no means have been registered on the mind by outside influence. Many significant and useless concepts also arise in the same manner. But the fundamental categories have been cumulatively extended and reinforced because of their value when applied to concrete instances and things of experience. It is therefore not the origin of a concept, it is its application which becomes the criterion of its value; and here we have the whole of pragmatism in embryo. A phrase of James very well summarizes its import: "the popular notion that 'Science' is forced on the mind *ab extra*, and that our interests have nothing to do with its constructions, is utterly absurd."

Given the point of view which we have just specified, and the interest attaching to a logical theory of conception and judgment, and there results a theory of the following description. The adaptations made by inferior organisms, for example their effective and coordinated responses to stimuli, become teleological in man and therefore give occasion to thought. Reflection is an indirect response to the environment, and the element of indirection can itself become great and very complicated. But it has its origin in biological adaptive behavior and the ultimate function of its cognitive aspect is a prospective control of the conditions of the environment. The function of intelligence is therefore not that of copying the objects of the environment, but rather of taking account of the way in which more effective and more profitable relations with these objects may be established in the future.

How this point of view has been applied to the theory of judgment is too long a story to be told here. We shall confine ourselves here to saying that, in general, the "subject" of a judgment represents that portion of the environment to which a reaction must be made; the predicate represents the possible response or habit or manner in which one should behave towards the environment; the copula represents the organic and concrete act by which the connection is made between the fact and its signification; and finally the conclusion, or the definitive object of judgment, is simply the original situation transformed, a situation which implies a change as well in the original subject (including its mind) as in the environment itself. The new and harmonious unity thus attained verifies the bearing of the data which were at first chosen to serve as subject and of the concepts introduced into the situation during the process as teleological instruments for its elaboration. Until this final unification is attained the perceptual data and the conceptual principles, theories, are merely hypotheses from a logical point of view. Moreover, affirmation and negation are intrinsically a-logical: they are acts.

Such a summary survey can hardly pretend to be either convincing or suggestive. However, in noting the points of resemblance and difference between this phase of pragmatism and the logic of neo-hegelian idealism, we are bringing out a point of great importance. According to the latter logic, thought constitutes in the last analysis its object and even the universe. It is necessary to affirm the existence of a series of forms of judgment, because our first judgments, which are nearest to sense, succeed in constituting objects in only a partial and fragmentary fashion, even to the extent of involving in their nature an element of contradiction. There results a dialectic which permits each inferior and partial type of judgment to pass into a more complete form until we finally arrive at the total judgment, where the thought which comprehends the entire object or the universe is an organic whole of interrelated mental distinctions. It is evident that this theory magnifies the rôle of thought beyond all proportion. It is an objective and rational idealism which is opposed to and distinct from the subjective and perceptual idealism of Berkeley's school. Instrumentalism, however, assigns a positive function of thought, that of reconstituting the present stage of things instead of merely knowing it. As a consequence, there cannot be intrinsic degrees, or a hierarchy of forms of judgment. Each type has its own end, and its validity is entirely determined by its efficacy in the pursuit of its end. A limited perceptual judgment, adapted to the situation which has given it birth, is as true in its place as is the most complete and significant philosophic or scientific judgment. Logic, therefore, leads to a realistic metaphysics in so far as it accepts things and events for what they are independently of thought, and to an idealistic metaphysics in so far as it contends that thought gives birth to distinctive acts which modify future facts and events in such a way as to render them more reasonable, that is to say, more adequate to the ends which we propose for ourselves. This ideal element is more and more accentuated by the inclusion progressively of social factors in human environment over and above natural factors; so that the needs which are fulfilled, the ends which are attained are no longer of a merely biological or particular character, but include also the ends and activities of other members of society.

It is natural that continental thinkers should be interested in American philosophy as it reflects, in a certain sense, American life. Thus it should be clear after this rapid survey of the history of pragmatism that American thought continues European thought. We have imported our language, our laws, our institutions, our morals, and our religion from Europe, and we have adapted them to the new conditions of our life. The same is true of our ideas. For long years our philosophical thought was merely an echo of European thought. The pragmatic movement which we have traced in the present essay, as well as neo-realism, behaviorism, the absolute idealism of Royce, the naturalistic idealism of Santayana, are all attempts at re-adaptation; but they are not creations *de novo*. They have their roots in British and European thought. Since these systems are re-adaptations they take into consideration the distinctive traits of the environment of American life. But as has already been said, they are not limited to reproducing what is worn and imperfect in this environment. They do not aim to glorify the energy and the love of action which the new conditions of American life exaggerated. They do not reflect the excessive mercantilism of American life. Without doubt all these traits of the environment have not been without a certain influence on American philosophical thought; our philosophy would not be national or spontaneous if it were not subject to this influence. But the fundamental idea which the movements of which we have just spoken have attempted to express, is the idea that action and opportunity justify themselves only to the degree in which they render life more reasonable and increase its value. Instrumentalism maintains in opposition to many contrary tendencies in the American environment, that action should be intelligent and reflective, and that thought should occupy a central position in life. That is the reason for our insistence on the teleological phase of thought and knowledge. If it must be teleological in particular and not merely true in the abstract, that is probably due to the practical element which is found in all the phases of American life. However that may be, what we insist upon above all else is that intelligence be regarded as the only source and sole guarantee of a desirable and happy future. It is beyond doubt that the progressive and unstable character of American life and civilization has facilitated the birth of a philosophy which regards the world as being in continuous formation, where there is still place for indeterminism, for the new, and for a real future. But this idea is not exclusively American, although the conditions of American life have aided this idea in becoming self-conscious. It is also true that Americans tend to underestimate the value of tradition and of rationality considered as an achievement of the past. But the world has also given proof of irrationality in the past and this irrationality is incorporated in our beliefs and our institutions. There are bad traditions as there are good ones: it is always important to distinguish. Our neglect of the traditions of the past, with whatever this negligence implies in the way of spiritual impoverishment of our life, has its compensation in the idea that the world is recommencing and being remade under our eyes. The future as well as the past can be a source of interest and consolation and give meaning to the present. Pragmatism and instrumental experimentalism bring into prominence the importance of the individual. It is he who is the carrier of creative thought, the author of action, and of its application. Subjectivism is an old story of philosophy; a story which began in Europe and not in America. But American philosophy, in the systems which we have expounded, has given to the subject, to the individual mind, a practical rather than an epistemological function. The individual mind is important because only the individual mind is the organ of modifications in traditions and institutions, the vehicle of experimental creation. One-sided and egoistic individualism in American life has left its imprint on our practices. For better or for worse, depending on the point of view, it has transformed the esthetic and fixed individualism of the old European culture into an active individualism. But the idea of a society of individuals is not foreign to American thought; it penetrates even our current individualism which is unreflective and brutal. And the individual which American thought idealizes is not an individual *per se*, an individual fixed in isolation and set up for himself, but an individual who evolves and develops in a natural and human environment, an individual who can be educated.

If I were asked to give an historical parallel to this movement in American thought I would remind my reader of the French philosophy of the enlightenment. Every one knows that the thinkers who made that movement illustrious were inspired by Bacon, Locke, and Newton; what interested them was the application of scientific method and the conclusions of an experimental theory of knowledge to human affairs, the critique and reconstruction of beliefs and institutions. As Hoffding writes, they were animated "by a fervent faith in intelligence, progress, and humanity." And certainly they are not accused today, just because of their educational and social significance, of having sought to subordinate intelligence and science to ordinary utilitarian aims. They merely sought to free intelligence from its impurities and to render it sovereign. One can scarcely say that those who glorify intelligence and reason in the abstract, because of their value for those who find personal satisfaction in their possession, estimate intelligence more truly than those who wish to make it the indispensable guide of intellectual and social life. When an American critic says of instrumentalism that it regards ideas as mere servants which make for success in life, he only reacts, without reflection, to the ordinary verbal associations of the word "instrumental," as many others have reacted in the same manner to the use of the word "practical." Similarly a recent Italian writer, after having said that pragmatism and instrumentalism are characteristic products of American thought, adds that these systems "regard intelligence as a mere mechanism of belief, and consequently attempt to re-establish the dignity of reason by making of it a machine for the production of beliefs useful to morals and society." This criticism does not hold. It is by no means the production of beliefs useful to morals and society which these systems pursue. It is the formation of a faith in intelligence, as the one and indispensable belief necessary to moral and social life. The more one appreciates the intrinsic esthetic, immediate value of thought and of science, the more one takes into account what intelligence itself adds to the joy and dignity of life, the more one should feel grieved at a situation in which the exercise and joy of reason are limited to a narrow, closed and technical social group and the more one should ask how it is possible to make all men participators in this inestimable wealth.

VI. *Pluralism*

INTRODUCTION

As the twentieth century began, William James said of American philosophy: "It lacks logical rigor, but it has the tang of life." Pragmatism was lively and earthy. James expressed it in metaphors that occurred to him while hiking in the Adirondacks. John Dewey pronounced it, with a Vermont grocery-store twang and Yankee matter-of-factness, in the side remark that working with your hands is no disgrace. Charles Peirce, isolated in a rural Pennsylvania town, regularly wrote to James how, if his dwindling food supply were replenished, he could live to incubate the first stirrings of some revolutionary insight. To their admirers these philosophers seemed to find their ideas on mountain trails and in country kitchens, not in libraries or campus clubrooms; they appeared as frontiersmen who had hacked through the underbrush of European intellectualism into the opening of Life and Experience.

For many, the new American philosophy was fresh because unacademic, rebellious because unauthoritarian, individualistic because exploratory, and authentic because in tune with Life, Experience, and Reality. A lack of logical rigor did not trouble some pathfinders who had abandoned "logic-chopping" after hearing real timber fall. But, as American philosophy settled down and took its seat among the professions, thinkers such as Morris Cohen found the invocation of "life," "experience," and "reality" flamboyant and disquieting. They worried about the evils attending any derision, however unintentional, of reason.

Cohen warned Pragmatists against exaggerated praise of the "life of action" that disparages the "life of reflection." Impatience in deliberation causes remorse in conduct, and the bane of lazy thinking is not the lazy but the horrendous action it too often permits. Those who praise the life of action, saying "Move ahead, let's stop quibbling," also suggest that *life* itself is exclusively valuable. But this, Cohen argued, makes a shambles of morality. If hanging on to life without regard to whether it is good or evil is urged, if moving life along without concern for its direction is urged, then the sacrifice of life for honor and conscience is senseless. We cannot afford to shirk the baffling task of distinguishing the *good* from both the *evil* and the *indifferent* life. Sometimes "the distaste for arduous intellectual tasks is natural, blameless, and in some cases even providential. But when such distaste sets itself up as a philosophy of life it is only ridiculous."

Morris Cohen understood the metaphysical subsoil of our culture, the subject of the preceding chapter. He appreciated how the religious roots of the culture spread, below the concrete of material, industrialized America, a network of occultism. Many readers of Melville, Hawthorne, Emerson, and James felt themselves confronted by the supernatural, and what church and home could not provide might be sought through a secret society, a promising horoscope, a reader of signs, a dream. It troubled Cohen, as it did Santayana (who accused James of "slumming"), that William James composed his *Varieties of Religious Experience* out of personal, often eccentric experiences while ignoring the major historic religions. If Pragmatism seemed a testimonial to the revelatory capacities of personal experience, what kinds of quackery, Cohen wondered, could it not be used to defend? There was the danger that professional philosophy, in its unguarded praise of Experience as the Key to Life, could be exploited for dignifying all sorts of whacky claims and enterprises. A word in *dispraise* of "experience" and "life" may serve to remind that the intimations of my personal experience, like those of yours, require our rational scrutiny as rational men.

The development of professional philosophy witnessed further modifications of early Pragmatism. Other thinkers shared Cohen's concern that the philospher's assist to the individual, earnestly trying to define his world philosophically, ought to include a careful account of concepts like *experience* and *reality*. For this, a patient, technical, and occasionally tedius train of reasoning was unavoidable. Professional philosophy, as Ralph Barton Perry described it, attempts to answer the questions of the ordinary man but with a greater and more persevering patience. Clarence Irving Lewis, the distinguished Harvard philosopher, was speaking to the ordinary man willing to listen in saying: "When the vast and impressive institution of human education—in its wider sense—is remarked, the assumption that such community is simply native or ready-made is seen to be superfluous. My world is my intellectual achievement; our common world, a social one." But behind and preceding this assertion was some very patient and technical reasoning devoted to the concepts of "reality" and "experience," also representing, Lewis thought, significant modifications of early Pragmatism.[1]

When I "experience" my environment, discriminate and identify things surrounding me, do not suppose that I am merely registering, like a passive camera, the details of my environment. C. I. Lewis, in following Kant, argued that I am *actively* interpreting and classifying what is impressed upon my senses from "out there"; what is impressed upon me altogether beyond my control is called "the given." It is the kernel of my experience of the environment, but the full-bodied experience of *recognizing* something seen, heard, etc., is the result, not just of the "given," but of the concepts and categories which I apply to the given. Experiencing the world involves, besides registering the given, interpreting or applying concepts to it. The character of my experience is formed by the given but also by how I classify it. My experience, when I judge the thing before me to be a desk and no part of the object to my left, obviously differs from my experience, when I judge the thing before me to be a chair and a part of the object to my left. Conceivably, the given is the same or at least indistinguishable in both experiences, in which case the manifest differences between them are due to the differences in my interpretations, in the concepts I apply to the given. To this extent, my world *is* an intellectual or conceptual achievement, and our common or shared world is a mutual, social conceptual achievement. In seeing the same desk, you and I are brothers-in-interpretation.

Scientific knowledge is the employment of *systems* of concepts— logic, mathematics, and physics. Which of these systems is "true of" our world is, in the end, a matter of convenience and pragmatic choice. Lewis wrote: "This thesis, by itself, seems implausible and highly paradoxical; the stronghold of pragmatism supposedly lies in the empirical; logic is the citadel of rationalism . . . Pragmatism, as ordinarily understood, seems to take things wrong end on; it is the element which mind contributes, in truth and knowledge, which may be pragmatic; the empirical brute fact of the given is absolute datum." According to Lewis, earlier Pragmatists denied any "absolute" in experience, declaring that absolute truths are found only in logic and mathematics, in the relations between concepts. Stating something in one's experience to be "absolutely there," independent of all interpretation and applica-

---

[1] My colleague John J. McDermott has written provocatively about reinterpreting the pragmatists' concept of *experience* for our own time. See his *The American Angle of Vision* (West Nyack, N.Y.: Cross Currents, 1966), especially pp. 437 *ff.*

tion of concepts, is either nonsense or can only be justified as a *decision* arrived at because *intellectually convenient*. But, Lewis argued in reply, labeling his own position "conceptual pragmatism," it is the choice of the concepts and the logic, by which we organize and classify our experience, that is pragmatic and finally justifiable only on the grounds of intellectual convenience. There is nothing absolute in the application of our concepts; we will replace our present "systems of thought," if convenient, with new ones. But "the given" in experience *is* absolute, its presence and character undetermined by our choice of concepts; it is what it is, no matter what systems of interpretation we find convenient to apply to it.

We next note, according to Lewis, that "the given" is not the same as "the real." What one declares as "real" is some particular conception of the given, but that, we saw, may change. The philosopher's job is to prescribe the criteria for distinguishing the real from the unreal, to work out the implications of those criteria, realizing of course that it may sometimes be more convenient to replace those criteria with others. What is real is always, in the end, a matter of our decision; what is given can never be our decision. As Lewis saw it, the fundamental difference is this: The real can be said; but the given is *ineffable*. We can never regard a particular experience, pick out some part of it, and say, "That is *the given* element in my experience." Identifying the given means identifying it independently of all conceptual interpretation, so it is impossible to verbalize the nature of the given, since using words, even silently to oneself, is conceptualizing and interpreting.

Lewis emphasized the consequence of this, that ordinary and scientific "knowledge" of the *given-absolute* in experience is impossible. Knowledge is restricted to what can be conceptualized. But that all-important element in experience cannot be expressed or communicated. We can be aware of it, can appreciate it, and thus testify to its significance. "Evaluation can hardly be indifferent to the quality of the given. Nor can the basis of ethics be laid without reference to the felt character of experience in another mind. And the religious sense, if it is to take reality as the matrix of human values, will likewise transcend the interests of knowledge in this restricted sense." What cannot be said can only be felt, and we must be guided by what we feel as well as by what we know; this is what a pragmatic understanding of logic and science teaches us.[2]

---

[2] For an excellent critical discussion of Lewis' theory of "the given," see Israel Scheffler, *Science and Subjectivity* (Indianapolis: Bobbs-Merrill, Inc., 1967).

One occasionally encounters the misconception, not always outside professional philosophy, that turning a logician loose in philosophy is like unleashing a bull in a china shop; everything held precious is bound to be shattered. But that was not true of C. I. Lewis, nor does it apply to the contemporary logician-philosopher, Willard Van Orman Quine. Some logicians and philosophers of mathematics are really "softies," compared with some existentialists, when it comes to criticizing tradition in philosophy. Today's technical philosophy is where yesterday's technical philosophy is kept alive. Quine, for instance, is friendly toward the old ontological and metaphysical questions, however sharply he may speak his own answers.

What exists? What sorts of things does the world contain? How are you to go about deciding what there is? How do you decide whether there are such entities as attributes, relations, classes, numbers, and functions? Quine helps you to make some progress here by noting, first, that ontological assertions ("There is . . .") are automatic consequences of the conceptual scheme with which one is working. "One's ontology is basic to the conceptual scheme by which he interprets all experiences, even the most commonplace ones. Judged within some particular conceptual scheme—and how else is judgment possible?—an ontological statement goes without saying, standing in need of no separate justification at all." If, for example, your conceptual scheme holds that red houses, red noses, and red sunsets *have something in common*, what you call "the attribute of redness," then your ontological assertion "There is an attribute" is assured, and it would be absurd of you to think it might need some additional argument. Given the conceptual scheme you have in mind, "There is an attribute" follows immediately from "There are red houses, red noses, red sunsets."

But, of course, your particular conceptual scheme is not necessarily mine. In mine, "There is an attribute" might be false. My conceptual scheme might not admit that red things have "something" in common, and though I say truly "There are red houses, red noses, red sunsets," the statement "There is an attribute of redness" does not follow automatically. The issue here may seem grander and more impressive in the context of mathematics. For, as Quine points out, it is not a matter of indifference as to what ontology one should adopt. The contemporary counterparts to the medieval ontologies of *realism*, *conceptualism*, and *nominalism*, are *logicism*, *intuitionism*, and *formalism;* choosing among these, says Quine, is "no mere quibble; it makes an essential difference in the amount of classical mathematics to which one is willing to subscribe." Logicists and intuitionists, for example, split over infinity.

Ontological questions, then, are questions about what conceptual schemes we ought to adopt. That is, we have to decide which scheme *to choose*, and the decision, since it has consequences, ought not be made idly or arbitrarily. How do we choose then? "Our acceptance of an ontology is, I think, similar in principle to our acceptance of a scientific theory, say a system of physics: we adopt, at least insofar as we are reasonable, the simplest conceptual scheme into which the disordered fragments of raw experience can be fitted and arranged." Quine is quick to admit that, in practice, simplicity can be a difficult criterion to employ for choosing between rival philosophical ontologies. In fact, where two conceptual schemes compete, simplicity can be used to justify both. The issue between the *physicalistic* scheme in which "There are physical objects" is true and the *phenomenalistic* scheme in which "There are no physical objects, only sensations" is true, is a case in point. As Quine sees it, for epistemological purposes the phenomenalistic scheme is simpler, but for everyday purposes the physicalistic is more economical. Thus, ultimately, it depends upon your particular interest and purpose as to which ontology is simpler and ought to be adopted. Put this way, it illustrates Quine's thought that "the obvious counsel is tolerance and an experimental spirit." One can also detect similarities between Lewis' "conceptual pragmatism" and Quine's "ontological relativism."

Logic and the philosophy of science, in response to developments in mathematics and sciences, have occupied increasingly prominent places in the curricula of American universities, so prominent in some graduate schools as to turn many unsuspecting students against philosophy as a career. But, though most schools now insist upon technical training for potential philosophers, American philosophy is not—to dispel another misconception—exclusively or mainly logic and the philosophy of science. Philosophy of religion and religious philosophies still flourish, and not only in religious-affiliated schools and seminaries. One hears periodic and contradictory reports about the decline and surge of interest in religion in this country, but, whatever the long-range trends may be, the old close ties between American philosophy and religion seem far from severed. After the Second World War, perhaps more attention was paid to the religious existentialists, from Soren Kierkegaard to Paul Tillich, than to atheistic existentialists such as Jean-Paul Sartre or to the "God is Dead" theologians. The fact is that philosophy in the schools substantially reflects the continuing orientation toward religion of the surrounding culture.

Charles Hartshorne is a respected descendant of a long line of thinkers who find intimate connections between religion and philosophy. He rejects the idea that religion offers only the illusion of security, that science and technology can now provide us with genuine security. Hartshorne argues that the two great threats to security today are the possibilities of global war and famine. International conflict and population growth menace the future, and, on the basis of what science can tell us, we are hardly equipped to lay bets on the outcome. If the kind of security provided by science is the psychological security enjoyed through possessing probable knowledge about the future, then science, also, leaves us *insecure* in the face of today's two looming disasters. But if science and technology will not yield it, where can we find the security with which to face the unforeseen?

"My answer is the old one: security is found more in *principles* than in conditions. It consists, not in the absence of danger or in banishing the unsettled status of the future, but in the ideas and ideals whereby danger and the ambiguities of the future can be faced with courage and with joy." The first principle, says Hartshorne, is that our response to events is as important as the events themselves. Security is often achieved through our own resolution, especially through the resolve to act in the faith that in virtually all situations a creative, hopeful response is possible. According to the second principle, "each moment of life is an event in itself, and not just a means to some future goal." The meaning of life is partly in the here-and-now, and one ought not to live exclusively with an eye to the future. Too many people really ignore the living present because of anxious preoccupation with the past and with the future.

On the other hand, according to Hartshorne's third principle, we cannot afford to live just for the passing moment. The "meaning of life is its relation to something more ultimate than the future, in the everyday sense. The biblical phrase for this relation to the ultimate is the love of God or, as the Jewish doctors have expressed it, for the Holy One, Blessed be He!" What we do of value is, as it were, preserved in a hidden treasure or treasury that is more permanent than any mortal thing. For the believer, this hidden treasury, in which our every moment is retained as if remembered, is identified with the Holy One. This is superior to making the identification with our own, possibly imperishable souls, since, for one thing, that makes us look like little gods; for another, it leaves unanswered the question of how or in what sense we are immortal. The superior answer is that our passing moments are preserved in a special way by God because He cherishes them and only He knows how to do justice to their value. We could not ourselves, in some future state, equal in our recollection God's appreciation of our own past moments. We ought to live, not for ourselves primarily, but for God, the hidden reality in which we are enveloped. Life is holy in the sense that the One gives every moment of every life its full due; each pulse of life receives an absolute appreciation. We need not, if this is understood, worry about the "everyday" future "since the future of every moment, its essential destiny, is to present itself as a gift to the One from whose possession it can nevermore be cast out." For Hartshorne, the consolation of philosophy, its capacity to provide security in a shaky world, depends upon its ability to express the way in which the transience of our lives is divinely preserved.

There are of course professional philosophers who not only reject Hartshorne's religious philosophy but also deny that it reflects the prevailing temper of American life. Ernest Nagel, for instance, distinguished for his contributions to the philosophy of science, sees the contemporary American scene as receptive to a frankly "this-worldly" philosophy. But, before saying this, he makes some very interesting preliminary observations.

Nagel notes—what was emphasized in our Introduction to Chapter III—that there is no "official" philosophy in America since a democratic society and a national philosophy to which all must give allegiance are mutually contradictory. There is not even a uniquely American philosophy. All important movements in this country, including Pragmatism, have European influences. It has been said that theology is created in Germany, corrected in England, and corrupted in America. Nagel offers something similar, when mentioning the variety of European imports: "There is at least a grain of truth in the witticism that philosophies which become moribund in Europe obtain a second lease upon life when transplanted to America." Before assessing the scene more finely, Nagel points to the variety of philosophies that are visible today as well as to foreign influences.

He finds traditional ones like Calvinistic theologies still in evidence. Nor have those "rosy-hued philosophies of progress" disappeared. Influential thinkers revive the Augustinian concept of man as inherently sinful and the idea that salvation is won through abandoning the ambitions of this world. Absolute Idealism has its defenders; Hegel still lives. Thomism is characterized as "militant" and making converts in nondenominational quarters. A "lush growth" of Phenomenology is attributed to the migration of European scholars during the Second World War, and there is *Existenzphilosophie*, "suddenly fashionable in literary circles because of French influence, though at the moment without energetic advocates among professional philosophers." Nagel perhaps understates the interest taken by professional philosophy in Existentialism, and he may pass over Phenomenology too quickly. Certainly, there are excellent spokesmen for these philosophies in our schools, and courses devoted to them are highly popular, indicating a waxing rather than waning of interest in these areas. For the moment, however, we seem without an American Husserl or Merleau-Ponty, and that is possibly inevitable, given that Phenomenology is an explicit import. We have no American Heidegger or Sartre, perhaps similarly inevitable for the same reason. Or it could be that Heideggerian thought is unsuited to the prevailing temper of American culture, and it could be that, unlike the French, our culture tends not to encourage the philosopher and the creative writer to be so close as to be the same person.

We must add to Nagel's list two other philosophies: Logical Positivism and Wittgenstein-ism. Positivism is nowadays considered dead or dying, but the influence of its attack, between the wars, on traditional metaphysics is very much alive. Reports that American metaphysics is alive and well are often exaggerated. The authors of these reports are too often found, not to be doing metaphysics, but instead composing another funeral oration over the corpse of Positivism. The living embodiment of American metaphysics is as elusive as an American McTaggart. Wittgenstein-ism, the multiple ways in which the philosophy of Ludwig Wittgenstein was appropriated by young American philosophers following the Second World War, is probably declining too. Yet the belief persists in many quarters that philosophical problems are basically linguistic problems and are linguistically resolvable. More important, it is quite possible that the American philosophers who feel they are not merely expounding Wittgenstein but are, because of him, doing original philosophical work, outnumber those who feel they are not merely expounding Phenomenology or Existentialism but are actually innovating in those areas. But, of course, this is a kind of sleuth-playing to be checked immediately. Out into the open—Is there or is there not a *wave* of the future forming now?

Ernest Nagel, if we read him accurately, thinks there is. It is what he calls "Contextualistic Naturalism," which strikes him as expressing, more adequately than the other philosophies just now mentioned, the spirit of contemporary American culture. "For it is a movement which is profoundly influenced by the achievements of both theoretical and applied science, and which makes its largest appeal to a people filled with a sturdy faith in the power of intelligent thought and action to solve the problems besetting mankind." Nagel detects a movement in the culture toward the philosophy for which Morris Cohen spoke. It is a "this-worldly" philosophy that is sensibly optimistic, regarding this world not as hostile and alien to man but as the place for rewarding accomplishments. Reason and natural, not supernatural, forces are the guides to action. It is a mistake to identify Naturalism with the Pragmatism of James, Peirce, and Dewey. Pragmatism is credited with originating American Naturalism, but little of the earlier movement survives in its original form and vitality. The older theories about truth and knowledge may be rejected by today's Naturalist, and many of the polemics of Dewey and James are relegated to historical essays—but largely because their battles were won and taken for granted long ago. New investigations of scientific method and of developments in the biological sciences feature contemporary Naturalism. It is the philosophy of many established thinkers, "but it also prides itself on the fact that it has the vigorous support of many of the keenest and best disciplined minds among the younger men. It is without question America's most significant contribution to philosophic intelligence."

Naturalism's conception of the world is pluralistic and loose-fitting. Events have causes and effects, but they had no beginning, and they converge toward no special purpose. Events are not related to each other in the same way, they are not all relevant to each other, and none of them are connected through "bonds of necessity." Nature is disorderly and unpredictable when compared with formal systems that philosophers may invent, and Naturalism accordingly emphasizes the scientific need to substitute controlled observation for *a priori* arguments. The central theme of Naturalism is the "fundamentally plural character of existence, in which no overarching pattern of development can be discerned, and in which qualitative discontinuities and loose conjunctions are as ultimate features as are firm connections and regular cycles of change." Naturalism's distaste for the traditional distinction between Appearance and Reality leads to its full name of Contextualistic Naturalism. The point is that every occurrence is a real aspect of some complex process or context and is not to be banished to a World of Appearance. No context is absolutely privileged or inherently superior to others, all contexts in which natural things occur and are identified being equally real.

Given the appreciation of the plural nature of existence, Naturalism is naturally antireductionistic; it does not say, for instance, that the human mind is reducible or is "nothing but" particles in the brain. "Unlike earlier forms of naturalism, it maintains that the world contains at least as many qualitatively distinct features as are disclosed in human experience, and not a fewer number of them." What is emphasized is man's part in nature, his life and death in a wholly natural setting, not his "reducibility" to certain special things that are also parts of nature. Owing to his possession of consciousness and intelligence, man properly assigns himself a unique place in the hierarchy of existence. But however unique and wonderful man discovers he is, his nature is always understood as the product of natural forces exclusively. Looking at his fellows and society, the Naturalist is equally pluralistic. There is no one moral problem, solution, or code; there are of course many, and the task is, in specific circumstances, to find specific remedies for eliminating suffering and promoting constructive outlets for human energy. Naturalism advocates the extension of scientific method to human affairs because the method of science is the only one that is self-corrective. Scientific method does not offer a security against error and uncertainty, but it does promise assurances against perpetual self-deception. And it is employed in the scientist's faith that solutions exist, in the philosopher's faith that one can approach the future basically optimistic that those solutions can also be discovered by sane and sympathetic men.

But the individual who is trying to define his world philosophically may be left persuaded but dissatisfied by the declaration that the world is just a plurality of natural things in a plurality of loosely related natural contexts. He appreciates how seventeenth-century philosophical and theological systems are too tidy to fit the facts of a sprawling, disorderly world. He understands why, in view of this, today's "analytic" philosophy is preoccupied with piecemeal clarification and analysis of concepts. He senses the new eclecticism in the schools, the decline of polemicizing, the spentness of recent debates like those between formalists and ordinary-language philosophers, between positivists and traditionalists, etc. Professional philosophy is a chorus of rival voices competing for the student's attention, and it is an increasingly administrative concern that curricula give each an adequate hearing. He understands this, perhaps does not care whether a wave of the future is forming or not, is content not to have one voice dominate the others. But, he wonders, can't philosophy do more than summarize the world and itself as *pluralities?* Like Roquentin in Sartre's *Nausea*, he may feel overwhelmed by the proliferation of existents. He may experience an ancient craving, a longing for some *unity* in the many-ness. Our individual, the student or the intelligent inquiring citizen, wonders if today's philosophy can give his world a focus, what vaguely might be called a meaning and point of view. Does nothing remain of the old idea that philosophy is a meeting place for the arts and sciences, a place where voices speaking from different experiences and disciplines do communicate?

John Hermann Randall, Jr., colleague of Nagel at Columbia University and another well-known spokesman for Naturalism, has addressed himself to these questions. He is concerned that an ancient function of philosophy may be forgotten in the contemporary emphasis upon pluralism, and, undoubtedly, his thoughts here echo the thinking of large numbers of younger as well as older teachers of philosophy. There are many who, while rejecting Naturalism, can enthusiastically agree with Randall's reflections on the attempt to achieve some *unification of knowledge*.

"It is a fundamental fact that the world is radically and ineradicably plural. But equally basic is the fact the world can be unified in human vision. Again and again the wit of man has been able to turn the trick." The anonymous poets of primitive cultures, says Randall, did it in myth and symbol, in visions that were great achievements even if intellectually unsophisticated. We may dare to hope today that unifying visions are still available to men of genius. Developments in the physical sciences, particularly in physics, may signalize an on-going movement toward a 'unity of science' as an approachable ideal. Knowledge and science may supply the unifying vision more appropriate to our time than myths and symbols.

But, Randall stresses, envisioning the world as a unity does not make the world a unity. What he is talking about is human achievement, the ability, despite the plurality and heterogeneity of the world, to bring it into a focus, to get a perspective on it, to illuminate it from a new vantage point. Nor is *vision* the same as *knowledge*. A man's vision is what he "sees" or "finds" in the world, an expression of what the whole thing means to him. But the vision, as in the case of poets and saints, of life on earth is not necessarily knowledge or understanding of life on earth. So, then, what is there to understand? Three different things: understanding the vision itself, grasping what it means, and discovering how it originated. "Broadly, we can say that the arts give the first understanding, the humanities the second, and the sciences the third." You really have to share in the vision to understand what it is, participating in the languages of art and religion that make communication and sharing possible. "What the vision *means* can only be understood by relating it to other things; this is the function of interpretation, clarification, and criticism, which belongs to the humanities as disciplines; and here I would place both theology and philosophy." And science explains the *why* of the vision, what caused it. This division, says Randall, is too simple, and all three disciplines can function as arts, though not as sciences, but, properly qualified, the division is helpful.

What kind of *unity* is exhibited by art, philosophy, and science? Very little in the arts, which is to be expected, since the idea of a "unity of vision" is really distasteful. We actually treasure the plurality of vision in art and religion, each one revealing new possibilities in the world and new meanings given to it. There is considerable talk today about the "unity of science," but, as Randall sees it, the world is not yet proved to be a unity and such "unifying" talk seems to interest philosophers more than the scientists themselves. Nevertheless, "the world does still reveal, if not unity, at least a continuity of the conditions by which it does all it does—a continuity of those devices by which all its processes are brought about." Nature is a labyrinth if not a unity, making continuity of scientific inquiry indeed possible. Given this, talk about an ultimate unity of scientific knowledge is not obviously unreasonable.

But the "world with man in it" is a different story. Here continuity breaks down, and *uniqueness* and *individuality* are the salient characteristics. Here is the subject matter for the interpretation and criticism that is *philosophical*. It tries to "relate the many things a world with man in it does, to each other, and to the way it does them—trying to relate possibilities to each other and to their conditions, trying to find what they mean." This is a never-ending search for increasing unification of knowledge, since it is an attempt to establish an endless number of relations between the actualities and possibilities of the "world with man in it." The world's possibilities do not spiral into a simple totality, so, in this sense, there is no unity, only many *human unifications* and visions of the world. "But here is the opportunity for more and more comprehensive unifications—as men learn more of the world's possi-

bilities, and come to understand more of the other meanings that other
men and cultures have found."

Thus described, the philosophical enterprise is seen by Randall as
the one to which the arts, the sciences, and the humanities all contribute.
The artist makes his contribution through his creation, the scientist by
his discoveries. The scientist may also achieve a remarkable unification
of knowledge. "But the unity of science achieved would not be the
unification of the world. No, our common enterprise seems to be the
enterprise of the critic and interpreter, of the humanist and philosopher,
of the searcher after more adequate meaning. Drawing on both the
others, he can hope to unify the world for knowledge with a meaning
found. He must indeed see the world from a selective focus, but he can
hope to see it steadily and whole." We will not agree in our answers
about what the world "means," and the selective focus will vary from
philosopher to philosopher. But we will have participated in what we
want to do, what the world prompts us to do, to seek more "adequate
meanings" by finding more and more relations within and between the
worlds of art, science, and daily affairs.

The proposal is attractive—treacherous too. For the human world,
anyway, is a scene of plurality and discontinuity. The connections you
philosophers make can be thrown back in your faces by those who
prefer it that way. So it is tempting to retire into private visions. But
you can never define your world philosophically through private
visions alone. You have to return to following the tracings "out there,"
bearing in mind that what you find or seem to find will inevitably cause
a controversy. Locating one's context philosophically is, unlike relaxed
dreaming, learning to accept the eternal tensions and controversies in
one's own brain as a part of the game.

MORRIS R. COHEN

Morris R. Cohen (1880–1947) was born in Russia and educated in New York City. He graduated from the College of the City of New York and received his PhD from Harvard in 1906. He exercised great influence as teacher, lecturer, and author during a long career at City College in New York. Cohen represented a variety of interests in philosophy, ranging from logic to the philosophy of history. His Carus Lectures were published as *The Meaning of Human History*. He was a political liberal, making important contributions to the philosophy of law. Other books include *The Faith of a Liberal, Law and the Social Order*, and *Reason and Law*. Cohen was a noted defender of reason and scientific thinking, and this is apparent in the following selection taken from his book *Reason and Nature*.* It is an excellent statement to juxtapose with some things typically said by earlier American Pragmatists.

In Dispraise of Life

In speaking of the new philosophic movement which began with the present century, William James remarked: "It lacks logical rigour, but it has the tang of life." It is strikingly significant of the temper of our age that this was intended and has generally been taken as praise of the new philosophy. To any of the classical philosophers, to whom not life, but the good life was the object of rational effort, James's dictum would have sounded as a condemnation. For life devoid of logic is confused, unenlightened, and often brutish. Indeed the new philosophy itself maintains that it is precisely because unreflective life is so unsatisfactory that it gives rise to logic. Why then should the word *life* itself be a term of praise except to those who prefer the primitive and dislike intellectual effort?

I can imagine that a classical philosopher living long enough amongst us to penetrate some of our bewildering ways might conclude that our worship of mere life, rather than the good or rational life, reflects the temper of an acquisitive society, feverishly intent on mere accumulation, and mortally afraid to stop to discriminate between what is worth while and what is not. The same preference for terms of promiscuous all-

* Reprinted by permission of The Macmillan Company. Copyright 1931 by Morris Cohen, renewed 1959 by Leonora Cohen Rosenfeld.

inclusiveness, rather than for those that involve the discrimination essential to philosophic clarity, shows itself also in the use of the terms *experience* and *reality*. It is of course true that surface clarity can readily be obtained by ignoring fundamental difficulties, and that we cannot dispense with terms indicating the unlimited immensities of which our little formulated systems are but infinitesimal selections. But if the world contains many things and therefore distinctions between them, ignoring these distinctions is not the same as profundity. The honorific use of non-discriminating terms can only serve to darken counsel. That this has actually been the case in ethics and in theories of knowledge, in religion and in art, is the burden of this brief epilogue.

That the continuance of mere physical life is an absolute moral good seems to be axiomatic in current ethics. It serves as a basis for the unqualified moral condemnation of all forms of suicide and euthanasia. Now I do not wish to question the biologic proposition that there are forces which make the organism continue to function after we have lost all specifically human goods, such as honour and reason. What I do wish to point out is that this setting up of mere life as an absolute moral good, apart from all its social conditions, is inconsistent with the moral approval of the hero or the martyr who throws away life for the sake of honour or conscience. It would be pathetically absurd to praise the abandoning of life by John Huss or Giordano Bruno on the ground that it increased or prolonged the total amount of life. Indiscriminate increase of population beyond any definite limit is of very doubtful moral value—despite the arguments of those who oppose all forms of birth control. We must not lose sight of the fact that life always carries with it not only the seeds of disease and inevitable death, but also the roots of all that is vicious and hideous in human conduct. We cannot, therefore, dispense with the classical problem of defining the good and discriminating it from the evil of life—a difficult and baffling problem, to be sure; but those who find it profitless are under no obligation to pursue moral philosophy.

The confusion of moral theory by the eulogistic use of the word *life* can be readily seen in the Nietzschean ethics—all the more instructive because Nietzsche himself starts from the classical perception of the inadequacy of ordinary utilitarianism in face of the moral values of heroism. The good life involves the sacrifice of ease and comfort, the receiving as well as the giving of hard blows. But just because Nietzsche is impatient of definition he falls into the easy error of sharply opposing the pursuit of life to the pursuit of knowledge—witness his essay on

History. But the pursuit of knowledge is itself a form of life. This fact cannot be obscured by rhetorical contrasts between the life of the closet philosopher and the open-air or what is euphemistically called *real* life. To the eye of philosophic reflection the scholar or persistent thinker shows as much life or vitality as those who have to cover their naked restlessness by a gospel of strenuous but aimless perpetual motion—in no particular direction. This is not the occasion to sing the praises of the intellect and what it has done to humanize life. We may grant that the distaste for arduous intellectual tasks is natural, blameless, and in some cases even providential. But when such distaste sets itself up as a philosophy of life it is only ridiculous.

This brings us to our second point, the vitalistic theory of knowledge —or perhaps we should refer to it as the theory of a vitalistic intuition superior to knowledge—I mean the widespread notion that by mere living we get an insight superior to that of the intellect operative in mathematical and natural science. To prevent misunderstanding, let me say that I am not referring here to genuine mysticism which asserts that all intellection and language move in the mist of appearances and cannot reach the ineffable reality. Genuine mysticism always holds fast to the idea that the substance of reality is altogether beyond the power of language, and hence it does not use language to describe this reality. It holds that language can at best only indicate its own shortcomings and thus point the way beyond itself. When, however, as in the Bergsonian theory, the claim of the scientific intellect is set aside for an instinctive intuition, and when this is held to provide a superior explanation of empirical phenomena like the formation of the eye of the scallop, it seems to me that philosophy is then not far removed from glorified quackery where the philosopher's stone is expected to remove the effects of the evil eye or cure toothaches and other empirical ailments. We may grant that biology as a natural science does not carry us very far into the mystery of life. But it does not follow that our ignorance can be cured in any other way. The fallibility of scientific reasoning is best corrected only by definite experiments and the critical reasoning of science itself. When men despair of solving theoretic problems and appeal to undefined words like *life* they show themselves devoid of intellectual stamina. It is doubtless true that in the process of living our ideas develop, mature, and receive a solid amplitude through an enriched content. Time tests our judgments and eliminates clever, plausible sophistries. But it is also true that the older a lamb grows the more sheepish he gets. Nothing seems so solidly established by anthropology and history as that men will not learn from what has actually happened to them unless they have developed the power of reflection. The idea that experience alone will teach everybody is a thin optimistic illusion.

The use of the word *experience* without any ascertainable meaning is perhaps the outstanding scandal of recent philosophy. In its original sense, which it still retains in ordinary, intelligible discourse, and from which we cannot altogether liberate ourselves in philosophy, experience denotes conscious feeling or something which happens to us personally. Thus I make my meaning clear when I say, "I did not experience any pain during an operation," or "I have never experienced what it is to be struck by lightning." I may also speak of not having experienced the panic of 1872 or the other side of the moon. The absence of such experience need not, however, prevent me from knowing a good deal about the operation, the lightning, the panic of 1872, and the other side of the moon—more indeed than about many of my own experiences. For experience in this personal and ordinary sense is but an infinitesimal portion of what is going on in the world of time and space, and even a small part of the world of ordinary human affairs. To identify the substance of the world with the fact of our experience of some part of it is to set up an anthropocentric universe, compared to which the mediaeval one is sane and respectable. For the mediaeval one rebuked the silly and arrogant pretensions of humanity by setting against it the great glory of God.

The absurdity of identifying the whole realm of nature with our little human experience of it is obscured in two ways—to wit, (1) by confusing the nature of possible experience, and (2) by stretching the word *experience* until it *excludes* nothing and therefore includes no definite meaning.

That things known are all objects of a conceivable possible experience to some possible being more or less like us need not be denied. But the object of a possible experience is a matter of intellectual consideration, not the object of actual personal experience. If, on the other hand, we stretch the meaning of the word *experience* and make it include everything that we can think about, e.g. the state of the earth before the advent of life, then there remains no difference between an object considered and an object experienced, and the proposition that knowledge rests on experience ceases to have significance. It is vain to define words so as to deny the fact that we know many things to be beyond our experience. In general, the term *experience* either means something personal and therefore limited, or it becomes so promiscuously all-inclusive that it ceases to have any intelligible negative. Without an alternative term to denote what is not experience it cannot have any pragmatic meaning. With characteristic sensitiveness to the difficulties of his own account, Professor Dewey has realized something of this dilemma in which the use of the term *experience* involves him. He has tried to defend it by the analogy of the use of the terms *zero* and *infinity*. But zero and infinity indicate at least definite directions. They indicate which of two definite terms is to the left or right of the other in a series. The term *experience*, however, in Professor Dewey's thought is equally applicable to everything that is an object of consideration. I cannot therefore see that it serves any definite intellectual function beyond carrying the faint aroma of praise.

In general, when familiar words are stretched and put to new uses, confusion is bound to result. For the meaning we attach to words is based on habits which arbitrary resolutions cannot readily change, and we invariably drag the old meaning into the new context.

An instructive instance of the confusing use of the term *experience* is the current phrase *religious experience*, used by those who regard it as a substitute for rational theology. Here again, I have no quarrel with any one who claims to have had the beatific vision of God or a special revelation of the truths of religion. One who makes such a claim puts himself beyond argument except when he asks others to believe what he believes. Then the doubt which Tennyson applied to his own vision certainly becomes relevant. Nor is my quarrel with those who assume the truths of their religion on the authority of an historic church or revelation fortified by the necessary truths of reason. The current fashion which talks about religious experience distrusts the great streams of historic tradition as it does the claims of systematic theology—witness James's *Varieties of Religious Experience*, in which none of the great historic religions receives any attention. He thinks he can establish "piecemeal supernaturalism" by the methods of natural science and the rules of empirical evidence. An elementary consideration, however, of the logic of induction shows the impossibility of proving the existence of miraculous or supernatural interventions on the basis of the postulate of the uniformity of nature involved in induction. Indeed, the naturalist can well maintain that as instances of mystic experiences have their parallel in the effects of drugs, starvation, etc., the naturalistic explanation of them is the only one that is scientifically worth investigating. In any case, the spiritualistic hypothesis does not lend itself to the crucial test of affording us veritable predictions. Not only a scientist but even a court of law would be derelict if it accepted as proved anything which rests on no better evidence than that offered by abnormal psychology for a finite, personal God and the immortality of the individual soul.

It is of course true that most people do not hold these beliefs as scientific hypotheses at all. Indeed, most people regard the cold, logical analysis of their religion with a horror like that which would be evoked by a funeral orator who proceeded to give a scientific examination of the character of the deceased. We come to mourn and praise our friend, not to hear him psychoanalyzed. But all this is irrelevant in moments of reflection or when our beliefs are challenged by the contrary beliefs of others. One may say: I hold these truths and the faith in them strengthens my life. But such assertions cannot keep out the lurking doubt that it is the psychologic attitude rather than the truth of what is assumed that produces the practical effects. The pragmatic glorification of belief contains the deep poison of scepticism as to what really exists, and this like a Nessus shirt will destroy any religious belief that puts it on. Religion may begin in ritual and conduct, but it inevitably goes on to reflective belief that must submit to the canons of logic. The popular and superficial contrast between religion and theology ignores the fact that where a diversity of religion exists it is impossible to stop a process of reflection as to which of two conflicting claims is true. In such a society, religious creed or theology (including the possibility of a negative or atheistic theory) becomes inescapable. Hazy talk about religious experience will not adequately meet the difficulties.

If terms that have no genuine negatives are to be condemned as devoid of significance, the word *reality* should head the list. I am not unmindful of the many attempts to define the unreal. But the question is: What corresponds to these definitions? The Hindoo mystic is deeply irritated when the wise Chinese suggests that the realm of Maya or illusion does not really exist, or that it is not worth while worrying about it. The reality of illusion is the emphatic centre of the Hindoo's philosophy, and similarly, of all those who sharply contrast reality and appearance. The difficulty here is classic. What I am more especially concerned about, however, is to call attention to the fact that the word *reality* maintains itself as a term of praise rather than of description. To be "in touch with reality" is our way of expressing what our less sophisticated brothers and sisters do by the phrase "in tune with the infinite." It is an expression which carries an agreeable afflatus without dependence on any definite meaning. Such edification is pleasing and would be harmless if it did not also cause intellectual confusion. This the eulogistic use of the word *reality* certainly does in the theory of art, especially in its realistic and expressionistic form.

Professor Neilson defined the realistic motive, in poetry and art generally, as the sense of fact. But whatever else art may involve, the process of selection is certainly essential to it in all its forms, useful as well as ornamental. Hence, the honourific use of a non-discriminating term like *reality* undoubtedly tends to justify the introduction of the inept and the ugly, which certainly cannot be denied to have real existence. But it is not only realism that is thus encouraged to escape or confuse the fundamental problem of what is relevant, fitting, or beautiful in representation and ornament. Expressionistic theories glorify the same lack of discrimination between the beautiful and the ugly. For expressionism is but a subjective realism. This becomes clear when we reflect that the real denotes, first, human affairs, then physical things, and now vivid impressions or emotions, so that abstractions are not real to us. The praise of reality, therefore, now has as its core the glorification of vivid impressions or violent expressions, regardless of fitness or coherence. This shows itself in an indiscriminate admiration for the breaking of all hitherto accepted rules of art—as if all rules were necessarily hindrances. But rules of art like the so-called rules of nature are at bottom only statements of what is relevant and what irrelevant to any given case. Hence it is doubtless true that new situations in art cannot always be profitably decided by old rules. But this again is a question of specific fitness, not to be disposed of by the violent assertion that the expression of inner reality is inconsistent with all rules.

It is doubtful, for instance, whether such a convention as the rules of the sonnet ever hindered a great poet from expressing himself, though it doubtless has aided many minor ones, perhaps unduly so.

To conclude, we cannot praise life without including in our praise moral and physical evil, corruption and death. As experience certainly includes error and illusion, we cannot priase it indiscriminately as a support of truth. Finally, as reality undoubtedly includes the useless and the ugly, its praise cannot but confuse the arts.

Instead of life we want the good life. Instead of accepting experience science discriminates between the experience of truth and the experience of illusion. Not all reality, but only a reality free from ugliness and confusing incoherence is the aim of art. Conduct, science, and art thus depend on rational discrimination. Rational philosophy tries to meet this need by defining the good, the true, and the beautiful. The essence of the romantic use of the terms *life*, *experience*, and *reality* is that it avoids this necessary task, and is therefore flattering to those to whom the use of reason is irksome. But the way to serenity and happiness through wisdom is more arduous and requires a purified vision into our hearts as well as courage to face the abysmal mystery of existence.

CLARENCE I. LEWIS

Most of Clarence I. Lewis' (1883–1964) career was spent at Harvard, where he had received his PhD in 1910. He held teaching appointments at Stanford and the University of California as well. His work in symbolic logic and the development of what he called "strict implication" attracted considerable attention. He was an influential teacher, and many of his students became distinguished contributors to analytic philosophy. More recently, Lewis' work in analytical ethics has interested professional philosophers perhaps more than his earlier writings in symbolic logic. His books include *A Survey of Symbolic Logic* (with C. H. Langford), *Symbolic Logic*, *Mind and the World-Order*, and *An Analysis of Knowledge and Valuation*. The following selection, in which he describes his intellectual development and the philosophy in which it culminated, is from *Contemporary American Philosophy: Personal Statements*.*

Logic and Pragmatism

The most powerful single influence in my intellectual development was an old lady whom I met when I was fifteen. A year or two earlier I had begun a period of the most intense and furious thinking I shall ever experience. The combination of native scepticism and an orthodox upbringing had proved to be an explosive mixture: I had been plunged into doubts and questions which went on and on until I faced the universe with something of the wonder of the first man. The old lady, with compassionate understanding, confessed that she too was a heretic, and after establishing our agreements we went on to the much more enticing matter of our disagreements. Our discussions continued, at intervals, over a period of about two years, at the end of which time I had worked out my own answers to the puzzles which beset me. Some of these, I am sure, must have startled and amused my mentor, but she always agreed solemnly to consider them.

*　　*　　*

Nothing comparable in importance happened after that until I became acquainted with Kant. I was now safely under academic

* From Vol. II, "Logic and Pragmatism," George P. Adams and William Pepperell Montague, ed. (1930) (New York: Russell & Russell, 1962). Reprinted by permission.

auspices, and thinking was no longer a lone adventure. Kant compelled me. He had, so I felt, followed scepticism to its inevitable last stage, and laid his foundations where they could not be disturbed. I was then, and have continued to be, impatient of those who seem not to face the sceptical doubt seriously. Kant attracted me also by his intellectual integrity and by the massiveness and articulation of his structure. The evidence of Kant in my thinking ever since is unmistakable, however little I may achieve the excellences which aroused my youthful admiration.

Of my teachers at Harvard, Royce impressed me most. His ponderous cogency kept my steady attention, even though I never followed to his metaphysical conclusions. James, I thought, had a swift way of being right, but how he reached his conclusions was his own secret. Royce was, in fact, my paradigm of a philosopher, and I was prone to minimize the difference from him of such convictions as I had. It was Royce himself, finally, with my doctor's thesis before him, who pointed out the extent of these differences. He concluded by saying, with his usual dry humour, "I thought you were principally influenced by Perry, but I find he thinks you are principally influenced by me. Between us, we agreed that perhaps this is original."

Royce was also responsible for my interest in logic, or at least for the direction which it took. In 1910–11 I was his assistant in two courses in that subject, and he put into my hands one of the first copies of *Principia Mathematica*, volume i, which came to Cambridge. It is difficult now to appreciate what a novelty this work then was to all of us. Its logistic method was so decidely an advance upon Schroder an~~d~~ ~~....o.~~ The principles of mathematics were here deduced from definitions alone, without other assumptions than those of logic. I spent the better part of a year upon it.

* * *

It had become apparent from my little experiments with strange "logics" that two minds which followed different systems in their modes of inference need not be unintelligible to one another—that, in fact, they might be so related that when their premises were common neither (outside of logic itself) would ever reach a conclusion which the other must repudiate as false. But, as between two such, the road from premise to conclusion would be more or less direct, more or less impeded. Fundamental psychological bent might here dictate a choice. Or again, if the general course of experience were other than it is—if, for example, all processes in nature should be reversible—then, although no different choice of modes of inference would be dictated, a different "logic" would apply with more facility. Thus the ultimate ground of accepted logical principles, as against other self-consistent modes, might be criteria of convenience (a poor word, but the best I can think of), somewhat like those which Poincaré suggested as determining our choice of Euclidean geometry.

This thesis, by itself, seems implausible and highly paradoxical; the stronghold of pragmatism supposedly lies in the empirical; logic is the citadel of rationalism. Nevertheless I became more and more convinced that this was right. Pragmatism, as ordinarily understood, seems to take things wrong end on; it is the element which mind contributes, in truth and knowledge, which may be pragmatic; the empirical brute fact of the given is absolute datum. Logic contains no material truth; it is independent of the given precisely because it dictates nothing whatever with regard to the content of experience, but determines only the mind's mode of dealing with it. This thought suggested others, which soon came to keep it company and mitigate the paradoxical air which it exhibited in isolation.

*   *   *

Logic, and that which is certifiable on logical grounds alone, constitutes the a priori element in knowledge. The Kantian cross-classification, by which *synthetic* judgments a priori become the foundations of science, has more and more clearly been proved to be without foundation, as mathematics and exact science have developed. Mathematics has been shown to be capable of purely logical development, by analysis alone, and without recourse to any synthetic element, such as geometric constructions, which represent an appeal from pure conception to intuition. *Principia Mathematica* represents the final state of the movement in this direction: we see here the deductive developments of mathematics merely from the logical analysis (definition) of the mathematical concepts. There is and must be a synthetic element in judgment about the *applications* of mathematics, about real space, or about concrete collections of things. At the same time that mathematics becomes purely logical and analytic, it becomes abstract. Which of the various abstract geometrics applies to space becomes a separate and extra-mathematical question, and, as Poincaré and relativity have shown, one which is to be determined either upon empirical grounds; in which case the answer is probable only, or by some pragmatic choice, or by some interplay between these two.

Hume was right in his somewhat wavering conviction that the truths of mathematics represent necessary connections of ideas, and likewise right that this by itself does not prove any necessary connection of matters of fact. The line between the a priori and the a posteriori coincides with the division between conceptual and empirical; and it likewise coincides with the distinction between what mind itself contributes or determines and what is given as datum of sense.

A priori truth is independent of experience because it is purely analytic of our conceptual meanings, and dictates nothing to the given. Logic, mathematics, and in general whatever has structure and order and system, may be developed in abstraction from all consideration of the empirical by purely logical analysis. It depends upon nothing but its own conceptual integrity for that kind of truth which is possible to abstract systems.

* * *

If, however, all truth which can be certain in advance of the experience to which it applies is of this purely analytic and definitive sort, then we might be led to remark that such abstract a priori truth tells us nothing of the nature of reality beyond our own minds, and is significant only of our own consistency of thought. This conclusion would be a mistaken one; paradoxical as it may sound, we can predict the nature of reality without prescribing the character of future experience. What the mind meets in experience is not independent *reality*, but an independent *given;* the given is not, without further ado, the real, but contains all the content of dream, illusion, and deceitful appearance.

In fact, the criteria of reality represent a peculiarly illuminating example of the a priori. The word "real" has a meaning, and represents a definite conception which, when applied to the content of experience, leads to the interpretation of this content sometimes as "real," sometimes as "unreal." The formulation of the criteria of the real constitutes a merely analytic or definitive statement, representing our interpretative attitude. Such criteria of reality can neither be supplied by experience (since direct generalization from an unsorted experience, not already classified as real, would not serve) nor can experience invalidate them. Whatever in experience does not conform to the criteria of reality is automatically thrown out of court.

We can and must prescribe the nature of reality. We cannot prescribe the nature of the given. The paradox of this is mitigated somewhat when we observe that the word "real" is systematically ambiguous.

"Reality" is of different sorts, physical, mental, mathematical—the easily named categories do not cover the easily recognized distinctions. A mirror-image, for example, is its own particular kind of reality, neither "physical" nor "mental," as is also a mirage and "appearances" in general. Each category of reality has its own peculiar criteria, and what is unreal in one sense will be real in some other. *Any* content of given experience will be real in some category or other—will be that kind of reality which is ascribed to it when it is "correctly understood." The categories are neither a Procrustean bed into which experience is thrust nor concepts whose applicability depends on some pre-established harmony between the given and the mind. Rather they are like the reference system which the mathematician stretches through all space and with respect to which whatever positions and motions are there to be described will inevitably be describable. Categorial criteria are neither insignificant and verbal tautologies nor empirical prophecies, but exhibit definitive criteria of intelligent classification and inter-pretation.

The content of a properly conceived metaphysics is the analytic truths which exhibit the fundamental criteria and major classifications of the real; it is definitive of "real"-ity, not descriptive of the universe *in extenso*. In fact, all philosophy has for its task such analytic depiction of the a priori—to define the good, the right, the true, the valid, and the real.

It will be evident that the absoluteness of such a priori principles, whenever and wherever they are held, is entirely compatible with their historical alteration, just as modes of classification or alternative reference systems, expressible in definitive principles or initial prescriptions, would be absolute while adhered to, but might be subject to considera-tions of usefulness and to historical change. The assurance of perpetuity for our categories is no greater than the assurance that our basic human nature and the broad outlines of experience will never alter. There is an eternal truth about our abstract concepts—the given is absolute datum; but the chosen conceptual systems applied to the interpretation of the given are subject to possible change. In the field of metaphysical concepts particularly, such change would seem to be a fact—as the history of such concepts as "matter," "mind," and "cause," bears witness.

The categories differ in no wise from concepts in general except in degree of comprehensiveness and fundamental character. Every con-cept whatever exhibits criteria of its own little kind of reality. In so far as experience is intelligible and expressible only when grasped in some framework of conceptual interpretation, this a priori element of the definitive is all-pervasive.

It is the conceptual order of experience alone which is communicable or expressible. The given, apart from such conceptual interpretation, is ineffable. If, so to speak, one sensory quality could be lifted out of the network of relations in which it stands and replaced by another, the aesthetic character of experience might be altered, but everything which has to do with knowledge and with action would remain precisely as before. Community of thought and knowledge requires community of concept or of relational pattern, but if there should be idiosyncrasies of sense which do not affect discrimination and relation, these would be immaterial to our common understanding and co-operation. In fact, in the face of all those *verifiable* differences of sense which are evidenced by our different powers of discrimination, we possess a common understanding and a common reality through the social achievement of common categories and concepts. When the vast and impressive institution of human education—in its wider sense—is remarked, the assumption that such community is simply native or ready-made is seen to be superfluous. My world is my intellectual achievement; our common world, a social one. The frequent objection of the sceptic, that knowledge is implausible in view of the subjectivity of sense, is an *ignoratio elenchi*.

Knowledge grasps conceptual structure or order alone. It was Berkeley who, almost without noting it himself, first phrased this nature of our knowledge. One idea is "sign of" another in the order of nature. If it be a reliable sign—that is, if it bear constant and orderly relationships— one empirical *quale* is as good as another to serve this function of cognition. Knowledge of the external world consists of relations between one item of experience and another, not in the content of experience somehow matching the quality of an external real. Such qualitative coincidence of idea and object—if the notion means anything—would be extraneous to knowledge. This conclusion is quite independent of idealism.

*   *   *

One further note I should like to make in closing. As the word "knowledge" has been used above, it is narrowed somewhat from its usual meaning. It comprises what have sometimes been called the "truths of description" which, as it is here conceived, depend exclusively upon conceptual order. It excludes "truths of appreciation," the aesthetic quality of the given, and all that depends upon sympathy and upon that communion of minds which requires coincidence of immediate experience. Evaluation can hardly be indifferent to the quality of the given. Nor can the basis of ethics be laid without reference to the felt character of experience in another mind. And the religious sense, if it is to take reality as the matrix of human values, will likewise transcend the interests of knowledge in this restricted sense. There is, then, a line of division between such interests and cognition of the type of science. And it is suggested that the foundation of these, not being found in knowledge alone, may rest upon some postulate.

WILLARD VAN ORMAN QUINE

Willard Van Orman Quine (1908–) is generally considered
one of America's most original and influential logicians and
philosophers. After graduating from Oberlin College and receiving
his PhD from Harvard in 1932, Quine became identified with
Harvard. He has taught in South America and Japan, was a
member of the Institute of Advanced Studies at Princeton, has
received honorary degrees from Ohio State University and the
University of Chicago, is a former president of the Association
for Symbolic Logic and the American Philosophical Association,
Eastern Division. His books include *Set Theory and Its Logic*,
Methods of Logic, *Mathematical Logic*, and *Word and Object*.
The following selection is a well-known essay and is from his
From a Logical Point of View.* It shows how Pragmatism and
logical analysis combine in Quine's thinking about the status of
ontological issues.

On What There Is

Now let us turn to the ontological problem of universals: the question
whether there are such entities as attributes, relations, classes, numbers,
functions. McX, characteristically enough, thinks there are. Speaking
of attributes, he says: "There are red houses, red roses, red sunsets;
this much is prephilosophical common sense in which we must all agree.
These houses, roses, and sunsets, then, have something in common; and
this which they have in common is all I mean by the attribute of redness." For McX, thus, there being attributes is even more obvious and
trivial than the obvious and trivial fact of there being red houses, roses,
and sunsets. This, I think, is characteristic of metaphysics, or at least
of that part of metaphysics called ontology: one who regards a statement
on this subject as true at all must regard it as trivially true. One's
ontology is basic to the conceptual scheme by which he interprets all
experiences, even the most commonplace ones. Judged within some
particular conceptual scheme—and how else is judgment possible?—
an ontological statement goes without saying, standing in need of no
separate justification at all. Ontological statements follow immediately
from all manner of casual statements of commonplace fact, just as—

* From Chapter I, "On What There Is" (Cambridge, Mass.: Harvard University
Press, 1953). Reprinted by permission of *The Review of Metaphysics* and the author.

THE SPIRIT OF AMERICAN PHILOSOPHY

from the point of view, anyway, of McX's conceptual scheme—'There is an attribute' follows from 'There are red houses, red roses, red sunsets.'

Judged in another conceptual scheme, an ontological statement which is axiomatic to McX's mind may, with equal immediacy and triviality, be adjudged false. One may admit that there are red houses, roses, and sunsets, but deny, except as a popular and misleading manner of speaking, that they have anything in common. The words 'houses', 'roses', and 'sunsets' are true of sundry individual entities which are houses and roses and sunsets, and the word 'red' or 'red object' is true of each of sundry individual entities which are red houses, red roses, red sunsets; but there is not, in addition, any entity whatever, individual or otherwise, which is named by the word 'redness', nor, for that matter, by the word 'househood', 'rosehood', sunsethood'. That the houses and roses and sunsets are all of them red may be taken as ultimate and irreducible, and it may be held that McX is no better off, in point of real explanatory power, for all the occult entities which he posits under such names as 'redness'.

*   *   *

Classical mathematics, as the example of primes larger than a million clearly illustrates, is up to its neck in commitments to an ontology of abstract entities. Thus it is that the great mediaeval controversy over universals has flared up anew in the modern philosophy of mathematics. The issue is clearer now than of old, because we now have a more explicit standard whereby to decide what ontology a given theory or form of discourse is committed to: a theory is committed to those and only those entities to which the bound variables of the theory must be capable of referring in order that the affirmations made in the theory be true.

Because this standard of ontological presupposition did not emerge clearly in the philosophical tradition, the modern philosophical mathematicians have not on the whole recognized that they were debating the same old problem of universals in a newly clarified form. But the fundamental cleavages among modern points of view on foundations of mathematics do come down pretty explicitly to disagreements as to the range of entities to which the bound variables should be permitted to refer.

The three main mediaeval points of view regarding universals are designated by historians as *realism*, *conceptualism*, and *nominalism*.

Essentially these same three doctrines reappear in twentieth-century surveys of the philosophy of mathematics under the new names *logicism*, *intuitionism*, and *formalism*.

Realism, as the word is used in connection with the mediaeval controversy over universals, is the Platonic doctrine that universals or abstract entities have being independently of the mind; the mind may discover them but cannot create them. *Logicism*, represented by Frege, Russell, Whitehead, Church, and Carnap, condones the use of bound variables to refer to abstract entities known and unknown, specifiable and unspecifiable, indiscriminately.

Conceptualism holds that there are universals but they are mind-made. *Intuitionism*, espoused in modern times in one form or another by Poincaré, Brouwer, Weyl, and others, countenances the use of bound variables to refer to abstract entities only when those entities are capable of being cooked up individually from ingredients specified in advance. As Fraenkel has put it, logicism holds that classes are discovered while intuitionism holds that they are invented—a fair statement indeed of the old opposition between realism and conceptualism. This opposition is no mere quibble; it makes an essential difference in the amount of classical mathematics to which one is willing to subscribe. Logicists, or realists, are able on their assumptions to get Cantor's ascending orders of infinity; intuitionists are compelled to stop with the lowest order of infinity, and, as an indirect consequence, to abandon even some of the classical laws of real numbers. The modern controversy between logicism and intuitionism arose, in fact, from disagreements over infinity.

Formalism, associated with the name of Hilbert, echoes intuitionism in deploring the logicist's unbridled recourse to universals. But formalism also finds intuitionism unsatisfactory. This could happen for either of two opposite reasons. The formalist might, like the logicist, object to the crippling of classical mathematics; or he might, like the *nominalists* of old, object to admitting abstract entities at all, even in the restrained sense of mind-made entities. The upshot is the same: the formalist keeps classical mathematics as a play of insignificant notations. This play of notations can still be of utility—whatever utility it has already shown itself to have as a crutch for physicists and technologists. But utility need not imply significance, in any literal linguistic sense. Nor need the marked success of mathematicians in spinning out theorems, and in finding objective bases for agreement with one another's results, imply significance. For an adequate basis for agreement among mathematicians can be found simply in the rules which govern the manipulation of the notations—these syntactical rules being, unlike the notations themselves, quite significant and intelligible.

I have argued that the sort of ontology we adopt can be consequential—notably in connection with mathematics, although this is only an example. Now how are we to adjudicate among rival ontologies? Certainly the answer is not provided by the semantical formula "To be is to be the value of a variable"; this formula serves rather, conversely, in testing the conformity of a given remark or doctrine to a prior ontological standard. We look to bound variables in connection with ontology not in order to know what there is, but in order to know what a given remark or doctrine, ours or someone else's, *says* there is; and this much is quite properly a problem involving language. But what there is is another question.

*   *   *

It is no wonder, then, that ontological controversy should tend into controversy over language. But we must not jump to the conclusion that what there is depends on words. Translatability of a question into semantical terms is no indication that the question is linguistic. To see Naples is to bear a name which, when prefixed to the words 'sees Naples', yields a true sentence; still there is nothing linguistic about seeing Naples.

Our acceptance of an ontology is, I think, similar in principle to our acceptance of a scientific theory, say a system of physics: we adopt, at least insofar as we are reasonable, the simplest conceptual scheme into which the disordered fragments of raw experience can be fitted and arranged. Our ontology is determined once we have fixed upon the over-all conceptual scheme which is to accommodate science in the broadest sense; and the considerations which determine a reasonable construction of any part of that conceptual scheme, for example, the biological or the physical part, are not different in kind from the considerations which determine a reasonable construction of the whole. To whatever extent the adoption of any system of scientific theory may be said to be a matter of language, the same—but no more—may be said of the adoption of an ontology.

But simplicity, as a guiding principle in constructing conceptual schemes, is not a clear and unambiguous idea; and it is quite capable of presenting a double or multiple standard. Imagine, for example, that we have devised the most economical set of concepts adequate to the play-by-play reporting of immediate experience. The entities under this scheme—the values of bound variables—are, let us suppose, individual subjective events of sensation or reflection. We should still find, no doubt, that a physicalistic conceptual scheme, purporting to talk about external objects, offers great advantages in simplifying our over-all reports. By bringing together scattered sense events and treating them as perceptions of one object, we reduce the complexity of our stream of experience to a manageable conceptual simplicity. The rule of simplicity is indeed our guiding maxim in assigning sense data to objects: we associate an earlier and a later round sensum with the same so-called penny, or with two different so-called pennies, in obedience to the demands of maximum simplicity in our total world-picture.

Here we have two competing conceptual schemes, a phenomenalistic one and a physicalistic one. Which should prevail? Each has its advantages; each has its special simplicity in its own way. Each, I suggest, deserves to be developed. Each may be said, indeed, to be the more fundamental, though in different senses: the one is epistemologically, the other physically, fundamental.

The physical conceptual scheme simplifies our account of experience because of the way myriad scattered sense events come to be associated with single so-called objects; still there is no likelihood that each sentence about physical objects can actually be translated, however deviously and complexly, into the phenomenalistic language. Physical objects are postulated entities which round out and simplify our account of the flux of experience, just as the introduction of irrational numbers simplifies laws of arithmetic. From the point of view of the conceptual scheme of the elementary arithmetic of rational numbers alone, the broader arithmetic of rational and irrational numbers would have the status of a convenient myth, simpler than the literal truth (namely, the arithmetic of rationals) and yet containing that literal truth as a scattered part. Similarly, from a phenomenalistic point of view, the conceptual scheme of physical objects is a convenient myth, simpler than the literal truth and yet containing that literal truth as a scattered part.

Now what of classes or attributes of physical objects, in turn? A platonistic ontology of this sort is, from the point of view of a strictly physicalistic conceptual scheme, as much a myth as that physicalistic conceptual scheme itself is for phenomenalism. This higher myth is a good and useful one, in turn, in so far as it simplifies our account of physics. Since mathematics is an integral part of this higher myth, the utility of this myth for physical science is evident enough. In speaking of it nevertheless as a myth, I echo that philosophy of mathematics to which I alluded earlier under the name of formalism. But an attitude of formalism may with equal justice be adopted toward the physical conceptual scheme, in turn, by the pure aesthete or phenomenalist.

The analogy between the myth of mathematics and the myth of physics is, in some additional and perhaps fortuitous ways, strikingly close. Consider, for example, the crisis which was precipitated in the foundations of mathematics, at the turn of the century, by the discovery of Russell's paradox and other antinomies of set theory. These contradictions had to be obviated by unintuitive, *ad hoc* devices; our mathematical myth-making became deliberate and evident to all. But what of physics? An antinomy arose between the undular and the corpuscular accounts of light; and if this was not as out-and-out a contradiction as Russell's paradox, I suspect that the reason is that physics is not as out-and-out as mathematics. Again, the second great modern crisis in the foundations of mathematics—precipitated in 1931 by Godel's proof [2] that there are bound to be undecidable statements in arithmetic—has its companion piece in physics in Heisenberg's indeterminacy principle.

In earlier pages I undertook to show that some common arguments in favor of certain ontologies are fallacious. Further, I advanced an explicit standard whereby to decide what the ontological commitments of a theory are. But the question what ontology actually to adopt still stands open, and the obvious counsel is tolerance and an experimental spirit. Let us by all means see how much of the physicalistic conceptual scheme can be reduced to a phenomenalistic one; still, physics also naturally demands pursuing, irreducible *in toto* though it be. Let us see how, or to what degree, natural science may be rendered independent of platonistic mathematics; but let us also pursue mathematics and delve into its platonistic foundations.

From among the various conceptual schemes best suited to these various pursuits, one—the phenomenalistic—claims epistemological priority. Viewed from within the phenomenalistic conceptual scheme, the ontologies of physical objects and mathematical objects are myths. The quality of myth, however, is relative; relative, in this case, to the epistemological point of view. This point of view is one among various, corresponding to one among our various interests and purposes.

CHARLES HARTSHORNE

Charles Hartshorne (1897–   ) received his PhD at Harvard and an honorary LHD from Haverford College in 1967. Currently the Ashbel Smith professor of philosophy at the University of Texas, he taught at the University of Chicago, Emory University, and Harvard. He has been the Terry Lecturer at Yale, Fulbright professor at Kyoto, and president of the American Philosophical Association, Western Division. Hartshorne's contributions are primarily associated with metaphysics and the philosophy of religion. His books include *The Divine Relativity*, *Philosophers Speak of God*, *The Philosophy and Psychology of Sensation*. The following selection is from *The Logic of Perfection*.* It is one of the many statements by Hartshorne about the role of a religious philosophy for our time. A recent book testifying to Hartshorne's influence is by Ralph James, *The Concrete God: A New Beginning for Theology—the Thought of Charles Hartshorne* (1969).

Science, Insecurity, and the Abiding Treasure

"God has said, ye shall fail and perish,
But the thrill ye have felt tonight
I shall keep in my heart and cherish
When the worlds have passed in night."
RICHARD HOVEY, in *More Songs from
Vagabondia* (with Bliss Carman)

Religion, we have sometimes been told, originated in man's weakness and fear, his inability to understand and control nature. Through the gods, man acquired an illusory sense of security. But now that we have science and technology, can we not be secure without religion? Still, there are grounds for discounting this possibility.

*   *   *

Perhaps the impossibility of a net increase in foresight is one source of the demand for what is called "social security." And it is indeed possible for a society to spread its risks, through insurance or organized

---

* Charles Hartshorne, *The Logic of Perfection and Other Essays in Neoclassical Metaphysics* (La Salle, Ill: The Open Court Publishing Company, 1962). Reprinted by permission.

charity, so that the danger of extreme poverty will be limited to the possibility of catastrophe for the society as a whole. This possibility of catastrophe seems to comprise war, international and civil; population growth beyond the immediately available means of production (for, alas, one cannot eat food grown through inventions not yet made); and gross mismanagement of the financial system, or other basic economic arrangements. The last of these dangers we appear to be learning to avoid; the other two remain major threats concerning which we may make guesses, entertain hopes, and try to take preventive measures. But serious prediction on a scientific basis is here out of the question. And think of the vast extent which our uncertainty thus spans. One of the following might occur: much of civilization and its peoples destroyed; *or* vast hordes of human beings barely kept alive; *or*, finally, immense increases in material benefits for that half of it which now enjoys practically nothing of such benefits except some elements of hygiene whose chief effect is the perpetuation of poverty through rapid increase in the number of persons to be cared for. An Indian chief, five centuries ago, was not able to foresee very precisely the near future of his tribe, but his uncertainty was over a much more moderate spread of possibilities than ours. Thus our growth in collective power means greater range in the possible uses of power and hence a greater span of uncertainty. Where, then, is security to be found?

My answer is the old one: security is found more in *principles* than in conditions. It consists, not in the absence of danger or in banishing the unsettled status of the future, but in the ideas and ideals whereby danger and the ambiguities of the future can be faced with courage and with joy. What are these ideas or principles?

First, the principle that life depends as much upon our response to events around us as upon the events. As Rufus Jones once said, it is "the steady swing of the will" which chiefly makes life. If we fear that others will reject us, we can at least resolve that we will not reject them. We can bear in mind that the hostilities, the aggressions, in our own hearts may be more destructive, as they are certainly more within our power to influence, than those around us. The determination to be a friend is part of the cure for the anxiety to have friends. The readiness to cultivate other and now neglected resources is part of the cure for the anxiety lest we lose certain resources. For instance, some persons fear the failing of their eyesight. But at least, music will remain, conversation will remain, listening to lectures, the fragrance of flowers, the touch of those we love, these and much more will remain. In the helpful words of one of the greatest contemporary preachers, who happens to be a Negro, Howard Thurman: "It must be possible to act creatively in any situation."

The second principle is that each moment of life is an end in itself and not just a means to some future goal. Not only is the evil of the day sufficient thereof, but so is the good. Consider a fawn with its mother, in a spot remote from man. A short time hence the fawn may be struck down by a wolf or mountain lion. But this does not poison the beauty of life for the fawn. The harmony of its impulses and perceptions is not less perfect for all the presence of the deadly menace down wind and out of sight. Now suppose a man alone in the forest, knowing that wolves are somewhere about and are hungry from the privations of a prolonged snowstorm. The man is superior to the fawn by his understanding, but this superiority tends to mean anxiety. Man, it appears, has lost a privilege enjoyed by the humbler creatures, that of not suffering from any but immediately present dangers. Should understanding be thus a source of evil? What is the adequate compensation for this evil? Is the sole virtue of understanding that it enables us better to avoid dangers? Fawns avoid dangers to all the extent that is necessary in order for them to exist in such numbers as the food supply can provide for. Something is wrong if understanding robs us of peace in the present, only so that we may, given luck, prolong our anxious existence into old age. Understanding should mean a higher mode of existence, not just the preservation of a given mode. Bacteria look after themselves quite well, thank you. They may die, but so do we. Surely, understanding must justify itself by enriching the present, as well as by providing for the future. Yet it cannot furnish this enrichment if we insist too much upon foreknowledge of a desirable future course of events. To have understanding without loss of serenity, we must also understand, or have faith, that the meaning of life does not lie solely in what we ordinarily think of as the future. Did the lives of those who, with perhaps their closest relatives and friends, teachers perhaps with pupils, died in an instant at Hiroshima lose all meaning at that instant? Does each moment borrow all its value from what may come after it? On the other hand, after life is over, what becomes of its qualities of happiness or nobility?

We now arrive at a third principle, which is that the meaning of life is its relation to something more ultimate than the future, in the everyday sense. The biblical phrase for this relation to the ultimate is the love of God or, as the Jewish doctors have expressed it, for the Holy

One, Blessed be He! So long as we do not consciously relate ourselves to Him, by whatever name, we are in the following situation. We may, at one extreme, try to live merely for the passing moment. But this will be folly so far as our own interest goes, besides being largely selfish; for to help others we must make plans and consider long-range consequences of our acts. And wise men agree that the beauty of life is in self-forgetful interchange, in generous creative response to one another's wishes, needs, and interests. Love is essential to human life. But if we love, do we not thereby compound our anxiety for our own futures with apprehension for the future of others and the race? Utopians may try to find a remedy in the ideal perfecting of civilization taken as a settled future fact. But how can they know this fact or know to what extent their lives will have contributed to the ideal outcome? They may not have at all! Is Robinson Crusoe's sole inspiration to be the hope that he may be rescued or his story become known? Suppose the island should sink into the sea, as sometimes happens. Is there no hidden meaning of life that such an outcome could not obliterate?

It is such a hidden meaning that the religions and the philosophies have sought to explain—never, it seems, with complete success; yet, also, it may be held, never with complete unsuccess. And must not the attempt be made? If we care for our human fellows, we care for perishable beings, whose benefit from our efforts is problematic, partial, and, for all we can possibly know, temporary. Yet care for our perishable fellows we must; there is no choice. The question, however, is, What are the final dimensions of this human reality we cherish? Is there nothing permanent about the quality of the moment of life—nothing beyond this, that we may for a time faintly recall this quality ourselves or give others (also only for a time) an echo of it through words or other means of expression? Or, on the contrary, is the harmony of the moment, in fawn or human being, an imperishable contribution to some ultimate treasure, "Where neither moth nor rust doth corrupt, and where thieves do not break through nor steal"? I sometimes call the affirmative view "contributionism." It does not imply that we are mere means to some end beyond ourselves. The fawn enjoys its harmony, and it is this enjoyed harmony which is its primary or most direct contribution. The fawn contributes itself, its own self-fulfillment, not merely the effects of its acts upon others. Our human privilege consists in this, that we may make our contribution *consciously*. We may partially understand our relation to the hidden treasury. Understand, yet so that it remains a mystery.

The minimal, most noncommittal way to express this is to say that the universe contains our entire past histories, our every moment, and it forevermore *will have* contained them. In the total truth, Crusoe's joys and sorrows are indelibly written—somehow, once and for all, there. Were this not so, it would not even be true that he had lived on the island. If it be true, then reality or whatever makes truth true must contain this feature, Crusoe-having-lived-on-such-and-such-an-island-with-such-and-such-thoughts-and-feelings. Thus the permanence of life's values cannot consist simply in what each of us does for our human posterity. For the book of truth must be more comprehensive and durable than the tablet of human memories and human reception of benefits from the past. The religious view is that this book of truth, in which all value is inscribed, is a divine book, to be understood by a mysterious analogy with human memory. Our abiding value is indeed what we give to posterity, to the life that survives us; but is there not one who survives all deaths and for whose life all life is precious? For the believer, it is the Holy One who is our final posterity.

Some readers may have been asking themselves, Is not the abiding treasure, to which each moment contributes, simply ourselves, as immortal souls, destined to reap the reward of our good actions everlastingly? This view almost seems to set us human beings up as immortal gods—rivals, to that extent, of the One God. Theologians have traditionally defended the doctrine by arguing that surely God will not destroy those He loves. Let us grant this, let us admit that in some sense we must be imperishable. But wherein does this imperishable reality consist? The question we have been discussing is, How can the passing moment have value, once for all, and, in this sense, security? Our answer has been that the passing moment is cherished forevermore by One who knows how to do justice to all its beauty and value. For God to love the earthly creatures which we are for our own sake is one thing; for Him to love us for our alleged capacity to be transformed into pseudo-angels is another thing. It begs the whole question to identify these two loves, or deduce the second from the first. Even should I be there, in some future state, to look back upon my present state, since I am not divine and my memory is faint and entertains but one thing at a time, I could not give just appreciation to this present moment. Must we not rather wish to contribute every experience, in which, after all, our present actuality consists, to the One who alone is capable of accepting the gift in its fullness—the Holy One, Blessed be He? True, no science can predict, as future facts, either His survival or His cherishing of our gifts. But this is because He is not to be regarded as a mere fact, among other facts, present or future. He is rather the very principle by which facts have meaning. Our faith then is as follows: we live not ultimately for self alone, nor yet even for mankind, or "all sentient creatures," but for that hidden reality which enfolds us all, with all that we can rightly claim to be, the book of truth which some envisage as a divine life. That this life is holy means that it gives to every moment of every life its full due—not in subsequent reward (for who can ask a reward for responding to the beauty of life and the joy of fellowship among men?) but rather in absolute appreciation for the worth of each moment. The present need not, then, be poisoned by cares for the future, since the future of every moment, its essential destiny, is to present itself as a gift to the One from whose possession it can nevermore be cast out.

ERNEST NAGEL

Ernest Nagel (1901–   ) is generally considered one of America's
most important philosophers of science. He has, however, written
on topics throughout the whole range of philosophic concern.
Born in Czechoslovakia, Nagel was educated in New York City;
he received his BA from City College and his PhD from Columbia,
with which institution his teaching career is identified and where
he was recently named University Professor. He has been a
Howison Lecturer at the University of California, an American
Philosophical Association Carus Lecturer, a Fellow of the
American Academy of Arts and Sciences, a past president of the
Association for Symbolic Logic, and the American Philosophical
Association, Eastern Division. His books include *Logic Without
Ontology*, *Principles of the Theory of Probability*, and *The Structure
of Science*. The selection, giving Nagel's thoughts on the temper
of American philosophy, is from his *Sovereign Reason.** A recent
book is *Philosophy, Science, and Method: Essays in Honor of
Ernest Nagel*, edited by S. Morgenbesser, P. Suppes, and
M. White.

Philosophy and the American Temper

A nation committed to a democratic way of life, but which prescribes
for its citizens a set of beliefs concerning the nature of the cosmos and
man's place in it, is a contradiction in terms. When permitted to reflect
freely upon fundamental questions, men are stimulated to thought by
diverse experiences and divergent traditions; and under these circumstances the world comes to be viewed from many different perspectives
and portrayed in many different colors. But the freedom to develop
alternative conceptions of nature and man, even though some of them
may be grossly inadequate to their subject matter, is an essential part
of the liberal, democratic tradition. There is accordingly no official
American philosophy.

Nor is there, contrary to the tales repeated by many foreign observers,
any unique American philosophy, stemming from native seed, nourished
exclusively by native soil, and flowering in all but lonely profusion in
all parts of the land. Only unfamiliarity with the variety of doctrines

* Ernest Nagel, *Sovereign Reason and Other Studies in the Philosophy of Science*
(New York: The Free Press, 1954). Reprinted by permission.

professed by academic teachers and reflective men of letters in America, or inability to resist an impulse for popular caricature, can produce such a claim. Ever since the settlement of the American continent, the commerce of ideas between it and Europe has been continuous, and the fundamental beliefs and habits of mind of American intellectuals have always been swayed by winds of doctrine coming from foreign shores. Even those modes of thought which have often been identified as distinctively American (for example, Puritanism, New England Transcendentalism, and Pragmatism) are historically related to intellectual movements which have flourished across the Atlantic—to British Deism and Empiricism, to the many varieties of German Philosophical Idealism, and to French Positivism and Voluntarism. There is at least a grain of truth in the witticism that philosophies which become moribund in Europe obtain a second lease upon life when transplanted to America. In any event, it is not possible to cite a type of philosophy current in America which has not its identical counterpart, or at least its unmistakable analogue, in other countries.

It would indeed be strange if it were otherwise. For although the political and social experience of America has in many respects been unique, contemporary America shares with western Europe a comparable literary and religious heritage, a similar social and economic structure, and above all an identical science. Geographical distance does not by itself produce differences in fundamental attitudes and beliefs. There is, to be sure, scarcely any evidence for the widespread view that systems of philosophy, like other manifestations of the human spirit, are simply the "reflections" of the prevailing economic structure of a society, and that there is therefore a point-to-point correspondence between the history of ideas and the socio-economic changes in the life of a people. But even in its most abstract reaches philosophy is surely a commentary upon experience, so that men steeped in similar cultural traditions and confronted with similar materials for reflections will in general adopt comparable modes of viewing their place in the world.

Nevertheless, when proper qualifications are made, it is not untrue to claim that a certain habit of mind and a set of general convictions characterize the writings of many professional philosophers in America which contrast sharply with the temper and the content of much foreign thought. But one must hasten to add that these convictions also contrast sharply with many intellectual currents long and firmly established in the country, as well as with recent importations that promise to acquire a wide following: with the still influential survivals of the once dominant Calvinistic theologies; with the rosy-hued philosophies of progress, which for a time replaced these latter in popular favor and which continue to exercise a hold on many contemporary minds; with the current revivals of the Augustinian emphasis on the inherent sinfulness of man, and with the many calls to salvation through renunciation of wordly effort; with absolute idealism in its many forms, still not without defenders among the older generation of philosophers as well as among the younger ones; with a militant Thomism, which in recent years has acquired vigorous camp-followers in lay seats of learning; with phenomenology, stimulated to lush growth by the recent influx of European scholars; and with *Existenzphilosophie*, suddenly fashionable in literary circles because of French influence, though at the moment without energetic advocates among professional philosophers.

An adequate portrayal of the contemporary American scene would have to give more than incidental mention to these contrasting currents of thought. If they receive but scant notice in the present account, it is because the movement in philosophy to be briefly described appears to express more adequately than any of these the dominant temper of American life. For it is a movement which is profoundly influenced by the achievements of both theoretical and applied science, and which makes its largest appeal to a people filled with a sturdy faith in the power of intelligent thought and action to solve the problems besetting mankind. Without being narrowly practical-minded or philistine in its loyalties, without undervaluing the liberalizing functions of art, contemplative reflection and theoretical inquiry, it voices a frankly "this-worldly" philosophy. It expresses the aspirations of a people still young enough to believe that the good life can be achieved through an overt participation in worldly affairs, rather than through a melancholy resignation. It subscribes to the view that the things most dear to mankind are brought into existence and are sustained in their functions by natural forces; and it therefore finds only a romantic sentimentalism in the conception according to which men are wanderers in an inherently hostile world who must take their directions from supernatural guides. It counts among its adherents a number of the older generation of philosophers, but it also prides itself on the fact that it has the vigorous support of many of the keenest and best disciplined minds among the younger men. It is without question America's most significant contribution to philosophic intelligence.

This philosophy has been variously designated as objective relativism, functional realism, contextualism, naturalism, and process philosophy.

Its central conceptions concerning man and nature have sometimes been identified with the pragmatism or instrumentalism of Peirce, James, Mead and Dewey. This identification is both mistaken and misleading. Although contextualistic naturalism has historical roots in pragmatism, and although Dewey himself is an exponent of both, those professing the former do not in general feel committed to the technical pragmatic doctrines concerning the nature of truth or the function of knowledge, and in the main they have no liking for the pragmatic or instrumentalist label. Indeed, the specific pragmatic conceptions propounded by James and Dewey, which caused such a flurry of excitement in the first quarter of the present century, now appear to be of little more than historical interest to the younger generation of American philosophers—in part, no doubt, because the intellectual storm raised by those conceptions has cleared the air of the traditional complacencies and barren self-deceptions against which pragmatism was a protest. Unlike contextualistic naturalism, it is problematic whether, except in some training schools for teachers and in centers of learning where the personal influence of the founders of pragmatism is still alive, pragmatism retains the expansive dynamism of a growing movement. Nonetheless, pragmatism is the matrix out of which, at least in America, contextualistic naturalism has emerged. For certain features of pragmatic philosophy that had been subordinated to its theory of truth and knowledge, have subsequently received an independent development; and fortified by fresh analyses of scientific method as well as by the findings of biological inquiry, they have been forged into a distinctive outlook upon man and nature.

Contextualistic naturalism is not a finished intellectual edifice, and perhaps it will never develop into one. Though much periodical literature indicates whence and whither it is tending, there certainly is no one treatise that could be cited as the *Summa* of its doctrines. However, many of the later writings of John Dewey, W. H. Sheldon's *America's Progressive Philosophy*, and various essays in the recent collection entitled *Naturalism and the Human Spirit* (edited by Y. H. Krikorian) contain at least its basic ground plan. Those out of sympathy with it are likely to judge it as eclectic, loose-jointed, and at a number of essential points even distressingly vague. But those who subscribe to its main tenets believe that a working philosophy cannot be more tidy and architectonically complete than the subjects of which it treats.

For a cardinal thesis of contextualistic naturalism is the essentially incomplete but fundamentally plural character of existence, in which no overarching pattern of development can be discerned, and in which qualitative discontinuities and loose conjunctions are as ultimate features as are firm connections and regular cycles of change. Events are recognized to have causes and consequences, without beginning and without preordained end. But though events are genuinely related to other events, they are not related to all events in the same way, not everything is relevant to the occurrence of everything else, and no events are related to others by logical necessity. Indeed, things may be caught up in some eddy of the flux of change which can alter their customary modes of behavior and transform them in a manner not always deducible from the known conditions of their normal existence. Novelty, contingency, and alternative possibilities of development, are accordingly basic features of nature. The disciplined human perspective upon the flux of events does not betray its observers, and the mixture of direction and chaos which that perspective reveals is not the superficial appearance of a fixed plan working itself out with inexorable logic.

In consequence, contextualistic naturalists exhibit a profound distrust of philosophic systems which attempt to catch once for all the variegated contents of the world in a web of dialectical necessity. They are keenly conscious of the limitations of purely formal analysis even when they engage in it. For they recognize that a logic, no matter how subtle, provides no warrant concerning matters of fact unless it is supported by controlled observation. Indeed, they sometimes show an almost pathological fear that those concerned with formal analysis may be deceived into supposing that nature is as coherently organized and as simple as are their intellectual constructions.

Nor does the familiar distinction between appearance and reality play any role in their thinking about nature, since the term "reality" designates no inherently basic substance in the world but at best only a humanly valuable phase of existence. Accordingly, every quality and event is a genuine occurrence in some complex process or context, and possesses ascertainable relations and functions in that context. There is, however, no one context which is relevant to the occurrence of everything, there is no absolutely privileged context. It is this emphasis upon the contextual conditions for the occurrence and for the manifested properties of everything whatsoever—upon the fact that a quality is an objective constituent of nature even though its existence depends on the relations in which it stands to other things—which explains the adjective in the label "contextualistic naturalism."

It is inevitable that on these assumptions contextualistic naturalism should be vigorously anti-reductionist. Unlike earlier forms of naturalism, it maintains that the world contains at least as many qualitatively distinct features as are disclosed in human experience, and not a fewer number of them. The widespread view exemplified in such claims as that the playing of a Bach *Chaconne* is "nothing but" a scraping of horsehair across catgut, or that the human scene is "nothing but" an aggregation of certain allegedly "ultimate" elements, is therefore rejected as resting upon patent confusions. Modern physics and modern biopsychology are taken seriously by contextualistic naturalists, and current theories concerning the electrical structure of matter and the biophysical basis of human action are assumed to be well-grounded in competent evidence. But they fail to see any merit in the argument according to which, simply because complex organizations of the elementary particles of modern physics constitute the conditions for the occurrence of familiar events and processes, the characteristic behaviors of such complex wholes are indistinguishably identical with the behaviors of their differently organized parts.

It follows that the human scene is as much an integral part of nature, and as valid a subject for the philosopher's concern with basic features of existence, as is any of its other sectors. As contextualistic naturalism views them, man and his works are not inexplicable occurrences, incomparable in every respect with other natural processes. Men come into being and act the way they do only because of the operations of natural forces, and they perish or cease to behave as men when forces no less natural disrupt the normal organization of their bodies and of their fields of behavior. On the other hand, though the conditions of man's life are thus continuous with the rest of nature, his behavior exhibits features which are discontinuous with other parts of existence. For man is not simply another odd item in the inexhaustible catalogue of created things. He possesses the apparently unique gift of an inquiring mind, which enables him not only to act under the compulsion of internal springs of action and external pressures, but also to direct his impulses and to master many of the forces in his environment.

This gift of intelligence man owes to the organization of his body and the character of his environment, and no supernatural agency or disembodied soul is required to explain it. It is this organization, complicated by the structure of his surroundings, which also accounts for men's moral and evaluative behaviors. The possession of needs and preferences, and the exercise of reflection upon them in the interest of fulfilling and harmonizing them, are as natural to man as is, for example, the property of a magnet to repel or attract another magnet. In any event, it is in the radical plurality of men's needs and in the limitations which their physical and social environment impose upon their fulfillment, that contextualistic naturalism locates the source and urgency of moral problems. Accordingly, it does not conceive the primary moral problem to be that of discovering or actually instituting some fixed set of ethical norms valid everywhere and for all time. For basic moral problems are plural in number and specific in character, and are concerned with the adjustment, in the light of causes and consequences, of competing impulses occurring in specific environmental contexts. There can therefore be no general or final solution to the moral predicaments of mankind; the moral problem is the perennial one of finding ways and means for eliminating needless suffering and for organizing in a reasonable manner the energies of men.

The advocacy of a responsible intellectual method, especially in matters pertinent to social and ethical issues as well as in philosophy, is thus an emphatic strain in the writings of contextualistic naturalists. For reliable knowledge is the end-product of a reflective process, involving the use of experimental controls over ideas which initially have the status of tentative hypotheses; and it is this procedure which must be employed if reliable knowledge and reasonable evaluations are to be attained in the settlement of social and moral conflicts. This method of science supplies no guarantees against error, it does not preclude alternative solutions to problems, and it certifies none of its conclusions as eternally valid. But since it is in essence a self-corrective method, and involves the continued criticism of its findings in the light of evidence capable of public inspection, it is a method which can discover its own errors. It is in any case the sole method which has historically shown itself able to yield intellectual and practical mastery over various segments of nature. From the systematic extension of the use of this method to the problems of men, contextualistic naturalists confidently anticipate an increased moral enlightenment.

Compared with many fashionable philosophies contextualistic naturalism is almost prosaically sober. It contributes to the current intellectual scene no apocalyptic visions, no thunderous absolutes, no unshakeable certainties. It offers no spectacular promises of salvation. It is essentially scientific and secular in temper, but confident that the concentration of scientific methods upon specific problems will yield a rich harvest of genuine knowledge. It is sane and reasonable at a time

when the tides of irrationalism run high in the world and when sub-
stitutes for the Apollonian virtues are at a premium. It expresses the
convictions of a people confident that a bold but disciplined intelligence
is still a creative power in the world.

JOHN HERMAN RANDALL

The career of John Herman Randall, Jr. (1899–   ) is associated with Columbia University, where he received his PhD and an honorary DHL in 1968, a year after receiving an honorary degree at the University of Padua. He is a former president of the American Philosophical Association, Eastern Division. Randall is a distinguished historian of philosophy, and his original contributions are always worked out with a concern for historical precedent. He is a noted and outspoken defender of Naturalism, helping to create the impression for many years of Columbia as a center of that philosophic outlook. His books include *The Making of the Modern Mind*, *The Career of Philosophy*, *The Role of Knowledge in Western Religion*, and *Aristotle*. This selection is from his *Nature and Historical Experience;** it presents a traditional concept of the function of philosophy that many accept without accepting Naturalism. It is one that many consider vital to keep alive today.

Unifications of Knowledge

However far men in their craving for "unity" may try to overlook or minimize it, this thoroughgoing diversity or plurality of the world is a fundamental fact. It augurs well for the progress of philosophical inquiry in our day that some form of pluralism has come to be accepted by most responsible philosophers. Only the philosophical "nothing-butter"—the brusque apostle of the method of reductive analysis—has ever managed to get all the world's immense variety of miscellaneous stuff unified into a neat system following from a few "first principles," or dependent logically on a single "first cause." That can be done only if we happily forget everything that refuses to fit snugly into the Procrustean bed of our tidy framework. And even when we succeed in bringing forth a unified system that will somehow embrace all we know of the world, that is no proof that the world is really "one," but only that we have found a system. The wise man cannot forget that in its time the world has patiently tolerated a host of others, and that in due course it will doubtless bring forth countless more.

* From John Herman Randall, "Unifications of Knowledge" in *Nature and Historical Experience* (New York: Columbia University Press, 1958). Reprinted by permission.

It is a fundamental fact that the world is radically and ineradicably plural. But equally basic is the fact that the world can be unified in human vision. Again and again the wit of man has been able to turn the trick. Now surely such works of unification are a tremendous achievement. They need not, however, be the product of great intellectual sophistication. The unknown poets responsible for the creation myths of the most "primitive" cultures—like those men of genius whose inspired thought is preserved in the opening of Genesis—were the first to see the world whole. And we dare to hope that the world can be likewise unified in the vision that is knowledge and science, even as it has so often been unified in the vision that is myth and symbol. It has been the dream of physics, which its history has surely gone far to encourage, that men might some day discover a single unified formula of calculation and prediction. Fortunately, the practice of physics has not had to await the consummation of that hope. But physics has exhibited a significant trend toward unification, and scientists have been able to institute progressively more general ideas or principles, in terms of which the available facts do fall into a systematic and intelligible order.

But the fact that the world can be unified in vision through myth and symbol, even the fact that it has been slowly approaching unification in knowledge and science, is no proof that the world constitutes in sober truth a "unity." It is proof only that the world *can become* unified in vision, and more doubtfully in knowledge. No one—not even a Creator —could generate the world, with all its infinite and inexhaustible variety, out of physical theory. Physics certainly did not create the world. The world rather gave birth to physics and physicists. And if our best established unified knowledge cannot be said to have created the world, still less can our many other unified visions and systems be credited with the responsibility for what is. Such unification is a human achievement, man's bringing of the world to a focus.

*   *   *

But what can we mean by understanding what men have found and seen, out of all that is and all that might be, of the world and its possibilities? We can, it seems, mean at least three different things: understanding what the vision is, understanding what it means, and understanding how what is seen and the seeing are brought about. Broadly, we can say that the arts give the first understanding, the humanities the second, and the sciences the third. What the vision *is* can only be understood by sharing it; and the many languages of the many arts, including the art of religion, are devices for communicating and sharing what has been found and seen. What the vision *means* can only be understood by relating it to other things; this is the function of interpretation, clarification, and criticism, which belongs to the humanities as disciplines; and here I would place both theology and philosophy. How the vision, the seeing and what is seen, is brought about, the devices by which the world has produced it, belong to the sciences, of nature and of man. But this is far too simple a division of labor. For all three are arts, in finding and revealing what is and what might be, though they are not all sciences; and all are humanities, in clarifying and criticizing meanings. It is functions rather than disciplines that are here distinguished.

We have, then, three major ways of understanding the world of vision—of understanding what man finds in the world. Are we to call what each of the three gives us, equally "knowledge"? The question seems idle, and any answer gratuitous. Would we deny knowledge to Plato and Dante, to Shakespeare and Goethe, because they are poets and not scientists? Surely they have seen the world. And who would deny knowledge to Kant and to Thomas, yes, to Dewey and to Niebuhr, who, being poets who have seen the world, are also critics and interpreters who have explored the meanings and the relations of what they have seen?

Do we have then three kinds of "knowledge"—vision, interpretation and criticism, and science? If we take knowledge broadly, so it can be said. But in what sense can these three kinds of knowledge hope to find a "unity"? How are they related? Surely they are not rivals—their aims, their ways of understanding are too different for them to compete. And surely they do not just lie side by side, supplementing each other, though they all alike exist and are sought in a world with man in it. Their cooperation seems more intimate than that. The knowledge that is vision of what a world with man in it contains has a kind of primacy—it presents to the others the subject-matter to be understood, what men have found there. The specific knowledge of the artist—the man who finds—is an understanding how to make us see and find what he has seen and found. The knowledge that is science tries to discover the conditions of the being and the finding of what is found, the devices that make both possible, on which they depend. The knowledge that is interpretation and criticism seems to require both the others. In seeking the meaning of what is found, in relating it to other findings and other meanings, it must know both what a world with man in it can do, and how it does it. It must seek to relate possibilities to their conditions, outcomes and eventuations to the devices by which they are achieved. This third kind of knowledge seems thus to call for a fuller understanding than either of the others alone.

What sort of "unity" may we hope to find within each of these three kinds of knowledge? In the knowledge that is vision and finding, the outlook is not promising. Many radically different things have been found, and so long as the world has man in it, many more will be. Every new poem, every new prophet's vision, will reveal new possibilities in the world, and these possibilities are in no significant sense "one." Visions are many, and many are the unified visions to which they can be pushed; but there is no unity of visions. The very idea is unintelligible and repellent. If, then, there be no unity in what is found, save that it is all found in the same world, is there a discoverable unity in the way of finding? This is the problem the experts on method must wrestle with— do all the various arts, with their various media and symbolic devices, pursue any common way in coming to see what they see? Is there indeed a common way in a single art even, like poetry or music or religion? Or are there rather many ways of making poems and songs and finding the Divine? Is there a common language in which all the arts tell us what they have found? Or if the tongues remain many, are they in any sense mutually translatable?

In the knowledge that is science, great claims have been made for unity. Science has indeed been unified in terms of a single scientific method—again and again, for the particular method for which the claim has been advanced has never proved able to embrace all fields and all subject-matters, and men have had to try once more, with a method more adequate. The claim is perhaps idle, for different fields notoriously demand differing procedures, and the unity of method can always be maintained by excluding from the single method these varying procedures. More recently, science has been unified in terms of a single language of science, though again the common language clearly requires different vocabularies in the various sciences, and the attempt to formulate a language of "basic science" is still an ideal.

These "unities" of science remain as yet human unifications of the world of science, more interesting to the interpreter, the philosopher, than to the scientists themselves. But the world does still reveal, if not a unity, at least a continuity of the conditions by which it does all it does—a continuity of those devices by which all its processes are brought about. However distinctive their outcomes—whether they eventuate in a star, a dog, or a poem—they seem bound up together in a network of common interactions without which they would not be. And this network can be followed out indefinitely—there is no field into which it does not lead us. It can be, and has been, pursued into man and all his works. The conditions and devices found elsewhere are found also in the life of man. Nothing has proved more futile than the repeated attempts to set barriers to the tracing out of this network. Our successive dualisms, claiming that man, or at least something in man, is not like all else caught up in it, have always broken down. The world for science knows no limits—it is coextensive with the world of vision, with everything man finds in the world. Tracing this network of causes and conditions may not tell us all we want to know, about the world, or about man; but it always tells us something, and what it tells is truly told. There can be no gainsaying the story. It encounters many complications at many points—when it comes to tell us about living things, or when it comes to man; and new chapters are required. But there is no fresh start. The world for science may not be a unity. But it is at least a continuity of processes and conditions, making possible a continuity of inquiry, a continuity of analysis, a continuity of scientific method.

This continuity of processes found has suggested to many an eventual unification of the causes and conditions of things into a single system— an eventual unity of the knowledge that is science. This seems a not unreasonable hope. It clearly possesses great value as an ideal of science—as what Kant called a regulative idea. Surely here if anywhere in our knowledges we may hope to look for system, coherence, even "unity." Doubtless it will always remain what it has been heretofore, a process of unification. But the notion of an ideal limit to be approached seems not wholly inappropriate.

But the world approaching unification through science is not identical with *the* world for knowledge. That world contains much else besides. It contains also everything these processes and conditions are able to accomplish, all the manifold eventuations and outcomes found in a world with man in it. And here is not even continuity, in any sense that would obliterate encountered distinctions of importance, of value, of meaning. Uniqueness and individuality are characteristic of the products and outcomes that man finds. Here are many dimensions and many levels, new beginnings and fresh starts. And it is just here that the knowledge that is interpretation and criticism operates, trying to relate the many things a world with man in it does, to each other, and to the way it does them—trying to relate possibilities to each other and to their conditions, trying to find what they mean.

The knowledge that is criticism and interpretation, since it is trying to establish relations, is itself a never-ending process of unification. When pushed, it becomes, in the philosopher, the attempt to understand *the* world in the light of the totality of its possibilities and of their conditions. But the world's possibilities have no discoverable totality—man is forever finding out more. Even their conditions are not unified in any existent science. Hence the unifications of meaning are many, and must so remain. We can understand the world whole in many ways—find many meanings in terms of which to unify it. Here is no unity. But here is the opportunity for more and more comprehensive unifications—as men learn more of the world's possibilities, and come to understand more of the other meanings that other men and cultures have found.

Do our three ways of understanding, then, commit us to three kinds of truth? I think and hope not; it seems more confusing than clarifying so to speak. The knowledge that is vision is what it is. We can ask of the poet or the painter or the saint or the prophet only if his vision be genuine or authentic. The only test is whether he knows how to make us see what he sees, and find what he has found. The knowledge that is interpretation and criticism is better called an understanding of significance or meaning than of truth. "Adequacy" seems the best name for its test. It is well to keep "truth" for the knowledge that is science, with all its complex procedures and criteria for verifying propositions that can be stated. We should then be left with vision, truth, and meaning.

But perhaps the scientists themselves are abandoning "truth" as the name for their knowledge, for some other property like "confirmability" or "warranted assertibility." And in calling the understanding of meaning something to be judged by its "adequacy," I remember the old definition of truth as "adequation of thing and understanding." Perhaps after all we have come the full circle, and it is now the unifications of the world in the light of some meaning understood that we are permitted to call "true." If so, this "truth" of meaning is not to be confused with the knowledge that is science. It is rather the Truth of which it was said of old, "Ye shall know the truth, and the truth shall make you free."

And so we come back to our central question: Is there a common enterprise of inquiry to which all our arts and sciences and humanities contribute? Have we found it? It is not the enterprise of the artist—the poet, the musician, the saint. His contribution is essential, but his own enterprise is not to contribute: it is to make what he makes and find what he finds, though his makings and findings tell us what we have to understand. It is not the enterprise of the scientist, though that too is essential to it: his enterprise is to explore the processes and conditions he sets out to explore. He can indeed hope for a unification of his own, a unification of the sciences in terms of their method, their language, their continuity of processes. But the unity of science achieved would not be the unification of the world. No, our common enterprise seems to be the enterprise of the critic and interpreter, of the humanist and philosopher, of the searcher after more adequate meaning. Drawing on both the others, he can hope to unify the world for knowledge through a meaning found. He must indeed see the world from a selective focus, but he can hope to see it steadily and whole. In asking our question, for a coherent and adequate view of the world, whatever our special knowledges, we are all in the end humanists and philosophers. The answers will be ours, and we shall not agree. But the question is not ours alone. It is the question the world poses to the searcher after more adequate meaning. What is the world, that man is mindful of it? What is man, that he is mindful of the world? These questions—no, this single question, in all its ramifications—is what the world for knowledge asks of him who seeks to know the world. The answers are many; the question at least is one.

Suggestions for Further Reading

The following sources have been carefully selected and are especially recommended.

PART I.   General Studies

COHEN, MORRIS R., *American Thought*. Glencoe, Ill.: The Free Press, 1954.

HOFSTADTER, RICHARD, *The American Political Tradition*. New York: Vintage Books, 1954.

——— *Anti-Intellectualism in America*. New York: Knopf, 1963.

MCDERMOTT, JOHN J., *The American Angle of Vision*. West Nyack: Cross Currents, 1966.

MORISON, SAMUEL ELIOT, *The Oxford History of The American People*. New York: Oxford University Press, 1965.

PARRINGTON, VERNON LOUIS, *Main Currents in American Thought*. New York: Harcourt, Brace & Company, 1927.

RIESMAN, DAVID, *The Lonely Crowd*, rev. ed. New York: Doubleday, 1950.

SCHLESINGER, ARTHUR M., JR., and WHITE, MORTON O., eds., *Paths of American Thought*. Boston: Houghton Mifflin Company, 1963.

SCHNEIDER, HERBERT, *A History of American Philosophy*, second ed. New York and London: Columbia University Press, 1963.

SMITH, JOHN E., *The Spirit of American Philosophy*. New York: Oxford University Press, 1963.

THAYER, H. S., *Meaning and Action: A Critical History of Pragmatism*. Indianapolis and New York: The Bobbs-Merrill Company, Inc., 1968.

PART II.   Specialized Studies

ALDRIGE, ALFRED OWEN, *Franklin and His French Contemporaries*. New York: New York University Press, 1957.

——— *Man of Reason: The Life of Thomas Paine*. Philadelphia and New York: J. B. Lippincott, 1959.

BARKER, CHARLES ALBRO, *Henry George*. New York: Oxford University Press, 1955.

BAYLES, ERNEST E., and HOOK, BRUCE L., *Growth of American Educational Thought and Practice*. New York: Harper & Row, 1966.

BEARD, CHARLES A., *The Enduring Federalist*. New York: Frederick Ungar Publishing Company, 1948.

BEMIS, SAMUEL FLAGG, *John Quincy Adams and the Foundations of American Foreign Policy*. New York: Knopf, 1949.

BOWEN, CATHERINE DRINKER, *Yankee from Olympus*. Boston: Little, Brown & Company, 1944.

BROWN, ARTHUR W., *William Ellery Channing*. New York: Twayne, 1961.

CHRISTIAN, WILLIAM A., *An Interpretation of Whitehead's Metaphysics*. New Haven: Yale University Press, 1959.

CONNER, PAUL W., *Poor Richard's Politicks: Benjamin Franklin and His New American Order*. New York: Oxford University Press, 1965.

CONWAY'S, MONCURE, DANIEL, *Life of Thomas Paine*. New York and London: G. P. Putnam's Sons, 1892.

COTTON, JAMES HARRY, *Royce on the Human Self*. Cambridge: Harvard University Press, 1954.

DE MILLE, ANNA GEORGE, *Henry George; Citizen of the World*. Chapel Hill: The University of North Carolina Press, 1950.

DORFMAN, JOSEPH, *The Economic Mind in America*, Vol. 3. New York: The Viking Press, 1949.

—— *Thorstein Veblen and His America*. New York: The Viking Press, 1934.

FAUST, CLARENCE H., and JOHNSON, THOMAS H., *Jonathan Edwards*, rev. ed. New York: Hill and Wang, American Century Series, 1963.

FUSS, PETER, *The Moral Philosophy of Josiah Royce*. Cambridge: Harvard University Press, 1965.

GALLIE, W. B., *Peirce and Pragmatism*. New York: Penguin Books, 1952.

GRANGER, BRUCE, *Benjamin Franklin, An American Man of Letters*. New York: Cornell University Press, 1964.

HARASZTI, ZOLTAN, *John Adams and the Prophets of Progress*. New York: Grosset & Dunlap, Universal Library Edition, 1964.

HONEYWELL, ROY JOHN, *The Educational Work of Thomas Jefferson*. Cambridge: Harvard University Press, 1931.

HOOK, SIDNEY, *John Dewey: An Intellectual Portrait*. New York: John Day, 1939.

JOHNSON, A. H., *Whitehead's Philosophy of Civilization*. Boston: Beacon, 1958.

KLINE, GEORGE L., *Alfred North Whitehead*. Englewood Cliffs, N.J.: Prentice-Hall, 1963.

KOCH, A., *The Philosophy of Thomas Jefferson*. New York: Columbia University Press, 1943.

KRUG, EDWARD A., *Salient Dates in American Education: 1635-1934*. New York: Harper & Row, 1966.

LERNER, MAX, *The Mind and Faith of Justice Holmes*. New York: The Modern Library, 1943.

——— ed., *The Portable Veblen*. New York: The Viking Press, 1948.

MARCEL, GABRIEL, *Royce's Metaphysics*, trans. Virginia and Gordon Ringer. Chicago: Henry Regnery Company, 1956.

MILLER, PERRY, and JOHNSON, THOMAS, *The Puritans*, 2 vols. New York: Harper & Row, Torchbooks, 1963.

MORISON, SAMUEL E., *The Intellectual Life of Colonial New England*. New York: New York University Press, 1956.

MUMTZ, MIHONK, *The Moral Philosophy of George Santayana*. New York: Columbia University Press, 1939.

PERRY, RALPH BARTON, *The Thought and Character of William James*, 2 vols. Boston: Little, Brown and Company, 1935.

RIESMAN, DAVID, *Thorstein Veblen: A Critical Interpretation*. New York: Charles Scribner's Sons, 1953.

SCHILPP, P. A., ed., *The Philosophy of Alfred North Whitehead*. Evanston, Ill.: Library of Living Philosophers, 1941.

——— *The Philosophy of John Dewey*. New York: Tudor, 1939.

——— *The Philosophy of Santayana*. Evanston, Ill.: Northwestern University Press, 1940.

SMITH, JOHN E., *Royce's Social Infinite: The Community of Interpretation*. New York: Liberal Arts Press, 1950.

SMITH, PAGE, *John Adams*, 2 vols. Garden City, N.Y.: Doubleday, 1962.

STARR, HARRIS ELWOOD, *William Graham Sumner*. New York: H. Holt and Company, 1925.

THOMAS, BENJAMIN PLATT, *Abraham Lincoln: A Biography*. New York: Knopf, 1952.

THOMPSON, MANLEY, *The Pragmatic Philosophy of C. S. Peirce*. Chicago: The University of Chicago Press, 1953.

VAN DOREN, CARL, *Benjamin Franklin*. New York: The Viking Press, 1938.

WHITE, MORTON G., *The Origin of Dewey's Instrumentalism*. New York: Columbia University Press, 1943.

WIENER, PHILIP P., and YOUNG, FREDERICK H., eds., *Studies in the Philosophy of Charles Sanders Peirce*. Cambridge: Harvard University Press, 1952.

WILD, JOHN, *The Radical Empiricism of William James*. New York: Doubleday, 1969.

WILSHIRE, BRUCE, *William James and Phenomenology*. Bloomington: Indiana University Press, 1968.

WILTSE, CHARLES M., *The Jeffersonian Tradition in American Democracy*. New York: Hill and Wang, 1960.